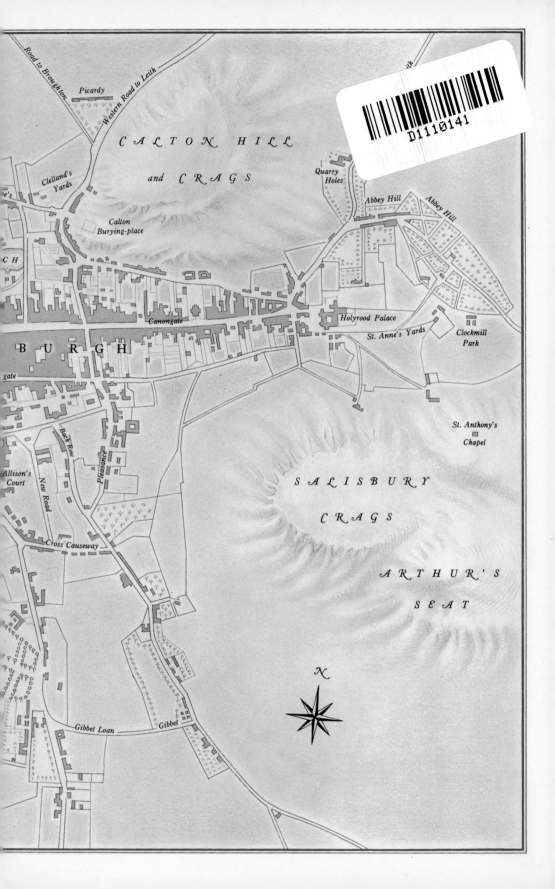

Road to Broughton

Western Road to Leith

Picardy

CALTON HILL

and CRAGS

Clelland's
Yards

...e's

Quarry
Holes

Abbey Hill

Abbey Hill

Calton
Burying-place

Canongate

Holyrood Palace

St. Anne's Yards

Clockmill
Park

BURGH

...gate

St. Anthony's
Chapel

Back Row

Pleasance

Allison's
Court

New Road

SALISBURY

CRAGS

Cross Causeway

ARTHUR'S

SEAT

N

Gibbet Loan

Gibbet

THE YALE EDITIONS OF

The Private Papers of James Boswell

Margaret Montgomerie (? 1738–1789), from the oil painting in the collection of Sir Gilbert Eliott of Stobs, Bt.

Boswell

IN SEARCH OF A WIFE

1766-1769

EDITED BY FRANK BRADY

ASSISTANT PROFESSOR OF ENGLISH

AND FREDERICK A. POTTLE

STERLING PROFESSOR OF ENGLISH

YALE UNIVERSITY

McGraw-Hill Book Company, Inc.

NEW YORK   TORONTO   LONDON

FIRST EDITION

EDITORIAL COMMITTEE

ADVISORY COMMITTEE

The Yale Editions of the Private Papers of James Boswell will consist of two independent but parallel series planned and executed for different types of readers. One, the "research" edition, will give a complete text of Boswell's journals, diaries, and memoranda; of his correspondence; and of "The Life of Johnson," from the original manuscript: the whole running to at least thirty volumes. It will preserve the spelling and capitalization of the original documents,, and will be provided with extensive scholarly annotation. A large group of editors and a permanent office staff are engaged in this comprehensive undertaking, the first volume of which may appear by 1957. The other, the reading or "trade" edition, will select from the total mass of papers those portions that appear likely to interest the general reading public, and will present them in modern spelling and with annotation of a popular cast. The publishers may also issue limited de luxe printings of the trade volumes, with extra illustrations and special editorial matter, but in no case will the trade volumes or the de luxe printings include matter from Boswell's archives that will not also appear in the research edition.

The present volume is the sixth of the trade edition.

CONTENTS

LIST OF ILLUSTRATIONS

NOTE OF CORRECTION

The map of Edinburgh in 1765 which follows this page was ready for printing before we discovered in it a number of errors that go back to the original." Edgar's map of 1765" is a revision by an unknown hand of a map drawn in 1742. The revisions were patched into the old plate, which in most respects remained unchanged. One of these revisions was the insertion of the Royal Exchange (built 1753–1761), which replaced three entire closes of the old map: Mary King's Close, Stewart's Close, and Pearson's Close. The reviser, who wished to leave the sequence of numbers on each side of the Exchange as they were, assigned the numbers of those closes to buildings in various parts of the city: the Royal Bank, St. Cecilia's Hall, and Dr. Alexander Monro's new theatre for dissections and lectures in anatomy (Nos. 19, 20, 21 of our map). The engraver misunderstood his directions, or could not find the new numbers, and so fitted them in around three sides of the courtyard of the Exchange. Actually, the Royal Bank (built 1727) was in No. 70, the close which Edgar calls Steil's (it was later called Royal Bank Close); St. Cecilia's Hall (built 1762) was at the foot of Niddry's Wynd (No. 87) on the right-hand side looking up from the Cowgate; and "Dr. Monro's New Class" (built ?1765) would have been somewhere in the area of the University of Edinburgh ("College" on our map).—The mysterious "Chander" (No. 101), which appears both in Edgar's map of 1742 and the revision, is probably a misreading of Chanclor, and is equated by H. F. Kerr in his composite "Map of Edinburgh in the Mid-Eighteenth Century" (*Book of the Old Edinburgh Club,* 1922) with the structure called "The Chancellor's House" in earlier accounts of Holyrood Palace.

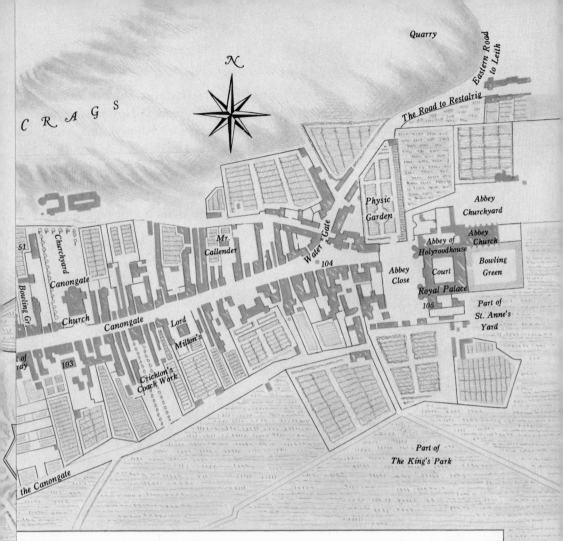

Quarry

Eastern Road to Leith

The Road to Restalrig

C R A G S

N

Physic Garden

Abbey Churchyard

Water Gate

Mr. Callender

104

Abbey of Holyroodhouse

Abbey Church

Court

Bowling Green

Abbey Close

Royal Palace

105

Part of St. Anne's Yard

51

Churchyard

Canongate

Bowling Gr

Church

Canongate

Lord Milton's

Crichton's Coach Work

103

Chander

of ray

the Canongate

Part of The King's Park

A PLAN OF THE CITY
OF EDINBURGH

NISI DOMINUS FRUSTRA

INTRODUCTION

§ I

The onset of maturity is marked by one definite sign: a moment of sudden realization that the future has turned into the present. Whether James Boswell ever experienced such a moment it is difficult to say. His determination, during the period covered by this volume, "if possible to maintain a propriety and strictness of manners" after the publication of his *Account of Corsica*, looks in another direction; it illustrates the impossible desire to reach a stage of static perfection that tantalized him throughout his life. But during the years 1766–1769, whether he knew it or not, he arrived at the greatest degree of maturity he was to reach. What had come before — his education, sexual and religious experiences, the Grand Tour — must be seen in a new perspective. It served to prepare him for the crucial particular situations he now faced, which, moreover, he was to deal with successfully. He became a lawyer, wrote a fine, popular, and influential book, and got married. These were his marvelous years.

To enter into the main stream of society, as Boswell now did, entails the adoption of a number of attitudes towards oneself, others, and one's work; it impels the individual to acquire a number of public and private roles. The roles chosen depend, in turn, not only on the context of the society in which he is to play a part, but also upon his past: the framework of relationships he has built up, and the fundamental principles or passions that rule him. "You may just keep in mind," Boswell wrote to Margaret Montgomerie, "that a disposition to melancholy and the most violent passion for the family of Auchinleck make a part of my very existence." Here are the bases of his actions and attitudes.

Melancholy and family are intertwined elements which can be illuminated by a look at Boswell's society and his early relationships. Modern, and especially American, readers are likely to forget that eighteenth-century society, though like our own in its stress on property and money, differed from ours in one important respect: it was a "lineal" society. A man thought of himself and was judged by others in terms of his family, its position and traditions, a good deal more than in terms of what he was or made of himself as an individual. For Boswell, then, what he was or did as a person counted less in itself than it did in relation to the family of Boswell of Auchinleck.

Such an attitude immensely complicated his most significant relationship up to this time, that with his father. He loved his timid and pious mother, but she lacked his father's force of character and the prestige he commanded in a patriarchal society. Lord Auchinleck, his son felt, was a man of "real worth" with a "strict regard to truth and to honour." As a judge he was known for his integrity, intelligence, and devotion to his duty. But to Boswell he seemed cold and unimaginative, with a talent for checking conversation and for putting what he despised in a contemptible light. More important, though he acted fairly towards his son and perhaps even loved him, he neither understood nor approved of Boswell's actions and character.

Boswell had spirit enough to rebel against his father's unflattering view; his survival as an individual demanded that he do so. His papers refer again and again to quarrels with his father, sullen interviews, remonstrances, defiant letters. But he was incapable of ever shaking himself really free from his father's opinion of him, of attaining "the privileges of an independent human being." Material factors played a part: his father provided him with a necessary allowance and other money on occasion; eventually the property of Auchinleck and the position it gave its owner were at stake. (Though Boswell could not actually have been disinherited, his father could have made difficulties for him.) But beyond these considerations and the basic struggle which defying a parent involves was the fact that Boswell's picture of himself was confused. Much as he loved the roles of the "great man" and the "playhouse buck," to run around London and chase after girls in the streets, he also had "agreeable, family, sober ideas" — he shared many of his father's values. He clung passionately to the idea of the House of Auchinleck of which his father was not merely the representative, but also the living spirit of its grave, shrewd ideals. To twist a phrase of Samuel Johnson's somewhat, the issues between Boswell and his father were often "matters of sensation not of judgement," which brought out differences of temperament rather than opinion. Therefore, Boswell could never be sure that he had a right to oppose his father and to follow his own course of action. The feelings of guilt and resentment that ensued account, in part at least, for his melancholy.

Lord Auchinleck's intention, three years after his wife's death, to remarry brought their relationship to its greatest crisis. Though such a decision might seem but mildly objectionable to most sons, Boswell wildly resented it. He saw it as a slur on his mother's memory, and as an ungrateful return for his submissive behaviour. He feared that remarriage might estrange his father from himself and his brothers, that Lord Auchinleck might even leave his estate to children by his second wife. (He did provide his widow with a large jointure.) His proposed bride was an "infamous woman" so to "impose on an old man worn out with business, and ruin the peace of a family!" Boswell had felt himself an "old Roman" in disputing with his father over the entail to the estate; now he conjured up visions of leaving Scotland, his prospects, and his career, to become a "wild Indian" in America if his father remarried. The violence of his emotion indicates how profoundly he was disturbed, and suggests that he feared something more central than any of the facts mentioned could warrant; he may have been afraid that remarriage signified the final alienation of his father's affection from him and from the mother with whom he had, to some extent, identified himself.

From such deep disappointment it was a relief for him to turn to Johnson, the other great older figure in his life. Instead of greeting him with cool Scots sarcasm, Johnson, Boswell records of one meeting, "took me all in his arms and kissed me on both sides of the head, and was as cordial as ever I saw him." Here was a father who, whether he approved of him entirely or not, demonstrated his love for him.

Boswell's attitude towards Johnson, however, was a complicated one. It included first the obvious roles of the dutiful son, the enthusiastic friend, and the eager student. He loved and admired Johnson, defended him, and wished to learn from him. He may even have sought and enjoyed being reprimanded on certain occasions; experience had taught him that fathers condemned. But the range of subjects they discussed, and even more important the particular topics to which Boswell constantly chose to return, indicate that he could also play the equal and the sceptic. Boswell questioned Johnson, of course, about problems immediate to his life: law, Corsica, his father's prospective marriage and his own; but he also pressed him about death and free will, matters tense with significance for both of them, and which Johnson wished to avoid. Furthermore, he felt secure enough to mention almost any thought that came into his head, and to pursue it even when Johnson showed annoyance: what would you do if you were shut up in a castle with a new-born child? There is a futile air about Boswell's struggles with his father, since neither seemed willing or able to learn from the other. But in Boswell's dealings with Johnson, enough affection and tolerance existed on both sides so that a give-and-take situation could often, though not always, be established. It was not a closed system in which nothing new could develop, but a meaningful and productive relationship.

§ II

In the landed and contentious society of eighteenth-century Scotland, the law was the great profession. Boswell clearly reveals his mixed attitude towards it, as his destined vocation from early years, in an anecdote in *Boswelliana*. After complaining that he disliked the law as a career and had entered on it only to please his father, he added: "I am pressed into the service here; but I have observed that a pressed man either by sea or land after a little time does just as well as a volunteer." Boswell did make a much better lawyer than one would have predicted; as a contemporary wrote: "Called to the bar, he distinguished himself in his first appearances by an ingenious invention of arguments, a brilliancy of eloquence, and a quickness of wit."[1] His early earnings were considerably better than the average for young advocates, though to be sure his father's position as a judge helped to make him sought after. Boswell grew used to his work, and even to like it at times. A stabilizing influence, it provided him with a place in society and a comfortable status in his own eyes; whatever roles he adopted temporarily, he was permanently James Boswell, advocate.

[1] Quoted in Percy Fitzgerald's *Life of James Boswell*, 1891, i. 109. Fitzgerald's source is unknown.

The case that most interested him in his early years at the bar was the Douglas cause, the greatest civil trial held in Scotland during the period. Archibald, Duke of Douglas, died in 1761 without direct heirs. His sister, Lady Jane Douglas, at forty-eight had married Colonel (later Sir) John Stewart, and two years later, in 1748, had announced the birth of twins at Paris in very obscure circumstances. One of the children died young. The guardians of the Duke of Hamilton and his brother, acting for them, and another relative who had an arguable claim to the estate if Archibald Douglas, the surviving child, were disinherited, brought suit maintaining that the children were spurious. The Hamilton lawyers thought they had discovered that Archibald and his brother were French children fraudulently obtained, and when the case, after having been fought through the courts since 1762, came to a decision in July 1767, the Court of Session agreed with them by a vote of eight to seven. In February 1769, the House of Lords reversed this decision upon appeal.[2]

Boswell did not need to be pressed into this cause; he became an ardent volunteer for Douglas. As well as composing ballads (sung to admiring audiences) and contributing items to the newspapers about it, he wrote a slightly disguised fictional account of the case called *Dorando*, while the trial was going on. In this little work the facts are twisted with an easy facility to favour Douglas. Speeches upholding his claim are inserted into the mouths of characters representing Robert Dundas, Lord President of the Court of Session, who was strongly opposed to it, and the Earl of Chatham; Douglas's victory is triumphantly predicted; and in a flight of fancy at its conclusion, the Prince of Dorando (Douglas) rescues the Prince of Arvidoso (the young Duke of Hamilton) from a wild boar, restoring peace between the two families. For this and other literary services, Douglas rewarded Boswell by making him a regular counsel in the cause after the main victory had been won.[3]

The major issue in the Douglas cause, so far as Boswell was con-

[2] A. Francis Steuart's *The Douglas Cause*, 1909, a volume in the Notable Scottish Trials series, contains the best short account of the case, together with illustrative documents. Lillian de la Torre has made an accurate and exhaustive study of the affair, and has come up with an ingenious solution to its difficulties in her lively and entertaining *The Heir of Douglas*, 1952.

[3] Boswell's other efforts to help Douglas are discussed on pp. 69 and 87.

cerned, was "that great principle of law — *filiation* — on which we all depend." Doubt a man's parentage, he felt, and you cut the very ground from under his feet. Why Boswell felt so strongly about an abstract principle can be understood if Douglas's problem is transposed into terms of his own situation. Boswell's own inheritance was threatened; in a metaphorical sense his parentage was questionable, for the differences between his father and himself must have made him wonder if he was a worthy son of the family of Auchinleck. The resentment aroused by such uncertainty found a happy release. During the rioting in Edinburgh that followed the news of Douglas's victory, Boswell headed the mob which broke the judges' windows — not excepting his father's.

§ III

Boswell's visit to Corsica in 1765 arose from a desire to see something which the ordinary young man on the Grand Tour missed; it ended by giving him a cause and a reputation. In the Corsican fight for independence, first from the Genoese and after May 1768 from the French, he saw externalized his own rebellious struggle for liberty, with none of the conflict which his respect for authority aroused in his personal situation. Authority, in this instance, could legitimately be defined as oppression, and in all his efforts on behalf of the Corsicans Boswell could be sure that he had the unqualified approval of another much-respected older man, Pasquale de Paoli, the gallant Corsican leader.[4]

As soon as he returned to the Continent from Corsica, Boswell started an elaborate newspaper campaign intended first to bring Corsica and his connection with it to public attention, and ultimately to persuade the British government to aid the Corsicans. In this campaign, "facts" and "inventions," as he distinguished them in his marked file of *The London Chronicle*, were mingled in a fashion calculated to mislead any but the most knowing reader; all furthered his

[4] The political and social implications of Corsica and the Corsican rebellion for eighteenth-century Europe, and Boswell's conception of the Corsicans are discussed in the introduction to the *Journal of a Tour to Corsica* in *Boswell on the Grand Tour: Italy, Corsica, and France*.

grand design. He also raised money to buy arms, and edited a volume
of essays "in favour of the brave Corsicans."

His most important effort, however, and the climax to his attempt
to rouse his countrymen, was his *Account of Corsica; The Journal of
a Tour to That Island, and Memoirs of Pascal Paoli*, published in
February 1768. His "little monument to liberty," as Boswell called
it, made a strong impression on the public: a book of the hour, it ran
to three editions in England, three in Ireland, and was translated into
Dutch, German, Italian, and twice into French. Because of *Corsica*,
Boswell was as well known on the Continent as Johnson during their
lifetimes. It impressed the French government, which had a translation made, and undoubtedly influenced the decision of the British
government to send secret supplies of arms to the Corsicans. But the
ministry had no intention of entering on a large-scale war over a com-
paratively unimportant island, and the attempt of a group in Parliament in November 1768 to force a more open stand against the
French was badly defeated. The French were then able to proceed
against their much inferior enemy without fear of British intervention, and by June 1769 had effectually overcome all resistance.

Though his book did not succeed in its object, it deeply affected
Boswell himself. His identification with the Corsican cause was so
complete that he was still known as "Corsica Boswell" twenty-five
years later. Johnson might deprecate his enthusiasm for the Corsicans, and others smile at its apparent excess, but the cause was a noble
one and commanded respect for its most famous adherent. Furthermore, *Corsica* made Boswell secure in another social role, that of author. He had "an ardent ambition for literary fame," as he remarks in
its Preface, for he felt that a successful author had "established himself as a respectable character in distant society, without any danger
of having that character lessened by the observation of his weaknesses."

Boswell could display weaknesses, however, at closer range, as
well as an open and very human mixture of motives. His appearance
in the figure of "an armed Corsican chief" at the Shakespeare Festival
in 1769, after the Corsican cause had been definitely lost, served no
larger purpose than to gratify his yearning for flamboyant exhibition-
ism by playing his Corsican role to the utmost. But his bid to save

Corsica was essentially a serious affair, no matter how it was tricked out, and might have had serious consequences. After Paoli's escape from Corsica, his former adjutant returned to Ajaccio with his pregnant wife, and a few weeks later their child was born. If Boswell had been successful in securing his government's intervention, Napoleon Bonaparte might have been born a British subject.

§ IV

Nowhere did Boswell strike more poses, or assign roles more rigidly to himself and others, than in his relations with women. Many of those in whom he had any serious interest he characterized by certain repetitive key words or phrases. These identifications were all the more hard and fast because Boswell needed women enormously and yet was often timid with them. Though he boasted that women of all ages and tempers were fond of him, it is doubtful that he really felt this to be the truth: the confidence displayed by the Don Juan is more apparent than real. Casting a woman in a particular role defined her for him, making her far easier to cope with than if he had tried to understand her personality in full. His concept of his own sexual role ranged erratically from "Mark Antony" to "Don Quixote," and his judgment of women was liable to be even less sound, especially when he was further unnerved by the prospect of marriage.[5]

The glittering procession of women that passes in this volume can be divided into two groups: those whom Boswell could marry and those he could not. In the latter category belong his "Italian angel," Girolama Piccolomini, that pathetic reminder of his stay in Siena; the gardener's daughter; and the pert, rompish "Circe" of Moffat, Mrs. Dodds. Among the theoretically eligible, Boswell was confronted by the brilliant and frightening Dutch "termagant," Zélide; the "Yorkshire beauty," Miss Bosville; and the unidentified Miss B., whose personal "charms" were enhanced by her position as heiress to certain valuable mining properties.

The question of choice was complicated by the sometimes united,

[5] Chauncey B. Tinker treats certain of Boswell's love affairs perceptively in his *Young Boswell*, 1922, ch. 7.

sometimes conflicting claims of love and fortune. Among the more important prospects, fortune was the predominant factor in the instance of Catherine Blair, known to Boswell as "the Heiress" or "the Princess." Social and property considerations made her an extremely desirable match: a distant relative and Lord Auchinleck's former ward, she was heiress to the estate of Adamtown. Boswell found her at eighteen a "handsome, stately woman" with a good countenance, as well as "sensible, good-tempered, cheerful, pious," but a sober and prudential estimate did not satisfy him. He had to idealize her, to convince himself that he lay entirely in her power, to adore her "like a divinity" in the romantic groves of Auchinleck. And divinity was not an end Miss Blair was shaped to. Temple thought her "a woman of sense and prudence"; Boswell's reports of her conversation show her to have been naïve and candid, a straightforward Scots young lady far from the Dulcinea del Toboso or even Cleopatra that his "feverish constitution" demanded. He must have sensed the disparity, however, between the actual Miss Blair and his conception of her even before she made it plain to him; his confession to Temple that he saw his love for her as another chapter in his adventures indicates that he saved himself from any real emotional commitment by safely "distancing" her. When he finally proposed, he could be sure of rejection.

Fortune also played a considerable part in Boswell's affection for "la belle Irlandaise," Mary Ann Boyd: "just sixteen, formed like a Grecian nymph" — and almost certain of a comfortable inheritance. This was Boswell's Horatian romance; she was an Arcadian shepherdess and he a "Sicilian swain." He carved her initial on a tree, and cut off a lock of her hair. But his pursuit of her into Ireland in the spring of 1769 was hampered by a growing interest in Margaret Montgomerie, his companion on the trip. Momentarily in the exhilaration of this Irish jaunt he may have seen himself as Macheath, his early hero from Gay's *Beggar's Opera:*

> How happy could I be with either
> Were t'other dear charmer away,

but his heart had made its choice.

Margaret Montgomerie emerges as the most real figure in the Boswellian gallery of women, partly because a good number of her letters have survived, and also because the ways in which Boswell saw her converge with what she was actually like. She was his first cousin, poor, and two years older than he. Though Boswell did not think her a beauty, he found her sexually very attractive, a "heathen goddess." Essentially she was a strong woman, neither hard nor aggressive, but patient and enduring. She lacked Boswell's extraordinary appetite for experience, preferring instead to live in peace with the world; she realized, as he did not, the necessity for compromise and prudent reserve. But she knew what she wanted, and she was willing to take it if offered. What she wanted was James Boswell.

The relationship between them is moving in its gradual development. Margaret had been Boswell's confidante for a number of years before he took his interest in her seriously. Then he began to test her and himself: did he love her enough, was she interested in someone else, how much did she love him? Quarrels were followed by *rapprochements*. Her meagre dowry was a serious barrier; Lord Auchinleck was opposed to the marriage because she would bring neither property nor sufficient money nor useful new connections to the family, and Boswell felt the force of these objections. But seeing her now as "my lady" and "my valuable friend," Boswell slowly began to realize that love was more important to him than fortune. His final test was severe: would she be willing to go off to America with him and live on almost nothing? When she answered that she would, even Boswell was convinced that she loved him.

After this crisis, the two were on firmer ground. Their mutual love and respect gave each confidence and a sense of value. Margaret felt it her duty to be submissive, to study his happiness, to be entirely guided by him, but she did not hesitate to speak her mind, whether it meant offering advice about a cold or admitting her wish to see him. Boswell insisted on his faults and his melancholy, feared that their happiness might be too great to last, but he had a due appreciation of her "admirable heart and spirit," which strengthened him for the responsibilities of marriage. A new note of maturity sounds in his letters: whatever Lord Auchinleck or the world might think, their attachment to each other was a credit to both. Boswell had found the woman who best suited him.

§ V

Any edition like the present is a desperate undertaking, since it seeks to fulfil the double demands of truth and art, while it is inevitably bounded by the nature and inflexibility of the documents that have happened to survive. In fiction one can impose whatever form is desired on the cycles of nature; here the documents insist in part on creating their own structure. Still, despite these limitations, it is possible to establish them within a framework, and this the editors have tried to do. Basically we have presented Boswell as a private individual rather than as a public figure, realizing fully that the documents selected emphasize certain aspects of a complex personality at the expense of others. How different an impression might be given if Boswell's letters to Mrs. Dodds had survived instead of those to Miss Montgomerie! Only a full-scale biography, such as the one Professor Pottle is now writing, can correct these deficiencies in perspective.

What Boswell reports, and how he reports it, are also of great significance in determining the nature of this volume. He himself defied "any man to write down anything like a perfect account of what he has been conscious of during one day of his life, if in any degree of spirits"; a man could mark external circumstances, "but the variations within, the workings of reason and passion . . . the colourings of fancy, are too fleeting to be recorded." Literally this is true, but it is amazing how evocative his own writing is in its nice mixture of description and incident, and in its apparently uncalculated selection of significant detail. What he reports is the scene before him, whether it is the Edinburgh court room or the London stage-coach, and he reports it as directly and undistortedly as he can. He avoids periphrasis and elegant variation in his Journal, or rather they never seem to enter his head.[6] Simplicity, vitality, and precision are the essential characteristics of his writing. It is a triumph of the normal vision.

Such a style could not be sustained unless it reflected the man within. George Colman, Boswell noted, "very justly observed that my character was simplicity: not in a sense of weakness, but of being plain and unaffected." This is the truth to which both his life and

---

[6] A phrase like "cherished the risible exertion" (21 February 1768) is extremely unusual; perhaps, indeed, the only example of elegant variation in the volume.

writings lead. One should not be misled by his candour or his uncertain self-estimation into thinking him eccentric; the strengths and especially the weaknesses that can be confided to a journal are not necessarily those exhibited in society. "Blending philosophy and raking," as he did, is no unusual matter, especially considering that the philosopher he most admired was Thomas Reid with his belief in "common sense." (The common-sense vision, too, tends to be comic, in the broadest sense, rather than tragic, though it is only coincidence that this volume ends, like most English comedies, in marriage.) Boswell's actions, like his aims, were for the most part ordinary; what distinguishes him is the extraordinary expressiveness of the great writer.

§ VI

The principal manuscripts from which this book has been compiled are the following:

1. Journal in Scotland, 10 January to 3 June 1767: 61 quarto pages and a title-page, numbered by Boswell 1–73, but pp. 1–2, 7–12, and 25–28 are now missing; ranging in size from $7\frac{3}{8}$ by 6 to $7\frac{3}{4}$ by $6\frac{1}{4}$ inches, unbound.

2. Journal in Scotland, 1 January to 27 February 1768: 34 quarto pages and a title-page, numbered by Boswell through p. 32; roughly $7\frac{7}{8}$ by $6\frac{1}{8}$ inches, unbound.

3. Journal in London and Oxford, 16 March to ?April 1768: partly filled bound half-calf quarto notebook, 70 pages (that is, 35 leaves), numbered by Boswell 1–108, but pp. 21–22, 65–70, 73–84, 89–102, and 105–108 are missing. Pp. 21–22 are printed from a typescript made while that portion of the text was intact, and the greater part of p. 108 has been recovered from the "off-set" on the blank page following.

4. Notes for Journal in London, 21 April to 16 May 1768: 7 unpaged octavo leaves, written on both sides, roughly $7\frac{1}{4}$ by $4\frac{3}{8}$ inches, unbound. Notes for 24 to 30 March are written on the verso of the third leaf.

5. Journal in London, 20 to 22 May 1768: 10 unpaged octavo leaves, the last blank, roughly $7\frac{1}{4}$ by $4\frac{3}{8}$ inches, unbound. These leaves are enclosed in a wrapper endorsed by James Boswell, the Younger,

"Conversations with Lord Mansfield," and contain on the inside in his hand an extract from the page of notes which originally preceded them.

6. Journal of Journey to Ireland, 25 April to 7 May 1769: "Journal of the first part of my jaunt to Ireland in 1769 with Miss Peggie Montgomerie. I regret that I ceased when it would have been most interesting": bound half-calf quarto notebook, 33 pages and a title-page (17 leaves), numbered by Boswell 1–9, 8–25, 24–25, 25–27, 30, but continuous and complete; roughly $7\frac{1}{2}$ by 6 inches.

7. Journal in Scotland, 12 June to 27 August 1769: enclosed in a wrapper endorsed by Boswell, "Journal, Summer Session, 1769": 100 numbered octavo pages (50 leaves); most are roughly $7\frac{1}{2}$ by $4\frac{1}{4}$ inches; unbound.

8. Journal in England, 28 August to 26 September 1769: "Journal of my jaunt to London, the Jubilee at Stratford upon Avon in memory and honour of Shakespeare, and to visit my old and most intimate friend, the Reverend Mr. Temple in Devonshire, &c., &c., &c. Autumn, 1769": written from the other end of the notebook containing No. 6; it consists of 122 pages and a title-page (62 leaves), numbered by Boswell 1–113, 104–114, but continuous. The lower half of the leaf bearing pp. 39–40 has been cut away, and pp. 41–42 are missing. The promise of the title is more ample than the performance, for the account breaks off in London a month before the trip to Devonshire.

9. Memoranda and Notes for Journal in London, 3 September to 17 October 1769: 14 unpaged duodecimo leaves, roughly $6\frac{1}{8}$ by 4 inches, stabbed and sewn. A fragment, leaves being missing both at the beginning, and (apparently) at the end. There are no entries for September 6, 8–10, 19, 22–23, 28, 30 and October 6, but the portion preserved seems to be complete as Boswell wrote it.

10. Notes for Journal in London, 24 September to 3 October, and 17 October 1769; 4 unpaged quarto leaves, ranging in size from 9 by $7\frac{1}{2}$ to $8\frac{3}{4}$ by 7 inches, unbound.

11. Papers Apart, Manuscript of *Life of Johnson*, after 28 May 1768: Corrections and Additions for p. 333 of Boswell's manuscript: 7 unnumbered quarto pages on 5 leaves; most are roughly $9\frac{7}{8}$ by 8 inches, unbound.

12. Papers Apart, Manuscript of *Life of Johnson*, 30 September

1769: Corrections and Additions for p. 335 of Boswell's manuscript: 10 quarto leaves, rectos numbered by Boswell 1–10, some with additions on versos, roughly 9¾ by 8 inches, unbound; an octavo leaf (roughly 8 by 4¾ inches) inserted at verso of p. 4.

13. Manuscript of *Life of Johnson*, 16–26 October 1769: 18 quarto leaves, rectos numbered by Boswell 335–352, some with additions on verso, roughly 9⅞ by 8 inches, unbound.

14. Papers Apart, Manuscript of *Life of Johnson*, 26–27 October 1769: Corrections and Additions marked "RC" [Roman Catholic?] for p. 352 of Boswell's manuscript: 22 octavo leaves, rectos numbered by Boswell 1–22, some with additions on versos, roughly 8 by 5 inches, unbound.

15. Manuscript of *Life of Johnson*, 8–10 November 1769: 3 quarto leaves, rectos numbered by Boswell 351–353; matter of this quotation on 351 v., 352 r. and v., 353 r.

16. Upwards of 550 letters sent or received by Boswell between 23 February 1766 and 25 November 1769. All but 62 of these letters are at Yale. The letters to Boswell in the Yale collection are originals, as are Boswell's letters to John Johnston and W. J. Temple. (He retrieved his letters to Johnston from Johnston's executor, and Temple returned the few letters of this period that are now at Yale. The others to Temple, which are in the Morgan Library, were discovered about 1840 in Boulogne, France.) Almost all the other letters by Boswell at Yale are drafts or copies. The originals of the letters from Margaret Montgomerie to Boswell with one exception were lost sometime after the transfer of the papers to Colonel Isham. A typescript had been made previously, from which our text of the letters is taken. Boswell's Register of Letters, now at Yale, covers the period from the opening of this volume to 21 October 1766, and from 10 June to 9 November 1769: while neither complete nor entirely accurate, it is often useful for fixing dates and for proving the existence of lost letters.

17. Miscellaneous documents, 23 February 1766 to 25 November 1769. These include such items as Boswell's Consultation Book (the original of which is in the National Library of Scotland), verses, two assorted notebooks, and legal papers.

The Journals included in this volume and the Notes for 21 April to 16 May 1768 were published in 1930 by Frederick A. Pottle in the seventh and eighth volumes of the *Private Papers of James Boswell from Malahide Castle, in the Collection of Lt.-Colonel Ralph Heywood Isham*, an expensive limited edition of which only 570 copies were printed. Some fifty-five of the eighty-five letters included in the present volume have also previously appeared, most of them in the *Private Papers* or in Professor Chauncey B. Tinker's *Letters of James Boswell*, Clarendon Press, 1924. Most of Boswell's letters to Temple included here and in Tinker had been previously published in *Letters of James Boswell Addressed to the Rev. W. J. Temple* [ed. Sir Philip Francis] 1857, and reprinted with an introduction by Thomas Seccombe in 1908. A group of newspaper items mainly about Corsica composed by Boswell has been collected from *The London Chronicle*, 1767. Outstanding among the material that now appears in print for the first time are Boswell's letters to Temple about the gardener's daughter, Temple's letters to Boswell, notes of a conversation between Boswell and Johnson, and the manuscript versions of certain scenes in *The Life of Johnson*. The fully written Journal is printed without cuts, but other documents have been abridged whenever it has seemed desirable. Notes saying that certain letters have not been recovered should not be taken as indicating a policy of including all the letters we have that are mentioned in the Journal. Such notes are intended to explain why letters that sound important enough to be included in this edition do not appear here.

The spelling, capitalization, and punctuation of both manuscripts and previously printed material have been reduced to accepted modern norms, and abbreviations and contractions have been expanded at will. All quotations have been standardized in the same fashion. The standard of spelling for all but proper names is *The Concise Oxford Dictionary* (1951). For place names F. H. Groome's *Ordnance Gazetteer of Scotland*, J. G. Bartholomew's *Survey Gazetteer of the British Isles*, and *London Past and Present* by Peter Cunningham and H. B. Wheatley have been followed. Family names have been brought into conformity with the usage of *The Dictionary of National Biography*, Mrs. Margaret Stuart's *Scottish Family History*, G. E. Cokayne's *Complete Baronetage* and *Complete Peerage*, Sir James Balfour Paul's *Scots Peerage*, and various other special books of reference. Names of speakers in conversations cast dramatically, whether supplied by Boswell or the editors, are put in small capitals without distinction. A few clear inadvertencies have been put right without notice. Square brackets indicate words added where the manuscript shows no defect, and where there is no reason to suspect a slip on the part of the writer; angular brackets indicate reconstruction of words lost through defects in the manuscript, where the reconstruction is not entirely certain. Those who wish to examine the unnormalized and unmodified text of the Journal are reminded that it is available in Colonel Isham's *Private Papers*.

The annotation and editorial notes to this volume have been designed for the general reader, though it is never easy to estimate how much the general reader knows or wants to know. We have attempted to provide essential information when it is available, and occasionally to add sidelights which are intended to characterize a person or event more firmly, but complete annotation — such as full explication of Boswell's legal cases — has been reserved for the research edition. The indexes of this series are not mere finding tools, but supplement the annotation. In particular, we usually reserve for the index the function of supplying Christian names and professions of persons mentioned.

An edition such as the present one is based extensively on previous published and unpublished work; it is, in fact, a highly collective and co-operative enterprise, which draws on the minute and multiple accumulation of facts, inferences, and guesses of at least a generation of scholarship. As has been mentioned above, F. A. Pottle published a text of Boswell's Journals and certain of the Notes for this period in Colonel Isham's privately printed *Private Papers of James Boswell*. He also published the correspondence between Boswell and Margaret Montgomerie, almost all of which appears in the eighth volume of the *Private Papers*. Certain other letters and documents reprinted here also first appeared in these volumes. As also mentioned above, Professor Tinker published many of Boswell's letters included here in his *Letters of James Boswell*.

The basic annotation for this volume has been collected from various sources. We have made grateful use of certain of the notes to Professor Tinker's edition of the *Letters*, as well as, on occasion, of notes from the Hill-Powell edition of *The Life of Johnson*. Sir James

Fergusson has generously answered many questions on Boswell's Scottish background. We have drawn upon Professor Joseph Foladare's unpublished Yale dissertation, "James Boswell and Corsica" (2 vols., 1936), and Dr. Richard C. Cole's unpublished Yale dissertation, "The Correspondence of James Boswell in 1769" (1955). The text of the Journal for 10 January to 3 June 1767 and 1 January to 27 February 1768 was reviewed and annotation for it collected by Professor Eleanor T. Lincoln as a class exercise in the Yale Graduate School. Similar services were performed for the Journal and Journal Notes from 16 March to 22 May 1768 by Dr. Joseph L. Walsh; for the Journal from 25 April to 7 May 1769 and from 12 June to 27 August 1769 by Professor Irving McKee; and for the Journal and Notes and Memoranda from 28 August to 17 October 1769 by Professor John P. Kirby. Dr. Charles H. Bennett reviewed the entire text of the Journal, Notes, and Memoranda for the period, and made additions to the annotation, especially for the Journal from 10 January to 3 June 1767 and 1 January to 27 February 1768. He also drafted annotation for a trade or reading edition. Using these materials and others resulting from his own researches, Professor Pottle completed a text for a trade edition over fifteen years ago. The subsequent recovery of papers from Malahide Castle and other documents of the first importance necessitated the planning of a quite different volume and extensive revisions of and additions to the annotation.

ACKNOWLEDGMENTS

The general plan of this volume, worked out by the editors, has benefited considerably from the advice of the Editorial Committee. Also, Mr. Liebert provided the artist with materials for the maps, and Dr. Metzdorf, who has been of assistance at every stage, assumed responsibility for collecting the illustrations. Both they and Professor Hilles read the proofs. Of the larger Advisory Committee, Professor Clifford and Sir James Fergusson read the proofs and provided corrections and suggestions for the notes.

In addition to those mentioned specifically elsewhere, we gratefully acknowledge the assistance of the following: C. Colleer Abbott, Frederick B. Adams, Jr., Cleanth Brooks, Herbert Cahoon, W. Kenneth Cornell, Miss Lillian de la Torre, Robert W. Hill, Dr. Harry M. Keil, James M. Osborn, Paul Pickrel, Marshall Waingrow, Robert Warnock, and Charles McC. Weis. Our next-door neighbours in the Walpole Office, George L. Lam and Warren H. Smith, have, as usual, often taken time from their own pursuits to help us with one of our problems. Finally we heartily thank all members of the office staff of the Yale Editions of the Private Papers of James Boswell during the past year: Miss Harriet Chidester, William F. Hawthorne '57, Robert E. Murphy '58, Mrs. Marion S. Pottle, and Mrs. Phyllis C. Warfel. Mrs. Hope G. Waingrow is mainly responsible for the index.

F.B.

Yale University, New Haven

15 August 1956

BOSWELL IN SEARCH OF A WIFE

1766–1769

This, my dear Peggie, is, I think, a just and true abstract of our story. It does you great honour, and I appear a better man than people have imagined. [BOSWELL TO MARGARET MONTGOMERIE, 21 AUGUST 1769]

Boswell in Search of a Wife

1766–1769

SKETCH OF BOSWELL'S LIFE TO MARCH 1766. James Boswell was born in Edinburgh on 29 October 1740, the eldest son of Alexander Boswell, whose title, Lord Auchinleck, indicated his position as a judge of the supreme courts of Scotland. Of an old family and an important land-owner in his home county, Ayrshire, Lord Auchinleck imparted his strong sense of tradition and family pride to his son. Boswell studied law at the Universities of Edinburgh and Glasgow, but his real inter-ests were writing and attending the theatre. In the spring of 1760, he ran away to London and briefly became a Roman Catholic. The Earl of Eglinton, his father's Ayrshire neighbour, reclaimed him from this lapse (which would have seriously disabled him in public life), and introduced him "into the circles of the great, the gay, and the in-genious." Admiring everything about London, Boswell tried to per-suade his father to secure him a commission in the Foot Guards, but Lord Auchinleck kept him at his studies in Edinburgh until he passed the civil law examination in June 1762. Then, although refusing to purchase a commission in the Guards, his father permitted him to return to London to see if he could obtain one through influence.

Boswell's ensuing year in London had two solid results: he wrote the first long stretch of his great Journal,[1] and near the end of his stay he met Samuel Johnson. The Journal vividly records his London im-pressions and experiences, from parties at Northumberland House to his affair with the actress Louisa and encounters with streetwalkers in the Strand, while Johnson was to exert a permanent moral and intel-lectual influence upon his life. Having failed to secure a commission, Boswell agreed to become a lawyer as his father wished, and crossed

[1] The journal for this year was discovered by Professor C. Colleer Abbott at Fettercairn House in 1930, and published in 1950 under the title of *Boswell's London Journal, 1762–1763* by the McGraw-Hill Book Company, Inc. (New York) and William Heinemann, Ltd. (London).

over to Utrecht in August 1763 to continue his study of civil law. His year in Holland was unhappy: he disliked the Dutch, and a combination of hard work and unaccustomed chastity profoundly depressed him. But near the end of this year a relaxation of his religious and moral standards and his interest in Belle de Zuylen (Zélide), a Dutch girl of noble family, helped to revive his spirits.[2]

In June 1764, Boswell started off on his Grand Tour proper. He visited a good number of the German courts, and, though he failed to meet Frederick the Great, he was presented to many people of the first rank and became close friends with the Margrave of Baden-Durlach. But greater successes were reserved for Switzerland, where he met Rousseau and Voltaire. Rousseau, though unwilling to become his father-confessor, did encourage and reassure him. With Voltaire Boswell had a delightful conversation on religion.[3] Having made the two great, antithetical spirits of the age conscious of his existence, Boswell headed happily over the Alps to Italy in January 1765. Here he pursued John Wilkes, sightseeing, and women with equal pertinacity, travelled with Lord Mountstuart, the Earl of Bute's eldest son, and had a serious love affair in Siena with Girolama Piccolomini. The most important event of his Continental tour, however, was his visit to Corsica in October and November 1765. He was profoundly influenced by the sight of this small nation fighting for its liberty and by the memorable character of its leader, Pasquale de Paoli. From Corsica he travelled to Genoa, and then through France to Paris. Hearing there of his mother's death he hurried home, after stopping briefly in London, where he saw Johnson and Rousseau, and informed Pitt about Corsica.[4] He arrived in Edinburgh about 7 March 1766.

---

[2] See *Boswell in Holland, 1763–1764*, 1952, McGraw-Hill Book Company, Inc. (New York) and William Heinemann, Ltd. (London).

[3] See *Boswell on the Grand Tour: Germany and Switzerland, 1764*, 1953, McGraw-Hill Book Company, Inc. (New York) and William Heinemann, Ltd. (London).

[4] See *Boswell on the Grand Tour: Italy, Corsica, and France, 1765–1766*, 1955, McGraw-Hill Book Company, Inc. (New York) and William Heinemann, Ltd. (London).

[Boswell to William Johnson Temple][5]

Auchinleck House, 28 April 1766[6]

MY EVER DEAR TEMPLE, — Many a curious letter have you had from me in my different situations. A more extraordinary one than this you have never had. I write to you while the delirium is really existing. In short, Sir, the gardener's daughter who was named for my mother,[7] and has for some time been in the family as a chambermaid is so very pretty that I am entirely captivated by her. Besides my principle of never debauching an innocent girl, my regard for her father, a worthy man of uncommon abilities, restrains me from forming the least licentious thought against her. And, therefore, in plain words, I am mad enough to indulge imaginations of marrying her. Only think of the proud Boswell, with all that you know of him, the fervent adorer of a country girl of three and twenty. I rave about her. I was never so much in love as I am now. My fancy is quite inflamed. It riots in extravagance.

I know as well as you can tell me that a month's or perhaps ten days' possession of this angelic creature would probably make her appear to me insipid as does to you Celia "who at Berwick deigns to dwell."[8] I have a clear remembrance of my being tormented with many such passions, all which went off in a little time, and yet, Temple, I am still dreaming of delightful nuptials. She and I were in a manner brought up together. As far back as I can remember, we used to build houses and make gardens, wade in the river and play upon the sunny banks. I cannot consider her as below me. For these six or seven years past I have seen her little. Before I went abroad she had begun to be timid and reserved, for Lord Eglinton admired her

[5] Temple, Boswell's one-time classmate at the University of Edinburgh, and closest friend, was now at Cambridge qualifying himself for holy orders. Though the two shared an interest in politics and literature, their intimacy was based on an unreserved trust and openness and an appreciation of each other's temperament.

[6] This letter was not sent until 17 May. See p. 5.

[7] Euphemia. Possibly the gardener's daughter's last name was Bruce.

[8] Celia is Ann ("Nancy") Stow, Temple's first cousin to whom he was more or less engaged. Thomas Gray later nicknamed her "Madame Minx." Boswell had stopped to see her at Berwick on his way north. The quotation is unidentified.

extremely and wanted to seduce her.[9] For my part I saw nothing more about her than in many good-looking girls in the neighborhood. But since my return from my travels, I have been quite enchanted with her. She has a most amiable face, the prettiest foot and ankle. She is perfectly well made, and has a lively, genteel air that is irresistible.

I take every opportunity of being with her when she is putting on fires or dressing a room. She appears more graceful with her besom than ever shepherdess did with a crook. I pretend great earnestness to have the library in good order and assist her to dust it. I cut my gloves that she may mend them. I kiss her hand. I tell her what a beauty I think her. She has an entire confidence in me and has no fear of any bad design; and she has too much sense to form an idea of having me for a husband. On the contrary, she talks to me of not refusing a good offer if it is made to her. Enchanting creature! must she be enjoyed by some schoolmaster or farmer? Upon my honour, it cuts me to the heart. If she would not marry anybody else, I think I could let her alone. That we may not be too often seen together, she and I write notes to each other, which we lay under the cloth which covers my table. This little curious correspondence, which to her is an innocent amusement, makes my heart beat continually. She has a fine temper. She has read a great deal, for I always supplied her with books. In short, she is better than any lady I know.

What shall I do, Temple? Shall I lay my account with all its consequences and espouse her? Will not the exquisite languish of her eyes charm away repentance? Shall I not pass a life of true natural felicity with the woman I love and have a race of healthy and handsome children? Good heavens! what am I about? It would kill my father. Have I returned safe from London, from Italy, and from France to throw myself away on a servant maid? You might apply to me what was said of St. Paul when the viper fastened upon his hand after the shipwreck: "Whom though he hath escaped the sea, yet vengeance suffereth not to live."[1]

I have got a lock of her hair which I dote upon. She allowed me to cut it off. If I should marry her, I would never suffer her to dress better than she does now. I think I could pass my whole life agreeably with

[9] For Alexander Montgomerie, tenth Earl of Eglinton, see p. 1.
[1] Acts 28. 4.

her assistance. I am not fit for marriage in all the forms. A lady would not be compliant enough, and would oblige me to harass myself with an endless repetition of external ceremony and a most woeful maintaining of *proper conduct*. Whereas my dear girl would be grateful for my attachment, would be devoted to me in every respect, would live with me just as a mistress without the disgrace and remorse. After all my feverish joys and pains, I should enjoy calm and permanent bliss in her arms. Was there ever such madness?

My friend, give me your hand. Lead me away from what is probably a delusion that would make me give up with the world and sink into a mere animal. And yet is it not being singularly happy that after the gloom I have endured, the dreary speculations I have formed, and the vast variety of all sorts of adventures that I have run through, my mind should not be a bit corrupted, and I should feel the elegant passion with all the pure simplicity and tender agitations of youth? Surely I have the genuine soul of love. When dusting the rooms with my charmer, am I not like Agamemnon amongst the Thracian girls? All this may do for a summer. But is it possible that I could imagine the dear delirium would last for life? I will rouse my philosophic spirit, and fly from this fascination. I am going to Moffat[2] for a month. Absence will break the enchantment. I charge you in honour not to mention it. Write me how you are affected by this letter. My dear Temple, I am ever yours,

JAMES BOSWELL.

[Boswell to Temple]

Moffat, 17 May 1766

MY DEAREST FRIEND, — I have been a week here, and to prevent that rodomontade of which you have frequently accused me, let me tell you at once that my love for the handsome chambermaid is already like a dream that is past. I kept the extravagant epistle which was to inform you of it till I should see if absence would not free me from the delirium. I can now send you with a good grace what would certainly have alarmed you, but will now be truly amusing. Romantic as I am, it was so strange a scene in the play of my life that I myself

[2] A watering-place in Dumfriesshire, about a day's journey away.

was quite astonished at it. I give you my word of honour it was literally true. There are few people who could give credit to it. But you, who have traced me since ever I fairly entered upon the stage, will not doubt of it. It is a little humbling, to be sure. It was the effect of great force and great weakness of mind. I am certainly a most various composition. Pray recollect my letter from Rotterdam,[3] and compare it with the inclosed. They are both genuine effusions, both original pictures of the same man at different times.

I can tell you though, Temple, such a man as I am must be very much upon his guard. I believe my safest way will be to give you a promise that I never will marry without your approbation; indeed you would not do amiss to make me such a promise too, for you was as seriously resolved to marry that girl at Berwick as ever I was to do a thing in my life! And had you married her, what a pretty figure would you have made by this time! For she has an old look, an auntish wisdom, awkward manners, and I imagine a narrow heart. She would grudge me coffee.

I am persuaded, Temple, that true exalted friendship never was stronger than it is between you and me. It has grown with ourselves and is in more vigour than ever. It has stood the trial of many a long absence and of my extensive travels, notwithstanding which you have kept up with me, as I told you with sincere joy in London. It has one more severe trial to stand — our marriage. Few have ever enjoyed the singular happiness that we have. Let us value it and preserve it. If we cannot have wives that will be united as are their husbands, let us take care to have such as will not offend us, as will be complaisant and agreeable and entertain us with elegance. I confess, my dear Temple, that you are the best adviser. You are more clear and determined than I am. After having seen your lovely Nancy, who upon honour looked so sour that I suspected she was the elder sister,[4] instead of giving you a spirited admonition to have nothing to do with her, I indolently thought: let him please himself. His grand ideas of rising in the state,

[3] Boswell had been extremely depressed when he first arrived in Holland in 1763: "Would you believe it? I ran frantic up and down the streets, crying out, bursting into tears, and groaning from my innermost heart" (*Boswell in Holland*, 16 August 1763).

[4] When Boswell sent a visiting-card to Ann Stow, her elder sister had burned it in front of the boy who delivered it.

of climbing the rocky steep of exalted ambition, and rivalling the most renowned in every age are now as if they never had been. Why should not his gay ideas of an angelic partner of his soul share the same fate? I ask you pardon, Temple. To rise in the world is not always given to superior merit, unless we allow a brazen assurance and unceasing forwardness to be superior to the merits which you and I now value so much. But an amiable wife and elegant living may be obtained by such philosophical men as we are, without either surprising strokes of chance or uncommon assistance from patrons; and therefore, my dearest friend, let us still please ourselves with the prospect of family happiness.

Miss Bosville is a charming young lady.[5] I got her to speak a good deal before I left London and found her extremely sensible. She never dances. That I should have insisted,[6] for no man shall ever pull about my wife. She loves reading and walking, and does not tire of six months in the country. But she is very fond of routs. What can that mean? Will she not cure of it? She speaks French very prettily. I dined three or four times a week at her father's while I stayed in London. He has written to me since I came to Scotland. I am to go and see them in Yorkshire. We must take time.

As to Zélide I am quite at my ease.[7] I have had a letter from her father telling me that he took my proposal in very good part; at the same time he informed me that things were so far advanced between his daughter and M. le Marquis, that the Marquis was actually applying to the Pope and the King of Sardinia for leave to marry a Protestant, and that therefore he and his daughter were bound in honour to fulfil their promises to him. As, however, the event of this application

---

[5] Elizabeth Diana, eldest daughter of Godfrey Bosville of Gunthwaite, Yorkshire, whom Boswell regarded as the chief of his "clan." Boswell thought her "vastly pretty: black hair, charming complexion, quite modest" (*Boswell on the Grand Tour: Italy, Corsica, and France*, 16 February 1766). The three names Bosville, Boswell, and Boswall are variants of the original French, Boisville.

[6] That is, insisted upon.

[7] Belle de Zuylen, whom Boswell always refers to as "Zélide," was the attractive, intelligent, and unconventional daughter of a noble Dutch family. Boswell, alternately fascinated and repelled by her, had made a very tentative proposal of marriage to her through her father the previous January. For a connected account of the whole Zélide affair, see *Boswell in Holland*, Correspondence with Belle de Zuylen.

was uncertain, if I continued to be of the same mind after they were free of the Marquis, he would then mention my proposal to Mademoiselle and have the honour to be umpire between us.[8] Nothing could be more genteel and friendly. I am glad I am off with Zélide. A *bel esprit* would never do at Auchinleck. My father and I have talked fully of her. He could not bear such a woman. You may remember you laughed very heartily at my finding fault with a *pretty* Dutchwoman. But my father judges extremely well when he finds fault with a *clever* Dutchwoman. "I love," says he, "one who has been accustomed to play in concert, be the music heavy or be it lively. For such a person will make harmony in any country. But one who has played in discord with those around her will hardly play in tune at all." *Cum fueris Romae, Romano vivito more* is sound sense;[9] and Otway says with much truth,

> Avoid
> The man that's singular . . .
> His spleen outweighs his brains.[1]

Zélide who must always *shine*, and Stockdale who is *sublimated* and thinks you below him in *genius* are weak beings, and would make one miserable to live with them.[2] 'Tis true they can't help their levity. Very well. Neither could they help it were the one humpbacked and the other palsied. I am sorry for them. But I would not join my existence with theirs.

After all, Zélide may perhaps *take up*.[3]

But this is a flight. Now, Temple, let me explain to you how I am already so free of the charming chambermaid. Absence alone was not enough. But I have found at Moffat a lady just in the situation of the one whom you formerly dallied with in Northumberland. But mine has no hope of ever being as yours now is, so that she is at full liberty, and therefore the king can do no wrong. I am quite devoted to her. I

[8] Belle's Catholic suitor was the Marquis de Bellegarde, a noble of Savoy and a colonel in the Dutch Service.

[9] "When in Rome, live as the Romans" (St. Ambrose, "cum" for "si").

[1] Altered from Otway's *Orphan*, III. i. 75–77.

[2] The Rev. Percival Stockdale, a friend of Temple's, one-time army officer turned clergyman, became a minor poet, critic, and dramatist.

[3] Obsolete for "reform."

dare write no more, but when we meet — you shall hear of Elysium. Love reconciles me to the Scots accent, which from the mouth of a pretty woman is simply and sweetly melodious. It is indeed, and I could engage to make Temple himself swear so in a few months. I am all health, affection, and gratitude.

I came to Moffat to wash off a few scurvy spots which the warmer climates of Europe had brought out on my skin. I drink the waters, and bathe regularly, and take a great deal of exercise,[4] and have a fine flow of spirits. I am as happy as an unmarried man can be. The *felices ter et amplius*[5] enchants me as the mitre or the genteel chintz arm-chairs in a handsome parlour do you. This shall be my last irregular connection. I shall be attached to the generous woman for ever. I am plaguing you with romantic sallies, my Temple. Forgive me, and it shall be made up to you before I sleep.

I wrote you a glowing letter from Prussia and observed that our fellow collegians had got before us in life. Do you remember what you and I used to think of Dundas? He has been making £700 a year as an advocate, has married a very genteel girl with £10,000 fortune, and is now appointed His Majesty's Solicitor General for Scotland. I should like to hear your remarks upon what I tell you.[6]

If you have not taken orders, I shall be out of all patience. Down with you to Devonshire, you dilatory dog.[7] And do not use your living as you have done the sighing and vulgar Celia.[8] I will abuse her. So let

[4] Moffat lies among some of the most impressive scenery of the Border, and serves as a centre for excursions.

[5] "Thrice happy and more [are they who are united in passionate love]" (Horace, *Odes*, I. xiii. 17–18).

[6] Henry Dundas, of the great legal family of Dundas of Arniston, was the younger half-brother of Robert Dundas, Lord President of the Court of Session. He later became Lord Advocate, Treasurer of the Navy, Home Secretary, and the political boss of Scotland. His wife, Elizabeth Rennie, ran away with a Captain Fawkener in 1778. Temple, Boswell, and Dundas had been schoolmates at the University of Edinburgh, Dundas being a couple of years younger than Boswell.

[7] Temple was ordained priest in the Church of England on 21 September 1766. His cousin once removed, Wilmot Vaughan, fourth Viscount Lisburne, presented him with the living of Mamhead in Devonshire, worth about £80 a year.

[8] Temple confessed his irresolution in regard to Miss Stow in his letter of 17 March 1766 to Boswell: "It was foolish of me to think of marrying any person in

me alone. I must make you laugh, though. One morning before I left
London as I was going along Great Russell Street, Bloomsbury, to Miss
Bosville's, whom did I meet but our friend Clack. BOSWELL. "Your
servant, Mr. Claxton." CLAXTON. "Your servant, Sir." BOSWELL. "Any
news from Temple?" CLAXTON. "No, but there's a letter come for him
in a woman's hand." BOSWELL. "It is from *her*, I dare say. We must
have him married." CLAXTON. "Yes, yes, he wants to be off, but he
shan't be off." BOSWELL. "No, no, the dog shan't be off. Do you watch
him there and I'll watch him here, and I defy him to break away."[9]
— Thus, Temple, upon honour did your two friends commune concerning you.

Mr. Pitt wrote me a most polite ministerial letter in answer to the
one which I sent him with your approbation. He said he would be glad
to "have the honour of my acquaintance" when he came to town. I
accordingly waited on him and had a noble conference, all which I
have in manuscript and hope to feast you most luxuriously with it.
Mr. Pitt is a great admirer of the Corsican Chief: "It may be said of
General Paoli what Cardinal de Retz said of the great Duke of Mon-
trose, 'C'est un de ces hommes qu'on ne trouve plus que dans les *Vies*
de Plutarque.' "[1] Thus did Demosthenes talk of Epaminondas.

So Mr. Gray thinks I should publish my Account of Corsica soon.[2]
I am afraid he has had a fit of ennui and just wished for something to
amuse him. I am, however, certainly to give you something concerning Corsica next winter, and am to do it with my father's approbation.
Pray offer my respectful compliments to Mr. Gray, and tell him that
as I was but five weeks in Corsica, I cannot be expected to have materials enough to furnish anything like a complete account of it. But

---

that part of the world, but especially one so disagreeably connected. . . . The
girl has some sense but no constancy."
[9] This expands a conversation already printed in *Boswell on the Grand Tour:
Italy, Corsica, and France*, 21 February 1766.
[1] Boswell's correspondence with Pitt here referred to and the record of the
"noble conference" are printed in *Boswell on the Grand Tour: Italy, Corsica, and
France*, 17–23 February 1766. He used Pitt's remark about Paoli, "He is one of
those men who are no longer to be found but in the *Lives* of Plutarch," as the
last sentence of *Corsica*.
[2] For Boswell's interest in Corsica, see Introduction, p. xiv. Thomas Gray, the
poet, was a cherished friend of Temple's at Cambridge.

that I hope to tell my countrymen so much concerning the brave islanders and their glorious leader that all the true lovers of liberty must admire them and be interested for them. *Quorum pars magna fui*[3] was really the case; so that I shall be obliged to write like an egotist, and would keep my eye on Bishop Burnet.[4] Would Mr. Gray give me his advice as to the form in which I should write? Shall I make it a continued narration? or memoirs? or letters? What shall be the title? Some Account of the Present State of Corsica — An Account of the Island of Corsica — A Tour to Corsica — Letters written from Corsica — Memoirs concerning Corsica and General de Paoli? What shall be the motto —

Manus haec, inimica tyrannis,
Ense petit placidam sub libertate quietem?[5]

Would Mr. Gray advise me as to this?

I am going very well on with the law, which I now like. As we grow older we get a stronger relish for solid truth. The mind is comfortably nourished with jurisprudence. Metaphysics are made-dishes, and the *belles-lettres* are sweetmeats and liqueurs. In short, Temple, I am soon to be a counsellor. I am ever, with the warmest affection, your friend and servant,

JAMES BOSWELL.

[EDITORIAL NOTE: Having freed his mind of the gardener's daughter and entangled himself instead with Mrs. Dodds, the lady at Moffat mentioned in the preceding letter, Boswell arrived in Edinburgh in the middle of June to complete the preliminaries necessary for his admission to the bar. Here he printed his Latin thesis on a title of the Pandects, *De supellectile legata* (*Concerning Legacies of Household Furniture*), and having gone through the formality of defending it before the Faculty of Advocates, he was admitted advocate on 29 July.

[Young advocates working up practice commonly accepted court appointments as counsel for poor clients, and put themselves in the

---

[3] "I played a large part" (Virgil, *Aeneid*, ii. 6).

[4] Gilbert Burnet, Bishop of Salisbury, wrote a valuable *History of My Own Time*, but the egotism displayed in it has sometimes been ridiculed.

[5] "This hand, hostile to tyrants, seeks peace and quiet under liberty with the sword" (Algernon Sidney). It was not the motto adopted.

way of such business by attending the circuits of the Justiciary Court. Boswell had been a member of the Faculty only about eight weeks when, at Glasgow in the autumn of 1766, he was handed his first criminal client, one John Reid, a poor man of bad reputation who was accused of stealing no fewer than one hundred and twenty sheep from a farm in Peeblesshire, driving them off to Glasgow, and there offering them for sale to the butchers. The charge was of course capital. There is no doubt that Reid had on occasion stolen sheep, for he later confessed as much to Boswell; nor was there any question that in this case he had offered stolen sheep for sale. But he persisted in maintaining that he had been imposed upon: he had had the flock, he said, from another man who had commissioned him to drive them to Glasgow and sell them. Boswell, who became convinced of his innocence, threw himself into the case with greater ardour than the Court thought appropriate. He managed to get the trial postponed to 15 December, in Edinburgh, and secured the assistance of Andrew Crosbie, a fine but erratic lawyer who had a fondness for this sort of case. The Lord Advocate countered by clapping on a second charge of sheep-stealing, committed as far back as 1763. Reid lost his nerve and proposed to settle for transportation, but was persuaded to stick it out. Boswell provided him with physical and spiritual comfort: he paid for his food in the Tolbooth and gave him a religious book with an inscription saying that if he could not save him from punishment in this world, he hoped at least to assist him in obtaining mercy in the world to come. At the trial the prosecution presented many witnesses and the Lord Advocate, the Solicitor General, and three other advocates spoke for the Crown. Boswell and Crosbie presented no witnesses at all, but talked to such good effect that the jury returned a Scots verdict of "not proven," whereupon Reid was discharged. The judges of the Justiciary Court (one of whom was Lord Auchinleck) denounced the verdict as against the evidence, and the Lord Justice-Clerk a few months later made a spiteful reference to it in giving his decision in the Douglas cause. By such zeal and imprudence at the very start of his legal career, Boswell made practically certain that he would never attain to a commanding position in his profession.

[The work closest to Boswell's heart, however, was his projected book on Corsica. Despite recurrences of the malaria he had picked up in Corsica, he made a determined effort to collect the materials he needed, both from printed accounts and from manuscript information furnished by the Reverend Andrew Burnaby, who had also toured the country; John Dick, British consul at Leghorn; Count Antonio Rivarola, Sardinian consul at Leghorn; and through General Paoli himself. By March 1767, he was ready to write. Meanwhile, he continued a newspaper campaign he had begun on the Continent to engage sympathy for the Corsicans with various items, both true and invented, intended to keep Corsica in the public eye. The most bizarre of his "inventions," as Boswell called them, was a Corsican courier, Signor Romanzo, who travelled mysteriously from European capital to capital, conferring with high dignitaries about aid to the Corsican cause. These items, to Boswell's delight, were copied in good faith by other periodicals and circulated widely throughout Europe.]

[Received ?1 September, Lord Hailes to Boswell][6]

Newhailes, 29 August 1766

DEAR SIR . . . As to Corsica, work as hard as you can, while the ideas are fresh in your memory. But pray be very short in your topography. Rather correct the errors of others where they are wrong than transcribe their observations where they are right. Do not make your vestibule too large for your house. Make your revolutions as rapid as those in *The Rehearsal*;[7] ride post through the wilds of history; who cares to know the ancient history of Corsica? It is the virtues and actions of their present leader which renders the Corsicans an object of public curiosity. If you publish any letters, sacrifice to modesty and leave out yourself. By drawing a *score* where self was mentioned, you will make the world think that you write to instruct it, not to puff yourself. Let your anecdotes be characteristical, of rain and wind and bad lodgings as little as you please. *Paschal* is more pleasing to an English ear than *Pasquale*. Do not omit anything that can give us

[6] Sir David Dalrymple, a judge in the Court of Session with the style of Lord Hailes, was one of Boswell's early models, and a mediator of differences between him and his father. A scholarly and respected historian, he advised Boswell on literary and antiquarian matters.

[7] Buckingham's play, which ridiculed the heroic tragedy popular in the Restoration period.

a clear idea of that hero; remember he is the chief figure, he must come forward; the others, even yourself, must keep back. But why do I thus talk to you who have so lately seen painting in perfection; you are now to adapt the knowledge you have learnt; from history paint-ing to history writing the transition is obvious. . . .

I beg my best respects to your father, and ever am, dear Sir, your most obedient and faithful servant,

DAV. DALRYMPLE.

[Received *c.* 2 September, Samuel Johnson to Boswell][8]

London, 21 August 1766

DEAR SIR, — The reception of your thesis put me in mind of my debt to you. Why did you dedicate it to a man whom I know you do not much love?[9] I will punish you for it by telling you that your Latin wants correction. . . . [1]

I have now vexed you enough and will try to please you. Your resolution to obey your father I sincerely approve,[2] but do not ac-custom yourself to enchain your volatility by vows: they will some-time leave a thorn in your mind, which you will perhaps never be able to extract or eject. Take this warning, it is of great importance.[3]

The study of the law is what you very justly term it, copious and generous; and in adding your name to its professors, you have done

[8] Printed from *The Life of Johnson,* the second sentence restored as described in the following note.

[9] The *Life* has "Why did you **********," but the transcript of the letter which Boswell used as printer's copy contained the missing words, and they can easily be read through his deleting stroke. The thesis was dedicated to his old Italian travelling companion, Lord Mountstuart, the eldest son of George III's former Prime Minister and intimate friend, the third Earl of Bute. Handsome, conven-tional, and indolent, he thought Boswell had "fine old noble ideas," but mis-trusted the "strange incoherency" of his temper (Mountstuart to Boswell, 29 May 1766). They had quarrelled violently in Italy, but were now supposed to be on friendly terms.

[1] Johnson's animadversions on Boswell's Latin are omitted.

[2] For Boswell's relations with his father, see Introduction, p. x.

[3] Boswell remarks in the *Life* (21 August 1766) that in a previous letter to John-son he had complained of irresolution and "made a vow as a security for good conduct."

exactly what I always wished, when I wished you best. I hope that you will continue to pursue it vigorously and constantly. You gain, at least, what is no small advantage, security from those troublesome and wearisome discontents which are always obtruding themselves upon a mind vacant, unemployed, and undetermined.

You ought to think it no small inducement to diligence and perseverance that they will please your father. We all live upon the hope of pleasing somebody; and the pleasure of pleasing ought to be greatest, and at last always will be greatest, when our endeavours are exerted in consequence of our duty.

Life is not long, and too much of it must not pass in idle deliberation how it shall be spent; deliberation, which those who begin it by prudence and continue it with subtlety, must, after long expense of thought, conclude by chance. To prefer one future mode of life to another, upon just reasons, requires faculties which it has not pleased our Creator to give us.

If, therefore, the profession you have chosen has some unexpected inconveniencies, console yourself by reflecting that no profession is without them; and that all the importunities and perplexities of business are softness and luxury compared with the incessant cravings of vacancy and the unsatisfactory expedients of idleness.

> Haec sunt quae nostra potui te voce monere;
> Vade, age.[4]

As to your History of Corsica, you have no materials which others have not, or may not have. You have, somehow or other, warmed your imagination. I wish there were some cure, like the lover's leap, for all heads of which some single idea has obtained an unreasonable and irregular possession. Mind your own affairs, and leave the Corsicans to theirs. I am, dear Sir, your most humble servant,

SAM. JOHNSON.

[4] "Such are the counsels which I am able to give you; go, act" (altered from Virgil, *Aeneid*, iii. 461–462).

[Boswell to William Pitt, Earl of Chatham][5]

Auchinleck, County of Ayr, 18 September 1766

MY LORD: — When (to use your own words) you was "William Pitt, a plain member of Parliament," you expressed a high regard for the Corsicans and their illustrious Chief. I have ever remembered that conversation which Mr. Pitt honoured me with, and I own my hopes of relief to the brave Islanders have been very great.

May I presume to ask the Earl of Chatham if he will befriend a noble and unfortunate little nation whom I have seen with the enthusiasm of liberty, and for whom I shall be interested while my blood is warm? Pardon me, my Lord, if I intrude upon you, and believe me to be, with the highest consideration, your Lordship's most obedient and most humble servant,

JAMES BOSWELL.

[Boswell to Samuel Johnson][6]

Auchinleck, 6 November 1766

MUCH ESTEEMED AND DEAR SIR, — I plead not guilty to . . .

Having thus, I hope, cleared myself of the charge brought against me, I presume you will not be displeased if I escape the punishment which you have decreed for me unheard. If you have discharged the arrows of criticism against an innocent man, you must rejoice to find they have missed him, or have not been pointed so as to wound him.

To talk no longer in allegory, I am, with all deference, going to offer a few observations in defence of my Latin, which you have found fault with. . . .

Might I venture to differ from you with regard to the utility of

[5] This letter was not sent until November. The original is missing, but the copy of it which Boswell enclosed in his next letter (see p. 17) is among the Chatham papers in the Public Record Office. Boswell's draft, which is practically identical with his copy, also survives. Pitt had formed a ministry and been made Earl of Chatham in the summer of 1766.

[6] Printed from *The Life of Johnson*. The hiatus in the first sentence, as Boswell explains in a note, covers a "private transaction" referred to in Johnson's letter, that is, to Boswell's alleged dislike of Mountstuart. In this case the copy for the *Life* does not preserve the missing words.

vows? I am sensible that it would be very dangerous to make vows rashly, and without a due consideration. But I cannot help thinking that they may often be of great advantage to one of a variable judgment and irregular inclinations. I always remember a passage in one of your letters to our Italian friend Baretti,[7] where, talking of the monastic life, you say you do not wonder that serious men should put themselves under the protection of a religious order, when they have found how unable they are to take care of themselves. For my own part, without affecting to be a Socrates, I am sure I have a more than ordinary struggle to maintain with *the Evil Principle;* and all the methods I can devise are little enough to keep me tolerably steady in the paths of rectitude. . . . I am ever, with the highest veneration, your affectionate humble servant,

JAMES BOSWELL.

[Boswell to Chatham][8]

Edinburgh, 3 January 1767

MY LORD: — It is now more than three months since I took the liberty to write your Lordship a short letter in behalf of the Corsicans, of which a copy is now transmitted lest it should not have come to your hands.

I have received a letter from General Paoli in which he thus talks of Mr. Pitt: "La pubblica fama esalta fino alle stelle li talenti del Signor Pitt, ma la relazione che ella mi fa della conversazione avuta con esso lui mi riempie ancora di maggior ammirazione e di attaccamento per la buontà del cuore di questo Pericle della Gran Bretagna."[9]

My Lord, I wrote to General Paoli the many strong and noble expressions which you uttered to me in a private conference with as much eloquence as ever Mr. Pitt displayed in the fullest assembly. And, my Lord, I trust you will now show a generous sincerity.

I would recommend to your Lordship, Mr. Dick, His Majesty's Consul at Leghorn, as a gentleman of great information and judg-

[7] A translator and critic, whom Boswell had met in Venice in 1765.
[8] Boswell's draft. The original has not been recovered.
[9] "Public report exalts Mr. Pitt's talents to the stars, but the report you give me of the conversation you had with him fills me with even greater admiration and love for the goodness of heart of this Pericles of Great Britain."

ment as to everything that concerns the Mediterranean, and I would recommend him as a man of worth and spirit who is warmly attached to the brave Corsicans. He will give your Lordship all the light you can desire as to the advantages which Great Britain might derive from an alliance with Corsica, either in the way of trade or for the conveniency of war, and will faithfully execute whatever commands your Lordship may lay upon him.

Your Lordship knows that a proclamation stands in force by which the subjects of Great Britain are prohibited from holding any intercourse with the malcontents of Corsica. If your Lordship would only get us that proclamation annulled, it would be of great consequence in the mean time. Corsica seems to be particularly unlucky. The Swiss and the Dutch had powerful assistance in recovering their liberties. But the gallant Islanders for whom I am concerned have now been in arms for the glorious cause nine and thirty years, and not a state in Europe has interposed in their behalf.

Let me plead with your Lordship for Corsica. Let me put you in mind of the people animated with the spirit of liberty, whom the Romans stood forth and protected against the great King of Asia, and in so doing gained more real honour than by the most extensive conquests.[1] And let me recall to your Lordship the excellent old fable of the lion and the mouse. Far be it from me to attempt pointing out any measures to be taken by the Government of my country. But surely a great free nation may befriend a small one. Is Great Britain now afraid of France, or does she owe anything to Genoa?

As an advocate for Corsica I look up to the Earl of Chatham, and I cannot but hope for a favourable answer.

I have the honour to remain, &c.

[1] The eighth chapter of I Maccabees tells how the Jews appealed for protection to the Romans. Boswell quoted it at length in *Corsica*.

1767

[EDITORIAL NOTE: Boswell's Journal had lapsed since 23 February 1766. He started to keep it again in condensed form on 1 January 1767, but the first leaf, bearing the entries for 1 January to the middle of 10 January, is missing. When the record begins, the scene appears to be Arniston House, where Boswell is visiting Robert Dundas, Lord President of the Court of Session.]

SATURDAY 10 JANUARY . . . . Then in library; found some curious remarks on Corsica in Graevius. President took them up at once before you — amazing quickness. Hearty all afternoon; quite at home. Dams[2] with Miss Dundas.

SUNDAY 11 JANUARY. Laird of Dundas [invited the company to church] and all went. You alone here; library all forenoon. . . . Hearty at dinner. Bottle of claret [for] each; second one [being brought] I grumbled, "Shall leave the half till night." . . . Good strong conversation against infidelity, &c. Evening with ladies; read alternately, all of you, *Rambler* and Bible.

MONDAY 12 JANUARY. Breakfasted early. President walked you about in room, and told you with fire how Justiciary Court brought itself down sending one judge by himself to circuit [and by] not sending impertinent counsel to prison. Complained of putting improper people into that office; talked of political connections with masterly force. You came all in in coach. Miss Dundas, fine girl. Liked her very well; was *retenu*[3] for fear of appearing lover. Quite proper; was really sorry to think of her and her sister, who might perhaps become maiden aunts. Safe journey through monstrous deep snow to town. Sorry to part. Heard of Willy Webster's being drowned.[4] Sorry, but felt mind hardened. Mr. Frazer dined with you. Afternoon, Miss ——;[5] very well.

[2] A Scottish name for the game of draughts.
[3] Restrained.
[4] Webster was the son of Boswell's mother's sister.
[5] Mrs. Dodds. She had followed Boswell to Edinburgh, and had taken lodgings there so as to continue their liaison.

TUESDAY 13 JANUARY . . . . Before nine, Miss ——, quite fond. She reproved you for drinking so much. Home, and had clerk, and corrected Caithness memorial till twelve.

THURSDAY 15 JANUARY . . . . Evening called Miss ——; gentleman with her. Came away jealous. Erskine came; very happy together.[6]

FRIDAY 16 JANUARY . . . . At six, after torment with jealousy, went to Miss. She was gay. She declared [that she had] no fear [of you]. You was torn with passion, or, as Rose[7] used to say, your gloom fixed on love as its object. You was quite serious; said you was much obliged to her. She must not think you ungrateful; but really you could not be miserable altogether, therefore you'd try to cease. You'd be her friend, &c., &c. But you again grew fond. Note came; 'twas open. Said she: "We can understand one another, though [our letters are] open,"[8] and laughed. You said nothing, but like Spaniard mused on the fire. Murmuring between you. She [said she] would not make you uneasy. YOU. "Then show me card." She did so freely. 'Twas from a poor woman you had got into Infirmary. Bless me! She just tried my jealousy. You asked pardon for weakness. She smiled, as well she might.[9]

[*London Chronicle*][1]

SATURDAY 24 JANUARY. Extract of a letter from Hamburg, January 1. "A courier arrived here early this morning in a very extraordinary dress, said to be a Corsican express, with dispatches from General Paoli to my Lord Marischal of Scotland, and Sir Andrew

[6] Lieutenant the Hon. Andrew Erskine, brother to the sixth Earl of Kellie, was one of Boswell's close friends. In 1763 they had published *Letters Between the Honourable Andrew Erskine and James Boswell, Esq.*, a youthful bagatelle full of private jokes.

[7] A Scotsman whom Boswell had known well in Holland.

[8] Mrs. Dodds is teasing Boswell, saying that she and the "lover" Boswell is jealous of understand each other even if their letters are not sealed.

[9] Six pages, containing the record of 17 January to 3 February, are missing.

[1] Here begins the bizarre "invention" of Signor Romanzo (see p. 13). Both George Keith, tenth Earl Marischal, and Sir Andrew Mitchell mentioned in it were friends of Boswell from his German days.

Mitchell, His Britannic Majesty's Ambassador at the Court of Prussia. We hear that this courier was immediately carried to the Stadthouse and examined for upwards of two hours, but nothing has yet transpired. It was with some difficulty that our magistrates allowed him to pass, under a convoy of the city guards, who were to attend him for several leagues and take care that he was not followed by any of our sailors, who had gathered about him in great crowds on his first arrival. Our magistrates had also the precaution to stop the departure of the post some hours, in order that an account of this singular affair might be transmitted to Potsdam by a special messenger, before the letters of our idle politicians should make the news of it resound through Brandenburg and to Paris and Vienna. This Corsican courier had plenty of money about him; and by his air and manner, it was strongly suspected that he is a man of more distinction than he chooses should be known."

[Boswell to Temple][2]

Edinburgh, 1 February 1767

My dear Temple, — When I see lying before me your last letter, dated the 2d of December, and consider how long a time has passed without any communication between us, I am filled with wonder and regret. But I think both of us are arrived so far in the knowledge of human nature that we can calmly contemplate the vicissitudes of our own minds, and without fretting at our imperfections can be sorry for them while we are supported and cheered by the consciousness of our good qualities.

I am sincerely happy that you are at length the Reverend Mr. Temple. I view the profession of a clergyman in an amiable and respectable light. Don't be moved by declamations against ecclesiastical history, as if that could blacken the sacred order.[3] I confess that it is

[2] This and all of the following letters from Boswell to Temple, unless otherwise stated, are reprinted from the *Letters of James Boswell*, 2 vols., 1924, with the kind permission of the editor, Professor Chauncey B. Tinker, and of the Clarendon Press. The originals of all the letters to Temple printed by Professor Tinker are in the Morgan Library, New York. The present letter, which was written in installments, is here given in parts according to date.

[3] Temple had written to Boswell (20 November 1766): "The great truths of

not in ecclesiastical history that we find the most agreeable account of divines. Their politics, their ambition, their art⟩ and their cruelty are there displayed. But remember, Temple, you are there reading the vices of only political divines, of such individuals as in so numerous a body have been very unworthy members of the Church, and should have rather been employed in the rudest secular concerns. But, if you would judge fairly of the priests of Jesus, you must consider how many of the distressed they have comforted, how many of the wicked they have reclaimed, how many of the good they have improved. Consider the lives of thousands of worthy, pious divines who have been a blessing to their parishes. This is just, Temple. You say the truths of morality are written in the hearts of all men, and they find it their interest to practise them. My dear friend, will you believe a specious *moral essayist* against your own experience? Don't you, in the very same letter, complain of the wickedness of those around you? Don't you talk of the tares in society? My friend, it is your office to labour cheerfully in the vineyard, and if possible to leave not a tare in Mamhead.

You are tempted to join Rousseau in preferring the savage state. I am so too at times. When jaded with business or when tormented with the passions of civilized life, I could fly to the woods; nay, I could ⟨be⟩ the whinstone on the face of a mountain, were it possible for me to be conscious of it and to brave the elements by glorious insensibility. But these are the sallies of desperation. Philosophy teacheth us to be moderate, to be patient, to expect a gradual progress of refinement and felicity. In that hope I look up to the Lord of the Universe, with a grateful remembrance of the grand and mysterious propitiation which Christianity hath announced.

Thus far I got in my letter before breakfast. It is now late in the evening when I sit down again. But I sit down in the same frame in which I parted from you in the morning. In a word, my dear Temple, be a good clergyman, and you will be happy both here and hereafter.

---

morality are written in the hearts of all men, they find it their interest to practise them; but priests of all ages and nations and of every sect have constantly and upon principle endeavoured to fix their attention upon something else, by making religion consist in fopperies, absurdities, and nonsense to the scandal of learning and of their character."

I can well imagine your solitary state at the rectory when all your neighbours are gone to town, and in such a winter too. I hope you read Thomson, and made the clouds and storms

> exalt the soul to solemn thought
> And heavenly musing.[4]

. . . of it while my father lives. His notions and mine are so different that the wife whom I would choose would in all probability be very disagreeable to him. If he does not marry again, there is a duty upon me to live with him and be careful of him. His character is such that he must have his son in a great degree of subjection to him. Were I to marry, he could not alter his ideas, so I should be in a most awkward state between the subjection of a son and the authority of the father and master of a family . . .

. . . keep himself free. A bachelor has an easy, unconcerned behaviour which is more taking with the generality of the world than the behaviour of a married man possibly can be, if he acts in character. The bachelor has a carelessness of disposition which pleases everybody, and everybody thinks him a sort of a common good, *nunc mihi nunc aliis benignus*,[5] a feather which flies about and lights now here, now there. And accordingly the connections of a bachelor are always most extensive. Whereas a married man has a settled plan, a certain degree of care, and has his affections collected by one great attachment, and therefore he cannot be such good company to everybody he meets. But, in my opinion, after a certain time of life a man is not so desirous of this general flutter. The mind becomes more composed and requires some settled satisfaction on which it can repose. I am sensible that everything depends on the light in which we view it, and nothing more so than marriage. If you think of that weariness which must at times hang over every kind of society, those disgusts and vexations which will happen in the intercourse of life, you will be frightened to take upon you the serious charge of the father of a fam-

[4] *Winter*, ll. 4–5. — Half the leaf has been cut away, the hiatus involving this paragraph and the following. The mutilation had occurred before the first printing of the letter in 1857, though the editor attempted to disguise the fact by inventing some forty words to fill the gaps. Actually something more like two hundred and fifty words are missing.

[5] "Pleasant now to me, now to others" (altered from Horace, *Odes*, III. xxix. 52).

ily. But if you think of the comforts of a home where you are a sort of sovereign, the kind endearments of an amiable woman who has no wish but to make you happy, the amusement of seeing your children grow up from infancy to manhood, and the pleasing pride of being the father of brave and of learned men, all which may be the case and depends much upon our conduct as fathers — then marriage is truly the only condition in which true felicity is to be found. I think we may strike a good medium. Let us keep in mind the *nil admirari*[6] and not expect too much. It was from having too high expectations of enjoyment that I certainly suffered so severely. For the natural gloom of my mind was not sufficient to torment me in a degree so acute.

In the mean time, my friend, I am happy enough to have a *dear infidel*,[7] as you say. But don't think her unfaithful. I could not love her if she was. There is a baseness in all deceit which my soul is virtuous enough ever to abhor, and therefore I look with horror upon adultery. But my amiable mistress is no longer bound to him who was her husband. He has used her shockingly ill. He has deserted her. He lives with another. Is she not then free? She is. It is clear, and no arguments can disguise it. She is now mine, and were she to be unfaithful to me, she ought to be pierced with a Corsican poniard. But I believe she loves me sincerely. She has done everything to please me. She is perfectly generous, and would not hear of any present. She has hitherto been boarded here, which lays us under a restraint. I have found out a sober widow, in whose house is the rendezvous of our amours. But I have now prevailed with my love to let me take a house for her, and as it will be my family I shall provide what is necessary. In this manner I am safe and happy and in no danger either of the perils of Venus or of desperate matrimony.

I am now advancing fast in the law. I am coming into great employment. I have this winter made sixty-five guineas, which is a considerable sum for a young man. I expect that this first year I shall clear, in all, about a hundred pieces.[8]

[6] The "admire nothing" of Horace (*Epistles*, I. vi. 1).

[7] Temple, in referring to Mrs. Dodds, had written (20 November 1766): "What a dear *infidel* you have got (from *not faithful* you know, Boswell). Nothing so convenient as an eloped wife. How are you so lucky in mistresses?"

[8] Continued on p. 32. Boswell does not exaggerate his success. Sir Walter Scott, who passed advocate in 1792, in his fifth year at the bar received fees of £144, considerably less than Boswell's fees in his first full year.

WEDNESDAY 4 FEBRUARY. Was hurt to find soul ravaged by passion; determined to be firm, [as you] saw it hurt ideas of family. . . . Had been looking at houses for Miss ——; at last fell on one in Borthwick's Close, quite neat and light.

THURSDAY 5 FEBRUARY . . . . In morning went to Mrs. Leith and took house. Mind at ease; determined to be generous and let Miss —— do as she pleased. Very busy all day. Tea, Lord Hailes. [Was] going to write noble letter to Miss ——; sent for by her; went. She tender as ever, quite affectionate. Saw all was easy. You felt too much like married man, but 'twas gay. Then at nine, Clerihue's[9] and Mr. William Wilson and Bryce, [a] client. Saw [that law was a] form of fleecing poor lieges. Hurt, *tant soit peu*,[1] [soon] firm again.

SATURDAY 7 FEBRUARY. With honest Doctor [Boswell] and a Doctor Livingston walked out to Sir Alexander's.[2] Fine day. Was powerful like Johnson; very much satisfied. Evening with Miss ——. She had taken other house, so resolved to give up yours. A little gloom still, a little fever.

MONDAY 9 FEBRUARY. Robert Hay's trial. You opened and strongly protested his innocence; quite calm.[3] Lasted till eight. Jaded a little.

[9] The Star and Garter in Writer's Court, kept by John Clerihue, a favorite tavern for lawyers.

[1] Ever so little.

[2] Sir Alexander Dick, one-time President of the College of Physicians of Edinburgh, was now retired to his estate at Prestonfield where he kept open house. His most conspicuous trait was amiability. — Dr. John Boswell was an amusing, honest eccentric, very different from his brother, Lord Auchinleck. Boswell admired his scholarly attainments and responded to his affectionate nature, but complained of his loose conduct.

[3] Hay, a young soldier (said variously to be twenty, twenty-one, and twenty-two years old), was charged with having assaulted a sailor in the Cowgate, Edinburgh, and with having robbed him of £2 and a silver watch. It was admitted that he had tried to sell the watch on the day after the robbery. Boswell's defence (apart from such moving but irrelevant representations as that Hay was "the favourite child of an old and distressed mother . . . whose grey hairs must be brought with sorrow to the grave should her unfortunate son be condemned") was that on the night in question Hay had been drunk for the first time in his life and could give no clear account of himself; that he had "a dark remembrance" of having been in the company of "one Robertson, a soldier of most infamous character," and that the watch must have come from him. The jury in a unanimous verdict found Hay guilty, but recommended mercy.

TUESDAY 10 FEBRUARY. Very busy. Poor Hay condemned. Dined Mr. John Gordon's: George Wallace and James Stevenson — new scene or rather old one revived. Quite comfortable and plain; saw how various happiness is. Very good conversation. Busy all the evening.

WEDNESDAY 11 FEBRUARY. Visited Robert Hay. Why it is, I know not, but we compassionate less a genteel man [in affliction than a poor man]. He was very quiet. You had a kind of sentiment as if he was utterly insensible to good. But he said if he had got time, he would have been a new man as from his mother's breast, and wept. Had Bible. Spoke to him seriously and calmly; bid him free innocent people, but not impeach a companion if [he held information] in trust.[4] At eight, Miss —— a little.

[Received 12 February, Chatham to Boswell]

Bath, 4 February 1767

SIR: — The honour of your letter found me here confined with a severe fit of the gout and totally unable to write, or I should sooner have acknowledged that favour. I now write with some difficulty, but çan no longer defer expressing the sense I have of the great honour done me by the sentiments contained in the Italian passage of the letter you are so good to convey to me. I can assure you, Sir, I retain the same admiration of your illustrious friend, General Paoli, which I

[4] Some days after the trial (the date is not given in the copy preserved in the Boswell papers) Boswell forwarded to the King a formal petition in Hay's behalf, begging that the sentence be commuted to transportation. This petition states what were probably the real facts of the case: "He confesses that the night the robbery happened . . . he was unfortunate enough to drink too much, and to be persuaded to go along with John Butterfield, drummer in the Forty-fourth Regiment of Foot, who committed the robbery, while your petitioner stood by, and afterwards accepted of a watch as part of the spoil." The petition goes on to say that this appeal for clemency is being made because there is "reason to fear that . . . the judges will not transmit the recommendation of the jury, as their Lordships were much offended with your petitioner because from a mistaken principle of honour, he for some time refused to discover his accomplice, and, in order to divert the course of public vengeance, laid the guilt to the charge of another person." Butterfield, who appears in the list of witnesses, had meantime fled the kingdom.

once expressed to you, but, sincere as this admiration is, I must not at the same time forbear to acquaint you (in answer to your desire to know my sentiments) that I see not the least ground at present for this country to interfere with any justice in the affairs of Corsica. As I think nothing more natural and commendable than the generous warmth you express for so striking a character as that able Chief, so I doubt not you will approve the directness of my opinion upon an occasion which admits of no deliberation.

I am with great esteem and regard, Sir, your most obedient, humble servant,

CHATHAM.

SATURDAY 14 FEBRUARY. Had composed song on [the memorial for the] Hamilton cause.[5] Lord Hailes [said], "Very witty, but put it in the fire; you'll make yourself enemies." He had frightened you, such is still your weakness. Showed it to Sir Adam [Fergusson], David Hume, &c. All liked it; no venom. "No," said David Hume, " 'Tis not in you." Sung it in Parliament House with circle round you; had the *vivida vis*[6] of Wilkes. Resolved to follow your own plan. Walked down with Sir Adam and Nairne to Lord Alemoor's; viewed my Lord calmly. Felt the sentiment of awe for others gone. Afternoon very busy. Mr. William Wilson, S.,[7] at tea with you. At six, Miss —— at Philippi.[8] Had been indifferent for this week. You and she this night first cold and upbraiding, then kind as ever. Home, and labour again.

SUNDAY 15 FEBRUARY. Morning Erskine called; told you what applause you got. You was quite firm and gay. Church, forenoon. Home between sermons, then to prison. Such an audience!

[5] That is, a song attacking the memorial for the Hamilton plaintiffs in the Douglas cause (see Introduction, p. xiii). Sir Adam Fergusson, mentioned below, had written the memorial. He was a conscientious, respectable, somewhat humourless man, a considerable scholar and linguist, and best known to posterity because Dr. Johnson called him a "vile Whig."

[6] "Lively force" (Lucretius, *De rerum natura*, i. 72).

[7] This "S.," which follows William Wilson's name and no other, may stand for "Senior." But it is also possible that it indicates "Writer to the Signet."

[8] This probably means, "At six met Mrs. Dodds at the house of the sober widow who serves as a screen for our amours" (see p. 24). The use of Philippi to mean a place of assignation was probably suggested by *Julius Caesar*, IV. iii. 284: "To tell thee thou shalt see me at Philippi."

Young divine preached: "Be not slothful in business," &c.[9] — not at all applicable to his hearers. Great genius required for a jail preacher. You sat in the closet, like an isle.[1] You did not like to hear the divine in his prayer talk of a *disgraceful death*. 'Twas too shocking to his unhappy hearers. He should have preached on patience, on the necessity of punishment, on the corruption of man's nature, on the mercy of God. [They sang] psalms, with precentor reading [them] line [by line] with a doleful tone. Your mind now so strong [that such a scene produces] no impression. . . .

Went and saw poor Hay. He was bad and all heaving — could not speak. His aged mother there, and his wife (a soldier's wife), very well looked. Then David Hume's, who was next day to set out for London; tea with him. He agreed to manage your Account of Corsica with Millar. You very pleasantly maintained your happiness in being a Christian. Then Miss ——'s, where you met La Cara in black. Your love returned gay and fine. . . . Supped Lord Kames;[2] rather too high. What a variety you have made of Edinburgh!

[Received *c*. 15 February, Sir John Pringle to Boswell][3]

London, 10 February 1767

DEAR SIR . . . I continue to have the satisfaction of hearing from different hands of your application to business, and of the figure which you have made and are likely to make at the bar. I believe that I told you in a former letter, but I must repeat it, that my pleasure is the greater, as in this event I have had my vanity gratified in thinking that I judged well when I told you that your genius, however differently it then appeared to you, was most calculated for that profession,

[9] Romans 12. 10–11. The "prison" is the Tolbooth, the city prison of Edinburgh — the "Heart of Midlothian" of Scott's novel.

[1] The isle or "aisle" was a wing or lateral extension of the church, commonly where the laird had his seat.

[2] Henry Home, styled Lord Kames from his position on the Bench, was one of the able, wide-ranging, and eccentric members of the Court of Session. Author of works on law, philosophy, history, agriculture, and education, he is best remembered as a "hanging" judge, and for his treatise on aesthetics, *Elements of Criticism*.

[3] Pringle, a pioneer in military hygiene, was later physician to George III and President of the Royal Society. He was a great friend of Lord Auchinleck and very fond of writing Boswell admonitory letters.

which you seem now to have embraced in earnest. I will go further, since you must now give a little credit to my predictions, and tell you that if you continue to give application you will soon get the start of all our young men in the Parliament House, and will give the tone for a new eloquence very different from what prevailed there in my time. You have the advantage of possessing the English language and the accent in a greater degree than any of your rivals, and a turn for expressing yourself in a clear and energetic manner, without those hyperbolical modes of speech that were introduced long ago, and were still kept up during my youth, and which slipped from the bar to the tea tables at Edinburgh.

By letters which I have since my return had from my worthy friend your father (for I have had more than one upon the subject), I have the comfort to find that you have made him very happy; and I have the superstition to believe that whilst you go on in this train (I mean in sobriety, diligence in your business, and attentions to the best of parents) God will bless you, not only with conferring upon you his imperceptible favours, but will even condescend to gratify you with reputation and other worldly enjoyments, which we may desire but never set our hearts upon. You may be assured that your father's confidence in you and his affection will daily augment; for, between ourselves be it spoken, could you expect that after all that is passed, he should all at once consider you as arrived at the full maturity of your judgment? Permit me to predict once more. In a year, or two at furthest, if you persevere in this course, my sage friend, so far will he be from seeing you in the light of a boy that he will not only communicate to you all his most secret affairs, but will consult you upon them and show a regard to your judgement.

In order to hasten this confidence, I will presume to suggest what may be the most proper means: that is, I would advise you to look out for a wife, and to make such a match as he and the whole world shall approve of. After examining that affair with some attention, I am much for early nuptials, and indeed so much, that if I were in your place I should set immediately about them. I am persuaded that you would have a great deal of satisfaction in following that plan; for your temper is good, you would have joy in children, and I believe I may add that you have had too much experience of the vague and vicious pleasures not to relish the confined and virtuous ones as soon as you will make the comparison. This would give great contentment to your father, and, as I said above, nothing would so much ripen that confidence which he is beginning to have in you as that very action. Your reconciled friend (and you may depend upon the sincerity of the reconciliation) is a married man, and I am persuaded happy in that state, although the match was made upon prudential considerations only.[4]

With regard to your design of publishing an Account of Corsica, I wrote to your father my thoughts on that subject. You may remember with what pleasure and approbation Sir Andrew Mitchell and I heard your natural account of those travels; but to relate and to print are two very different things. If you had any encouragement from the Minister that would be another matter; but as he has not chosen to answer your letter on that subject, you may take it for granted that the publication would give him no satisfaction. At present be you and Paoli private friends. Possibly the time may come when the Ministry here may find it their interest to support him; in which event they will probably apply to you. Meanwhile, I hope you have not omitted to take an opportunity of sending that brave man the present which you proposed, as a just return for the civilities which he showed you during your stay with him.[5]

I am with great sincerity, dear Sir, your affectionate friend and humble servant,

JOHN PRINGLE.

TUESDAY 17 FEBRUARY . . . . Evening with Miss ———, dressed in the very black she had charmed you with on Sunday. You was delighted with her. . . .

SATURDAY 21 FEBRUARY. You was quite overpowered with papers to draw. Had been accustomed too much to make the law easy, and write papers like essays for a newspaper, without reading much. Saw labour and poring necessary, and reading long papers. Dined Samuel Mitchelson's with Sir Alexander Dick and family. Evening with Miss ———, again in black. Allowed you full sight; enchanted

---

[4] Pringle is talking about Lord Mountstuart, who had married Charlotte Jane Windsor, an ugly heiress. When Mountstuart and Boswell had quarrelled at the beginning of 1766, Pringle had acted as intermediary.

[5] The present was a collection of English books, which mainly dealt with politics and morality.

with her. She said, "Next night I'll wear black and let candles burn to keep you longer."

SUNDAY 22 FEBRUARY. . . . You stayed in the afternoon and wrote letters. Evening was with Miss _____, who came instantly on your sending [for her, and was] very kind.

WEDNESDAY 25 FEBRUARY. At five Miss _____ with you; pretty well. At eight, at Mrs. Dunbar's in Gosford's Close, low house but comfortable, with William Taylor and John Stobie[6] consulting on cause of old Barclay, [the] Quaker [of] London. Four bottles [of] good claret drunk, quite style of old consultations. Home and finished paper. Was with Father; was hearty. Asked him, "Am I not doing as well as you would wish?" HE. "Yes." Took his hand.

SATURDAY 28 FEBRUARY. . . . At six with Miss _____, in varying humour. She upbraided you; almost would give up *concert.*[7] Talked of expense offending you, [and] parted angry with you. [As you came out] met _____,[8] [and showed] alarm. You supped Lady Betty's with Grange, Dr. Gregory,[9] Arbuthnot and his ladies. Pleasant, but you was a little drowsy.

[Boswell to Temple, *continued*]

28 February. In this manner have I travelled on through seven folio pages. Every day I have intended to close my letter, and every night I have felt real pain of mind to think that I had not done it. Your kind favour of the 19th current is just arrived. It rouses me, and now I am resolved to give no longer quarter to my indolence.

I am at present leading the strangest life. You know one half of the

[6] For John Stobie, see p. 43 *n.*2.

[7] That is, common design.

[8] Lord Auchinleck? Boswell says in the entry of 2 March: "Father has been displeased."

[9] Lady Elizabeth Macfarlane was Andrew Erskine's sister and wife of the antiquary, Walter Macfarlane, who died in June 1767. The following year she married Alexander, seventh Lord Colville of Culross. — Next to Temple, John Johnston of Grange was Boswell's closest friend. An obscure "writer" (that is, solicitor or attorney) in Edinburgh, he was mild, indolent, melancholy, and a great lover of Scottish scenery and antiquities. — Dr. John Gregory was Professor of Medicine in the University of Edinburgh. He was chiefly known for his *Comparative View of the State and Faculties of Man with Those of the Animal World,* which had been published the previous year.

business before the Court of Session is carried on by writing. In the first instance, a cause is pleaded before the Lord Ordinary, that is to say one of the fifteen judges who sits in his turn for a week in the Outer House. But no sooner does he give judgment than we give him in representations and answers and replies and duplies and triplies, and he will sometimes order memorials to give him a full view of the cause. Then we reclaim to the Inner House by petition, and there again we give in variety of printed papers, from which the Lords determine the cause. For it is only in causes of great consequence that the Court orders a hearing in presence. This method of procedure is admirable, for it gives the judges a complete state of every question, and by binding up the session papers a man may lay up a treasure of law reasoning and a collection of extraordinary facts.[1]

SUNDAY 1 MARCH. Miss Blair of Adamtown in [our] seat [at church], handsome, stately woman; good countenance.[2] Dined Duchess of Douglas, very hearty.[3] . . . Before dinner had been with Miss ——, and settled plan how to explain last night's alarm. You and she were as fine as ever. At six she met you. By having lived luxuriously so much last week, you was confused and debilitate, [and] performed only one — a kind of ludicrous distress.

TUESDAY 3 MARCH . . . . Tea, Grange; Erskine there. Read part of your London Journal; delighted [them]. Talked of your fever for Mrs. Dodds.[4] They showed you weakness; you saw 'twas only sudden resolution to be free. Sat till near three — extraordinary night.

WEDNESDAY 4 MARCH. Was so much hurt to hear scandal of Miss —— would not visit her. Was on rack. . . .

[Boswell to Temple, *continued*]

4 March. Here I am still, and let me go on. It must be confessed that our Court of Session is not so favourable to eloquence as the Eng-

---

[1] Continued below, 4 March.

[2] For Catherine Blair, see Introduction, p. xvii. "Our" church was the New Church, the east end of St. Giles's cathedral.

[3] Ostentatious, vulgar, illiterate, and vigorous, Peggie Douglas, Dowager Duchess of Douglas, was one of the main forces behind Archibald Douglas in the Douglas cause.

[4] This is the only place in the Journal where Boswell gives the name of his mistress.

lish courts. Yet the Outer House here is a school where a man may train himself to pretty good purpose. I am surprised at myself I already speak with so much ease and boldness, and have already the language of the bar so much at command. I have now cleared eighty guineas. I am kept very throng.[5] My clerk comes to me every morning at six, and I have dictated to him forty folio pages in one day. It is impossible to give you an idea of my present life. I send you one of my law papers and a copy of my thesis. I am doing nobly. But I have not leisure for learning. I can hardly even answer the letters of my friends. But henceforth, Temple, I will write to you every two weeks. Trust me. It is very odd that I can labour so hard at law when I am so indolent in other things. Let you and I keep up a frequent intercourse and preserve our friendship in its full force and elegance, and assist each other to dispel every cloud.

You are right in preferring social life to retirement, for no philosophy is equal to action. You should not, however, have quitted your elbow-chairs and fine carpets.[6] They are amusements, and you must not be without them. You have had a fit of low spirits.

In a former part of this letter I have talked a great deal of my sweet little mistress. I am, however, uneasy about her. Furnishing a house and maintaining her with a maid will cost me a great deal of money, and it is too like marriage, or too much a settled plan of licentiousness. But what can I do? I have already taken the house, and the lady has agreed to go into it at Whitsunday. I cannot in honour draw back. Besides, in no other way can I have her. But I have had more intelligence of her former intrigues. I am hurt to think of them. I cry, "Damn her, lewd minx."[7] I am jealous. What shall I do?

Oh, my friend! were you but here; but, alas! that cannot be. Mamhead is not within a call. It ought to be so, for you should always be my pastor; and I might now and then be yours. Friend of my youth, explain to me how we suffer so severely from what no longer exists. How am I tormented because my charmer has formerly loved others!

[5] Scots for "busy."
[6] Temple had written (19 February 1767) that he had abandoned ideas of "elbow-chairs, fine carpets, and such trumpery." He now thought the man happiest "who has no more than the mere necessaries of life, cleanness, and decency."
[7] *Othello*, III. iii. 475.

I am disgusted to think of it. My lively imagination often represents her former lovers in actual enjoyment of her. My desire fails, I am unfit for love. Besides, she is ill-bred, quite a rompish girl. She debases my dignity. She has no refinement. But she is very handsome, very lively, and admirably formed for amorous dalliance. What is it to me that she has formerly loved? So have I. I am positive that since I first courted her at Moffat she has been constant to me. She is kind. She is generous. What shall I do? I wish I could get off, and yet how awkward would it be! And, after all, can I do better than keep a dear infidel for my hours of Paphian bliss? But, alas, since yesterday I am cooled. Think of your Berwick Celia and sympathize with me. One way or other, my mind will be settled before I can hear from you. This is a curious epistle to a clergyman. Admonish me, but forgive me.

Doctor Robertson will soon give the world his *Charles the Fifth.* Smith, I suppose, is in London. But I do not hear that his book on jurisprudence is in any forwardness.[8] David Hume, you know, is gone back to be a minister of state, being appointed secretary to Mr. Conway. I fancy he will hardly write any more. I was very hearty with him here this winter. Whenever you go to London, I will give you a letter of introduction to him. His quarrel with Rousseau is a literary tragicomedy. I wrote verses in the character of each of them. I also designed a ludicrous print. They have altered my idea and made a glister be applied to David. But you may have the substance of it from one of the London print-shops under the title of "The Savage Man." You must know Rousseau quarrelled with me too, and wrote me last summer a peevish letter with strong marks of frenzy in it. For he has never yet told me the cause of his offence. As you well observe, how different is our friendship![9]

I have got pretty well acquainted with Doctor Gregory. He was very desirous to know me. His book is ingenious and elegant, and he himself is one of the amiable, pleasant men alive.

---

[8] Adam Smith never did write a book on jurisprudence, though a collection of his lectures on justice, police, etc. was published long after his death. Possibly Boswell refers to his *Wealth of Nations*, published in 1776.

[9] Boswell's relations with Rousseau and his share in the quarrel between Rousseau and Hume are discussed in *Boswell on the Grand Tour: Italy, Corsica, and France*, after 23 February 1766.

The session will be up this day sennight. I shall then set myself down to my Account of Corsica, and finish it in the vacation. I have got more materials for it. I had some time ago a letter of sixteen pages from General Paoli, and lately a letter of three pages from my Lord Chatham. David Hume told me sincerely he imagined my Account of Corsica would be a book that will stand, and he is obliging enough to transact the publication of it for me with Andrew Millar. All your old friends here are well, *in statu quo*, Jeel and all, and remember you kindly.[1] Sinclair has never found his brother. I don't write often enough to Squire Bosville, but I shall give him a good letter tomorrow. His beauty, I am afraid, would be too fine for this northern air. Temple, will you allow me to marry a good Scots lass? Ha! ha! ha! What shall I tell you? Zélide has been in London this winter. I never hear from her. She is a strange creature. Sir John Pringle attended her as a physician. He wrote to my father, "She has too much vivacity. She talks of your son without either resentment or attachment." Her brothers and I correspond. But I am well rid of her. You say well that I find mistresses wherever I am. But I am a sad dupe, a perfect Don Quixote. To return to where it winces, might not I tell my little charmer that really I am an inconstant being, but I cannot help it? Or I may let my love gradually decay? Had she never loved before, I would have lost every drop of my blood rather than give her up. There's madness! There's delicacy! I have not had such a relief as this for I don't know how long. I have broke the trammels of business, and am roving unconfined with my worthy Temple.

My brother Davy is a prodigious fine fellow. He and I dined to-gether tête-à-tête on Christmas Day in an elegant manner, and went to chapel,[2] as you and I did long ago. He is in constant occupation as a banker . . . [3]

---

[1] Jeel is Scots for jelly. Boswell and Temple, while students at the University of Edinburgh, had been entertained at tea or dinner at the home of Robert Hunter, Professor of Greek, and had been amused by his broad Scots ("Will you hae some jeel?") "Jeel" consequently became their nickname for Hunter.

[2] That is, to the Church-of-England chapel in Carrubber's Close. Temple had introduced Boswell to Anglican worship there, probably on Christmas Day, 1755. See p. 124 n.3.

[3] Continued on p. 36. Brother David was an earnest young man apprenticed to a banking house in Edinburgh.

THURSDAY 5 MARCH. Had message from Miss ———; went to her. Could not conceal [you] was black and dreary. She was much affected. You begged of her to have patience. You was unhappy, but you would not tell why. Supped Lord Coalston's. Some young lawyers there, and Miss Nisbet of Dirleton, a most charming creature did not she speak too broad. Her mother, a genteel, amiable woman. You was much in spirits. You consented to sing your Hamilton song. You was asked about the prison, &c. You was well understood.

[Boswell to Temple, *continued*]

March 8, still here . . . . and thinks those weak men whose minds waver. He is doing as well as I could wish. He is to settle in London. I hope you will make him your banker. On Christmas Day he and I drank in great form, "The Reverend Mr. William Temple, Rector of Mamhead, Devonshire."

What is to be thought of this life, my friend? Hear the story of my last three days. After tormenting myself with reflecting on my charmer's former loves and ruminating on parting with her, I went to her. I could not conceal my being distressed. I told her I was very unhappy, but I would not tell her why. She took this very seriously, and was so much affected that she went next morning and gave up our house. I went in the afternoon and secured the house, and then drank tea with her. She was much agitated. She said she was determined to go and board herself in the north of England, and that I used her very ill. I expostulated with her. I was sometimes resolved to let her go, and sometimes my heart was like to burst within me. I held her dear hand. Her eyes were full of passion. I took her in my arms. I told her what made me miserable. She was pleased to find it was nothing worse. She had imagined that I was suspicious of her fidelity, and she thought that very ungenerous in me, considering her behaviour. She said I should not mind her faults before I knew her, since her conduct was now most circumspect. We renewed our fondness. She owned she loved me more than she had ever done her husband. All was again well. She said she did not reproach me with my former follies, and we should be on an equal footing. My mind all at once felt a spring. I agreed with her. I embraced her with transport.

That very evening I gave a supper to two or three of my acquaintance, having before I left Scotland laid a guinea that I should not catch the venereal disorder for three years, which bet I had most certainly lost and now was paying. We drank a great deal till I was so much intoxicated that instead of going home, I went to a low house in one of the alleys in Edinburgh where I knew a common girl lodged, and like a brute as I was I lay all night with her. I had still so much reason left as not to "dive into the bottom of the deep,"[4] but I gratified my coarse desires by tumbling about on the brink of destruction. Next morning I was like a man ordered for ignominious execution. But by noon I was worse, for I discovered that some infection had reached me. Was not this dreadful? I had an assignation in the evening with my charmer. How lucky was it that I knew my misfortune in time. I might have polluted her sweet body. Bless me! what a risk! But how could I tell her my shocking story? I took courage. I told how drunk I had been. I told the consequences. I lay down and kissed her feet. I said I was unworthy of any other favour. But I took[5] myself. I gloried that I had ever been firmly constant to her while I was myself. I hoped she would consider my being drunk as a fatal accident which I should never again fall into. I called her my friend in whom I had confidence, and entreated she would comfort me.

How like you the eloquence of a young barrister? It was truly the eloquence of love. She bid me rise; she took me by the hand. She said she forgave me. She kissed me. She gently upbraided me for entertaining any unfavourable ideas of her. She bid me take great care of myself and in time coming never drink upon any account. Own to me, Temple, that this was noble — and all the time her beauty enchanted me more than ever. May I not then be hers? In the mean time I must be shut up, and honest Thomas must be my guardian.[6] He does excellently well. Pray what do you hear of Nicholls[7] and Claxton? Make my compliments to them. There is a pretty book just now published,

[4] *I Henry IV*, I. iii. 203.

[5] That is, checked.

[6] Boswell's servant, who had been recommended to him by Temple.

[7] According to Boswell, the Rev. Norton Nicholls, a good friend of Thomas Gray as well as of Temple, was distinguished for "an amiable disposition, a sweetness of manners, and an easy politeness" (*Boswell's London Journal*, 13 May 1763).

An Essay on the History of Civil Society, by the Moral Philosophy Professor here.[8] Let me hear from you soon, and believe me, ever yours,

JAMES BOSWELL.

Postscript.[9] My dear Temple, you are by this time well acquainted with my present situation. Many a different one have you known me in. You must comfort me; for by the time I can have your answer my spirits will be very low.

My present misfortune is occasioned by drinking. Since my return to Scotland I have given a great deal too much into that habit which still prevails in Scotland.[1] Perhaps the coldness of the Scots requires it. But my fiery blood is turned to madness by it. This will be a warning to me, and from henceforth I shall be a perfect man. At least I hope so. Adieu, my friend. Let us correspond once a fortnight. Write me fully. Tell me sincerely, do I right to insist that my dear little woman shall stay? She was married very young. But she has three children. I hate to think of it. No matter. She is like a girl of eighteen. She has the finest black hair, she is paradisial in bed. Is it not right I should have a favourite to keep me happy? But, alas, I love her so much that I am in a kind of fever. This is unworthy of Paoli's friend. Lord Eglinton once observed very justly that a man may be in love with an Italian woman of gallantry, because by the custom of the country she does not think she is doing wrong, — so may be called virtuous. But in this country a woman of gallantry is a woman without principle. There is too much truth in this. But I cannot apply it to my angel. By the by, she is now more affected by my bad conduct than she was at first. *Adieu encore.*

WEDNESDAY 11 MARCH[2] . . . . a kind of gloom to think this was the last day of the session. You drank tea at Mr. Alexander Tait's.

[8] Adam Ferguson.

[9] This postscript is written on another sheet, which became separated from its letter. It seems to belong here.

[1] It is quite true that Boswell did not begin drinking to excess until about the time he was admitted to the bar. This is, we believe, the first record of real drunkenness that has appeared in these volumes.

[2] Four pages of the Journal, containing the entries from 6 to the middle of 11 March, are missing.

He was not in. You had for company Mrs. Tait [and] Mrs. and Miss Blair. You was quite easy. You liked Miss Blair more and more without any fever. Saw Miss ——— a little.

FRIDAY 13 MARCH. Had a kind card from Miss ———; went to her and stayed from twelve to two. . . .

MEMORABILIA, 1767 [3]

? MARCH. I am a singular man. I have the whim of an Englishman to make me think and act extravagantly, and yet I have the coolness and good sense of a Scotsman to make me sensible of it.

I have often found myself inclined to give praise in a great degree. The reason is that in giving praise one feels a pride similar to that of one giving money. When I deal out laudatory epithets I am like a great man bestowing his largesses. Our inclination to censure strongly is owing to the same imaginary dignity. We suppose ourselves men of power distributing punishments; such, indeed, are not often of much importance.

Lord Auchinleck used to pass his time in the country in continual attention to the improvement of his place, but would often busy himself with very small matters. He would, for instance, gather stones off the land for hours; nay, he would very gravely fill his pockets with them, and carry them to mend a broken part in some favourite part. His sons, though they had a high respect for him, could not but exercise their humour on such oddities in a great character. David said, "He carries the stones in this manner upon the principle of utility, and no doubt he does some good to the road. But he would also do some good were he to fill his nails with sand, and sprinkle it upon the road. Why does he not always do good in some more important manner?"

I have seen contemptible beings exceedingly vain of being satirical. They do not consider how very little a dog is yet capable to bite. The veriest cur may scratch the heel of the most generous horse.

I have sometimes fallen into a strange, wild reverie, looking upon the human species as produced merely to exist a little here, and then

[3] An undated group of thoughts in a notebook entitled "Memorabilia," placed here because they follow an extract of a letter from Boswell to Lord Marischal, dated 12 March 1767.

be destroyed by the course of nature; so that all the diversities of character and of virtues have appeared as of little consequence. Methought I could use the words of him who was born blind, when Jesus was curing him, "Methinks I see men as trees walking."[4]

I am a weaker man than can well be imagined. My brilliant qualities are like embroidery upon gauze.

SATURDAY 14 MARCH. Tea, Miss ——; provoked her with old stories. Grange had been with you in the forenoon, and insisted you had no morals. You was shocked. You saw Miss —— had no sentiment. You had sore conflict. But you resolved to try one winter, to enjoy fully so strong a passion. You then fancied you could inspire her with finer feelings. You grew fond. Her eyes looked like precious stones. Some delirium seized you. She seemed an angel. ——

SUNDAY 15 MARCH. Had message from Miss ——; she was to set out next day. Was in, quiet all this day. Captain Erskine and Houston Stewart drank tea with you. Houston was dissipated as ever. You felt calm superiority, but not to shock him you assumed dissipation a little. You had wrote earnestly to Miss ——. She came at eight, and sat a while with you. It was vastly kind.

MONDAY 16 MARCH. You called on Miss —— and passed a great part of the forenoon, as she was not to go till Tuesday. You again spoke of old stories. She was fretted. You were both very uneasy. You saw her temper such that no eloquence could touch her. But you was her slave. Returned at five to tea. She was young and vivacious. What a temperament! You gave word in honour you'd never again allow her to be ill spoken of by Grange in your presence. You were like man and wife. . . . Went to Lady Betty's. She had been ill; you was so. [She still] appeared invalid. Was restless, having promised to Miss —— to return. You talked much of Miss ——, and Lady Betty and the Captain rated you about her. At eleven you went to her. You was let softly in. She was quite kind. But the recollection of her former tricks galled you, for your heart was affected. You had been with Lord Monboddo and talked of your flame.[5] He quoted Ulysses and Circe: ·

---

[4] Mark 8. 24.

[5] James Burnett, a judge in the Court of Session with the style of Lord Monboddo, was an able lawyer, a passionate admirer of antiquity, and remarkable for his pre-Darwinian evolutionary views. Though a highly intelligent man, he was

"Sub domina meretrice vixisset turpis et excors."[6] You saw how lightly passions appear to those not immediately affected by them, for even to yourself will this afterwards seem light. You was all resigned to sweet Miss ———. You chased away all reflection. You drank in instant delight. You sat till one, and parted with great fondness in hopes of meeting. Home, Father still up. Lady Betty bore the blame of late hours.

TUESDAY 17 MARCH. [Was] feverish [and felt like] Mark Antony, quite given up to violent love. . . . Then Miss G—— and gave money for [your] house, &c. Had laboured hard all winter, but now passion made you at once give up the fruits of your labour, which you had carefully collected. . . .

WEDNESDAY 18 MARCH. Found a listlessness creeping on you. Reviewed winter; wondered at the variety of business you had gone through, having made fourscore and four guineas. Went to Lord Hailes to have him examined by Lord Eliock in Cairncross cause. The other party could not attend. You was hurt to find reverence for Lords ceasing. You feared that *caelum ipsum* might lose its dignity if you got to it. Wild idea! Can finite beings be at all compared to infinity? You had a tête-à-tête with Lord Hailes. He commended you in some causes, said you had fought a good battle; but in Warnock's cause you had drawn a paper with as unfair a state of the facts as Lockhart could have done.[7] You told him of feverish passion. He bid you break off, but he seemed not rigid.

Then Dr. Blair's.[8] Had not seen him of a long time. He was comfortable. Talked of Corsica. He was roused with it. Complained of sickly love. He talked of it calmly as a bad thing. Talked of marriage, how agreeable, and how suited to you. Talked of action as quite neces-

---

misled into maintaining vigorously that in some countries men had tails. This prompted Dr. Johnson's remark that Monboddo was as jealous of his tail as a squirrel.

[6] "He lived filthy and stupid ruled by a whore" (Horace, *Epistles*, I. ii. 25, "vixisset" for "fuisset").

[7] For Alexander Lockhart, see p. 116 *n.*9.

[8] The Rev. Hugh Blair was Professor of Rhetoric and Belles-Lettres at the University of Edinburgh, and later published some very popular sermons. Boswell described him as learned, ingenious, and full of an engaging simplicity.

sary. You said yes, but [only] as a remedy to distempered minds. The sound and perfect human being can sit under a spreading tree like the Spaniard, playing on his guitar, his mistress by him, and glowing with gratitude to his God. Music, love, adoration! there is a soul. The Doctor was struck and pleased with this warm effusion. Commissioner [Cochrane] dined with you.[9]

At five, Lady Betty's, comfortable tea. You was still in fever about Miss ——. She and the Captain[1] showed you what a weakness [this was], what want of firmness, and how in all such cases a man of imagination supposed his mistress to have virtues. Lord Kellie actually believed Miss Massey, a common whore, to be a most virtuous woman but in unhappy circumstances, and that for the first time her *heart* was engaged to him. Lady Betty talked to me as a Christian. In short, everything was said, and the Captain recalled all the scandalous stories, [her living with the] waiter and all, which revolted you. You resolved to be self, to break free from slavery. What strength of mind you have had this winter, to go through so much business and at the same time have so violent a passion! You held Lady Betty's hand. Owned error; said, "Have hope of me"; and gave honour you'd never again allow yourself to fall into such a scrape.

Home. David sat long with you. Told him fairly your situation (all but paradisial completion). He, like a man, advised you to get free; you'd ruin yourself. You would fain have indulged for one year. "No," said he, "you might acquire habit of slavery, and, besides, it would then be ungenerous to quit." You wavered and knew not how to determine. You saw yourself gone. You wondered how you would feel if a notorious villain; for, from your violent passions, you dreaded its possibility. Was stunned; resolved firm. To bed quite agitated.

THURSDAY 19 MARCH. Waked in tender anguish: "What, shall I give her up?" Your melting moments rushed on your mind: her generosity — ah! For some seconds a real fit of delirium [seized you], tossing in your distempered mind [the thought of] instant self-destruction. Bless me! is this possible? It was literally true. Got up, roused, grew better. Bad weather had kept you still in town yesterday.

[9] Basil Cochrane, Boswell's maternal grand-uncle, one of the Commissioners of the Customs in Scotland.

[1] Andrew Erskine.

However set out today, the same family form. John Bruce, Mr. Stobie, Matthew Dickie, [and] Bob Boswell all down with you to the Back Stairs.[2] This composed your mind. It was, as it were, quilted with good, comfortable, family ideas. Jogged on. Good conversation on law. Dined Livingstone; night, Bedlay's new house. Father gave you account of the Hamilton memorial after supper, [but] left it off. In your room begun letter to Miss ———. Was gloomy but resolved; considered she had not feeling [enough] to be much affected.

FRIDAY 20 MARCH. Heavy snow. Father resumed the Hamilton memorial. Astonished at his memory, and how all this time he has never said a word, and yet has it so perfectly. [He has a] prodigious strong mind, singular frame. Dined Strathaven; night, Sornbeg, [to which you] walked up from Galston. Comfortable and easy, reflected on the gradual course of things. Was contented. Sat up late and finished letter to Miss ———. Sent it; was firm as if it had been a year after.

SATURDAY 21 MARCH. Left Sornbeg in the morning. As you came along, talked of economy. You was sensible of your want of that virtue, and wanted to save yourself. BOSWELL. "Come, come, I see some people in this world have economy, and some not." "Very right," said my father, "but why don't they acquire it then? You may as well say, 'Some people have learning in this world and some not. Some people are thieves in this world, and some not.' That argument will serve for everything." How excellent was his reasoning! You resolved to exert your active powers. My father has done so, and is the man he is. Arrived safe at Auchinleck. Reflected on your emancipation from Circe. Enjoyed the noble seat after the *longa negotia*[3] of a winter session. But the evil complaint pained you. It was, however, pretty easy.

SUNDAY 22 MARCH. Lay abed long and reflected comfortably

[2] All evidently dependents on the Boswell family. John Bruce was Lord Auchinleck's major-domo, and John Stobie his law clerk. Matthew Dickie, whom Boswell once described as a kind of diminutive Falstaff, was later his law clerk. Robert Boswell was Dr. John Boswell's son, and a "writer" in Edinburgh. The party walked down the long flight of stone steps leading from the Parliament Close to the Cowgate instead of making the horses pull the coach by a roundabout route up the hill to the High Street.

[3] "Tedious business" (Horace, *Odes*, III. v. 53).

on being free from Laïs.[4] We did not go to church. I wrote to M. de Sommelsdyck a calm family letter which my father read, I am sure, with satisfaction.[5] We read some of old Mr. Robert Bruce's Scots sermons, and a chapter of the Greek New Testament, and a psalm of Buchanan. We were very happy. We are now friends as much as my father's singular grave and steady temper will allow; for he has not that quick sensibility which animates me. Since the beginning of last winter he has ceased to treat me like a boy. This evening I thought with astonishment, "Is it really true that a man of such variety of genius, who has seen so much, who is in constant friendship with General Paoli, is it possible that he was all last winter the slave of a woman without one elegant quality?"

MONDAY 23 MARCH. Mr. Dun, Hallglenmuir,[6] &c., here. I roused my mind and wrote the Introduction to my Account of Corsica.

[London Chronicle][7]

THURSDAY 26 MARCH. Extract of a letter from The Hague, dated March 1, 1767. "The Corsican courier who some time ago made such a noise at Hamburg stayed a week in this place, and had an audience of three hours of Sir Joseph Yorke, His Britannic Majesty's Ambassador, to whom he was introduced by the Reverend Mr. Richardson, his Excellency's chaplain, and by the Reverend Mr. Maclaine, minister of the English church here, in whose house he was lodged during his residence at The Hague. M. Formey, perpetual Secretary of the Royal Academy at Berlin, had recommended him to Mr. Maclaine. It seems he would not put up at either of our two great inns, the Maréchal de Turenne or the Parliament d'Angleterre. What was the reason of this nobody can say; very probably he thought he would be less exposed to the visits of idle people by having an apartment in a

---

[4] The name of a famous Greek courtesan applied to Mrs. Dodds.

[5] The Countess of Kincardine, Boswell's great-grandmother on his paternal side and great-great-grandmother on his maternal side, had been a Sommelsdyck. A partial copy of Boswell's letter which survives describes various documents and *objets d'art* at Auchinleck pertaining to her and her relatives.

[6] The Rev. John Dun was minister at Auchinleck and had once been Boswell's tutor. Alexander Mitchell of Hallglenmuir was a neighbour and distant relation.

[7] In this continuation of the adventures of Signor Romanzo, Boswell draws on his acquaintance with Holland and the English there.

private house. But some of our penetrating politicians of the Morning Society will needs have it that the courier meant to show that neither France nor England could be looked upon as friendly to his nation. To such extravagant lengths will some wise heads carry their divination. This courier passed by the name of Signor Romanzo. He appeared to be a man of profound learning and great address. The Stadtholder showed him particular marks of attention, and the Duke of Brunswick was much with him. His equipage was superb, and his servants had the richest clothes ever seen in Holland."

FRIDAY 27 MARCH. Began my Account of Corsica, [and found I] could labour well. Father studied Douglas memorials[8] and at intervals [read] *Don Quixote*. [He was] much entertained with him. Joked on my Account; called it quixotism.

SATURDAY 28 MARCH. Went on well; thought I was writing for Europe. Had kept the house all this week. Honest Dr. Johnston had been with me.[9] At night Mr. Brown arrived.[1]

SUNDAY 29 MARCH. At church. Mr. Brown went to Mauchline. Evening, [we read from the] Greek Testament; very comfortable. Quite firm; mind sound after the fever of love. Determined to support the ancient family; offered up sincere devotions to my Father above.

[Boswell to Voltaire]

Auchinleck, 29 March 1767

SIR: — The politeness with which you received me at Ferney has never faded from my remembrance. I often recall it with the liveliest pleasure, and I am happy to think that I can boast of having had several conversations with M. de Voltaire.[2]

After I left you, you was so good as to write me a letter in English, which I had the honour to receive at Naples. On my return to Rome, I sent you an answer. I know not if you received it.[3]

Since that time I have seen a great deal, and I think my travelling

[8] Memorials for the defendants in the Douglas cause.
[9] Daniel Johnston, a physician in Cumnock.
[1] James Brown, Boswell's clerk.
[2] Boswell's description of his visit to Voltaire at Ferney is printed in *Boswell on the Grand Tour: Germany and Switzerland*, 25–29 December 1764.
[3] These letters are printed in *Boswell on the Grand Tour: Germany and Switzerland*, 15 March and 4 April 1765.

has done me great service. It has at least furnished me with a stock of ideas with which I can entertain my mind while I live; and to a man of keenness of thought that is very important. For if he has not a good stock of ideas he is apt to turn his keenness against himself, and you philosophers know that the human mind cannot be nicely searched without certain pain. My philosophy appeared to you very gloomy, for I confessed to you that misery seemed to me to be the principal portion of thinking beings.

I have visited the Island of Corsica, where I saw with enthusiasm a brave people who have vindicated their liberty with as much real spirit as was ever found in antiquity. General Paoli is a most extraordinary man. His abilities in politics and in war, his learning, his eloquence, and his generous sentiments render him truly illustrious. He has been now ten years the commander of his countrymen from personal merit, a glorious distinction!

I am busy writing an Account of Corsica, with Memoirs of General Paoli, which will be published the beginning of next winter. Mr. David Hume is so obliging as to take the charge of the publication, as I cannot be at London myself.

What does M. de Voltaire think of the Corsicans? I am persuaded he feels for them as I do. Why do you not write something in their behalf to rouse the cold spirit of the times? Why does M. de Voltaire live in the same age with so gallant a nation and not compose a verse to their honour?

After all my travels, I am now fixed in Scotland half the year as an advocate and the other half as a country gentleman. If it is not presuming too much on your former goodness I would beg to hear from you. I entreat you may make my best compliments to Madame Denis and to Père Adam. I have the honour to be, Sir, your most obedient, humble servant.

My address is &c.

Je n'ai pas osé vous écrire en français. Je crois qu'il est mieux d'écrire dans sa propre langue, même quand on sait bien une langue étrangère; et à plus forte raison quand on en sait très peu.[4]

---

[4] I have not dared write to you in French. I believe it is better to write in one's own language, even when one knows a foreign language well; and with much greater reason when one knows it very badly.

MONDAY 30 MARCH . . . . Proceeded in Corsica. Received noble letter from Temple; was in great spirits.

[Received 30 March, Temple to Boswell]

Mamhead, 20 March 1767

BEFORE I PROCEED to what I am going to say, let me beg of you when we write to each other never to consider me in the light of a priest, but in that of your friend, of a philosopher in the modest and original sense of the word, in short in that of a man. Now for your letter.

Though your last favour, my dearest Boswell, affords me the sincerest pleasure and much entertainment, yet I must confess myself a good deal concerned to find your attachment to your Moffat acquaintance is become so serious. A little occasional amorous dalliance, it is to be hoped, all of us may innocently enough allow ourselves; I mean where the object is incapable of injury, and ourselves run no hazard of fame or health; but then such intercourse ought to be but *occasional*, when nature will not be denied; and the desire being satisfied, the object should be thought of no more. Perhaps this reasoning may shock your delicacy (it once would have shocked mine), but unhappily in our present circumstances it is but common sense and common prudence, and whoever acts otherwise is considered by people that think, and even by the world, either as the good-natured dupe of an artful woman, or the slave of his passions.

I know, my dear Boswell, that neither of these characters can be applied to you, but if you continue to cohabit with a married woman, the unnatural mother of three children, and by your own account noted for her former gallantries, have a care of the character of a bad citizen, an encourager and the support of vice, and the convenience of a lewd woman. To be convinced that this is not declamation, for a moment only put any of your friends in your circumstances. Poor Temple, I am really grieved for him, my heart bleeds to see him act with so little regard to the esteem of his friends, and even his character in common life; he is a promising young man coming fast into business, and cannot be too guarded in his conduct; and to keep another man's wife, to take a house for her, and at this time too when so many industrious poor can hardly procure a morsel of bread, a woman that has deserted three poor infants and whom any handsome fellow that has money [can] lie with, surely he must either be bewitched or utterly abandoned. Probably in these words, or somewhat like them, you would compassionate my unhappy turn of mind.

Now you, who think it possible for the God of nature to have a son whose blood alone can appease him for the crime a created being committed in eating an apple, do not flatter yourself that such a propitiation will atone for sins against the laws of our country and against mankind. In the vast continent of Ethiopia, where according to Diodorus men yet live in a state of nature, chastity and fidelity are not virtues, for women and children are there in common;[5] but in our polished Europe, where we have sacrificed many of our natural rights to the peaceable enjoyment of our persons and properties, the laws of our country are our religion, and can hardly ever be violated without impiety. The absolute necessaries of life are what we all have right to, can demand, and ought to obtain, but he who indulges himself in superfluities, not to say criminal excesses, when thousands of his fellow creatures are fainting with hunger, what must we think of such a citizen! But to talk more like myself. My dearest Boswell, if you love me let me entreat you to sacrifice this woman to our friendship. You know that there is not a person in the world who possesses such a share in my heart as you do; you know it is my affection for you that dictates this letter; if then you really love me, if you would not give your worthy father pain, if your own peace of mind, if your time, if your health, if your good name is dear to you, by all that is sacred in friendship, by all that is desirable in life, let me prevail with you to break your ignominious fetters, to assert the command of yourself, and be again my Boswell. . . . [6]

Adieu, dearest friend, let our affection increase with our years, and let our hearts be conscious of a friendship that might have done honour to Greece or Rome.

W. J. TEMPLE.

[5] Diodorus Siculus in his *Historical Library* attributes this state of affairs to neighbors of the Ethiopians, the Fisheaters.

[6] In the omitted portion of this letter, Temple tells Boswell that the "holy intercourse" of philosophy, history, and poetry is preferable to the "melting down" of his manhood in the arms of his Chloe.

P.S. Pray keep your promise in writing often. You shall hear from me again next week. Tell me if you are got well.

[Boswell to Temple]

Auchinleck, 30 March 1767

MY DEAR TEMPLE, — I have this moment received your kind letter of the 20th instant, which has been like an oration of Tully to my soul. I am happy that I can make you a good report, for as my Circe went to Moffat just after I wrote to you last, and I myself was to go to Auchinleck, I had time to think coolly and to call up that reason which I have so often contradicted. Johnston, an old friend of mine, a writer in Edinburgh, but too much of an indolent philosopher to have great business, being rather a worthy country gentleman with a paternal estate of £100 a year, was much distressed with my unhappy passion. He was at Moffat when it first began, and he marked the advance of the fever. It was he who assured me upon his honour that my fair one had a very bad character, and gave me some instances which made my love-sick heart recoil.

He had some influence with me. But my brother David had more. To him I discovered my weakness, my slavery, and begged his advice. He gave it me like a man. I gloried in him. I roused all my spirit, and at last I was myself again. I immediately wrote her the letter of which I inclose the scroll for your perusal.[7] She and I have always corresponded in such a manner that no mischief could come of it, for we supposed a Miss ____ to whom all my amorous vows were paid. You will observe my method. I wish you may be able to read the scroll. After reading the note to Mrs. ____,[8] read pages two, three, and four to Miss ____, then read what is below the second score in page one, and lastly read what is between the scores in page one. This is leading you an odd dance, but it is better than giving myself the labour of copying the letter, which I think you ought to see, and which you will please return to me. I have not yet got her answer. What will it be, think you? I shall judge of her character from it. I shall see if she is abandoned or virtuous, I mean both in a degree. I shall at any rate be

[7] The enclosure is missing. A "scroll" is a draft or rough copy of a letter.
[8] The name in this instance has been crossed out. The dashes elsewhere occur in the manuscript.

firm. What a snare have I escaped! Do you remember Ulysses and Circe?

> Sub domina meretrice vixisset turpis et excors.

My life is one of the most romantic that I believe either you or I really know of, and yet I am a very sensible, good sort of man. What is the meaning of this, Temple? You may depend upon it that very soon my follies will be at an end, and I shall turn out an admirable member of society. Now that I have given my mind the turn, I am totally emancipated from my charmer, as much as from the gardener's daughter, who now puts on my fire and empties my chamber-pot like any other wench; and yet just this time twelvemonth, I was so madly in love as to think of marrying her. Should not this be an everlasting lesson to me? It shall be so, and Mrs. _____ shall second it. By the by, Temple, I must tell you that I have never owned Mrs. _____'s real kindness to me except in my letters to you. I am much upon honour in all these affairs. So if by some strange accident anybody who knows her should enquire of you, laugh it off as a frolic.

You unrelenting dog! You have used my charmer cruelly. You say she is the unnatural mother of three children — ah, no! She loves her children, but a barbarous father keeps them from her. Her affection for her children makes her amiable to me. But I confess she ought, for the sake of her children, to conform to the strict ideas of the world. How strangely do we colour our own vices. I startle when you talk of *keeping another man's wife*. Yet that was literally my scheme, though my imagination represented it just as being fond of a pretty, lively, black little lady who, to oblige me, stayed in Edinburgh, and I very genteelly paid her expenses. You will see by my letter to her that I shall have a house and a servant-maid upon my hands. How she will settle that I know not. You rogue! don't bid me settle it this way: put the maid into the house and kiss the maid. At any rate, I shall not be *Limberham*.[9]

What say you to my marrying? I intend next autumn to visit Miss Bosville in Yorkshire. But I fear, my lot being cast in Scotland, that beauty would not be content. She is, however, grave. I shall see. There is a young lady in the neighbourhood here who has an estate of her

[9] The "kind keeper" of Dryden's loose comedy, *Limberham*.

own between two and three hundred a year, just eighteen, a genteel person, an agreeable face, of a good family, sensible, good-tempered, cheerful, pious.[1] You know my grand object is the ancient family of Auchinleck, a venerable and noble principle. How would it do to conclude an alliance with this neighbouring princess, and add her lands to our dominions? I should at once have a very pretty little estate, a good house, and a sweet place. My father is very fond of her. It would make him perfectly happy. He gives me hints in his way: "I wish you had her." No bad scheme this. I think a very good one. But I will not be in a hurry. There is plenty of time. I will take to myself the advice I wrote you from Naples, and go to London a while before I marry.

I am not yet quite well, but am in as good a way as can be expected. My fair neighbour was a ward of my father's. She sits in our seat at church in Edinburgh. She would take possession here most naturally. This is a superb place: we have the noblest natural beauties, and my father has made most extensive improvements. We look ten miles out upon our own dominions. We have an excellent new house. I am now writing in a library forty foot long. Come to us, my dearest friend. We will live like the most privileged spirits of antiquity. I am now seriously engaged in my Account of Corsica. It elevates my soul, and makes me *spernere humum.*[2] I shall have it finished by June. My brother David is quite to my mind. I inclose you a letter from him. You will see the young man as he is, in it. He has a portion of that sensibility which rendered you and me unhappy every moment, till time and experience taught us common sense and moderate desires. I am ever, my dearest friend, most affectionately yours,

James Boswell.

What *varios casus*[3] have you known your friend in, first and last, real and imaginary, only recollect. How do you get your letters, when my Lord Lisburne is in London? Must this go to his Lordship's town house? Return me David's letter with the scroll to Mrs. ———.

TUESDAY 31 MARCH. Began information for Gilkie. Read always a little of Hamilton and Douglas memorials after breakfast. At night you and Father both owned you were living very happily.

[1] Catherine Blair.
[2] "Spurn the earth" (adapted from Horace, *Odes*, III. ii. 21–24).
[3] "Varied hazards" (Virgil, *Aeneid*, i. 204).

THURSDAY 2 APRIL. Mr. Brown at Cumnock. Mr. Reid dined.[4] Gave him your time as a worthy old friend of the family. Talked of your grandfather, &c. Dr. Johnston drank tea. You was still bad. At night had fear of ghosts, [thinking of] poor Robert Hay.[5]

FRIDAY 3 APRIL . . . . You laboured hard and with spirit.

SATURDAY 4 APRIL. Accounts came of the Corsicans having made a descent on Capraja, with a letter from Mr. Dick confirming it and informing you that all your correspondence was safe. You was roused. You had not felt your blood in fermentation of a long time before. You only regretted that you don't feel *yourself* more manly. This your own fault. Resolved more guarded conduct.

SUNDAY 5 APRIL. Mr. Brown had gone yesterday to Kilmarnock. At church. Evening read Greek Testament and Hervey.[6]

MONDAY 6 APRIL. Corsica went on, and old charters. You saw everything is only practice.

TUESDAY 7 APRIL . . . . You was well enough. At night talked with Mr. Dun on the nature of God and of a future state. Felt yourself much unaccustomed to these subjects. Meditated seriously. Wonderful thought; alarming too. But God is good.

WEDNESDAY 8 APRIL. Dr. Johnston thought me better. Corsica still.

[Boswell to Chatham][7]

Auchinleck, 8 April 1767

MY LORD: — I have had the honour to receive your Lordship's letter from Bath, and I perfectly feel the sentiments which it contains. I

[4] The Rev. George Reid, minister of Ochiltree, had been chaplain to James Boswell, Boswell's grandfather, and domestic tutor to Lord Auchinleck. He was now about 70 and lived to be 90.

[5] Who had been hanged on 25 March.

[6] The Rev. James Hervey was author of such popular essays as *Meditations Among the Tombs, Reflections on a Flower Garden,* and *Contemplations on the Night.*

[7] Published in part in the *Correspondence of William Pitt, Earl of Chatham,* ed. W. S. Taylor and J. H. Pringle, 1838–1840, iii. 244–247, and in *Letters of James Boswell,* i. 110–111. Boswell's draft differs very little from the letter as sent. The original, which is followed here, is among the Chatham Papers in the Public Record Office.

only wish that circumstances were such that your Lordship could have an opportunity of showing the interest you take in the fate of a people who well deserve the favour of so illustrious a patron of liberty as your Lordship. I have communicated to General Paoli the contents of your Lordship's letter, and I am persuaded he will think as I do.

Allow me to give your Lordship another quotation from a letter of that hero. It is addressed to a friend of mine at Leghorn. "Essendo al Ministero il Conte di Chatham, voglio sperar tutto il buon successo alla generosa premura del Signore Boswell, per la rivocazione dell' ingiuriosa Proclama del 1763. Quel sublime genio della Gran Brettagna e quell' anima grande ne' propri sentimenti e nel sistema della sua politica, ritroverà i più efficaci motivi per far uscir la sua Corte dello stato di indifferenza sopra gli affari di Corsica."[8] I leave with the Earl of Chatham these words of General Paoli, and I am persuaded *quell' anima grande* will not forget them.

Your Lordship applauds my "generous warmth for so striking a character as the able Chief." Indeed, my Lord, I have the happiness of being capable to contemplate with supreme delight those distinguished spirits by whom God is sometimes pleased to honour humanity; and, as I have no personal favour to ask of your Lordship, I will tell you, with the confidence of one who does not fear to be thought a flatterer, that your character, my Lord, has filled many of my best hours with that noble admiration which a disinterested soul can enjoy in the bower of philosophy.

I think it my duty to inform your Lordship that I am preparing to publish an Account of Corsica. My plan is, first, to give a geographical and physical description of the Island; secondly, to exhibit a concise view of the revolutions it has undergone from the earliest times till now; thirdly, to show the present state of Corsica in every respect; and, lastly, I subjoin my Journal of a Tour to That Island, in which I

[8] "Now that the Earl of Chatham is in the Ministry, I venture to hope for good success to Mr. Boswell's generous concern in the revoking of the injurious Proclamation of 1763. That sublime genius of Great Britain, and that great spirit, will find in his own sentiments and in his own political views the most efficacious motives for causing his Court to emerge from its state of indifference to the affairs of Corsica." John Dick was the Leghorn friend who forwarded a copy of Paoli's letter to him. Although Boswell does not seem to have known it, Paoli, on 31 January 1767, had written directly to Pitt asking for English aid.

relate a variety of anecdotes and treasure up many memoirs of the illustrious General of the Corsicans — *memorabilia Paoli.*

While I was in Corsica I was careful to write down everything that deserved attention, and since my return home I have received many materials from different people of that country. I hope my book will be agreeable, and may do some service to the brave Islanders by representing them in a proper light. General Paoli is very impatient for my publishing it.

I beg to know what your Lordship thinks of my undertaking, for although I am so much engaged to the island that I must at any rate go on with it, the approbation of my Lord Chatham would make me advance with double spirit.

And I must entreat your Lordship's permission to take notice of your noble sayings concerning Corsica and General Paoli.[9] It will add much dignity to the subject and to the author. I promise to insert nothing that is improper to be read by all the world. But when I record General Paoli's grand ideas of your Lordship, I would also record your Lordship's grand ideas of him, that posterity may see how highly two such men thought of each other.

As for myself, to please a worthy and respected father, one of our Scots judges, I studied law, and am now fairly entered to the bar. I begin to like it. I can labour hard; I feel myself coming forward, and I hope to be useful to my country. Could your Lordship find time to honour me now and then with a letter? I have been told how favourably your Lordship has spoke of me.[1] To correspond with a Paoli and with a Chatham is enough to keep a young man ever ardent in the pursuit of virtuous fame. I ever am, my Lord, with the highest admiration, your Lordship's much obliged, humble servant,

JAMES BOSWELL.

P.S. I beg to know if I may address my letters to your Lordship by the public post?[2]

[9] See p. 10.

[1] Erskine wrote to John Johnston (2 June 1766): "I would tell Boswell what Pitt said of him at Bath, but why feed vanity?" Apparently no record survives of what Pitt did say.

[2] By the time Boswell's letter reached him, Pitt had sunk into a state of prostration close to insanity, and he remained unfit for business during the rest of his ministry.

THURSDAY 9 APRIL. Craigengillan[3] and Mr. Duff dined. You was quite easy and felt the effect of experience, which it is impossible for youth to conceive. Only most people are not so much surprised with it, because they did not look so far before them in youth as I did. In the evening came Captain Cuninghame-Montgomerie[4] and Matthew Dickie. Very comfortable.

FRIDAY 10 APRIL. Your toe was pretty well, and you walked in the Broomholm with Matthew. You talked of Miss Blair. I felt my openness too great. I might soon acquire a habit of telling everything. By doing so a man becomes quite easy, but loses delicacy and dignity. You thought it best to own a libertine misfortune and regret your fault. The same company continued all night, with honest Hallglenmuir. You found time, however, to advance a little in Corsica.

[*Scots Magazine*]

London, April 11. This morning M. Romanzo, agent from Corsica, had a private audience of the Earl of Shelburne.

SUNDAY 12 APRIL. Overton very kindly agreed to buy Dalblair[5] for me, and got a letter of commission from my father to the extent of £900. We had much good conversation on my being a well-doing laird, as the Jameses have been in this family. Overton went to church with us, from whence he went home. At night we read our Greek chapters, translating one in English, the other in Latin.

MONDAY 13 APRIL. Corsica advanced. Treesbank[6] and Polquhairn dined. The latter told you gross scandal of Mrs. ———. It hardly hurt you, so well are you grown. Dr. Johnston thought you not so

[3] John McAdam of Craigengillan, a wealthy landowner and close friend of the Boswell family, was later a friend of Burns, who addressed a poem to him.

[4] Captain Alexander Montgomerie-Cuninghame, eldest son of Sir David Cuninghame of Corsehill. His wife was Elizabeth Montgomerie, Lord Auchinleck's niece, and proprietress of Lainshaw.

[5] Part of the wild vale of Glenmuir, about ten miles east of Auchinleck. It probably bordered on the Auchinleck estates.

[6] James Campbell, laird of Treesbank, was Lord Auchinleck's first cousin. He married in 1768 as his second wife, Mary Montgomerie, sister to the late laird of Lainshaw.

well. Said your distemper had paroxysms, but could hardly go wrong
in the way you treated it. Mr. Brown returned.

TUESDAY 14 APRIL. Began information for Mackenzies against
Sir Alexander Mackenzie.[7] Made library [your] consulting room to
inspire you with noble ideas of antiquity of family while you wrote
in favour of entails. . . . Little was done to Corsica. You began
Dorando . . . .[8]

WEDNESDAY 15 APRIL. You was in great vigour of genius, and
in the library you dictated Dorando. You thought it excellent. Mr.
Brown, when writing it, often was struck with admiration, and cried,
"That's grand!" You considered it as an elegant mark of your attachment to the family of Douglas. You did nothing to Corsica. Mr. Andrew Mitchell was here.

THURSDAY 16 APRIL. Waterhead breakfasted. You and he
agreed that venereal disorders do not hurt the constitution. Only severe cures do. There may be a good deal in this. But Waterhead and I
have both been wild, so are not impartial judges, for no doubt such disorders do harm. Mr. Mitchell and I and Knockroon[9] rode up to Cumnock to the roup[1] of Dalblair. I dined in Mrs. Johnston's. The trustees
were hearty. Sundrum was there.[2] There was a kind of awkwardness
when he and I, who had formerly travelled pretty much in the same
way, and had now taken so very different roads, met again. I was as
much composed as I could wish to be. I felt myself insensibly grown
up.

About four we had the roup. Overton made at first an offer of
£2400. It had been set up at £2000. I bid £10 more. I sat as if pretty indifferent, but was very anxious, till at last it fell to me. The company
then took me by the hand as Dalblair. We went upstairs, and I gave

[7] Sir Alexander Mackenzie wished to break the entail which settled his estate on
his eldest son, in order to provide for his children by his second wife. He was unsuccessful.

[8] For *Dorando*, see Introduction, p. xiii.

[9] John Boswell of Knockroon was a distant cousin of Boswell's, and at one time or
other collector of taxes in Ayr. Boswell bought his lands in 1790.

[1] Auction.

[2] John Hamilton of Sundrum, an important landed proprietor, later for many
years Vice-Lieutenant of Ayrshire. He had been a college mate of Boswell's both
at the University of Edinburgh and the University of Glasgow.

them a bowl of punch. Polosh said he would give me £500 for my bargain, and, if I had not bid, he would have given a great deal more. So said Overton, perhaps in earnest. So said several. This showed the influence of the family of Auchinleck. It was most fortunately conducted. Had Overton bid a small sum, they never would have let it go for that, the ice would have been broke, and when once they had begun to bid they would have gone to their utmost stretch. Or had I bid £100 more, as I intended, I should have paid £90 more. Over and above the price, I was burdened with an annuity of £25 a year to young James Gib's wife, which, however, I believe may be compounded for £80. At any rate the price cannot be more than £2500. I drank tea at Dr. Johnston's, from whence I wrote to David acquainting him of my purchase. When I came home I found my father in the library. He imagined Dalblair would be bought by the Earl of Dumfries. But I told him, "It's our own," and the price. He took me by the hand as Dalblair and was very well pleased.[3]

FRIDAY 17 APRIL. At breakfast my father treated me with some fine honey. "For," says he, "you are a stranger laird — a parish laird." I finished Mackenzie; at night read it to my father. I was wrong towards the end. But upon the whole he thought it a good paper.

SATURDAY 18 APRIL. Corsica advanced. Mr. Brown went home. Sent Dorando to Foulis.[4] Imagined he might perhaps scruple to publish so strong an allusion to the Douglas cause; left him to himself.

MONDAY 20 APRIL. Corsica advanced. At night I began to write an account of the Boswells from my father's dictating.

TUESDAY 21 APRIL. Corsica still understood to advance. Also much entertained with the Douglas cause. Studied today Godefroi's [testimony] by [the] Pursuers.[5] At night came Captain McAdam and Mr. Robert Aiken. Felt a kind of wildness and awkward reluctance to be in society. 'Tis in the family.

[3] He did not continue to be so well pleased. Boswell still owed £1300 of the purchase price in 1776, and Lord Auchinleck, who had gone surety for part of it (see entry for 12 April), made a number of unpleasant scenes before finally advancing the money to pay off the debt.

[4] Robert Foulis, the noted Glasgow printer.

[5] The Hamiltons were trying to prove that at the time when Lady Jane was supposed to be lying in at a different house, she was actually at Godefroi's inn.

WEDNESDAY 22 APRIL. Corsica still. Read Godefroi's [testimony] by [the] Defender; amazingly strong. Captain McAdam and Fingland dined. At night continued account of [the] Boswells; very happy.

THURSDAY 23 APRIL. Corsica advanced. Mr. Dun, Mr. Hugh Campbell, and Mr. Smeaton, the seceding minister, dined. The seceder was jocular upon the established minister.[6] Mr. Dun went home after tea. Mr. Smeaton was my client, so had a right to my time. I went through his cause to him. It was curious to find myself the grave counsellor of an old seceding minister with his mind full of Presbyterian notions about the Covenant, the Act and Testimony, &c. At night he and I had a long tête-à-tête. I led him into metaphysical enquiry. I talked of original sin. I argued in defence of the metempsychosis, or of a pre-existence. I objected that indeed this could hardly be, as there is to be a resurrection. Now, in this state we know nothing of spirit. All that I know of a person is an animated body. If I do not see the animated bodies of my friends at the Resurrection, I cannot know them. Now, if there is but one soul, which has animated a variety of bodies, there must in every generation be numbers a-wanting at the last day; for not only does the same soul serve different bodies, but has different accidents and fills different spheres in life. To this I answered myself, that the Resurrection is a doctrine exceedingly dark. That in creeds we find the resurrection of the body, but that the Scriptures do not expressly contain it. Paul, in order to give some satisfaction to the curiosity of the Corinthians, says, "It is sown in corruption, it is raised in incorruption; it is sown a natural body, it is raised a spiritual body"; and, having illustrated this with a comparison to grain, he says, "And that which thou sowest, thou sowest not that body which shall be." Therefore I suppose [there will be] no resurrection of the body, in conformity with "flesh and blood shall not inherit the Kingdom of Heaven," and with "at the Resurrection there is neither marrying nor giving in marriage."[7]

Now, may it not be thus? A soul darts its view backward through all the stages of its existence; the earthy frames are totally forgot, and

[6] The Seceders were members of Presbyterian splinter groups that had left the Church of Scotland. They held, in general, rather old-fashioned views.

[7] I Corinthians 15 and Matthew 22. 30.

the spirits recollect each other by mutual ideas. A spirit remembers having been in different states of life, as a man recollects infancy, youth, and manhood; and, as it is by a communication of ideas only that spirits shall recollect each other, the spirits of every age will find their companions and friends in this spiritual intercourse. Only throw body out of the question and all is easy. Suppose the ideas of Alexander the Great and Luther to be repeated by the same spirit, those spirits who retain the ideas of Alexander's courtiers and those who retain the ideas of the first Reformers will find corresponding communications. The ethereal spirit, the air, affects us with sensations both of cold and of heat. We do not look for a distinct body out of which the qualities producing each of these sensations must issue.

Mr. Smeaton was struck with my subtle philosophy. He defended himself by some abstract doctrines of the schoolmen, and I let him off. I found he had afterwards said to James Bruce that he had conversed with many, but he had never found a gentleman who had such a foundation, and if I lived I must be a very great man.

[*London Chronicle*][8]

THURSDAY 23 APRIL. Letter from an English soldier in the Corsican service to his cousin at Salisbury.

Island of Capra, this 20th Day of March 1767.
Dir Bob, — This is to let you know I am piur and well, thank God. You knows as how I never coud be quaiet, bot was allwis awishing for somthing to do. And I had mi bellifool of it in Germani, and win I was dismist the servis as laim, I cryd lyk a nu born child to Doctor Armstrong, and that wurthi sowl gaiv me a guiny and a paiper all ful of diricshiuns how to git mi ligg heeld. So you knows as how I cumd hom and recuvert, and as how I next embarkt to Martinico [and had hot wurk enuff of it. I then went with my Captain to Itali][9] wer I heerd mooch tauk of them here Corsicans, so over I gos, and faith Bob

---

[8] In the following "invention," Boswell imitates illiterate letters in the novels of Fielding, Richardson, and Smollett, and anticipates such comic American characters as Mr. Dooley.

[9] The phrases in brackets were added in Boswell's hand to his marked copy of the *Chronicle.* The printer must have dropped them out inadvertently.

I never was better. The General on em Poli is as good a man as the King himself, whom God blis, I shall never sarv another whyl he his any thing to do. He speaks to us in inglish for you must know thair ar fyv mor on us inglish, two on em Scots, but they call us all inglish here. Wir not listit nor sworn befor a Justis, no, no, all Volonteers, and never a lash, all bold and free as as many lyons. We haiv littel pai to signifi but enuff of good vittals and drink, sweet mutton as any on the downs, and the best of wyns as plenty as smal bir in old Ingland. Youll see by the Paipers wiv had an expedishun to the Island of Capra. We landed saif and soon took thri forts, and ar now seeging the Sitedil. Thair drol littel fellows them Corsicans. Som on em can tauk to be understood, as we went briscly on they cryd well don Brother Inglish, well don Brother freemen. They fyt powrfuli, but I wish we had Gunner Robison and som mor of the train, for thair tilleri dos not plai so smart as I coud wish. If Duncan Drummond wer heer by Jove hid blow the Genoeses to hell.[1] We heer as how a fleet is cumin against us. But we will all dy on the spot befor we giv it up. No more at present but rests your loving Cousin

SAM: JONES.

FRIDAY 24 APRIL. My father and I went to the burial of the Justice Clerk's lady.[2] I was not affected by such solemn feelings as I used to be at burials. I did not see the rest so affected. A woman had paid the common debt to nature and we interred her decently; that was all. We had so heavy a rain that few of us came out of our chaises to go into the isle.[3] My father and I sat snug. We came home through the Trabboch. At night [received] many letters; a great packet from Temple, curious, &c.

[1] Boswell had met Duncan Drummond, Captain in the Royal Regiment of Artillery, in Genoa. There is no record of his having known David Robison, Lieutenant Fireworker in the Royal Irish Artillery.

[2] The Lord Justice-Clerk, acting head of the Justiciary Court, was Thomas Miller, a neighbour of the Boswells at Auchinleck. On Miller's elevation to this position David Boswell wrote Boswell: "It is a shame that such a *body* sprung from nothing should come before so many more worthy personages" (29 April 1766).

[3] The isle (see p. 28 *n.*1) was often used as a burial place for the laird's family. The burial probably took place in the family vault at Stair church.

[Received 24 April, Temple to Boswell]

Mamhead, 13 April 1767

MY DEAR BOSWELL, — I kept my promise in writing to you, but my letter is so unreasonably long that I must defer sending it till I get a frank from Lord Lisburne in town.[4] Indeed it is lucky I am going thither, for I am in some danger. O Boswell, what weak creatures are we! how apt to forget ourselves, how prone to folly and vice! I wrote to my friends in the North to get me a sober, careful maidservant to manage my house, and on whom I might entirely depend, for I cannot bear to suspect anybody and hate the trouble of ordering dinner, &c. They have sent me a young creature of two and twenty, not handsome indeed, but the very picture of health, modest, gentle, and even anxious to please me. I am a weak creature: good nature, affection destroy me, I cannot resist it, I cannot get this girl out of my head. How I despise myself! and what is worse, it makes me mad to think my man is always by her. What shall I do! I am miserable, it has affected my health, I wish to be dead. I know it is all owing to my situation; in any other I could never forget myself so much, but I see nobody, I am as bad as you were at Utrecht, I rave, I burst into tears, I almost say, why did you give me being? I cannot sleep, I call out aloud in my bed. O God, I hope I am not mad!

What shall I do! I'll go to town instantly, I'll go down to the North, I'll come to you. And the lady at Berwick. They tell me I shall be infamous there if I do not marry her. We must sacrifice our happiness to our good name. You must give me leave, you must approve, you must insist that I do not deceive her. How cruel it is that virtue and peace of mind should depend so much upon circumstances, situation! Aristippus said a man that can live alone must either be a god or a beast. A god — alas! A beast I may be. But I would not injure her for the world; I would not attempt it.

What I have said has given me some relief. My heart is not so heavy. I write incorrectly, but as I feel. You know your own weaknesses, you can pity mine. My constitution is rather a peculiar one. My passions seemed to sleep till I came hither. I am much altered. I

[4] Postage on letters was paid by the recipient, not the sender. It was customary for members of Parliament to frank covers for their friends.

am no longer that resigned, tranquil creature you knew me. My thoughts are too much turned upon myself. Discontent, ambition, a gentler passion, indolence, yet an insatiable thirst after knowledge tear my very soul in pieces and make me a torment to myself. What a picture have I drawn of myself! I cannot look at it. Pity your lost Temple. Farewell, O farewell, my dear Boswell.

W.J.T.

[Received 24 April, Temple to Boswell]

14 April 1767

MY EVER DEAR FRIEND, — I have just now received your letter from Auchinleck, and to find you are yourself again suspends the anguish of my troubled mind and is a most sensible relief to me. What a pleasure is it to me to feel that the interest, the honour, the happiness of another man are as dear to me as my own. I can never repent me of this double existence. It is the surest pledge of the goodness of my heart; it may increase my pains, but it must also double my pleasures. I thank your friend Johnston, I thank your brother David; they are good young men. Davy's letter is sensible, and I think very like our own at his age. I shall be curious to see Mrs. _____'s answer. Yours is very polite, delicate, and philosophical.

I am in a very good frame now. My Boswell has broken the shackles of a dishonourable connection, is happy at the seat of his ancestors, has thoughts of a union that will be a credit and happiness to him, and is employing his recess from business in creating an eternal monument to his love of letters and of liberty.[5] You see I almost flatter you to keep you in humour, for you are a very young man, and you know I regard no honours but personal ones worthily acquired; and it is not certain that your book will last.

What shall I say of myself? 'Tis a fine morning, the sun shines mildly and nature is reviving in every herb and flower. I am now quite calm, pleased with and thankful for my existence. I look up to the God of my being with silent gratitude. If we may say so, what should I have lost had I never been! many cares, many sorrows, many disgusts, but oh! what sensations, what thoughts, what pleasures.

[5] In the Preface to *Corsica*, Boswell spoke of his work as "my little monument to liberty."

How horrible the idea of never having existed, of existing no more. It makes my very blood run cold. Certainly, certainly, impossible! Wollaston says God cannot disappoint us! silly enough! We cannot be disappointed if we do not exist. And how are we accountable creatures? Are we not the workmanship of God? Don't we think and move and act through him? If he foreknows the tenor of our lives, where is freedom? These doubts can never be resolved. I give over the search. What then do we really know? That we are created beings, born to live with one another, to be grateful to God for what we enjoy, to be just, humane, temperate; this, I think, is all. 'Tis enough, Boswell. God bless you. Your most affectionate,

W.J.T.

P.S. Your letters come directly to me here. I inclose your brother's and the other with mine this afternoon to Lord Lisburne to frank. Don't write again till you hear from me from London. I propose going by Bath. I must amuse myself. Today I think the girl very ordinary, her features coarse, far too much red in her face; besides, she cannot write. Never was there such folly. Her lips too don't please me, and her breasts are too small. And think of the want of delicacy in that rank. The coarse jest, the lewd reply, the falseness, the unfeeling heart, and the inexpressible meannesses and low arts. The best can hardly resist example; water always tastes of the soil it flows through. Let this be buried in oblivion. Do not reproach me, my dear Boswell. Adieu.

MONDAY 27 APRIL. Corsica went on pleasantly. After dinner I got a letter from [Miss] ——— that the *black boy*, &c.[6] I was very composed; half delighted to obtain what I had wished, and half vexed to think of the expense, &c. — a curious example of the vanity of human wishes. A man loves a woman to distraction. He would give the world to have a child by her. It does not appear. He suffers, he quits his angel, his love cools. He hears she is pregnant. O world, world! But I resolved to behave with humour and generosity, and pleased my fancy with a thousand airy plans. I also got a proof of Dorando. What a variety of *productions!* My father argued with Mr. Connell, or rather joked, against reading books of controversy about religion. I

---

[6] Boswell and Mrs. Dodds were both very dark in complexion.

saw my father had never been uneasy upon these matters. His system has never been tried. He has had it like a man who has carried his walking-stick under his arm, being so strong that he has never had occasion to put it to the ground; but, had he leaned on it, he might perhaps have been obliged to seek for another, or at least to look well how he put his own to the ground.

TUESDAY 28 APRIL. Baillie Wilson of Kilmarnock and his son came in the morning, and, as clients, had a claim to my time. We walked about. I was very comfortable. At night I received a packet of papers brought from Holland by Captain Kinloch. But my Journal was a-missing. I was much vexed. I figured its being exposed to a hundred enemies. I wrote immediately to Mr. Brown at Utrecht, and to Mr. Kinloch of Gilmerton, the Captain's father.[7] James Bruce said it would *cast up* yet. So I suppose he would have me not *cast down*. Come, a pun is not a bad thing at times.[8]

SATURDAY 2 MAY. My father was to have gone with me to Lainshaw, but he was not quite well. I rode to it. I dined at Treesbank, a noble, hearty meeting with the honest Laird. I then called at Hill of Kilmaurs', and saw Mr. Smeaton and his wife. I was as solid and sagacious as I could wish. But I don't know how, I have not the vivid feelings of satisfaction that I expected. Well, is not this the *nil admirari* of Horace? — the

> prope res una,
> Solaque, quae possit facere ac servare beatum?[9]

[Reached] Lainshaw at night; easy and happy.

SUNDAY 3 MAY. Stewarton church all day. Many reflections on old stories. But calm and not shocked with the course of nature. Had thought I would be in love; was so.[1] Steuart Hall supped with us, a

---

[7] Boswell's Holland Journal never was found. See *Boswell in Holland*, p. 359 of McGraw-Hill's edition (p. 349 of Heinemann's).

[8] The next three days have an identical entry: "Corsica advanced."

[9] "To admire nothing [is] almost the one and only thing to make and keep a man contented" (altered from *Epistles*, I. vi. 1–2).

[1] With Jean Montgomerie, widow of James Montgomerie of Lainshaw, and sister-in-law of Lord Auchinleck's nieces. Boswell also calls her *La Vedova* (see entry for 8 May). He had not been at Lainshaw since Montgomerie's death in

genteel, lively man. At night a long walk, the Captain[2] and I; a solid, serious conversation. Relished much his strong sense. Curious pun at supper to ladies: "Is cod light? O, yes, fish is light; anything that swims is light." Mrs. ____ was so agreeable you formed romantic schemes. xxxx.[3] Lainshaw was really comfortable and orderly. You had no dreary ideas of death. All is soon easy and well again by a succession of good people.

MONDAY 4 MAY. Early this morning some rioters about meal at Stewarton were with you, being indicted against the circuit.[4] I counselled them as well as I could, and promised to let them know soon what to do. The ladies promised to come to Auchinleck. I set out, dined at Kilmarnock with Mr. Wilson; saw manufactory of carpets and the tannery. All well. Felt most agreeable change of the frame of my mind as I sat by my cousins of Sornbeg,[5] with whom I had formerly been most weak and dreary.

TUESDAY 5 MAY. Very early set off with James Bruce to see my lands of Dalblair. Took up Dr. Johnston at Cumnock. Rode on to Hallglenmuir, [where we had] a good breakfast. Then Polosh arrived and we all proceeded. Good fresh day; difficult riding. Now and then like to sink. When we came to the foot of Wardlaw the physician, as we called him, stopped. We made it out to the top; took a dram of rum. Immense prospect: Ayr, Ailsa, Ben Lomond, Jura, Galloway hills, Cairnsmore, Clydesdale hills. Resolved to erect a pillar here, but must do it without lime, as there is none but at a good distance, though there is plenty of stone, a quarry on the very top of the hill. We then came to the house, a very poor one, but might be repaired. Got plenty of bread and milk. It is a noble moor farm; a great extent — above three miles from Wardlaw to the march behind Benhill, and two

---

December 1766, which perhaps accounts for his remark about "the course of nature."

[2] Captain Montgomerie-Cuninghame.   [3] So in the original.

[4] The rioters, discovering that meal was being shipped out of the country in a time of scarcity, seized some and forced its sale to the local inhabitants. The charges against the four defendants who appeared to face trial were found "not proven."

[5] The Campbells, generally called of Barquharrie. Bruce Campbell, mentioned in the entry for 1 June, was of this family.

miles broad. Few places fit for planting; it may be tried on the west point, Craigengour. We rode up to Benhill, a very pretty hill. Unluckily my Lord Dumfries has one half of it. But I can make a plantation of a triangular or oval shape. There is in Dalblair variety of moorground, a tup park well inclosed, some arable land near the house, and a few trees which the snow hurts much. On the Gass water there is a great appearance of lead, [and] large and extensive veins of spar. It may be a noble quarry in time. . . .

THURSDAY 7 MAY . . . . In the evening arrived Mrs. Montgomerie, Mrs. Cuninghame, &c., from Lainshaw.

[*London Chronicle*]

THURSDAY 7 MAY. A letter from the Hague, dated April 28, says, "Signor Romanzo, the Corsican courier, passed by here lately in his return from London. He appeared remarkably gay, but made a profound secret of his negotiations. His *maître d'hotel* was heard to say that the taking of Capraja had gained Corsica £100,000 extraordinary credit from the English merchants."

FRIDAY 8 MAY. At night [came] Sir Adam Fergusson and George and Professor Wallace. You was quite *inamorato* of *La Vedova*. All went well. After supper somebody talked of *flirtation* with a married woman — nothing but trifles and jests, &c. Said my father: "Ay, ay; they begin wi' needles and prins and end wi' *horned* nowt."[6] The best conceit I have heard. The day had passed well, yet you was uneasy to have company, even your own relations. Curious turn. Worthy Sir Adam wondered you was "still on Douglas side." The Fall of Terni surprised me, but not like this.[7]

SATURDAY 9 MAY. Walked about with Mrs. Cuninghame; recalled old stories. Spoke of the family hypochondria quite seriously; saw it was believed in the country. Both you and honest David have a

---

[6] A Scottish proverb meaning that those who begin by stealing needles and pins end by stealing nowt (cattle). Lord Auchinleck is also alluding, of course, to the horns of the cuckold.

[7] Boswell had visited the Cascade of Velino at Terni on his trip to Italy, and thought it "prodigious wild" (*Boswell on the Grand Tour: Italy, Corsica, and France*, 14 February 1765).

certain pride to think of it to a certain degree. But it would be very bad should it be universally known. There are also two ways of viewing it. Either thus: there is a distemper in that family, all crackbrained; or thus: that family is remarkable for genius and worth, though they have a cast of melancholy, often the attendant of distinguished minds. I am now perfectly well upon the whole. Let my actions bear evidence.

[EDITORIAL NOTE: On 11 May, Boswell set out with his father to join the southern Justiciary circuit at Dumfries. "Want of sleep had hurt" him, and for the first time in "many months" he had a sharp attack of hypochondria, seeing the vanity of all things: "judges, chaises, men, and horses." Recovering by the time they reached Dumfries on the 12th, he divided his time between the law court during the day and assemblies at night. He became fond of a Mrs. Laurie ("Not yet firm against fine eyes"), and on 17 May after a long walk with her and others reported himself "in love like a madman," but "knew it would not last."

[He and his father started for home the next day, riding through Auchinleck village on 19 May with the trumpeters, attached to Lord Auchinleck in his position as judge, sounding their call. The next day on a "good ride to Ayr" for the session of the court there, Boswell composed *The Douglas Cause*, a companion ballad to his earlier *Hamilton Cause*. While at Ayr he rode out to Adamtown, Kate Blair's estate ("fine lands, large orchards, good house, but in disorder"); he "was much joked on having been viewing the premises." Business went well: he got a "handsome fee of six guineas" for defending some rioters from Galloway. He wrote for 24 May: "Felt now that former ideas of recommending myself to the county with anxious care were gone, and that I just did my duty and showed my talents free and unconcerned." Yet, he added later, his vivacity still appeared "feverish in this cold and composed country." He was home for breakfast on 27 May.]

THURSDAY 28 MAY. Mr. Claud[8] and I went to Adamtown, dined, passed the afternoon agreeably, [and] stayed all night.

[8] Claud Boswell of Balmuto, Lord Auchinleck's first cousin but a couple of years younger than Boswell. Later as a judge in the Court of Session he was styled Lord Balmuto.

FRIDAY 29 MAY. Mrs. Blair and Miss came with us to Auchinleck. We rode by the chaise. . . . After tea walked down to the old place, and from thence up the waterside to the Broomholm and so home.

SATURDAY 30 MAY. My father would not let them go. Wettish weather. We walked to the grotto and down the grotto walk, and then to the old place. Miss Blair and Mr. Claud and I walked to the top of the old castle, and then with Mr. Overseer Bruce we made the complete round of the avenues and came in by the Hern Gate.[9] Polquhairn, Mr. Thomas Wallace, &c. dined. Dr. Johnston called after dinner. We walked again to the natural bridge. I had a deep return of gloom. I wished the ladies away. I was quite discontented. At night recovered. Looked at medals.

SUNDAY 31 MAY. All at church. We had our dues. First [we drank] the twopenny, which was to be cleared off to make room for the strong ale to be decanted in the *stoup*. My father filled always the other *capful*[1] to Mr. Claud and me, and said he made slop-bowls of us. All went well. Honest Hallglenmuir was with us. Yet I looked some years before me, and saw that I would not feel then as I figure in prospect, no more than I feel now what I have figured in years past. At night walked at the old place, and down to the cave at the back of the garden.

MONDAY 1 JUNE. The ladies agreed to stay one day longer. But it was a wet day. My mind had been relaxed by elegant dissipation. I called myself to my post and wrote Corsica as well as ever. At night Bruce Campbell with us. [I was] too free and rampageneous. Time must cure all.

TUESDAY 2 JUNE. Went with the ladies to Coilsfield.[2] Fine day. [Played] at ninepins with Messrs. Claud, Bruce Campbell, and Sandy Montgomerie, and then all four in dining room with coats off played

[9] The "old castle" dated back to the days of the Auchinlecks of Auchinleck. James IV had granted their estate to Thomas Boswell in 1504. The "old place" had probably been built in the middle of the 16th century. It was superseded by Lord Auchinleck's handsome new mansion.

[1] A "cap" was a wooden cup or bowl; a "stoup," a deep, narrow vessel.

[2] The home of Alexander Montgomerie, next in line, after the Earl's brother, to the Earldom of Eglinton. The Sandy Montgomerie of the next sentence is probably his son Alexander.

at the handball, quite keen. Was pleased to relax a little into youthful frolic. Rather too impetuous here; better so than being too bashful. Home at night. Auchinleck seemed desolate without the ladies.

WEDNESDAY 3 JUNE. From this day till I left Auchinleck I omitted to mark daily the incidents of my life. In general I was at home, and much composed and happy. I went over one day and drank tea at Barquharrie; and one day when Gilmillscroft and Hallglenmuir dined at Auchinleck, I proposed to them to take a ride up and see the coalwork at Barglachan, which we accordingly did. As we returned by our village, I said, "Gilmillscroft, are you dry? Cooper Gib has good twopenny." The Laird relished the proposal. Up came the worthy physician (Doctor Johnston), and in we all went to Cooper Gib's (the provost), where we had twopenny with *cap* and *stoup* and drank like fishes, while the provost and the overseer (James Bruce), who was also of the party, drank punch at a by table. We drank "Agriculture," "Trade," "Mines and minerals," "Coal and lime," &c., and Miss Blair in all manner of ways: "Her speedy return to the loft of Auchinleck kirk," &c. We sung most nobly, and towards the end of the evening we got rum in gills and took a *papin*,[3] all the time eating bread and cheese, both raw and roasted. We then got in Halbert the schoolmaster and drank to the rising generation. Time galloped away. I loved to be a perfect Scots laird of the last age. We were vastly joyous. At ten Gilmillscroft went away.

[EDITORIAL NOTE: Boswell's Journal unfortunately lapses for the rest of 1767, one of the busiest and most amusing periods of his life. It can be replaced in part by his letters and other documents, particularly by his correspondence with Temple, which concentrates on their love affairs.

[The Douglas cause was much in the foreground at this time. *Dorando* was published anonymously on 15 June and became at once a *succès de scandale*, going into a third edition. And Boswell found another way of exciting interest in Douglas. On 19 May, a letter printed in *The London Chronicle* announced that "no less than five eminent writers of shorthand are preparing to set out for Edinburgh, in order to take the reports for the Scots judges on the Douglas cause."

[3] A combination of small beer and whisky.

These five shorthand writers, ranking with Signor Romanzo as one of Boswell's most elaborate and entertaining inventions, were to have a short but distinguished career. On 16 June they were reported to have passed through Berwick the previous day. On the 19th *The Edinburgh Advertiser* built them up in extended character sketches. Mr. Tracy, for example, had dissipated a fine fortune "by extravagant living with the late Duke of Hamilton and many of the first nobility." Of another, Mr. Burridge, it was reported that he "wears a brown coat and a cut wig, and looks as grave as a parish clerk; yet over his bottle he has the most droll and ludicrous sallies." He had been a government spy in the Rebellion of 1745. "It will be in vain to think of excluding the shorthand men from your court," the *Advertiser* announced. "They will appear like men of the highest rank and quality. Nay, they have often been known to dress themselves in women's clothes." By 26 June, they had actually been in court, and naturally were sympathetic to the Douglas side.

[At this point the joke ends. The publishing of extracts from *Dorando* and the continued reports of the progress of the shorthand men so infuriated Robert Dundas, the Lord President, that he hauled the publishers before the bench for publishing opinion upon a case *sub judice*. Boswell himself was engaged as counsel for *The Edinburgh Advertiser*, and wrote a brief filled with demure sarcasms against the Lord President and his Court. But however much *Dorando* might sway the multitude to the side of Douglas (and it was unquestionably very influential in that direction), it failed to impress the Lord President, who on 14 July, when seven of the judges had voted for Douglas and seven against, cast his deciding vote for the Hamilton party. The case was appealed at once to the House of Lords.

[In the mean time, Boswell was still advancing in Corsica, which he kept before the public eye through the career of Signor Romanzo and other newspaper items.]

[*London Chronicle*]

SATURDAY 6 JUNE. Extract of a letter from Marseilles, dated May 1. "Signor Romanzo, the Corsican courier, has been among us these ten days past. The Duke de ——, having said something very

Archibald Douglas, 1st Baron Douglas of Douglas (1748–1827), from an engraving in the Scottish National Portrait Gallery, after a portrait by George Willison. (Boswell was present in Willison's studio when this painting was begun. See the entry in his Journal for 22 July 1769)

impertinent against the British nation, and particularly against a great personage, the generous Corsican told him that the British were a nation of men, and their King the best prince in Europe. He said this with such an emphasis and so indignant a look that the Duke thought proper to call him out, and they fought behind the ramparts. The Duke was severely wounded, but Signor Romanzo escaped unhurt. This affair has done him great honour with everybody. *C'est un beau coup cela pour prendre congé*,[4] said a colonel of the *Gendarmes*. M. Romanzo is preparing to embark on his return to Corsica."

THURSDAY 11 JUNE. Toulon, May 9. It is said that when Signor Romanzo had an audience of General Paoli to render an account to the illustrious Chief of his different negotiations, his Excellency insisted that the conversation should be in English.

[Boswell to Temple]

Edinburgh, 12 June 1767

MY DEAR TEMPLE, — I have this moment received your letter of yesterday. All your letters have come safe. I may at times be a man of flight, but I am equalled if not exceeded by my friend. Now at Mamhead all passion for a pretty maid, yet profound, daring, and philosophical; then to London and desiring me not to write till I should hear from you; and now to my astonishment at Berwick upon Tweed.[5] Never surely were two men of minds more similar.

I am not surprised with what you tell me of your present views. Perhaps the plan you are now thinking of may be the surest for your happiness. The lady undoubtedly has merit: she has a genteel fortune, and her constancy shows that she has a real regard for you. But of this we shall talk at great length.

The lady in my neighbourhood is the finest woman I have ever seen. I went and visited her, and she was so good as to prevail with her mother to come to Auchinleck where they stayed four days, and in

[4] That's a good way of taking leave.
[5] Temple wrote from Berwick on 11 June that (1), the "innocent" servant-maid he had wished to make love to had had a child before coming to Mamhead; (2), that he now intended, though with reluctance, to marry Ann Stow, unless Boswell could raise serious objections; (3), that he wished to visit Boswell in Edinburgh.

our romantic groves I adored her like a divinity. I have already given you her character. My father is very desirous I should marry her. All my relations, all my neighbours approve of it. She looked quite at home in the house of Auchinleck. Her picture would be an ornament to the gallery. Her children would be all Boswells and Temples, and as fine women as these are excellent men. And now, my friend, my best adviser comes to hear me talk of her and to fix my wavering mind.

I must tell you my Italian angel is constant.[6]I had a letter from her but a few days ago, which made me cry. And what shall I tell you? My late Circe, Mrs. ———, is with child. What a fellow am I! Come to me, my Temple, and on that Arthur Seat where our youthful fancies roved abroad into extravagant, imaginary futurity shall we now consult together on plans of real life and solid happiness. We can now hear from each other every two days. How glad I am at this unexpected meeting! What a variety have we to talk of! I was at any rate to have insisted on your coming down to see my princess. Perhaps it would be well for me to be as much engaged as you are. It would fix my mind at once in women as the law has done in employments.

[Received ?18 June, Temple to Boswell]

[Berwick] Wednesday [17 June 1767]
MY DEAR BOSWELL, — Your last letter gives me both pleasure and pain. I am happy to think of the connection you have in view, but distressed at what you tell me of the consequence of your late unfortunate passion. It must not be known on any account: it would give all your friends much uneasiness and might disgust the young lady. Your own prudence will point out the best methods to keep it from the light; your humanity will protect and take all due care of it.

I am impatient to come to you. Pray name a week when you can give yourself entirely to me. Business must not interrupt us: no longwinded briefs, no importunate, noisy clients; friendship and philosophy ill agree with interest and clamour. . . .

You are too young a man to be retained in the Douglas cause, yet

[6] Girolama Piccolomini's letters to Boswell during the period covered by this volume are published in *Boswell on the Grand Tour: Italy, Corsica, and France,* Appendix A.

as I hate a crowd, and you will probably wish to hear the trial, I should not choose to come while it is in agitation. I intend, and indeed must return to Devonshire the middle of next month; name therefore your time, and let Thomas take a comfortable lodging for me for a week; yet not till I hear from you again. Yours, my dear friend,

W.J.T.

I am amazed at the constancy of your Italian friend. How must she write to force tears from you? But you are easily melted.

[Boswell to Temple]

Edinburgh, 22 June 1767

MY DEAREST FRIEND, — Your impatience is not greater than mine. Every hour since I heard you was at Berwick I have been for taking wing to meet you. I only regret that this is session time (term time) with me, which of necessity enslaves me more or less. This Douglas cause is still put off by some new delay. The Lords are to examine tomorrow Isabel Walker, who was one of Lady Jane Douglas's maids, and is the only person now alive who has been accused as an accomplice in the alleged crime of *partus suppositio*.[7] Her examination will be solemn and important. Though I am not a counsel in that cause, yet I am much interested in it. I doubt if it will be determined this week. But I am persuaded it will not be put off longer than next week.

The week after next my father is judge in the Outer House, and I shall have such a load of business that we could be together very little. I would therefore have you to come and stay next week when I hope to be in a great measure disengaged, and any hours that business absolutely demands shall be compensated by reading journals and letters which you will delight to peruse.

You will also have my Account of Corsica. How happy am I that my Temple comes to give it his friendly revisal. My Lord Hailes has given me seven folio pages of remarks upon it. He says, "I am much entertained and instructed." Is not this noble? You may have very good lodgings in the same stair[8] with us. When I get your answer fixing a particular day, I shall secure them for you. We shall live en-

[7] Supposititious birth. See Introduction, p. xiii.
[8] Lord Auchinleck's house was one of the floors of Blair's Land, Parliament Close, a multiple tenement served by a common stair.

tirely in the luxury of philosophy and friendship. We shall have the society of Dr. Blair, Dr. Gregory, Dr. Ferguson, and our other *literati*. But we shall keep the best portion of our time sacred to our intimate affection.

My dearest friend! is it not a distinguished felicity to participate of the highest friendship as much as the greatest and best of other ages have done? This is literally the case with you and me. We are divine madmen to the dull and interested many. Will you come on Saturday or on Monday? Why, O why, is it session time! Temple, you must be at Auchinleck. You must see my charming bride. If you cannot return in autumn, pray resolve to take a ride now, and on pretence of viewing the seat of your friend view also the woman who has his heart. Come, you have the fire of a Spaniard. I know you have. Oh, think of this.

I am ever, my dear, dear Temple, most sincerely yours,

JAMES BOSWELL.

My Circean charmer will probably be here by the time you come. You must see her. I have a great deal to tell you. My Signora is indeed a wonderful creature. You shall know all. But again let me entreat of you to take one romantic ride to oblige essentially your most cordial friend. God bless you.

Sir Alexander Dick, a *Corycius senex,*[9] quite a classical man and much of an Italian in pleasantness of disposition, has a fine seat just a mile from town. He is very desirous to see Mr. Temple. We shall be quite at home there. Well, I never was happier. Adieu till we meet.

[Received ?25 June, Temple to Boswell]

[Berwick] 24 June [1767]

THANK YOU, MY DEAREST BOSWELL, for your affectionate letter. Your friendship, I think, is the only happiness I enjoy in life. Indeed my relations are my greatest enemies: my father cruel, an ungrateful brother. I beg your pardon but cannot help complaining, for I feel to my very soul.

But, till I return, let me banish from my memory every disagreeable reflection. I am going to see my Boswell, my friend, my dearest

[9] "Old man of Corycus" (altered from Virgil, *Georgics,* iv. 127). Virgil describes him as a hospitable old farmer making the most of his unproductive land.

friend. O Boswell, believe me, I love you as I do myself, and when I die shall thank God above all things in life for your friendship. Indeed our intimacy little requires these declarations, but to have the virtue to make them with sincerity is a pleasure which I shall ever glory in. Let the boast of others be eloquence and wit and learning, let them too be our ornament, but let the basis of our fame be laid in virtue, humanity, and friendship.

God bless us! you talk as if you had more business than Norton or Mr. Yorke.[1] In time you may be worthy of as much, but *do not, do not* think such methods necessary to raise my esteem of you; 'tis an injury to yourself as well as to your friend.

I am greatly disappointed to find the young lady is not at Edinburgh. I fully expected to have had the pleasure of paying my respects to her there. I am the more grieved, as I fear it will hardly be possible for me to go to Auchinleck.

Let me now congratulate you on my Lord Hailes' approbation. I dare say he is a good judge, and I now begin to flatter myself that your Account of Corsica is a book *that will stand.*[2] I trust it will and hope it will make but a small segment of the *glorious circle* that is yet to surround my Boswell. I shall be abashed in the presence of your Gregories and Fergusons, but shall recover myself when I recollect I have seen a Gray. Yours ever,

W.J.T.

Expect me Monday evening.

[Boswell to Temple]

Edinburgh, Friday 26 June 1767

MY DEAREST FRIEND, — The first thing I must do is to defend myself against a charge of affected importance. Yes, indeed I do say neither Mr. Yorke nor Mr. Norton can be busier than I shall be the week that my father sits as judge in our Outer House. For you must know that the absurdity of mankind makes nineteen out of twenty employ the son of the judge before whom their cause is heard.[3] And

---

[1] Two former Attorneys-General of England.

[2] Hume's opinion as reported by Boswell. See p. 35.

[3] From 29 June to 4 July, Boswell was concerned in fourteen cases.

you must take it along with you that I am as yet but a very raw counsellor, so that a moderate share of business is really a load to me. So,
my dear Temple, you are wrong. Never suspect that I can pretend
to be a bit better to you than I am. You know me too well, and I am
perfectly satisfied with the genuine esteem which you have for me. I
may perhaps now and then assume some airs. For it is strange that it
should be so, but undoubtedly we are very well pleased that those
who cannot admire us for what we truly possess should admire us for
what we do not.

Thus far my defence, and now, my ever dear friend, let me enjoy
the agreeable prospect of our meeting. I have secured lodgings for
you. When you arrive you are to choose whether you will have one
room with a large alcove bedplace or two rooms. As you are to stay
immediately above us, Thomas will be always ready to attend upon
you, as I suppose you will not bring a servant with you.

I would not cloud the present frame of my mind with any gloomy
reflection that concerns either you or myself. It is better to communicate them when we meet, when our mutual sympathy and
friendly warmth may temper and relieve them. In the mean time,
I must tell you that on Tuesday last, drinking Miss Blair's health (for
that is the name of my angelic princess), I got myself quite intoxicated, went to a bawdy-house, and passed a whole night in the arms
of a whore. She indeed was a fine, strong, spirited girl, a whore worthy
of Boswell if Boswell must have a whore, and I apprehend no bad consequences. But I am abashed, and determined to keep the strictest
watch over my passions.

You *must* resolve to visit my goddess. You are a stranger, and may
do a romantic thing. You shall have consultation guineas as an
ambassador has his appointments. You see how I use you. In short,
between us two all rules and all maxims are suspended. Pray prepare
yourself for this adventure. We shall settle it, I hope. I cannot go with
you though. You are to see our county for a jaunt upon my recommendation, &c. Adieu, my dearest friend. Ever yours,

                                                    JAMES BOSWELL.

This is Friday. If you write me a line tomorrow, I shall have it on
Monday by dinner-time.

[Received ?29 June, Temple to Boswell]

[Berwick] Saturday 27 June [1767]

I confess myself much in the wrong, my dear Boswell, and beg your pardon. May you soon have *always* as much business as Mr. Yorke or Norton, and may I ever be thus mistaken when I apprehend anything to your disadvantage!

If any ill effects are the consequence of your last week's extravagant sally, you will be in a fine situation indeed! Your libation to Bacchus is excusable enough, but you might have omitted the sacrifice to Venus.

So Miss Blair is this angel's, goddess's name. Pray is she like anything human? Would Miss Bosville give one any idea of her, or could any of Lady Harrington's daughters serve by way of contrast?⁴ Indeed, Boswell, it gives me a good deal of concern that she should be in the country at this time.

You are good to get me a lodging so near you. I should imagine the alcove room will do well enough, for I am now learning to be an economist. I shall set out tomorrow evening after divine service and sleep at Old Cambus, so that I shall have an easy journey next day to Edinburgh. I bring a servant and horses, but shall send them back the morning after my arrival. Economy again, you see!

I dare say I shall like Sir Alexander Dick. I have heard of him, formerly a physician, and Mr. Spence sometimes spends a summer with him.⁵

There is a Cambridge acquaintance of mine too at Edinburgh at present, a Mr. Wyvill, a clergyman of a good living in Essex, a man of letters and merit, and more orthodox than your friend.⁶ He is upon a visit to his father, who has an employment in the customs. You must let me introduce him to you.

Would you believe it, but I really tremble to think of hearing you at the bar. 'Tis childish, for I have been told by several people that

---

⁴ Lady Harrington and at least one of her daughters were notable beauties.

⁵ Joseph Spence, literary and art critic, is best remembered for his collection of anecdotes about Pope and his friends. He had been Professor of Poetry at Oxford.

⁶ Christopher Wyvill became a noted parliamentary reformer and advocate of religious toleration.

you are beginning to make a figure. Persevere in the glorious career, my dear Boswell, and be the joy and boast of your worthy father's old age, and ever the dearest friend of your affectionate

TEMPLE.

Adieu till Monday evening.

[EDITORIAL NOTE: No records remain of Temple's visit except the following sheet of instructions, which Boswell gave to him for his tour to Auchinleck and Adamtown. Temple intended to arrive on Monday 29 June, as his letter printed immediately above indicates; he probably began his journey to the west of Scotland on the following Monday, 6 July, since he wished to be out of town during the period (7–14 July) when the judges were delivering their opinions on the Douglas cause.]

INSTRUCTIONS FOR MR. TEMPLE ON HIS
TOUR TO AUCHINLECK AND ADAMTOWN[7]

He will set out in the fly on Monday morning, and reach Glasgow by noon. Put up at Graham's,[8] and ask for the horses bespoke by Mr. Boswell. Take tickets for the Friday's fly. Eat some cold victuals. Set out for Kingswells, to which you have good road; arrived there, get a guide to put you through the moor to Loudoun; from thence Thomas knows the road to Auchinleck, where the worthy overseer, Mr. James Bruce, will receive you. Be easy with him, and you will like him much; expect but moderate entertainment as the family is not at home.

Tuesday. See the house, look at the front, choose your room, advise as to pavilions. Have James Bruce to conduct you to the cab house,[9] to the old castle, to where I am to make the superb grotto, up the river to Broomholm, the natural bridge, the grotto, the grotto walk down to the Gothic bridge; anything else he pleases.

Wednesday. — Breakfast at eight, set out at nine; Thomas will

---

[7] Published in *Letters of James Boswell Addressed to the Rev. W. J. Temple* [ed. Sir Philip Francis] 1857, pp. 97–99. These instructions were apparently written out on a separate sheet of paper, which is now lost.

[8] The Saracen's Head Inn, Glasgow.

[9] Probably Boswell wrote "old house."

bring you to Adamtown a little after eleven. Send up your name; if possible, put up your horses there, they can have cut grass; if not, Thomas will take them to Mountain, a place a mile off, and come back and wait at dinner. Give Miss Blair my letter.[1] Salute her and her mother; ask to walk. See the place fully; think what improvement should be made. Talk of my mare, the purse, the chocolate.[2] Tell you are my very old and intimate friend. Praise me for my good qualities — you know them; but talk also how odd, how inconstant, how impetuous, how much accustomed to women of intrigue. Ask gravely, "Pray, don't you imagine there is something of madness in that family?" Talk of my various travels — German princes — Voltaire and Rousseau. Talk of my father; my strong desire to have my own house. Observe her well. See how amiable. Judge if she would be happy with your friend. Think of me as the great man at Adamtown — quite classical too! Study the mother. Remember well what passes. Stay tea. At six, order horses and go to Newmilns, two miles from Loudoun; but if they press you to stay all night, do it. Be a man of as much ease as possible. Consider what a romantic expedition you are on; take notes; perhaps you now fix me for life.

Thursday. — Return to Glasgow from Newmilns or from Adamtown. See High Church, New Church, College, and particularly the paintings, and put half a crown into the box at the door. My friend, Mr. Robert Foulis, will show you all.

Friday. Come back in the fly. Bring your portmanteau here. We shall settle where you are to lodge.

N.B. You are to keep an exact account of your charges.

[Received *c.* 28 July, Temple to Boswell]

[Berwick, *c.* 27 July 1767]

My DEAR BOSWELL, — Forgive me for not writing to you immediately on my return hither, but really when I am at Berwick I am never myself, oppressed with low spirits, dissatisfied with myself and with everything around me.

---

[1] Not recovered.

[2] Miss Blair sent him chocolate as Boswell wrote to Sir Alexander Dick (21 August 1767), but nothing is known of the purse or the mare.

I had a very accurate letter from Dr. Gregory; I have begun my regimen and shall be punctual in observing it. Pray have you heard from Miss Blair? If she does not write favourably of me, mention not a word of what she writes. Her dear idea shall ever accompany me, and if you lose her you may be assured you will regret it as long as you live. Next week will probably unite me to one not so handsome, indeed, but I would fain hope almost as good. Make my best respects to your excellent father, and remember me to David, honest Johnston, and tell Wyvill I am ashamed of not taking my leave of him but shall write to him soon. I can say nothing more but that I am ever yours most sincerely,

W.J.T.

P.S. I hope poor Thomas is better. When the third edition of *Dorando* comes out, I must beg two copies.[3]

[Boswell to Temple]

Edinburgh, 29 July 1767

MY DEAR TEMPLE, — I have more reason to make an apology than you had, for I have been longer negligent. Let us guard against this vice and not subject ourselves to continual returns of remorse to a certain degree. For every instance of our doing those things which we ought not to have done and leaving undone those things which we ought to have done is attended with more or less of what is truly remorse. I am an unhappy man. The consequences of my debauch are now fatal, for I have got a disease from which I suffer severely. It has been long of appearing and is a heavy one. I shall stay a month here after the Session rises, and be cured. I am patient under it, as a just retribution for my licentiousness. But I greatly fear that Mrs. ———— is infected, for I have been with her several times since my debauch, and once within less than a week of the full appearance of mischief. In her present situation the consequences will be dreadful; for, besides the pain that she must endure, an innocent being cannot fail to be injured. Will you forgive me, Temple, for exclaiming that all this evil is too much for the offence of my getting drunk because I

[3] Curiously enough, the third edition of *Dorando* had been advertised as early as 29 June in *The Caledonian Mercury*.

would drink Miss Blair's health every round in a large bumper? But general laws often seem hard in particular cases. I am not, however, certain that Mrs. ——— will be ill. I would fain hope that she may have escaped. I have told her the risk she runs. Her good temper is astonishing. She does not upbraid me in the least degree.

I have not heard from Adamtown since you left me. I wrote to Miss Blair above a week ago, and thanked her for the polite reception she gave my friend. I told her how much you was charmed with her, and that I should not probably get a letter from you without some fine thing said of her. I made your compliments to her and Mrs. Blair. What can be the matter? Probably the letter you carried has been thought so strange, and so distant from any *rational scheme* that it has been resolved no longer to carry on so friendly and easy an intercourse with me. Or what would you say if the formal Nabob whom you saw there had struck in, and so good a bird in the hand has made the heiress quit the uncertain prospect of catching the bird on the bush?[4] I am curious to see how this matter will turn out. The mare, the purse, the chocolate, where are they now? I am certainly not deeply in love, for I am entertained with this dilemma like another chapter in my adventures, though I do own to you that I have a more serious attachment to her than I ever had to anybody. For "here every flower is united."[5] Perhaps the dilemma will be agreeably solved. So let me not allow my mind to waver. At any rate you have a tolerable hold upon me.

Smith is here just now. His Jurisprudence will be out in a year and a half. Hoping to hear of a very happy event being at length certain, I am ever most affectionately yours,

JAMES BOSWELL.

[Received ?8 August, Temple to Boswell]

[Berwick] 7 August 1767

DEAREST BOSWELL, — I just sit down to acquaint you that I was married yesterday. Do I repent? God knows; I'll tell you a twelve-

---

[4] The Nabob (that is, the man returned from India with a fortune) was apparently William Fullarton of Rosemount.

[5] From Macheath's song in act I of Gay's *Beggar's Opera*.

month hence. I own I can't yet perceive that it makes any difference. I awoke in the morning not at all surprised at myself. I got up, read, and eat and drank as usual. Indeed, I am apt to believe that almost all changes are much more in the idea than in the reality. The mind is a very complaisant and pliant gentleman, and easily suits himself to every situation. Thanks to your excellent father; I have in great measure adopted his idea.

But how can I talk so indifferently when you are so justly distressed. I feel with you most sincerely, both on your own account and that of the dear innocent exposed to such danger. Forgive me if I suspect Mrs. ——— herself, but I must suspect her; and dearest Boswell, *guard*, *guard* against her artful openness and vulgarity. But you see the consequence of such connections, and how dare I call the punishment unjust? It is according to the order of nature and Providence, and you will ever find, my orthodox friend, that *faith* without *works* is nothing, that virtue is happiness and vice misery; henceforth, never have the audacity to refuse drinking David Hume in my company, and learn to reverence his name till you can imitate his example. I know I write confusedly and incorrectly, but consider my situation. My respects to your father, compliments to David, Wyvill, and worthy Johnston. Most sincerely yours,

T.

From my wife's bedchamber, this 7th of August, 1767. In my next I shall not forget Miss Blair. Perhaps your jealousy of the Nabob is not groundless.

[Boswell to Temple]

Edinburgh, 11 August 1767

MY DEAR TEMPLE, — I sincerely congratulate you on your marriage, which from your manner of writing I take to be a very good, comfortable situation. You have removed half my apprehensions, and I suppose I shall likewise by and by experience the agreeable union. But what can you say in defence of this heiress? Not a word from her since you were there. You carried her one letter from me, and I wrote her another a week after, neither of which have been answered. You must know that my present unhappy distemper joined with a cold brought on a most terrible fever, and I was for several days in a very alarming situation. I am not yet got up, though I am in a fair way of recovery from every evil. Well, but to return. I wrote Miss Blair on Wednesday the 5th that I was afraid Mr. Temple had told her my faults too honestly, so that she found she was mistaken in having too good an opinion of me. That, however, she had *punished me* (only think of that, Temple!) too much. That I felt it the more, because I had been for some days confined to my bed by a feverish disorder, and had been dreaming a great deal of her.

Now, my dear friend, suppose what you please: suppose her affections changed as those of women too often are, suppose her offended at my Spanish stateliness, suppose her to have resolved to be more reserved and coy in order to make me more in love, nay suppose her betrothed to that man of copper, the formal Nabob — still politeness obliged her to give me some answer or other. Yet it is now four posts since that answer might have come. Is it not strange after such frankness and affability? What shall I think? As I am quite in the dark, I will take no resolution against her till you advise me; for I still cannot help thinking she is the best woman to be my wife whom I have ever seen. Perhaps her mysterious conduct may be quite cleared up.

I am in great hopes that my black friend is safe. No symptoms have yet appeared. O Temple, what an escape. I had the other day a letter from my Signora at Siena written with all the warmth of Italian affection. I am a strange man, but ever your most sincere friend.

JAMES BOSWELL.

David, Johnston, and all here wish you joy. So does Sir Alexander Dick and Doctor Boswell. The honest Doctor thinks you a good quiet philosopher, a kind of Parson Adams.[6] Inimitable! Wyvill was so good as to call when I was very ill. I shall send to him and have him to chat a while. I am to be a week or two here, quiet and studious. Mr. Dilly, bookseller in the Poultry, has purchased my Account of Corsica. I receive *one hundred guineas* three months after publication.[7] I shall be close employed all this autumn in revising it and correcting the proof sheets. Let me hear from you soon.

[6] The comic parson of Fielding's *Joseph Andrews.*
[7] Edward Dilly with his younger brother Charles ran a well-known publishing firm; Charles later published *The Life of Johnson.* It was at their house that Boswell managed to bring Johnson and Wilkes together for dinner.

[Boswell to Temple]

Edinburgh, 25 August 1767

MY DEAR TEMPLE, — Marriage is like to lose me a friend, for I have not had a line from you for near a fortnight, although my last letter was full of anxiety with regard to my amiable Miss Blair. What can have occasioned so long a silence? I conclude because you are not able to make an apology for the conduct of a lady for whom you are a kind of surety. I will therefore relieve you from this dilemma by informing you that she has made an apology herself. On Monday sennight I had the pleasure to receive a most agreeable letter from her, in which she told me that my letter to her had lain eight days at the post-house at Ayr, which was the occasion of her seeming neglect. You see, my friend, how appearances are often very deceitful. This never occurred either to you or me. I have refrained from communicating this to you from a curiosity to see how you would endeavour to excuse her conduct. But since I have waited so long in vain, I now make you as easy as myself. I would send you the letter, but it says so many fine things of you that I will not give you so much pleasure till I hear from you again.

Wyvill was so good as to come and sit a whole afternoon with me. He is an admirable critic on my Account of Corsica. He is gone on a jaunt to Glasgow, &c. with his father and sister. He sends you his best compliments. I hope to have him with me again in a day or two.

I ever am, my dear Temple, your most faithful friend,

JAMES BOSWELL.

[Received 26 August, Temple to Boswell]

Berwick, 25 August 1767

MY DEAR BOSWELL, — I thank you and all our friends for their good wishes. I make no doubt of being happy. My wife is a modest, sensible, good-natured girl, and always seems best pleased when we see least company. She studies my humour in everything, and will make an excellent country parson's wife.

I am glad I did not know of your illness. I trust you are now quite recovered, perhaps indeed once more happy at your princely retirement at Auchinleck. Pray endeavour to acquire a juster relish for natural beauties, let the fauns and naiads of your groves and streams view you oftener, and never neglect one evening to invoke the genius of the Broomholm.

There is no mystery in Miss Blair's conduct. The Nabob with bended knee has offered her his crown, and she is in doubt whether to accept of it, till by a little finesse the haughty Boswell is obliged to be explicit. Tell her immediately you love her, will marry her, or be content to lose her.

You are very lucky in selling Corsica so well. I hope it will bring you fame as well as money. I desired you to send me two copies of *Dorando* with the speeches;[8] pray don't neglect it. Thomas will easily find out the Berwick carrier.

I am quite sick of being here, but cannot yet get away. Nicholls is so kind as to go down to supply my living. There is even *now* such a thing as disinterested friendship.

Remember me in the kindest manner to Wyvill. I am sorry I have not spirits to write to him, but I shall be able to do nothing while I stay here.

Mrs. Temple sends her compliments to you. Pray write soon, and believe me, ever yours, my dear friend, most sincerely,

W.J.T.

[Boswell to Temple]

Edinburgh, 28 August 1767

MY DEAR FRIEND, — It seems you and I, like the magnetic needles of the two friends, have both turned towards each other at the same time. You would receive the day before yesterday a letter from me complaining of your long silence, and I by the same post received a very kind [one] from you.

Are you not happy to find that all is well between the prince of Auchinleck and his fair neighbouring princess? In short, Sir, I am one of the most fortunate men in the world. As Miss Blair is my great object at present, and you are a principal minister in forwarding the alliance, I enclose you the latest papers upon the subject. You will find the letter I wrote her when ill, where you will see a Scots word

[8] Presumably copies of the judges' speeches in the Douglas cause (see p. 87).

roving from the French *rever*, as if to dream awake.[9] I put it down as a good English word, not having looked[1] Johnson. You will next find the lady's answer; then a long letter from me which required an extraordinary degree of good sense and good temper to answer it with an agreeable propriety; then her answer, which exceeds my highest expectations.

Read these papers in their order, and let me have your Excellency's opinion.[2] Am I not now as well as I can be? What condescension, what a desire to please! She studies my disposition and resolves to be *cautious*, &c. Adorable woman! Don't you think I had better not write again till I see her? I shall go west in a fortnight. But I can hardly restrain myself from writing to her in transport. I will go to Adamtown and stay a week. I will have no disguise. We shall see each other fairly. We are both independent. We have no temptation to marry but to make each other happy. Let us be sure if that would be the consequence. Was it not very good in my worthy father to visit my mistress[3] in my absence? I have thanked him for it, and begged he may send his chaise for Mrs. Blair and her to come and stay some days with him.

I am recovering well, and my spirits are admirable. I shall send you two *Dorandos* by the carrier. He does not go till Thursday. Honest Johnston, who sits by me, sends you his most sincere congratulations. Pray make my best compliments to Mrs. Temple. I ever am, dear Temple, your most affectionate friend,

JAMES BOSWELL.

[Boswell to Temple]

Edinburgh, 29 August 1767

DEAR TEMPLE, — My letter of yesterday was so full of the Princess that I had not room for anything else. I cannot, however, delay expressing the great satisfaction I feel at your prospect of happiness in a married state. By what you say of Mrs. Temple I have no doubt of

---

[9] The *New English Dictionary* cites this dialectical word as rare, and gives but one example of its use, and that from the year 1789. Boswell's derivation of the word is incorrect.

[1] Scots for "looked in."

[2] These letters have not been recovered.

[3] Miss Blair, of course, not Mrs. Dodds.

your living agreeably, as I am persuaded you will make an excellent husband.

I like your way of representing marriage plainly and simply. For we have a strange custom of looking upon it as something quite mysterious, and have therefore twice as many apprehensions as we need have; for, I do say, we must have some apprehensions when engaging to have a fidelity and common interest for life. Not only will you be happy, but you will make your friend so too, by showing him the way to calm and permanent felicity as far as this life will allow. The packet I sent you yesterday would furnish you with an excellent subject for *a homily*, as worthy Sir Alexander Dick said. My old and intimate friend, can I be better? Can you suppose any woman in Britain with whom more circumstances could unite to engage me? All my objections arise from my own faults. Tell me, can I honestly ask so fine a woman to risk her happiness with a man of my character?

I am so well that I hope to be abroad in a few days. My health must be restored in the first place. Then I have Mrs. ⸺ to take care of. You may say what you please, but she is a good girl. She [has] a contented, cheerful temper, and is perfectly generous. She has not had a single guinea from me since you was here, nor has she given me the least hint as if she wanted money. It is my duty to be kind to her while she bears *Edward, the Black Prince.* I am indeed fond of her. But some tender feelings must be forgotten. She comes and drinks tea with me once or twice a week. This connection keeps me reasonable in my attachment to the Princess. Next month will probably fix our alliance, which may be completed next year.

I am glad Nicholls is so good a man. Do you wish to have the speeches of our judges? They are very imperfect. You will soon have a better edition. With compliments to Mrs. Temple, I ever am yours, &c.,

JAMES BOSWELL.

[EDITORIAL NOTE: Apart from his pursuit of Miss Blair and his successful legal practice, Boswell's main interests during the remainder of 1767 were the great Douglas cause and Corsica. The theatre of Douglas activities having shifted from Scotland to England, Boswell now provided his new audience with two publications, one intended to instruct and the other to move it. On 24 November was published

The Essence of the Douglas Cause, which reduced the four thousand pages of memorials and proofs to a neat, clear, and of course one-sided pamphlet of eighty. Four days later appeared the *Letters of Lady Jane Douglas*, an attractive but rather unscrupulous selection from Lady Jane's private correspondence. While these works can hardly have affected the Lords' decision, the latter especially had a profound influence on public opinion.

[With his publisher arranged for and Robert Foulis engaged as printer, Boswell also had to work hard on Corsica. The Account had probably been completed by the middle of June, and this could be sent to the press at once. He received his first proof of it by the beginning of September. The Dedication is dated "Auchinleck, 29 October 1767," which was his twenty-seventh birthday. But in spite of Dilly's promptings, the Journal of a Tour was still being revised in line with his friends' comments until well into November. Not until 30 December was the whole printed off, and Boswell able to sit back to wait for its publication.]

[Received ?4 September, Temple to Boswell]

Berwick, 3 September 1767

MY DEAR BOSWELL, — I received the packet and your letter by the next post, and am happy to find that not Miss Blair but we are in fault. To be sure we might easily have supposed that such an accident had happened, but where we are much interested, common sense often deserts us. Upon the whole, however, as it has been cleared up so agreeably I am far from repenting of our mistake.

I shall say nothing of your letter to the Princess; it is in your usual manner, quite characteristic. She writes easily and naturally, like a woman of sense and prudence. We must not look for wit and humour indeed, but for simplicity and unaffected freedom. It is the only style in which a wife should write.

I am glad you are in so fair a way of recovery. I love your humanity to Mrs. ——, but afterwards you should really think of her no more.

As you say there is a correct edition expected, you need not trouble yourself to send the speeches.

Probably I shall continue here a fortnight longer. You certainly should write to Adamtown. Do not forget my most respectful compliments, and tell your charming mistress it is impossible she can do anything to hurt herself in my esteem. I sincerely beg her pardon for my unworthy suspicion; it was natural enough, she will own, but Miss Blair stands single above her sex. . . .

I lead a very idle life. I read, I may well say, nothing, and at present take much more care of my body than of my mind. I am perpetually on horseback or walking in the fields; my wife is all my company, and I desire to see nobody else here. She desires her best compliments to you. Return mine to Johnston. Yours ever, my dear Boswell, most sincerely,

W.J.T.

[Boswell to Temple]

Edinburgh, 9 September 1767

MY DEAR TEMPLE, — How kind are you to take such a concern in what interests me. *We* have been to blame, you say; and throughout the whole of your last letter you talk in the plural number, as if the affection between Miss Blair and me were of equal importance to you as to your friend. I do think her the finest woman I have seen, take her altogether; nor could I wish to be happier in a wife.

But in this strange world it is hardly possible to be happy. If uneasiness does not arise from ourselves, it will come to us from others. How unaccountable is it that my father and I should be so ill together! He is a man of sense and a man of worth. But from some unhappy turn in his disposition, he is much dissatisfied with a son whom you know.

I write to him with warmth, with an honest pride, wishing that he should "think of me as I am." But my letters shock him, and every expression in them is interpreted unfavourably. To give you an instance, I send you a letter I had from him a few days ago. How galling is it to the friend of Paoli to be treated so! I have answered him in my own style. I will be myself. I have said: "Why think so strangely of my expression of being *primus Mantuae?*[4] Suppose I were married to Miss Blair, would I not be *primus Mantuae* at Adamtown? And why

4 "First in Mantua" (adapted from Virgil's *Georgics*, iii. 12).

not? Would not you be pleased to see your son happy in independence, cultivating his little farm, and ornamenting his nuptial villa, and fitting himself to fill one day, as well as possible, the place of a much greater man?"

Temple, would not you like such a son? Would not you feel a glow of parental joy? I know you would. And yet my worthy father writes to me in the manner you see, with that Scots strength of sarcasm which is peculiar to North Briton.[5] But he is offended with that fire which you and I cherish as the essence of our souls, and how can I make him happy? Am I bound to do so, at the expense not of this or the other agreeable wish, but at the expense of myself? The time was when such a letter from my father as the one I enclose would have depressed me. But I am now firm, and as my revered friend Mr. Samuel Johnson used to say, I feel the privileges of an independent human being. However, it is hard that I cannot have the pious satisfaction of being well with my father. I send you an extract from a letter of yours which gave him a very bad opinion of Temple in the year 1759.[6] It will divert you to read it at this distance of time. Pray return it together with my father's letter by the carrier who brings you this and *Dorando*, of which I have sent only one copy, as I have few here. When you get to London, I shall desire Mr. Wilkie, my publisher, to let you have two or three of them. Let me know if packets come safe by your carrier. . . .

The press is opened, and my book is fairly set a-going.

O navis, referet in mare te novum.[7]

The proof-sheets amuse me finely at breakfast. I cannot help hoping for some applause. You will be kind enough to communicate to me all that you hear, and to conceal from me all censure. I would not, how-

[5] Boswell probably mean to write "Britain."
[6] Temple had written to Lord Auchinleck, proposing that he and Boswell should go together to Geneva to study. The letter contained the words, "Voltaire! Rousseau! immortal names!"
[7] "O ship! [the flood] will bear you into a strange sea" (altered from Horace, *Odes*, I. xiv. 1). Boswell seems to have in mind principally the concluding lines of the *Ode:* "O you, so lately a cause of worry and fatigue, but now an object of tenderness and concern, may you escape those seas which race among the shining Cyclades."

ever, dislike to hear impartial corrections. Perhaps Mr. Gray may say something to you of it.[8] The last part of my work, entitled The Journal of a Tour to Corsica, is in my opinion the most valuable. You have not had an opportunity to see it. So soon as I find a sure hand I will send you it, and you must do me the favour to peruse it with care and write your observations and corrections on a separate paper, referring to the pages as my Lord Hailes did. Pray enquire and let me know if you can get a sure hand by whom you can venture to send it to Mr. Wyvill, who is also to revise it for me. Did you see him as he passed? He promised to me that he would call upon you.

I rejoice to hear of the continuance of your contentment. Laugh as you please or reason as you please, I think your present way of life very comfortable. Reading little, riding, walking, eating, drinking, and sleeping well, and enjoying the society of a wife whom you love:

> Parson, these goods in thy possessing
> Are better than the Bishop's blessing.[9]

My dear friend, I weary you with a letter of an intolerable length. I cannot, however, conclude without saying one word of the Princess. I shall write to her tomorrow; and so soon as I am quite clear of all evil, shall go and throw myself at her feet. I offer my best compliments to Mrs. Temple, to whom I hope to pay my respects next spring at Mamhead. My old friend, at this moment our first acquaintance at Hunter's class comes full into my mind. What a crowd of ideas since! Adieu,

JAMES BOSWELL.

[Boswell to Temple]

Edinburgh, 22 September 1767

MY DEAR TEMPLE, — I am really uneasy at not having heard from you since I sent you a packet by the Berwick carrier. Thomas took the packet to him on Thursday sennight. It contained *Dorando*, a long letter from your old friend, with one from his father. Pray

---

[8] Gray wrote to Horace Walpole that it was "a dialogue between a green-goose and a hero" (25 February 1768).

[9] Pope's imitation of Swift, *The Happy Life of a Country Parson*, ll. 1–2 ("goods" for "things").

write to me, and if you have not received the packet make the carrier give an account what he has done with it, for I should be vexed to think it has fallen into the hands of strangers. If my uneasiness is only occasioned by your indolence I shall be glad, though I shall not spare you.

I have written to the Princess in a style more and more as you would wish. I expect to hear from her soon. I have received a most polite letter from Sir James Steuart, in answer to one which I wrote to him with regard to a passage in his *Political Economy* which is injurious to the Corsicans. I shall settle that matter in my book in terms very respectful to Sir James.[1]

I see in the newspapers a specimen of *A Tour to the East* by Lord Baltimore, just published. It seems to be written with the most careless ease but with vivacity, and now and then you meet with admirable little anecdotes. Lord Baltimore has had a very good opportunity to know something of Eastern manners. He is a man of singular independence and whim. He lived a long time at Constantinople, wore the dress of the country, kept his seraglio of the finest women, and in short enjoyed the existence of a Turk.[2] Do you, my dear Temple, enjoy the existence of a worthy clergyman of the Church of England. Make my best compliments to your one wife, and believe me ever your affectionate friend,

JAMES BOSWELL.

[*London Chronicle*][3]

THURSDAY 24 SEPTEMBER. Extract of a letter from Civitavecchia, dated August 14. "The celebrated Prince Heraclius of Georgia hath sent General Paoli a present of six beautiful camels, with a letter full of the glow and metaphor of oriental eloquence. He concludes,

[1] Temple had asked Boswell, in the omitted portion of his letter of 3 September, how Sir James Steuart's new book had been received.

[2] Lord Baltimore continued in his supposed oriental ways, barely escaping conviction on a charge of abduction and rape the following year. Evidently Boswell knew his work only from the newspaper specimen referred to, since the book itself does not bear out Boswell's statements with regard to Baltimore's residence in Constantinople.

[3] Indexed as an "invention" in Boswell's own file of *The London Chronicle*, now at Yale.

'Great Sir, while in thy zenith of glory, deign to accept the tribute of him who is proud of being born in the same age with Paoli, and feeling the most exalted admiration of his character without one spark of envy.' "

[Received 30 September, Temple to Boswell]

Jermyn Street [London] 26 September [1767]

YOU WILL BE SURPRISED, MY DEAR BOSWELL, to find me apply to you for money, but at present I have a particular occasion for £30, which if you can I imagine you will send me a bill upon London for in a few posts. We set out for Mamhead Friday, the 2d of October. Direct for me there. I shall write to you soon with regard to your father's letter, and return it under one of Lord Lisburne's covers. My wife desires her best compliments. Yours affectionately,

W.J.T.

[Boswell to Temple]

Edinburgh, 2 October 1767

MY DEAREST FRIEND, — Your letter from London relieved me from a great deal of anxiety, both on your account and on that of the letters, which would have made a bad appearance to strangers. How can you let indolence occasion me so much uneasiness? Your letter came late, night before last; it was not in my power to get £30 ready for last night's post. You have along with this a draught for that sum.

I have sent you a copy of my Corsican Journal, which you will do me the favour to peruse in the shades of Mamhead in the tranquillity of your rectory, and write down on a separate sheet of paper your remarks and corrections, as my Lord Hailes did. You need not take the trouble to mark both page and line, only page. So soon as you have finished six sheets, send me your remarks, and transmit the sheets to Wyvill with franks addressed to me along with them so that he may send them to me. Wyvill, I fancy, will be in Essex. I expect a letter from him every day with his address if he is not, which I shall send to you. His address in Essex is Rector of Black Notely, near Braintree, Essex. You will find many various readings in my Journal; tell which you prefer. Now, Temple, I trust you will be diligent and clever to aid your friend, and will let me see that had your fortune made you a minister of state you would have been an able and expeditious one. I allow you a day to three sheet[s]. Transmit to Wyvill six and six, and to me your remarks. Pray be my Atticus.[4] I am very near well. I go west on Wednesday. There is again a little silence in the Princess. Compliments to Mrs. Temple. Ever yours,

JAMES BOSWELL.

[Received ?2 October, Margaret Montgomerie to Boswell][5]

Lainshaw, Thursday [1 October 1767]

DEAR JAMIE, — I beg the favour of you to take the trouble to bring out a gown of mine with you. I shall write the mantua-maker to bring it to you, but, if she neglect to do it, she is a Miss Tait who lives in Milne's Square; so I'll be obliged to you if you'll send to her.

I am glad you propose being here so soon. I hope you intend being at the October meeting at Ayr,[6] as I dare say your favorite Miss Blair will be there; and as the Duke of Gordon has convinced you he is in earnest, I hope you will continue fixed in resolutions of following his example.[7] I was at Pollok this week and left Mrs. Montgomerie in perfect health.[8]

I fancy you have seen Lord Eglinton, as I met him on his way to Edinburgh. I beg my compliments to Davy. All here join in best wishes to you and him. Adieu, dear James, and believe me, your affectionate cousin and obliged

M. MONTGOMERIE.

Will expect you and David the beginning of the week.

[*London Chronicle*][9]

THURSDAY 8 OCTOBER. A correspondent writes that a threatening incendiary letter has been lately sent to the author of *Dorando*,

[4] Cicero's friend and correspondent.
[5] For Margaret Montgomerie and the textual history of her letters to Boswell, see Introduction, pp. xvii and xxii.
[6] At the races.
[7] The Duke of Gordon was about to marry Miss Blair's cousin and friend, Jeanie Maxwell.
[8] Jean Montgomerie was the daughter of Sir John Maxwell of Pollok.
[9] A Boswellian "invention."

A Spanish Tale, declaring with horrid imprecations that if he does not retract the speeches and arguments therein contained before the appeal of a certain alarming cause, he shall be stabbed in the dark; and that a very considerable reward has been offered for the discovery of the author of the said letter.

[Boswell to John Johnston]

Edinburgh, 9 October 1767

MY DEAR SIR, — You will wonder to find me still here. But this unhappy distemper has been very obstinate, and as I have done so well hitherto I have determined to finish my course of medicines in the most complete [manner]. I am now, I may say, perfectly recovered. Tomorrow I go to Sir Alexander Dick's where I shall stay till Monday; and on Tuesday morning David and I set out for Auchinleck in a post-chaise, with trusty Thomas riding by us. We are to stay a night at Bothwell Castle. I wrote to the Duchess of Douglas to let me have a warm, orthodox room, and she with great good humour sent me word that the warmest bed in the house was her own, to which I should be welcome. How far this would be orthodox, your Honour and Mr. Joseph Fergusson may judge.[1]

Having said so much of myself, let me now treat of you, my friend. A letter which I had this morning from Mr. William Hay has thrown me into great concern. He tells me you have *a new attack of the old complaint*. Does he mean that some latent poison has broken out? Or that you have again been infected?[2] Either of the two suppositions is distressing. Pray take care of yourself, and let me know by the very first post how you are.

We are unhappy mortals, no doubt. But in the present state of society, a great part of our unhappiness is occasioned by our own vices

[1] The Rev. Joseph Fergusson at one time had been tutor to the Boswell children. He was now minister of Tundergarth, Johnston's parish.

[2] Johnston had reported his "complaint" in a letter of the previous spring (24 April 1767): "My good friend, I may in confidence tell you that it is owing to my own folly in indulging an irregular passion with a wretch full of disease. At first, when I found myself affected, my mind was so totally unhinged that for some days I was quite miserable, until reflection and cool philosophy brought me back to reason more justly and to think of attending to my own recovery." We have no further information as to the "new attack."

and follies. You know I am an austere philosopher in principle, and even my practice has often been so. Could either you or I act in consistency with our principles, we should not be in danger of suffering from a malady the most dreadful which nature has ever produced, and which has been well said is the cause of poisoning the very sources of the human species. As far as man can be depended on, I trust that I shall henceforth maintain such a conduct as is the best for this life and for that which is to come. I have been busy with the Douglas cause, and have made out the Essence of it, which I hope will be of considerable service. The scheme which I communicated to you will make a great noise.[3] Wishing to hear comfortable accounts of you, I ever am, dear Sir, your affectionate friend,

JAMES BOSWELL.

[Oath of David Boswell][4]

I, David Boswell, youngest son of the Right Honourable Alexander Boswell, Lord of Session and Justiciary, present representative of the family of Auchinleck, do by these presents declare that, according to the usage of the family when any branch of it is sent forth into the world, I have stood upon the old castle of Auchinleck and have there solemnly promised to stand by these old walls with heart, purse and sword, that is to say, that in whatever part of the globe my fortune should place me, I should always be faithful to the ancient family of

[3] The scheme was perhaps Boswell's intention of "editing" the letters of Lady Jane Douglas.

[4] An oath which Boswell requested his brother to take on the occasion of his leaving to become a merchant in Spain. Geoffrey Scott remarked that the oath "illustrates, better than anything else we possess, the highly romantic attachment which [Boswell] felt, and assiduously cultivated, for his feudal ancestry. . . . It is in its inspiration an eminently juvenile document. The romantically staged scene on the crumbling walls, the seal of investiture, the chaplains drawn from their pulpits at Auchinleck and Tundergarth and 'appointed for the occasion,' and the entire family of Bruces — mostly juvenile gardeners — proclaiming with one voice, at a suitable moment selected by Boswell, their fealty to his ancient line, — all this appears more like the device of a boy of fifteen than a man of twenty-seven." On his return from Spain in 1780, David added a ratification, and explained that the custom of swearing such oaths did not go back to time immemorial but had begun with this instance.

Auchinleck, and give a reasonable obedience to the representative thereof. In consequence of which I was invested with a ring according to the usage of the family. All this was done upon the nineteenth day of October in the year of our Lord one thousand seven hundred and sixty-seven years, in presence of James Boswell, Esquire, my eldest brother and heir of the family; the Reverend Mr. John Dun, minister at Auchinleck, and the Reverend Mr. Joseph Fergusson, minister at Tundergarth, chaplains appointed for the occasion; I departing for Valencia in Spain, there to settle as a merchant. Also in presence of Mr. James Bruce, overseer at Auchinleck, and Alexander, John, Andrew, and James Bruces, his sons, all present having with one voice wished the continuance and prosperity of the ancient family of Auchinleck, and that the family of Bruce might ever flourish there. In testimony of which I now subscribe these presents, and seal them with the seal of my investiture, they being written by the said James Boswell, Esquire, and subscribed on the twenty-seventh day of the said month and in the said year of our Lord. Amen.

DAVID BOSWELL.

JAMES BOSWELL, Witness.
JOHN DUN, Witness.
JOSEPH FERGUSSON, Witness.   (*Seal*)
JAS. BRUCE, Witness.

[Received ?28 October, Temple to Boswell]

Mamhead, Monday, seven in the evening,
19 October 1767

MY DEAREST BOSWELL, — I received yours of the 9th instant[5] on Friday last, but the packets only came to my hands this moment, being sent by mistake to Lord Lisburne at Bath. His Lordship is just arrived here and brought them with him to my great joy, for I own I began to have my apprehensions. The bill came also safe.

You complain of your father's letter, but I think without reason. How could you tell him "that were he anybody but your father, you could live in friendship with him and with satisfaction"; and "that you never will concern yourself with country business till he is dead."

---

[5] Not recovered.

Surely strange declarations from a son to a father, and very unbecoming and undutiful from such a child to such a parent. But you will take your own way; I find all I can say is in vain; I shall therefore interfere no farther, but leave you to your own inventions. Allow me, however, to assure you of one thing, that if any open rupture happens between you, the son alone will be blamed and will repent it as long as he lives. Undoubtedly there is some severe humour in the letter, but is there no foundation for it? And notwithstanding its severity, is it not full of the tenderest affection and regard? Indeed, my dear Boswell, if you do not endeavour in everything to please such a father, I can never think so well of you as I have done.

I will read your Journal with all possible care, but do not confine me to days. When I have finished a packet, I will dispatch it and the observations as you direct. I would fain hope that this book will do you some credit and make it remembered a century hence, *that there was one James Boswell.* I fancy you expect at least to be named with a Stanyan and a Molesworth.[6]

How can you expect to hear from the Princess? Does not she hope every day to see you at Adamtown? But I forgot myself; you are now at Auchinleck, and have you been to wait on her; and does she look as well, and did she receive you with as much ease as formerly? I trust not. Were there no blushings, nor hesitation, nor eyes afraid to meet? And did not your heart beat, my friend, and were there no tremors and anxieties on your side? Alas! my Boswell, where these symptoms are wanting, respect and esteem may inhabit, but the god of love will be sought for in vain. If she still deems you worthy of that honour, pray make my best respects to her and to Mrs. Blair, and say with what pleasure I shall ever remember the polite and friendly reception they gave me at Adamtown. When I return, I trust I shall salute her mistress of, though not a more sweet, yet a more princely seat.

And now, Boswell, you are at the retirement of your ancestors; let me beg of you to please your father a little and show some curiosity about flowering shrubs, trees, and the manner of laying out ground with some sort of taste. Let honest James Bruce and you persuade my Lord to cut down the row of trees that spoils the meadow, and not to make the wings to the house little bandboxes, but in proportion to the

---

[6] Abraham Stanyan, a diplomat, wrote *An Account of Switzerland.* Robert Molesworth, first Viscount Molesworth, wrote *An Account of Denmark.*

body of the building; otherwise, tell his Lordship from me that the whole will look like a giant with the arms of a dwarf. Most affectionately yours,

W.J.T.

My wife is even happy in my hovel. She begs her kind compliments to you.

[Received ?31 October, David Boswell to Boswell]

Glasgow, 30 October 1767

DEAR JAMES, — This is wrote at a place which I shall ever hold in contempt as being filled with a set of unmannerly, low-bred, narrow-minded wretches; the place itself, however, is really pretty, and were the present inhabitants taken out and drowned in the ocean, and others with generous souls put in their stead, it would be an honour to Scotland. I arrived here yesterday about three o'clock. My jaunt since I left you has been really very agreeable. I dined with Mrs. Wilson at Kilmarnock, where I had much respect shown me, and I thought by my behaviour I merited it; worthy Mr. Joseph was quite the same man, had his own little jokes about matrimony and was very happy. He never knows what it is to make any alteration in his behaviour; I verily believe that if he was in the presence of General Paoli he would not be ten minutes there before he would be saying, "General, can you recommend us to a goud wife."

I arrived at Lainshaw before it grew dark; was exceedingly well received. I have not better friends in the world than the Lainshaw family; they are not such friends, however, as you would wish me to have, for the Captain and Mrs. Cuninghame said they thought my father should give me £5000 patrimony. We talked a good deal about you; I related to them particularly how my father used you, and they owned it was a difficult task for you to live with him. My father has great confidence in Mrs. Cuninghame, and lets her into all his secrets; she often speaks to him about the strange way he lives in, and of the bad way in which he treats his children. She is to speak boldly to him next time she sees him, and I hope it will produce some good effect, for I must say I should be sorry you was to live separate from him; for although he seems to take little satisfaction in his sons when they are with him, yet when they are absent he wishes constantly for

them and thinks their presence would enliven him. This, I well remember, was the case before you came from abroad, and yet how
soon after your arrival did he grow displeased with you.

I left Lainshaw yesterday morning. I really appeared during my
stay there a sensible, well-behaved young man. Mrs. Cuninghame
was brought to bed while I was there of a daughter. She was, however,
so well that I sat with her yesterday morning half an hour, and had
much conversation about our family. My father had mentioned your
illness to her, and exclaimed against it, and do you know that she ex-
cused you by telling him that what occasioned it was now become
quite common. . . .

I hope to hear from you soon. Make my best respects to my father,
and my compliments to the worthy overseer. I ever am, with regard,
your affectionate brother and friend,

DAVID BOSWELL.

[Boswell to Temple]

Adamtown, 5 November 1767

MY DEAR TEMPLE, — The pleasure of your countenance on reading the date of this letter is before me at this moment. I imagine it
cannot be less than I felt glowing in my eyes when I received the last
of your letters with the elegant and, I am fully persuaded, sincere
commendations of my Corsican Journal.[7] In short, I am sitting in the
room with my princess, who is at this moment a finer woman than
ever she appeared to me before. But, my valuable friend, be not too
certain of your Boswell's felicity, for indeed he has little of it at present. You must know that Miss Blair's silence, which I mentioned to
you, was a silence notwithstanding of my having written three letters
to her and (here supper interrupted me; the rest is written in my own
room, the same where you slept) and when a former quarrel should
have taught her that she had a lover of an anxious temper. For ten
days I was in a fever, but at last I broke the enchantment. However,
I would not be too sullen in my pride. I wrote to her from Auchinleck
and *wished her joy, &c.*[8] She answered me with the same ease as ever,
that I had no occasion. I then wrote her a strange sultanic letter, very

[7] Not recovered.

[8] Boswell thought that the Nabob was pressing his suit successfully.

cool and very formal, and did not go to see her for near three weeks.

At last I am here, and our meeting has been such as you paint in your last but one. I have been here one night. She has insisted on my staying another. I am dressed in green and gold. I have my chaise in which I sit alone like Mr. Gray, and Thomas rides by me in a claret-coloured suit with a silver laced hat. But the Princess and I have not yet made up our quarrel. She talks lightly of it. I am resolved to have a serious conversation with her tomorrow morning. If she can still remain indifferent as to what has given me much pain, she is not the woman I thought her; and from tomorrow morning shall I be severed from her as a lover. I shall just bring myself (I hope) to a good, easy tranquillity. If she feels as I wish her to do, I shall adore her while my blood is warm. You shall hear fully from Auchinleck.

We have talked a great deal of you. She has made me laugh heartily with her ideas of you before you arrived, an old friend, an English clergyman. She imagined she was to see a fat man with a large white wig, a man something like Mr. Whitefield.[9] Upon honour, she said so. But she and Mrs. Blair were quite charmed with the young parson with his neat black periwig, and his polite address. They send you a thousand compliments. With my best compliments to Mrs. Temple, I am ever yours,

James Boswell.

[Boswell to Temple]

Auchinleck, Sunday, 8 November 1767

My dear Friend, — I wrote you from Adamtown and told you how it was with the Princess and me. Next morning I told her that I had complained to you that she would not make up our last quarrel. But she did not appear in the least inclined to own herself in the wrong. I confess that between pride and love I was unable to speak to her but in a very awkward manner. I came home on Friday. Yesterday I was extremely uneasy. That I might give her a fair opportunity I sent her a letter, of which I enclose you a copy.[1] Could the proud Boswell say more than you will see there? In the evening I got her answer. It was written with an art and an indifference astonishing

[9] George Whitefield, the famous Methodist preacher.

[1] The enclosures mentioned in this letter have not been recovered.

from so young a lady. "I have not yet found out that I was to blame. — If you have been uneasy upon my account, I am indeed sorry for it. I should be sorry to give any person uneasiness, far more one whose cousin and friend I shall always be." She refused sending me the lock, "because (in the eyes of the world) it is improper," and she says several very cool things upon that head. What think you of such a return to a letter full of warmth and admiration?

In short, Temple, she is cunning and sees my weakness. But I now see her; and though I cannot but suffer severely, I from this moment resolve to think no more of her. I send you the copy of a note which goes to her tomorrow morning. Wish me joy, my good friend, of having discovered the snake before it was too late. I should have been ruined had I made such a woman my wife. Luckily for me a neighbour who came to Auchinleck last night told me that he had heard three people at Ayr agree in abusing her as a d——ned jilt. What a risk have I run! However, as there is still a possibility that all this may be mistake and malice, I shall behave to her in a very respectful manner and shall never say a word against her but to you. After this, I shall be upon my guard against ever indulging the least fondness for a *Scots lass*. I am a soul of a more southern frame. I may perhaps be fortunate enough to find an Englishwoman who will be sensible of my merit, and will study to please my singular humour. By what you write of Mrs. Temple I wish I had such a wife, though indeed your temper is so much better than mine that perhaps she and I would have quarrelled before this time, had we been married when you was.

Love is a perfect fever of the mind. I question if any man has been more tormented with it than myself. Even at this moment as I write, my heart is torn by vexing thoughts of this fine Princess of ours. But I may take comfort, since I have so often recovered. Think of the gardener's daughter. Think of Mrs. D——. By the by, the latter shared in my late misfortune, but she is quite well again; and in a fortnight hence I expect a young friend, who if a male is to be George Keith after my good Lord Marischal, who has accepted of being his name-father.[2]

---

[2] Lord Marischal wrote to Boswell on 12 September 1767: "Bonny wark, Colonel, getting the lassies wi' bairns, and worse to yoursel. . . . What's done is done; get well; take care of Keith Boswell, who in time I hope shall become a nabob."

You are too hard upon me in judging of the differences between father and son. I never wrote to him that I would take no pleasure in country affairs till he was dead. I said, indeed, that I should hardly give my mind to them till I had a place of my own; and, I added, "Auchinleck will be well taken care of while you live, and you may be assured that it shall not be neglected after you are gone." You see how a temper anyhow out of tune can interpret. Perhaps I do the same by the Princess. However, I promise you I shall be conscientious in doing a great deal to make my worthy father easy and happy. He and I are at present very well. It is merely a jarring of tempers which occasions our differences.

One word more of the Princess. The two last days I was with her, she was more engaging than you can conceive. She and I had the most agreeable conversations together, and she assured me she was not going to be married to any other man; and yet, Temple, with what a cold reserve does she behave. Let her go.

Do you know I had a letter from Zélide the other day, written in English, and showing that an old flame is easily rekindled. But you will not hear of her. What say you? Ah, my friend, shall I have Miss Bosville? You see I'm the old man. I am much obliged to you for your remarks on my Corsican Journal. Please return the letters enclosed. My compliments to Mrs. Temple. Ever yours,

JAMES BOSWELL.

[Boswell to Temple]

Strathaven, 9 November 1767[3]

MY EVER DEAR TEMPLE, — Having left Auchinleck this morning in a hurry, I brought my letters to you in my pocket so far on the road; and as your kind packet of the 30th October has overtaken me I have opened one of my letters and add a few lines. Upon my soul, the madness of which I have a strong degree in my composition is at present so heightened by love that I am absolutely deprived of judgment. How could I possibly be in a rage at the Princess's last letter? I now sit calmly in this village and read it with delight. What could she do more? Like you, she thought I could not expect to hear from her when

---

[3] See 20 March 1767. Boswell is on his way back to Edinburgh for the opening of the Winter Session of the courts (12 November to 12 March).

she expected me every day at Adamtown; therefore she was not to blame, and she had too much spirit to own herself in the wrong when she was conscious of no fault. Yet how amiably does she comply with my request and tell me that she is sorry that I have been uneasy on her account. "I shall always be a cousin and friend. — I hope you will not look upon this as a new quarrel."

I love her, Temple, with my whole heart. I am entirely in her power. Were she a woman of such a temper as I have, how might she fret against me: "He comes to Auchinleck and is near three weeks without coming to see me. When he comes, not a tender word, not one expression of a lover. How can I allow my affections to fix on such a man!"

She has defended herself very well in refusing me the lock. I shall get it from her at Edinburgh. O my friend, be watchful over me in this precious period. If she does not write to me she is certainly unfeeling, and I must at any price preserve my own character. If she writes as I can imagine, I will consecrate myself to her for ever. I must have her to learn the harpsichord and French. She shall be one of the first women in the island. But let me take care. I know not what is in store. Do you think it possible that she can have any scheme of marrying another? I will not suspect her.

Your remarks are of great service to me. I am glad you show my Journal to Lord Lisburne. But I must have my great preceptor Mr. Johnson introduced. Lord Hailes has approved of it.[4]

Temple, I wish to be at last an uniform, pretty man. I am astonishingly so already; but I wish to be a man who deserves Miss Blair. (By the by, your expression, "Be perpetually with Miss Blair," is fine. It made me more affectionate towards you than ever.) I am always for fixing some period for my perfection as far as possible. Let it be when my Account of Corsica is published. I shall then have a character which I must support. I will swear like an ancient disciple of Pythagoras to observe silence. I will be grave and reserved, though cheerful and communicative of what is *verum atque decens*.[5] One

[4] Boswell had somewhat gratuitously brought Johnson into his *Journal of a Tour to Corsica* by relating how he had discussed him with Paoli. See *Boswell on the Grand Tour: Italy, Corsica, and France,* 22–27 October 1765.

[5] "Right and seemly" (Horace, *Epistles,* I. i. 11).

great fault of mine is talking at random. I will guard against it. My feudal signors are printed off in the Account.[6] Adieu, my best friend. I thank God for the comfort of such a friend. Ever yours,

J.B.

[Received *c.* 2 December, Temple to Boswell]

Mamhead, 22 November 1767

My dear Boswell, — I received your two packets today, and am now convinced that you are really in love with Miss Blair. Your anxiety, your perpetual change of resolution, your desiring yet not being able to break your fetters, are too certain proofs of the dominion of the Princess over your heart. As to her Highness, did I not suspect her mother I should with you accuse her of artifice. But, indeed, considering your behaviour, I think she only treats you in the manner you deserve. The defence you make for her is a very good one, and severe enough upon yourself.[7] Yet, after all, I must confess I am not altogether pleased with your mistress's indifference. Did she really love you, could she act with such prudence and caution? O my dear friend! be upon your guard, consider what you are about, and penetrate and explore her very soul before you surrender yourself irretrievably to her charms. Know that she loves *yourself:* that she loves and esteems you for those qualities for which I love and esteem you, not for your fine house, your estate, and your hopes. Converse with her on every subject, draw forth and examine her principles, her ideas, her notions of retirement and dissipation, of friendship, of pleasure, of domestic happiness, of society, of her fellow creatures, and all this with such address that she may not be aware of your intention, but be surprised in a manner into a confession of her real sentiments. When you have done this you will have done all that man can do; yet such is the dissimulation of the sex that you may still be deceived, and instead of an angel, wake with a serpent in your arms. Yet there [are] many good women, and I trust you will not be less fortunate than myself.

I wish our future George Keith may not bring into the world with him the marks of his father's irregularities! I need not desire you to

[6] That is, Foulis had printed through Boswell's remarks on the feudal organization of Corsica, or about two-fifths of the book.

[7] Two and a half lines are deleted here, presumably by Temple.

take care of his mother, but, for God's sake, when she is quite recovered break off all connection with her and see her no more. Surely she was not with child when she first told you so: artful baggage! she trusted to her good fortune. I would immediately take the child from her and send it to honest James Bruce to be brought up in the country. . . .

I was much entertained with your letter from Adamtown. I thought I saw you writing, Mrs. Blair sitting by the fireside, and the Princess walking about the room, interrupting you every now and then. Your pen in your hand, with eyes that speak what no language can express you heard her with ecstasy and unwillingly resumed your letter. After supper, she wished you a good night with a sweetness and expression that sent you to bed in a fever. I followed you up the stone staircase, I saw the unpainted room, I heard you invoke the goddess of your adoration, I pitied the poor pillow you squeezed so unmercifully, and then I left you asleep. Adieu, adieu, dearest Boswell.

W. J. Temple.

My wife commends herself to you.

[Received ?8 December, Pringle to Boswell]

London, 4 December 1767

Dear Sir, — By this time you will probably have heard that I have been abroad once more, for my health, and that it is not long since I returned. This will partly apologize for my long silence, after having received so obliging a letter from you, and one too that made a demand upon me for speedy advice. . . .

I should have the more regretted and apologized for my unmannerly silence, had I been persuaded that I could have influenced your judgment with regard to most of those articles which were the subject of your letter. Not that I consider you as more wilful or tenacious to your own opinion than others are, in general; but because the determination was to be about such things as a man, after asking the opinion of twenty friends, will either do or omit doing just as if he had no friends at all. I will therefore not pretend to give you my advice, but I will amuse you with my opinion. In the first place (as I am assured by Mr. Forbes that you have got entirely free from your disorder), I should think Miss Blair would be a very proper match if she has all those good qualities which you mention, and which I am the more inclined to believe she has, as you seem not to be blinded by love when you recite her good qualities, and especially as you are likely to have your father's approbation. How far you yourself are qualified for entering into the holy bonds and fitted for Miss Blair is another question, notwithstanding that point about which you were doubtful was settled fully to my satisfaction by Mr. Forbes. I should hope that principles of honour as well as prudence would engage you to keep those solemn vows, which too many make too lightly of.

I was amused, as I have been before on the like occasion, with your confidence about your success. I have commonly observed that vanity is for the most part punished by mortifying the person in the very thing in which he most prides himself; and, upon that principle, I could lay a bet that in this very affair you will meet with a disappointment. But we shall see.

You have had, it seems, too much success upon less honourable terms with a weak one of the sex. I hope you have as sincerely repented of that action, as you must have done of that act which brought you into the condition in which Mr. Forbes saw you. If you have not repented, and with great compunction too, be assured that your misfortunes are not at an end, and that Providence for your amendment will not cease to chastise you till you cry *peccavi*. Is it nothing to render ashamed and unhappy for life a poor silly creature whom you have catched off her guard? The damage is irreparable, but since the thing is done you ought to make amends as much as you can by money. In the first place, I hope you will apply that sum which you tell me you are to receive for the copy of your book. Not that I approve of that merchandise, but since you have made the bargain I take the liberty to tell you what my opinion is with regard to the disposal of the money.

I have always, you well know, used great freedom with you, not only when you have asked my opinion, but likewise whenever you afforded me matter to form opinions relating to your conduct and character. On the occasion of the book I must therefore tell you that, since contrary to my advice you have written it and will publish it, you have done, I am afraid, rather ungenteelly in selling the copy (before the publication) to a bookseller. This has too much the air of writing for gain, I mean for money, which is below a gentleman. I know this was not your only motive; nay, I will do you the justice as to say that I believe that this circumstance did not at first enter into the consideration at all, but you ought to have avoided the appearance of it. I shall keep your secret, but will your bookseller do it; or have you done it yourself? Were I the Heiress of Adamtown, be assured I should never listen to a lover who had been capable of so doing. See the consequences: your bookseller, in order to indemnify himself, must puff your work with a pompous title-page, and advertisements in the newspapers. He must tell that you give not only the political but the natural history of that Island. Now surely you could never call yourself a naturalist; or if you had had any genius or education for that branch of science, had you time to make observations that could claim an article in such a book? If it be not too late, I would advise you to change that at least. You see I take great liberties.

I shall conclude with telling you that with regard to separate houses in case of marriage, your father is too reasonable not to consent to it. But remember that by leaving him lonely, he may be tempted to take a companion likewise. Perhaps the best for you both would be for each to have a good one. I am most affectionately yours,

J.P.

[Boswell to Temple]

Edinburgh, 18 December 1767

MY DEAR TEMPLE, — You have reason to blame me for a too long silence, after having received all your friendly remarks on my Journal, and while you was incertain as to my negotiations with the Princess. I am sincerely obliged to you for your aid in polishing my Corsican monument. It is now complete, and I would fain hope it will do both the brave Islanders and myself a good deal of honour. As to the Princess, I sent the letter which you returned. She did not write, but bid her aunt tell me that she and I were as good friends as ever. This did not satisfy me, and for several weeks did I strive to break my chain. At last she came to town, and I have had a long conversation with her. She assured me she did not believe me serious or that I was uneasy, and that it was my own fault if ever she and I quarrelled. I in short adored her, and was convinced she was not to blame. I told her that henceforth she should entertain no doubt that I sincerely loved her — and, Temple, I ventured to seize her hand. She is really the finest woman to me I ever saw.

I am just now going to meet her at the concert, after which I sup with her at Lord Kames's along with her cousin, the beautiful young Duchess of Gordon. I am therefore in a hurry and a flutter and must break off. But in a day or two I shall write you fully. In the mean time, my friend, wish me joy of my present peace of mind, and make my best compliments to the woman to whom I see you owe a great deal. Adieu, my best friend. Ever yours,

JAMES BOSWELL.

[Boswell to Temple]

Edinburgh, 24 December 1767

MY DEAREST FRIEND, — In my last I told you that after I had resolved to give up with the Princess for ever, I resolved first to see her, and that when I did see her I was so lucky as to have a very agreeable interview, and was convinced by her that she was not to blame. This happened on a Thursday. That evening, her cousin and most intimate friend, the Duchess of Gordon, came to town. Next day I was at the concert with them and afterwards supped at Lord Kames's. The Princess appeared distant and reserved. I could hardly believe that it was the same woman with whom I had been quite easy the day before. I was then uneasy.

Next evening I was at the play with them. It was *Othello*. I sat close behind the Princess, and at the most affecting scenes I pressed my hand upon her waist. She was in tears, and rather leaned to me. The jealous Moor described my very soul. I often spoke to her of the torment which she saw before her. Still I thought her distant, and still I was uneasy.

On Sunday the Duchess of Gordon went away. I met the Princess at church. She was distant as before. I passed the evening at her aunt's, where I met a cousin of my princess, a young lady of Glasgow who had been with us at Adamtown. She told me she had something to communicate, and she then said that my behaviour to the Princess was such that Mrs. Blair and her daughter did not know how to behave to me. That it was not honourable to engage a young lady's affections while I kept myself free. In short, the good cousin persuaded me that the Princess had formed an attachment for me, and she assured me the Nabob had been refused. On Monday forenoon I waited on Miss Blair; I found her alone, and she did not seem distant. I told her that I was most sincerely in love with her, and that I only dreaded those faults which I had acknowledged to her. I asked her seriously if she now believed me in earnest. She said she did. I then asked her to be candid and fair as I had been with her, and to tell me if she had any particular liking for me. What think you, Temple, was her answer? *No.* "I really," said she, "have no particular liking for you. I like many people as well as you."

(Temple, you must have it in the genuine dialogue.) BOSWELL. "Do you indeed? Well, I cannot help it. I am obliged to you for telling me so in time. I am sorry for it." PRINCESS. "I like Jeanie Maxwell (Duchess of Gordon) better than you." BOSWELL. "Very well. But do you like no man better than me?" PRINCESS. "No." BOSWELL. "Is it possible that you may like me better than other men?" PRINCESS. "I don't know what is possible." (By this time I had risen and placed myself by her, and was in real agitation.) BOSWELL. "I'll tell you what, my dear Miss Blair, I love you so much that I am very unhappy. If you cannot love me, I must if possible endeavour to forget you. What would you have me do?" PRINCESS. "I really don't know what you should do." BOSWELL. "It is certainly possible that you *may* love me, and if you shall ever do so I shall be the happiest man in the world. Will you make a fair bargain with me? If you should happen to love me, will you own it?" PRINCESS. "Yes." BOSWELL. "And if you should happen to love another, will you tell me immediately, and help me to make myself easy?" PRINCESS. "Yes, I will." BOSWELL. "Well, you are very good" (often squeezing and kissing her fine hand, while she looked at me with those beautiful black eyes).

PRINCESS. "I may tell you as a cousin what I would not tell to another man." BOSWELL. "You may indeed. You are very fond of Auchinleck; that is one good circumstance." PRINCESS. "I confess I am. I wish I liked you as well as I do Auchinleck." BOSWELL. "I have told you how fond I am of you. But unless you like me sincerely, I have too much spirit to ask you to live with me, as I know that you do not like

me. If I could have you this moment for my wife I would not." PRIN-
CESS." I should not like to put myself in your offer, though." BOSWELL.
"Remember, you are both my cousin and my mistress. You must make
me suffer as little as possible. As it may happen that I may engage
your affections, I should think myself a most dishonourable man if I
were not now in earnest, and remember I depend upon your sincerity;
and whatever happens you and I shall never again have any quarrel."
PRINCESS. "Never." BOSWELL. "And I may come and see you as much
as I please?" PRINCESS. "Yes."

My worthy friend, what sort of a scene was this? It was most curious. She said she would submit to her husband in most things. She
said that to see one loving her would go far to make her love that person; but she could not talk anyhow positively, for she never had felt
the uneasy anxiety of love. We were an hour and a half together, and
seemed pleased all the time. I think she behaved with spirit and propriety. I admired her more than ever. She intended to go to her aunt's
twelve miles from town next day. Her jaunt was put off for some days.
Yesterday I saw her again. I was easy and cheerful, and just endeavoured to make myself agreeable.

This forenoon I was again with her. I told her how uneasy I was
that she should be three weeks absent. She said I might amuse myself
well enough. She seemed quite indifferent. I was growing angry
again. But I recollected how she had candidly told me that she had no
particular liking for me. Temple, where am I now? What is the meaning of this? I drank tea with her this afternoon and sat near four hours
with her mother and her. Our conversation turned all on the manner
in which two people might live. She has the justest ideas. She said she
knew me now. She could laugh me out of my ill humour. She could
give Lord Auchinleck a lesson how to manage me. Temple, what does
the girl mean? We talked a good deal of you. You are a prodigious
favourite. Now, my worthy friend, assist me. You know my strange
temper and impetuous disposition. Shall I boldly shake her off, as I
fear I cannot be patient and moderate? Or am I not bound in honour
to suffer some time and watch her heart? How long must I suffer?
How must I do? When she comes back, shall I affect any indifference
to try her? or shall I rather endeavour to inspire her with my flame? Is
it not below me to be made uneasy by her? Or may I not be a philoso-

pher, and without uneasiness take her if she likes me, and if not, let her alone? During her absence I have time to get a return from you. It is certainly possible that all she has said may be literally true, but is not her indifference a real fault? Consult Mrs. Temple and advise me.

Amidst all this love I have been wild as ever. I have catched another memorandum of vice, but a very slight one. Trust me in time coming. I give you my word in honour, Temple. I have nothing else to save me.

My black friend has brought me the finest little girl I ever saw. I have named it Sally. It is healthy and strong. I take the greatest care of the mother, but shall have her no more in keeping.

I have this day received a large packet from Paoli, with a letter in elegant Latin from the University of Corte, and also an extract of an oration pronounced this year at the opening of the University, in which oration I am celebrated in a manner which does me the greatest honour. I think, Temple, I have had my full share of fame. Yet my book is still to come, and I cannot doubt its doing me credit. Come, why do I allow myself to be uneasy for a Scots lass? Rouse me, my friend. Kate has not fire enough. She does not know the value of her lover. If on her return she still remains cold, she does not deserve me. I will not quarrel with her. She cannot help her defects. But I will break my enchanting fetters. Tomorrow I shall be happy with my devotions. I shall think of you and wish to be at Mamhead. Could you assist me to keep up my real dignity among the illiberal race of Scots lawyers? Adieu, my dearest friend. My best compliments to your amiable spouse.

J.B.

1768

FRIDAY 1 JANUARY.[8] Busy all day drawing replies in the Forfar elections.[9]

SATURDAY 2 JANUARY. Went with my father to Arniston. By the way talked of the antiquities and constitution of the election law in Scotland. Found it difficult to fix my attention. But by degrees wrought my mind into a knowledge of the subject. Was amazed at my father's memory and patience. Well at Arniston. All old ideas had no longer any force, but the traces of them diversified and amused my thoughts. At night played whist. Still had gloom, because I have never played at it when well so as to get free of former prejudices.

About nine my father was taken ill with his old complaint.[1] Thomas went express to Edinburgh. The President showed a friendly concern which will ever make him be regarded by me. For some hours my father was in agony. In the view of death he gave me the best and most affectionate advices. He spoke of Miss Blair as the woman whom he wished I would marry. How strong was this. I was in terrible concern. He said if business did not succeed with me after his death I should retire to the country. He charged me to take care of my brothers, to be a worthy man, and keep up the character of the family. I firmly resolved to be as he wished, though in somewhat a different taste of life. I looked my watch a hundred times. A quarter before one Thomas arrived with the catheter. In five minutes my father was easy. What a happy change! Went calmly to bed. It was an intense frost, and the ground was covered with snow.

[8] This Journal, written on loose sheets, is enclosed in a wrapper which Boswell endorsed: "Journal 1768, from January 1 to February 27."
[9] A new parliament was elected this year, and the complicated property qualifications of voters in the counties and burghs of Scotland were being contested by the various opposing interests.
[1] A suppression of urine, probably due to an enlarged prostate. The affliction had first appeared at the time of the Ogilvy trial of 1765 when Lord Auchinleck sat nine hours without rising from his seat (see *Boswell on the Grand Tour: Italy, Corsica, and France*, following 30 November 1765).

SUNDAY 3 JANUARY. My father was quite easy. I went out for an hour with the President in his chariot. Talked freely on the Douglas cause. Heard how it struck him in its various points. Saw how foolish the suspicions against him were. Resolved to take men as I find them. Was assured by the President that I should do well as a lawyer. Saw no difficulties in life. Saw that all depends on our frame of mind. Lord and Lady Hyndford were here. The day passed well. In the evening I adored my God; I had now no doubt of the Christian revelation. I was quite satisfied with my being. I hoped to be happy with Miss Blair.

MONDAY 4 JANUARY. After breakfast, set off. My father remarked how foolish and wicked evil-speaking was. The President afforded a good instance, as so many false reports had been raised against him as to the Douglas cause.[2] We dined at Newbattle. I experienced that calm tranquillity in presence of great people for which I have often wished and have now acquired. Much attention was paid me. Returned to town. Supped Sir George Preston's.[3]

TUESDAY 5 JANUARY. I was at home all day except calling half an hour for Sally's mother. Felt all inclination gone and that I now acted from principle alone.

WEDNESDAY 6 JANUARY. In all day. Matthew Dickie dined with us. The terrible cold weather made me consider keeping warm as almost business enough.

THURSDAY 7 JANUARY. Breakfast Mr. Webster's.[4] Old ideas revived in an agreeable manner. When my mind was weak, ideas were too powerful for me. I am now strong; I can discern all their qualities but am master of them. I was formerly, in many articles of thought, like a boy who fires a gun. He startles at the noise, and, being unable to wield it, he can direct it to no steady point. I am now master of my gun, and can manage it with ease. I called for Lord Leven, visited Mr.

[2] For an example, see p. 171.

[3] Preston's wife, Anne Cochrane, was Boswell's maternal great-aunt. She had brought up Boswell's mother, and Boswell had spent a good deal of time at the Prestons' estate of Valleyfield as a child.

[4] The Rev. Alexander Webster, D.D., was married to Mary Erskine, Boswell's aunt. He was a leader of the "High Flying" or fundamentalist faction of the Church of Scotland, but is best remembered for his early work on actuarial calculations. His love of a social bottle was well known.

George Frazer, called for Lord Dalhousie, visited Lady Crawford. Miss Montgomerie, John and George Frazers dined.

FRIDAY 8 JANUARY. In all day. Felt myself now quite free of fancies. Was amazed to find how much happiness and misery is ideal. Passed the evening at Mr. Moncrieffe's with the Chief Baron,[5] Miss Ords, &c. Felt myself now quite indifferent about making a figure in company. Am I grown dull? Or is it a calm confidence in a fixed reputation?

SATURDAY 9 JANUARY. Busy with election law. John Chalmer showed me an old opinion of Duncan Forbes, and reflected how curious it was that the opinion remained while the man was no more. A hint such as this brings to my mind all that passed, though it would be barren to anybody but myself. At home all day consulting and writing law papers till six. Went and saw *The Suspicious Husband* and *Citizen;* had my London ideas revived. Went home with Mr. Ross and supped and drank a cheerful glass. He gave me all the history of his marriage.[6] He put me into my old romantic frame. I wished again for adventures, for proofs of my own address and of the generosity of charming women. I was for breaking loose from Scots marriage. But my elegant heiress and the old family of Auchinleck brought me back again.

SUNDAY 10 JANUARY. In forenoon writing to Zélide, &c. Church afternoon. Heard Heiress was to have a knight.[7] Was not so much shocked as before. I did not indeed fully believe it. Visited Sally's mother. Was tired of her.

MONDAY 11 JANUARY. Busy with law. Lord Chief Baron, Mr. Moncrieffe, Lord Strichen, &c., dined.

TUESDAY 12 JANUARY. Went in coach with my father, visited

---

[5] Robert Ord, Lord Chief Baron of the Court of Exchequer, a witty and hospitable Englishman. For Moncrieffe, see p. 210 *n.*9.

[6] David Ross, a well-known actor, was patentee and manager of the Edinburgh Theatre Royal. Boswell had written a Prologue at its opening the previous December, which he himself credited with having saved the theatre in the face of strong local opposition. Ross was married to Fanny Murray, a famous courtesan and the main figure in Wilkes's obscene *Essay on Woman.* Upon his marriage, Ross is said to have received an allowance of £200 a year from Lord Spencer, whose father had "debauched" her.

[7] That Miss Blair was to marry Sir Alexander Gilmour. See pp. 117–118.

Mr. James Ker. Felt myself quite established. Dined Lady Alva's with Lord Chief Baron, Miss Ords, and Mr. John Mackenzie. Was well, but found I was ignorant and had no turn for the common affairs of life.

WEDNESDAY 13 JANUARY. Dined Mrs. Boswell's of Balmuto.[8] Found I had formed a habit there of constant jocularity, in so much that I never said one serious word. This must be corrected; they are good people. Relations should be regarded. In the immense multiplicity of human beings, the more attachments we can form, the better. Do as we please, they are all few enough. Saw Martin's portraits. Drank tea at Mr. Kincaid's. Mrs. Kincaid not in; just the father and son and his governor. I appeared a formed man of learning.

THURSDAY 14 JANUARY. Was entertained to find myself again in the Parliament House in all the hurry of business. Mr. Kincaid and his family dined with us.

FRIDAY 15 JANUARY. Breakfasted with Mr. William Alexander — genteel people. I thought myself among strangers and not in Edinburgh. Was busy with election causes; found the law fatigue me greatly, and from my indolent and anxious temper I was really harassed with it.

SATURDAY 16 JANUARY. This morning I was amazed when I thought of Mr. Lockhart, who is all the forenoon in the Parliament House and is never hurried or fretted, and yet goes through such multitudes of causes.[9] I told him he was just a *brownie* in business. In a few hours the work of a dozen of men is performed by him. He never talks of himself, or complains anyhow. He said he wondered how the story of *brownies* came ever to be believed. I never before saw him aim at philosophy. It is indeed odd how the existence of a being who actually performed work, as a *brownie* was said to do, came to be believed; for it is not like imagining one sees a vision or hears a noise. Miss Montgomerie and Doctor Boswell and I were carried out by

[8] Lord Auchinleck's aunt and Claud Boswell's mother.

[9] Alexander Lockhart, Dean of the Faculty of Advocates, was considered perhaps the most eminent lawyer practising at the Scottish bar. He was certainly one of the most successful. Boswell described him as always ready to cry and fond of getting his fees, and applied 2 *Henry IV*, IV. iv. 31–32, to him:

> He hath a *tear* for pity, and a *hand*
> Open as day.

worthy Sir Alexander Dick in his coach to Prestonfield. We were very happy. I don't believe there ever existed a man more continually amiable than Sir Alexander. Came home in his coach.

Had a consultation on the Forfar politics. In the forenoon, as we went along in the coach, the Earl of Eglinton was at the Cross. I jumped out, and he and I embraced most cordially. I had a strange pleasure in showing my intimacy with his Lordship before the citizens of Edinburgh. It is fine to be sensible of all one's various sentiments and to analyse them. After my consultation, I went to Fortune's and supped with Lord Eglinton, Lord Galloway, Matthew Henderson, and several more.[1] I saw a genteel, profligate society who live like a distinct nation in Edinburgh, having constant recruits going and coming. I was ill of a venereal disorder, but resolved to make myself easy and eat and drink, though not to excess, yet freely.

About one, Lord Eglinton and I went upstairs and had a friendly conference. I told him I loved Miss Blair much and wished to marry her if she liked me, and I gave him all our history. He said I was right to be honest with her; that her answers were very clever, and that it was probable she liked me. But he said I did not show her attention enough; that a woman had a right to be courted as much as a husband after marriage had a right to command. That if I insisted on a woman showing much love for me, I was certain of being taken in by any artful girl who wanted to have a man with a good estate. That I should tell Miss Blair, "If I have any chance, I'll do all in my power to be agreeable. If not, I'll make myself easy as soon as possible." He said my Yorkshire beauty[2] would not do so well, that she would be miserable in this country; and he quoted a blunt saying of the Highlanders that "a cow fed in fine Lowland parks was unco bonny, but turned lean and scabbed when she was turned out to the wild hills." Up came Matthew Henderson and swore he believed Sir Alexander

[1] Fortune's was the most fashionable Edinburgh tavern of the day. Matthew Henderson was a convivial antiquary, and later a friend of Burns, who said of him after his death: "Of all mankind I ever knew, he was one of the first for a nice sense of honour, a generous contempt of the adventitious distinctions of men, and sterling though somewhat *outré* wit" (*Letters of Robert Burns*, ed. J. De Lancey Ferguson, 1931, ii. 33). Boswell once described Lord Galloway as a quick, spirited, pleasure-loving politician.

[2] Miss Bosville.

Gilmour was to have the Heiress. My Lord advised me to write to her and know as to this. Such admirable advice did I get from a man of great genius who knows the world perfectly. He talked to me of my neutrality in the Ayrshire elections. I felt I was wrong. I was now quite free of hypochondria. Walking home after convoying my Lord to the Bow, I met a girl. Like a madman I would try the experiment of cooling myself when ill. What more mischief may it not bring!

SUNDAY 17 JANUARY. In all forenoon. At dinner my father was out of humour because I had been so late abroad. I bore with him quite calmly. At five met at Mr. Macqueen's[3] with Messieurs Rae, Alexander Murray, and Armstrong, as counsel for Raybould, the forger, as I allow myself to consult on criminal business on Sundays. Went to bed at nine that I might be up early next morning.

MONDAY 18 JANUARY. Rose at three. Wrote a reply in the Forfar politics, and prepared a charge to the jury for Raybould. Went to the Justiciary Court at nine. Dull reading of the decreet of the Court of Session for many hours.[4] At two I went home, dined and drank a

[3] Robert Macqueen, a coarse, vigorous, gifted lawyer, well known for his Scots dialect and accent. Later a judge in the Courts of Session and Justiciary with the style of Lord Braxfield, he was notorious for his severity in the sedition trials of the 1790s. He is supposedly the model for the judge in R. L. Stevenson's *Weir of Hermiston.*

[4] John Raybould, who seems to have been an Englishman living in New Merchiston, Stirlingshire, had already been found guilty by the Court of Session of forging bank-notes. If the indictment was true (as there seems no reason to doubt), he had hired an engraver in Birmingham to engrave a copper plate duplicating a twenty-shilling note of the Thistle Banking Company, Glasgow, and had caused five hundred impressions to be struck from this plate. Having been unable to hire the engraver to fill in with a pen dates, numbers, and subscriptions for the notes, he brought them back to Scotland and filled in some himself and got other persons to fill in others. At least fifty notes were completed in this fashion, and at least twenty-two were put in circulation. Raybould's counsel had caused one postponement by demanding proof that he was the same as the person who had been tried by the Court of Session; on this day they seem to have limited their efforts to an attempt to establish that he did not himself fill in the signatures on some of the forged notes. The case raised an important and interesting legal point on which the authorities were disagreed: was the jury in the Court of Justiciary bound to accept the finding of the Court of Session, or could it acquit if it thought the prisoner in fact not guilty? Raybould's counsel argued for the latter view, and the judges of the Court of Justiciary upheld them. It made no difference, for the jury returned a unanimous verdict of guilty. Boswell

glass or two of malaga, and wrote another reply. Returned to the court. The Solicitor[5] charged the jury for the Crown. I was very uneasy and frightened. I however began, and was soon warm and in spirits, and recollected all my arguments. I really spoke well for above half an hour. I saw my imperfections, and hoped in time to make a real good speaker. I felt sound ambition and clear faculties. At eight went to Crosbie's[6] and had tea and a consultation with Mr. James Hay, Writer to the Signet. He revived in my mind worthy Scots family ideas. What a variety do I enjoy by observation! I went to bed in good time.

[Received ? 18 January, Temple to Boswell]

Mamhead, 8 January 1768

MY DEAR BOSWELL, — I have read your letter with some care, and must confess am rather at a loss what to think of Miss Blair's conduct. Though she chooses to coquet it with you a little, yet she certainly may love you, and perhaps the dance she seems to intend leading you is no more than you deserve, considering the unaccountable manner in which you have behaved to her. For what woman can bear to see a man so long an admirer professedly, and yet at the same time so cautiously insensible as always to guard against the least advance to any engagement. At last, indeed, she finds you are caught and is resolved to punish you for your former temerity. Alas! the proud Boswell, to what humiliations, to what entreaties, to what pardons, to what insults do I not see him destined! The great Baron, the friend of Rousseau and Voltaire, the companion of Paoli, the author of that immortal work, the Account of Corsica, is dwindled into a whining, fawning lover, the slave of a fair hand and a pair of black eyes.

---

does not seem to have been much involved emotionally in this case, partly because Raybould was unquestionably guilty, partly because he was "a genteel man" (see above, 11 February 1767).

[5] Henry Dundas.

[6] Andrew Crosbie, Boswell's fellow advocate in the John Reid trial, was noted for his learning and the originality of his thinking and arguments. He pleased Dr. Johnson on one occasion by discoursing on alchemy. In later life he was ruined in a disastrous banking venture, and died in great poverty. Though Scott denied using him as a model, he was taken for the original of Counsellor Pleydell in *Guy Mannering*.

Jesting apart, my dear friend, I dare not venture to say whether Miss Blair loves you or no. As she now has reason to think that you really love her, why does she not ingenuously confess that your flame is reciprocal? But you have told her your character; you have told her that you are inconstant, fickle, and jealous, and never sure of yourself for two days together. Has she not reason then to examine every step that she takes, lest imagining she is walking upon flowers she meets with nothing under foot but thorns and poison? But is such caution consistent with tenderness, with love, with genuine passion? Undoubtedly it is, my dear Boswell; the romance of knight-errantry is no more, and good folks nowadays agree to run the race of life together because it is convenient; not because they love, but because they do not hate. Does not this shock the sensibility of your enthusiastic soul? However, in general, it is but too true, and if you want a wife upon more refined conditions, I fear you must go seek her in the wilds of America, or in that stage of society in which mankind have not yet learnt to prefer paltry conveniences and gilded trifles to the genuine feelings of nature and passion.

I am much pleased with her being so amiably affected at *Othello;* for to feel even for imaginary distresses is the sign of a tender and generous heart. But I am not fond of the mediation of her Glasgow cousin. It looks artful. However, considering your strange conduct, perhaps it was necessary and probably more owing to the prudence of a wary mother than to anything else. Upon the whole, I dare say Miss Blair is a good girl. When she returns, therefore, continue your assiduity and professions of eternal love; if you cannot melt her that way, then affect a careless indifference, which, if there is the least spark of love in her breast, will certainly blow it into a flame; at any rate you must not lose her, for she surely is destined by fate to continue the race of the lords of Auchinleck. . . .

My wife desires her kind remembrances to you. She seems in a fair way to bring me a boy. Adieu, my dear friend,

W.J.T.

TUESDAY 19 JANUARY. Was at the anniversary meeting of the Faculty of Advocates.[7] Had the true old sensations, and felt myself

---

[7] "Anniversary" seems simply to mean "annual." Its purpose was the election of officers and committees.

Mr. James Boswell, comfortable and secure. Recollected how formerly I should have been wretched with a life so void of vivid enjoyment, but now had force of mind enough to be content. At Clerihue's we were very merry. The Dean after many ladies had been drank called out, "Here is a toast: a young lady just in her teens — Miss Corsica. Give her a gentleman!" All called out, "Paoli!" I drank too much. I went to a close in the Luckenbooths to seek a girl whom I had once seen in the street. I found a natural daughter of the late Lord ⟨Kinnaird⟩,[8] a fine lass. I stayed an hour and a half with her and drank malaga and was most amorous, being so well that no infection remained. I felt now that the indifference of the Heiress had cured me, and I was indifferent as to her. I was so happy with Jeany Kinnaird that I very philosophically reasoned that there was to me so much virtue mixed with licentious love that perhaps I might be privileged. For it made me humane, polite, generous. But then lawful love with a woman I really like would make me still better. I forgot the risk I run with this girl. She looked so healthy and so honest I had no fears.

WEDNESDAY 20 JANUARY. Mr. George Frazer and Mr. Orme drank tea and claret with me, consulting on a plan for Lochmaben manse.

THURSDAY 21 JANUARY. Lords Stonefield and Barjarg, Walter Campbell, George Cockburn, &c., dined. I drank tea with Johnston. Supped with Dempster at Peter Ramsay's.[9] Had a most pleasant evening.

FRIDAY 22 JANUARY. My father and I dined at Lord Coalston's. I had written to Miss Blair to tell me if she was going to be married to Sir Alexander Gilmour, and if she was disengaged and did not write me so I should *upon honour* consider it to be the same thing as if she was engaged. No answer had come yet, so I began to exert all my spirit to be free. I drank tea at Mrs. Hamilton of Bangour's, and made my peace for not having visited her since I came home.

SATURDAY 23 JANUARY. My father and I dined at Lord Galloway's. Old ideas of true people of quality revived. I then went to the play, to Mrs. Hamilton's box. It was *Venice Preserved:* Jaffier, Ross; Pierre, Sowdon; I relished it much. The Heiress began to lose her do-

---

[8] There is a hole in the manuscript here, but Boswell supplies the name below.
[9] An inn at the bottom of St. Mary's Wynd. For Dempster, see p. 173 *n.*5.

minion over me. I supped at Ross's after the play. Sowdon was there and Cullen, &c. Felt myself now calm and improved, as I used to wish.

SUNDAY 24 JANUARY. In all forenoon. Afternoon, church; then tea, Marchioness Dowager of Lothian. Miss Bothwell, a sister of the late Lord Holyroodhouse, was there. We had good solid conversation on the advantages of the Christian religion. Then drank coffee at the Marquess of Lothian's. Found myself as in a London family of fashion. Then visited Lady Crawford, a most amiable woman. Sir John Cathcart and lady there.

MONDAY 25 JANUARY. In all day. M. Dupont drank tea with me;[10] had two consultations. Supped Mrs. Hamilton of Bangour's, an Edinburgh evening. Found I was fit for any company. Before my Account of Corsica came out, I was desirous to have all my visits paid, as I thenceforward intended if possible to maintain a propriety and strictness of manners.

TUESDAY 26 JANUARY. All the evening was employed in writing to Paoli, Mr. Burnaby, &c., before the great era of the publication of my book. I sat up till past two.

WEDNESDAY 27 JANUARY. My father and Claud and I dined at Lord Barjarg's. It was just a family dinner. I felt myself palled with insipidity, so high is my taste of society grown. I drank tea at Mrs. Hunter's of Polmood, and revived Sommelsdyck and Auchinleck ideas.[1] I then came home and wrote papers busily till seven. Then had a consultation at the Hon. Alexander Gordon's. Then supped Mrs. Cockburn's.[2] A great company there. Felt myself quite easy, but still subject to fall in love with the woman next me at table. I have from nature a feverish constitution which time has moderated and will at last cure. Mrs. Cockburn said a man much versant in love was not so valuable. I maintained he was, for a hack, if not lamed or too much worn down, is the cleverest horse when put on good pasture.

THURSDAY 28 JANUARY. My father was confined with a se-

[10] The Rev. Pierre Loumeau Dupont was minister of the Huguenot congregation in Edinburgh.

[1] Mrs. Hunter, like Boswell, had a Sommelsdyck ancestor, which explains the association.

[2] Alicia Cockburn was a poetess who in person somewhat resembled Queen Elizabeth. Her supper parties were well known for the distinguished circle she gathered. Burns admired her lyrics, and Scott her conversation.

vere cold. I saw his great worth and value to me, when I was reminded of the danger of losing him. I resolved to act towards him in such a way as to make his life comfortable, and give me the consolation after he is gone that I have done my duty, and may hope for the same attention from my son. I was not abroad but at the Parliament House and dining at Lord President's.

FRIDAY 29 JANUARY. Had Hallglenmuir and Knockroon to dine. Went after supper to Bailie Hunter's, and sat a while with Lady Crawford and a good many more company. Sat too late. I resolved to be more regular, as I really had a constant fever and sweating every morning.

SATURDAY 30 JANUARY. I stayed in all forenoon writing replies for Hardriggs, in the division of Dornock commonty. Dined John Chalmer's with Hallglenmuir, James Neill, Knockroon, &c.

SUNDAY 31 JANUARY. Forenoon at church. Dined Mr. Moncrieffe's with Prebendary Douglas and lady, Lady and Miss Eden, all from Durham, who wished much to see the author of *The Essence of the Douglas Cause*. Lord John Murray was there. All was elegant and really agreeable. At night went to Sally's mother and renewed gallantry.

MONDAY 1 FEBRUARY. Was busy all day with law till five, when I drank tea at Miss Montgomerie's. At seven consulted at Solicitor's.

TUESDAY 2 FEBRUARY. At seven met Mr. Alexander Orme and Holmains, George Frazer, William Hay, and Jamie Baillie at Clerihue's at a treat given by the heritors of Lochmaben. Mr. Ross had come up to me and asked me to sup with him; so I went and found Sir Johns Cathcart and Whitefoord. We were very merry and pleasant. I drank a great deal, though I was not well yet. Between two and three I went to Sally's mother's and renewed again. What a life do I lead!

WEDNESDAY 3 FEBRUARY. I awaked so ill I could hardly rise, and all forenoon I was quite out of order and feverish after my debauchery. I felt myself a very rake as I pleaded a cause before Lord Monboddo.

THURSDAY 4 FEBRUARY. I was busy and regular.

FRIDAY 5 FEBRUARY. I supped at Lord Monboddo's with Lords

Coalston and Kennet, Mrs. Murray of Stormont, &c. I was quite easy. I saw lords of session in a quite different light from what I have done by looking only at awful judges. Claret fevered me, and I again went to Sally's mother and renewed.

SATURDAY 6 FEBRUARY. Breakfasted at the President's. Was too late for a cause before Lord Monboddo. Determined to confine myself to the Parliament House all the forenoon. Considered the law is my profession, my occupation in life. Saw it not to be such a mystery as I apprehended.

SUNDAY 7 FEBRUARY. Church forenoon. Heard Mr. Butter in St. Paul's Chapel,³ afternoon. Drank tea with Mrs. Montgomerie-Cuninghame. Then visited Lady Maxwell. Was quite cheerful and well. Mr. Fullarton (the Nabob) came in. Miss Blair was now arrived. He proposed we should go and visit her. We went. She was reserved and distant. I saw plainly all was over. Yet I could not be quite certain. Fullarton and I came away together. I liked the man. I asked him freely how he was. We owned candidly to each other that we were both for Miss Blair. I insisted that he and I should not part that night. I carried him to sup at Mrs. Montgomerie-Cuninghame's and then we adjourned to Clerihue's. I opened the Nabob's mind, and he and I gave each other a fair recital of all that we hoped from the Heiress. It was agreed I had her heart once, and perhaps still, if she was not engaged to Sir Alexander Gilmour. "Come," said I, "we shall be at our wits' end. If you'll ask her tomorrow, upon honour I'll ask her." We shook hands and wished all happiness to him who should succeed. Never was there a more curious scene. At two in the morning I went to Sally's mother, and, being flushed with claret, renewed my love.

MONDAY 8 FEBRUARY. Between nine and ten went to Miss Blair. "Come, before they come in, are you engaged or no?" She seemed reserved. I said, "You know I am much in love with you, and, if you are not engaged, I would take a good deal of trouble to make

³ Not "Old St. Paul's," the Scots Episcopal church whose present beautiful structure on the east side of Carrubber's Close is believed to cover the site of its eighteenth-century chapel, but a "qualified" congregation meeting at the foot of the close in the luckless theatre which Allan Ramsay had opened in 1737, only to have it promptly shut by the authorities.

myself agreeable to you." She said, "You need not take the trouble. Now you must not be angry with me." "Indeed no," said I. "But is it really so? Say upon your word, upon honour." She did so. I therefore was satisfied. My spirit was such that, though I felt some regret, I appeared quite easy and gay. I made her give me breakfast, and with true philosophy I put my mind in a proper frame. It was agreed that we were not to ask her if she was engaged. She gave me a lecture on my conduct towards her, in talking without reserve. At twelve the Nabob was with her, and she treated him with the greatest coldness. He and I met at the Cross at two and joked and laughed with all our acquaintance. I did the Nabob much good, for I relieved him from serious love by my vivacity. I have one of the most singular minds ever was formed.

[Boswell to Temple]

Edinburgh, 8 February 1768

MY DEAR FRIEND, — All is over between Miss Blair and me. I have delayed writing till I could give you some final account. About a fortnight after she went to the country a report went that she was going to be married to Sir Alexander Gilmour, Member of Parliament for the county of Midlothian, a young man about thirty who has £1600 a year of estate, was formerly an officer in the Guards, and is now one of the Clerks of the Board of Green Cloth,[4] £1000 a year; in short, a noble match, though a man of expense and obliged to lead a London life. After the fair agreement between her and me which I gave you fully in my last, I had a title to know the truth. I wrote to her seriously, and told her that if she did not write me an answer I should believe the report to be true. After three days, I concluded from her silence that she was at last engaged. I endeavoured to laugh off my passion and I got Sir Alexander Gilmour to frank a letter to her, which I wrote in a pleasant strain and amused myself with the whim. Still, however, I was not absolutely certain, as her conduct has been so prudent all along.

At last she comes to town, and who comes too but my old rival, the Nabob. I got acquainted with Mr. Fullarton, and he and I joked a good deal about our heiress. Last night he proposed that he and I

[4] A judicial and financial department of the King's Household.

should go together and pay her a visit for the first time after her return from the country. Accordingly we went, and I give you my word, Temple, it was a curious scene. However, the Princess behaved exceedingly well, though with a reserve more than ordinary. When we left her, we both exclaimed, "Upon my soul, a fine woman." I began to like the Nabob much, so I said to him, "I do believe, Mr. Fullarton, you and I are in the same situation here. Is it possible to be upon honour and generous in an affair of this kind?" We agreed it was. Each then declared he was serious in his love for Miss Blair, and each protested he never before believed the other in earnest. We agreed to deal by one another in a fair and candid manner.

I carried him to sup at a lady's, a cousin of mine, where we stayed till half an hour past eleven. We then went to a tavern, and the good old claret was set before us. He told me that he had been most assiduous in attending Miss Blair, but she never gave him the least encouragement, and he declared he was convinced she loved me as much as a woman could love a man. With equal honesty I told him all that has passed between her and me, and your observation on the *wary mother.* "What!" said he, "did Temple say so? If he had lived twenty years in the country with them, he could not have said a better thing." I then told him Dempster's humorous saying that all Miss Blair's connections were in an absolute confederacy to lay hold of every man who has a £1000 a year, and how I called their system *a salmon fishing.* "You have hit it," said he. "We're all kept in play; but I am positive you are the fish, and Sir Alexander is only a mock salmon to force you to jump more expeditiously at the bait." We sat till two this morning. We gave our words as men of honour that we would be honest to each other, so that neither should suffer needlessly; and to satisfy ourselves of our real situation we gave our words that we should both ask her this morning, and I should go first. Could there be anything better than this? The Nabob talked to me with the warmth of the Indies, and professed the greatest pleasure on being acquainted with me.

Well, Temple, I went this morning, and she made tea to me alone. I then asked her seriously if she was to be married to Sir Alexander. She said, "It was odd to believe everything people said, and why did I put such a question?" &c. I said that she knew very well I was much in love with her, and that if I had any chance I would take a good deal of trouble to make myself agreeable to her. She said I need not take the trouble, and I must not be angry, for she thought it best to tell me honestly. "What then," said I, "have I no chance?" "No," said she. I asked her to say so upon her word and upon honour. She fairly repeated the words. So, I think, Temple, I had enough.

She would not tell me whether she was engaged to the Knight. She said she would not satisfy an idle curiosity. But I own I had no doubt of it. What amazed me was that she and I were as easy and as good friends as ever. I told her, "I have great animal spirits and bear it wonderfully well. But this is really hard. I am thrown upon the wide world again. I don't know what will become of me."

Before dinner the Nabob and I met, and he told me that he went, and in the most serious and submissive manner begged to know if she was engaged. She would give him no satisfaction, and treated him with a degree of coldness that overpowered him quite, poor man.

Such is the history of the lovers of this cruel princess, who certainly is a lucky woman to have had a sovereign sway over so many admirers.

I have endeavoured to make merry on my misfortune.

A Crambo[5] Song on Losing my Mistress

Although I be an honest *laird*,
In person rather strong and brawny,
For me the Heiress never cared,
For she would have the Knight, Sir Sawney.

And when with ardent vows I swore,
Loud as Sir Jonathan Trelawny,[6]
The Heiress showed me to the door,
And said she'd have the Knight, Sir Sawney.

[5] That is, with a constantly recurring rhyme-word.
[6] Sir Jonathan Trelawny, a militant bishop of the late seventeenth and early eighteenth centuries, was tried for seditious libel under James II. It is to him that the song refers:

And shall Trelawny die?
Then twenty thousand Cornishmen will know the reason why.

> She told me with a scornful look
> I was as ugly as a tawny;[7]
> For she a better fish could hook,
> The rich and gallant Knight, Sir Sawney.

N.B. I can find no more rhymes to *Sawney*.

Now that all is over, I see many faults in her which I did not see before. Do you not think she has not feeling enough, nor that ingenuous spirit which your friend requires? The Nabob and many other people are still of opinion that she has not made sure of Sir Sawney, and that all this may be finesse. But I cannot suspect so young a creature of so much artifice, and whatever may be in it I am honourably off; and you may wonder at it, but I assure you I am very easy and cheerful. I am, however, resolved to look out for a good wife, either here or in England. I intend to be in London in March. My address will be at Mr. Dilly's, bookseller. But I expect to hear from you before I set out, which will not be till the 14 of March. I rejoice to hear that Mrs. Temple is in a good way. My best wishes ever attend you and her. I am your most affectionate friend,

JAMES BOSWELL.

11 February. I have allowed my letter to lie by till this day. The Heiress is a good Scots lass. But I must have an Englishwoman. My mind is now twice as enlarged as it has been for some months. You cannot say how fine a woman I may marry; perhaps a Howard or some other of the noblest in the kingdom.

TUESDAY 9 FEBRUARY.[8] Mr. Claud and I visited the Heiress. She seemed very ordinary today. My Lord President and his lady, Mrs. Montgomerie-Cuninghame, Professor Stevenson, &c., dined. Mrs. Dundas and I danced at a private ball at Fortune's, a very good company. The Nabob was there, and I made him talk easily and be quite cheerful. After supper I gave for my toast, "May we bear our

[7] Mulatto.

[8] Boswell, bringing up his Journal at a later date, began to misnumber the days here, calling this 2 February, until he came to his supposed 8 February (really the 15th) when his memory naturally failed him. He then wrote, "I cannot say what I did" for this day, and for the next, "I have also forgotten what I did, only one day this week I visited Raybould under sentence of death." The next "week" is blank, until the entries pick up again correctly on the 15th.

misfortunes with spirit," and sung, "The mind of a woman." Lord Monboddo was there and highly pleased. All my prejudices against Edinburgh were worn off. I saw the company quite agreeable and elegant enough, with a great deal of virtuous manners.

WEDNESDAY 10 FEBRUARY. I breakfasted at Lord President's.

FRIDAY 12 FEBRUARY. Lord Justice-Clerk, Mr. David Kennedy, Ilay Campbell, Mr. Alexander Tait, John Davidson, &c., dined.[9]

SATURDAY 13 FEBRUARY. I dined at Lord Justice-Clerk's with my father. Lords Kinnoul, Coalston, Kames, Baron Winn, &c., were there. I drank pretty freely, and after five went to Sally's mother and renewed. She told me she was again, she believed, as before.[1] I was a little embarrassed, but just submitted my mind to it. I then went to Crosbie and had some tea. Then he and I went to Mr. James Hay's and had a consultation with Mrs. Smith of Forret. It was quite in old style, and when it was over honest Mr. Hay gave us a couple of bottles of claret. This inflamed me again and I went back to Sally's mother. She really looked pretty.

SUNDAY 14 FEBRUARY. I sat in all forenoon. Afternoon went to church. Tea at home, then went to the good Doctor's.[2]

MONDAY 15 FEBRUARY. This day I heard from Mr. Dilly that my Account of Corsica was ready for publication, so I ordered Mr. Neill[3] to give out copies in Scotland.

TUESDAY 16 FEBRUARY. I was busy with law.

THURSDAY 18 FEBRUARY. I breakfasted with Lord Hailes and gave him my book. I dined with my father, Lord Coalston, &c., at the Solicitor's with the ladies of Cromartie. Lady Augusta, the famed beauty, did not strike me. I then went to an Ayrshire ball at Fortune's. My book was published this day, and felt my own importance. I danced with the Countess of Crawford, so opened the ball. I was quite as I wished to be; only I am positive I had not so high an opinion of

[9] A legal gathering. David Kennedy, an advocate, was M.P. for Ayrshire and later tenth Earl of Cassillis. Ilay Campbell, one of the Douglas counsel, was later Lord President of the Court of Session, and a baronet. Tait was a principal clerk of session, and Davidson a crown agent.

[1] Boswell does not make any further mention of Mrs. Dodds's possible pregnancy, so perhaps she was mistaken.

[2] Dr. Boswell's.

[3] Adam Neill, printer in Edinburgh, and a business connection of Dilly's.

myself as other people had. I look back with wonder on the mysterious and respectful notions I used to have of authors. I felt that I was still subject to attacks of feverish love, but I also knew that my mind is now firm enough soon to recover its tone.

FRIDAY 19 FEBRUARY. I called on Lady Crawford in the forenoon. I felt that I could easily relapse into dissipation, but I also saw that I was become strong; and though, when I allowed myself to be indolent, I was carried down the stream, I might if I pleased swim up against the current.

SATURDAY 20 FEBRUARY. I dined at Lord Dundonald's. There had been a coldness between that family and me, and I had not seen them of a long time. All was well again, and old ideas of Major Cochrane, my dear mother, &c., &c., &c. revived.[4]

SUNDAY 21 FEBRUARY. In all forenoon. I had dreamt of Raybould under sentence of death. I was gloomy. Afternoon, church. Tea home, then visited Raybould, that my gloomy imagination might be cured by seeing the reality. I was shown up to him by Archibald, the soldier who was to be tried for murder.[5] The clanking of the iron-room door was terrible. I found him very composed. I sat by him an hour and a half by the light of a dim farthing candle. He spoke very properly on religion. I read him the 4 Chapter of the 1 Epistle of John and lectured upon it. On verse 18 I discoursed on *fear* very appositely,[6] by an illustration taken from Robert Hay, the soldier who was hanged last year. "There, John," said I, "did he lie quite sunk, quite desperate, and neither would eat nor drink, and all for *fear*, just terror for dying. But the comfortable doctrine of Christianity prevents this." I was quite firm, and I was astonished to compare myself now with myself when a boy, remarkably timorous. Raybould seemed wonderfully easy. I therefore talked quite freely to him. "But, John, have you no fear for the immediate pain of dying?" "No," said he, "I have had none as yet. I know not how it may be at the very moment. But I do

[4] Thomas Cochrane, eighth Earl of Dundonald, was Boswell's maternal granduncle. He had been known as Major Cochrane before his accession to the title. The "coldness" may have been occasioned by the Douglas cause, Lord Dundonald being a violent partisan of the Hamilton interest.

[5] James Archibald, accused of murdering a fellow labourer, was found not guilty because he had used no weapons but his fists.

[6] "There is no fear in love, but perfect love casteth out fear."

AN
ACCOUNT
OF
CORSICA,
THE JOURNAL OF A TOUR
TO THAT ISLAND;
AND MEMOIRS OF
PASCAL PAOLI.

BY JAMES BOSWELL, Esq;

ILLUSTRATED with a New and Accurate MAP of CORSICA.

Non enim propter gloriam, divitias aut honores pugnamus, sed propter liber-
tatem solummodo, quam nemo bonus nisi simul cum vita amittit.
Lit. Comit. et Baron. Scotiae ad Pap. A. D. 1320.

GLASGOW,
PRINTED BY ROBERT AND ANDREW FOULIS FOR
EDWARD AND CHARLES DILLY IN THE POULTRY, LONDON:
M DCC LXVIII.

Title-page of the first edition of Boswell's *Account of
Corsica*, published in February 1768

think I shall be quite composed." I looked steadfastly at him during this and saw he was speaking truly. One certain sign of his being much at ease was the readiness with which his attention was diverted to any other subject than his own melancholy situation; for, when a man is much distressed, he is still fixed in brooding over his calamity. But Raybould talked of his wife's journey down in all its particulars, just as if he had been an indifferent, ordinary man.

He told me when he came first to Scotland he did not know the difference between an agent and an advocate.[7] I saw him beginning to smile at his own ignorance. I considered how amazing it would be if a man under sentence of death should really laugh, and, with the nicest care of a diligent student of human nature, I as decently as possible first smiled as he did, and gradually cherished the risible exertion, till he and I together fairly laughed. How strange! He very calmly examined whether a man dying of sickness or one in his situation was worst. He said one in his situation. I argued that one dying of sickness was worst, because he is weakened and unable to support the fear of death, whereas one in his situation was quite well but for the prospect before him. Raybould, however, maintained his proposition, because, he said, the man weakened by sickness was brought to a state of indifference. I bid him farewell. It was truly a curious scene. I went and sat a while at the worthy Doctor's.

WEDNESDAY 24 FEBRUARY. I went to see Raybould's execution. I was invited up to the window of one ———, a merchant by ———, who knew me. I tried to be quite firm and philosophical, and imagined Raybould in some future period telling what he felt at his execution. The most dreadful event seems light when past, and I made it past by imagination. I felt very little; but when he stood long on the ladder I grew impatient, and was beginning to have uneasy sensations. I came home. Mr. William Wilson, S., Mr. Walter Scott,[8] &c. dined. At night I was with Lady Crawford at *The Beggar's Opera*, which quite re-

[7] An advocate is a counsellor-at-law or barrister, who does the actual pleading in court. An agent or "writer" (the English equivalent is "solicitor") is a member of the legal profession who advises clients and manages cases, but does not present them in court. The position of agent was less distinguished socially, but was likely to be more remunerative. Boswell was an advocate, John Johnston an agent. A "Writer to the Signet" belongs to a special, superior class of agents.

[8] Sir Walter Scott's father, a Writer to the Signet.

lieved any gloom. The songs revived London ideas, and my old intrigues with actresses who used to play in this opera.[9] I was happy in being free of Miss Blair. The farce was *The Vintner Tricked*. It was curious that after seeing a real hanging I should meet with two mock ones on the stage. I went with Houston Stewart and renewed our old acquaintance at Caddie[1] Miller's with oysters and claret. We sat till two, very agreeably. When I came home I was a little dreary, but it went off and I slept well.

THURSDAY 25 FEBRUARY. My father and I dined at the Marquess of Lothian's.

SATURDAY 27 FEBRUARY. Sir Alexander Dick carried me out in his coach to Prestonfield. No other person was there. We were quite happy.

[Boswell to Horace Walpole][2]

Edinburgh, 26 February 1768

SIR: — I beg your acceptance of a copy of my *Account of Corsica*, to which you have a better claim than you perhaps imagine, as I dare say you have forgotten what you said to me at Paris, when I had the honour of giving you a few anecdotes of what I had just come from seeing among the brave Islanders. In short, Sir, your telling me that I ought to publish something in order to show the Corsicans in a proper light was my first incitement to undertake the work which has now made its appearance.[3]

If it gives any pleasure to Mr. Horace Walpole I shall be particularly happy. I shall think that I have been able to make him some small return for the pleasure which his elegant writings have afforded me. I have the honour to be, Sir, your most obedient, humble servant,

JAMES BOSWELL.

[9] One of these actresses was Mrs. Love, wife of James Love, once manager of the Edinburgh theatre, and an early friend of Boswell's.

[1] A caddie was a street messenger, *valet de place*, and odd-job man in general.

[2] Printed in *Letters of James Boswell*, i. 146–147 and in *Supplement to the Letters of Horace Walpole*, ed. Paget Toynbee, 1918, ii. 138–139. The original is in the collection of Mr. and Mrs. Donald F. Hyde.

[3] For this visit, see *Boswell on the Grand Tour: Italy, Corsica, and France*, 22 January 1766. Though Boswell did not know it, Walpole had disliked him at sight.

[Received ?9 March, Temple to Boswell]

Mamhead, 1 March 1768

DEAR BOSWELL, — If I am at all sorry you have broke with Miss Blair, it is only lest it should give your father pain and lest he should think it owing to your own imprudence; otherwise I could almost congratulate you upon it, as I cannot help suspecting the mother of interested views and the daughter of great insensibility, and even want of sincerity and candour. Miss Blair's conduct, till you declared yourself passionately her admirer, was prudent and blameless, but since that time I should think that neither her reserve nor want of feeling can be at all justified. "The woman that wants candour where she is addressed by a man of merit wants a very essential virtue; and she who can delight in the anxiety of a worthy mind is little to be pitied when she feels the sharpest stings of anxiety in her own," so says Lady Betty in the new comedy.[4] If she even loves you then (which is almost impossible) she is justly punished; if she does not, you must own you are happily off.

So it is as we suspected with regard to the Nabob. I trust he has not taken the advantage of your candour and openness. I hope you do not forget that the Princess did not give him an absolute refusal. Take care you are not duped. Yet perhaps all this time I am accusing Miss Blair very rashly and unjustly; perhaps she has heard of your unfortunate connection with Mrs. ——; and if so, who then will be to blame? And pray do not take any merit to yourself in bearing this disappointment so calmly; perhaps some of it may be placed to that vulgar creature's account; and if not, I am sure you never loved Miss Blair. Pray tell me how the little infant does and where you have placed it.

So you are going to town — to publish your book, I fancy. How have you swelled it into a six-shilling volume? Though so far on the way, I will not formally invite you to proceed to Devonshire. My parsonage is in a wretched condition, and I cannot have a spare room till autumn. This, my dear Boswell, gives me a good deal of un-

[4] Hugh Kelly's *False Delicacy*, act 2, scene 2. Garrick had produced it at Drury Lane about six weeks before in competition with Goldsmith's *Good-Natured Man.*

easiness. However, if you do come, I'll endeavor to get a bed for you at Lord Lisburne's. I know you will think I write unkindly here, but you cannot imagine what a vile house I live in, and I own I am weak enough to be almost ashamed to receive you in it. However, take your own way, and be assured that I can be no place where I would not rather see you than any man I know. Adieu, and write to me when you get to town.

W.J.T.

P.S.[5] I have just heard to my great concern that my unworthy brother has completed the measure of his follies by eloping to Edinburgh with a woman of very low condition and not worth a guinea.

Claxton gives me a very good account today of your *Corsica;* he commends it much. Pray do not forget to call upon him. As I expect a copy, *from the author*, directed to the Reverend Mr. Temple of Mamhead, near Chudleigh, Devon, to be left at the London Inn, Exeter, I shall not think of buying Boswell's book. Is it not a shame I should have occasion to mention this? But perhaps you have now bound yourself by the same promise you did with regard to your *Letters*. Such promises are very convenient.

WEDNESDAY 16 MARCH.[6] It is very odd that it is hardly possible to set out upon a journey without being in confusion. I was so not a little this morning. My worthy friend Johnston came and stayed by me while I packed my trunk, the sign of a real friend. He who can stand by a man while he packs his trunk would attend him to the place of execution were he going to be hanged; for really one packing his trunk and one going to be hanged are pretty much the same company to a friend. My travelling companion was Mr. Robertson near Alloway, one of the contractors for paving the streets of London, but who was going thither for the first time. Mr. John Small, one of the macers[7] of the Court of Session, was to ride by us all the way. He could not get a horse this morning, so we took him into the chaise to Haddington, where we had a beefsteak, having set out at two o'clock. We seemed hearty and easy. Only I, whose combustible, or rather inflammable, soul is always taking fire, was uneasy at hav-

[5] A postscript preceding this one has been omitted.

[6] To symbolize the importance of his jaunt to London, Boswell started a new Journal, the first to be kept in a bound notebook.

[7] A petty official who executes indictments and keeps order in the court.

ing left *Mary*, a pretty, lively little girl whom accident had thrown in my way a few days before. She was one of those females who either from wickedness or misfortune are the slaves of profligate men. She was very young, and I resolved to try if there was virtue in her; so I left her as many guineas as she said she could live upon till my return. I got two of my friends to promise to go to her and offer her a high bribe to break her engagement to me, and to write me what she did. I find I am still somewhat of a Don Quixote, for now am I in love with perhaps an abandoned, worthless being; but we shall see. We went to Dunbar at night, where we drank the finest small beer I ever tasted in my life, and had a good supper and warm punch.

THURSDAY 17 MARCH. We set out about half an hour after four and went two stages to Berwick to breakfast. Captain Webster came and saw me.[8] The elections were very dead here. The landlord offered any of us a premium to set up as candidate and make a stir. We were obliged to take four horses to Belford, but we went all in the chaise. By the way we came to a place called Longbridgend, where there is an arm of the sea and a river meeting which crosses the road on the sands, which we took as easier than the turnpike road. The sea was out, so we had to wait an hour. We played at drawing straws and at odds and evens for halfpence. We did not dine, but came to Alnwick at night to the house of Turnbull, the family of Northumberland's old piper, who gave us many tunes with amazing dexterity. My attention had still been fixed on Mary. It was a moment diverted by a glance from a girl standing at a door in Alnwick. We supped heartily and drank warm punch.

FRIDAY 18 MARCH. We set off very early. Small galloped on first and had breakfast ready for us at Morpeth. He had travelled the road a hundred times as Lord Cathcart's master household.[9] So he bullied waiters, postilions, and ostlers, and carried us on like smoke. We got to Newcastle about noon. I sent for my brother, the Lieutenant,[1] and he carried me to dine where he was boarded, at Dr. Wilson's.

[8] Captain (later Lt.-Colonel) James Webster, Dr. Alexander Webster's second son, was full of vivacity and lively humour according to David Boswell. He served with distinction in the American Revolution and died of wounds received at the battle of Guilford Court House.

[9] The Scottish equivalent of a steward in a nobleman's household.

[1] Lt. John Boswell, Lord Auchinleck's second son, suffered from intermittent attacks of insanity, possibly initiated by a fall on a flight of stairs in 1762.

The Doctor was not at home. But his lady, a fine, pretty, amiable little woman, entertained us. I had on my journey an old French black suit, but I here put on my green and gold and made a good figure. After dinner the Doctor came in, a worthy, sensible man. He showed me a little essay he had written on the Douglas cause. It was well. But I had already seen so much upon it in a more masterly style that it did not strike me greatly. My brother and I went and drank tea with old Mr. Aitken, the dissenting clergyman who was my father's governor, and there much plain, old-fashioned, cordial conversation passed. I then went to my inn and sent for Mr. Spearman, the attorney. He was a young, smart, talking fellow. He and Dr. Wilson and my brother supped with me. I was pleased to see the kind of people in the north of England. But hasted south.

SATURDAY 19 MARCH. Small acquitted himself so nobly that Mr. Robertson and I constituted him Lord President, and we were the Court of Session. He was very droll. "Come, my lords, we have done a great deal of business. Tomorrow your lordships have a church cause." (That was to see the Minster at York.) "We shall make a good session of it." We got to York at night and put up at Bluitt's Inn. We were dusty, bustling fellows, and no sooner was our baggage taken off than we posted to the theatre. We went into the back seat of one of the boxes, and indeed there was a pretty company. I loved to see so many genteel people in their own county town, in place of crowding to London. The play was *False Delicacy*, and the farce, *A Peep behind the Curtain*. Wilkinson, the mimic, played, and several of the performers did very well. We returned to our inn and had an excellent supper, the President encouraging the court to eat heartily. I never saw a better inn. The waiters had all one livery: brown coats and scarlet vests. We had hitherto been raised very early, but we now resolved to take sufficient repose for a night. Upon my word, eating, drinking, and sleeping are matters of great moment.

SUNDAY 20 MARCH. After a long sleep and a copious breakfast, we went and saw the cathedral. It is a prodigiously noble Gothic edifice. Small and Robertson stayed all the time of service. But I slipped away to a coffee-house where I fell into conversation with a Sir George (I believe, Armytage) about Corsica. He talked very warmly for them and seemed to know a good deal about them. I began to think he must have learnt his knowledge of me. So I asked him if the Corsicans had any seaports. "Oh, yes, Sir," said he, "very good ones. Why, Boswell's *Account of Corsica* tells you all that." "Sir?" said I, "what is that?" "Why, Sir," said he, " a book just now published." "By an officer in that service, Sir?" said I. "No," said he. "I have not the pleasure of being acquainted with the gentleman, but Mr. Boswell is a gentleman who was abroad and who thought he would pay a visit to Corsica, and accordingly went thither and had many conversations with Paoli" (Pioli he pronounced it), "and he has given its history and a full account of everything about the island, and has shown that Britain should make an alliance with Corsica." "But, Sir," said I, "can we believe what he says?" "Yes, Sir," said Sir George, "the book is authentic and very accurate." I was highly pleased.

About twelve we set out, having first seen the assembly room, which is really very noble, with columns all round it, and a spacious passage with lifters behind each box for gentlemen to get in, and then let them down and sit behind the ladies. I call the seats between each column, boxes. I lost Mary in the crowd at York, but I found her again upon the road. How strange is this! the author of the *Account of Corsica* the sport of a frivolous passion. Shall my mind ever be all solid and rational? Yes. A room which is hung with the slightest chintz and gaudiest paper may by and by be hung with substantial velvet or even thick arras hangings with scripture stories wrought upon them. My walls are good, so they will bear any sort of hangings. Often have they been substantially hung. But as yet I have changed my furniture as whim suggested. Small insisted we should dine at Ferrybridge, at the inn of his old acquaintance, Landlord Lowe. We did so, and were very jolly. Lowe had travelled in Italy with the Marquess of Rockingham, but had not weakened a bit his honest old English bluffness. This was the only dinner our President allowed us upon the journey. He was our purser and studied economy as well as dispatch. Lowe was very desirous to see my *Corsica*. Many a curious reader I have.

We went at night to the inn on Barnby Moor. We were now jumbled into old acquaintance. I felt myself quite strong, and exulted when I compared my present mind with my mind some years ago. Formerly my mind was quite a lodging-house for all ideas who chose to put up there, so that it was at the mercy of accident, for I had no

fixed mind of my own. Now my mind is a house where, though the
street rooms and the upper floors are open to strangers, yet there is
always a settled family in the back parlour and sleeping-closet behind
it; and this family can judge of the ideas which come to lodge. This
family! this landlord, let me say, or this landlady, as the mind and the
soul are both she. I shall confuse myself with metaphor. Let me then
have done with it. Only this more. The ideas — my lodgers — are of
all sorts. Some, gentlemen of the law, who pay me a great deal more
than others. Divines of all sorts have been with me, and have ever[2]
disturbed me. When I first took up house, Presbyterian ministers
used to make me melancholy with dreary tones. Methodists next
shook my passions. Romish clergy filled me with solemn ideas, and,
although their statues and many movable ornaments are gone, yet
they drew some pictures upon my walls with such deep strokes that
they still remain. They are, indeed, only agreeable ones. I had Deists
for a very short while. But they, being sceptics, were perpetually
alarming me with thoughts that my walls were made of clay and
could not last, so I was glad to get rid of them. I am forced to own that
my rooms have been occupied by women of the town, and by some
ladies of abandoned manners. But I am resolved that by degrees there
shall be only decent people and innocent, gay lodgers.

MONDAY 21 MARCH. We started betimes. We breakfasted at
———.[3] Small, as President, said, "Come, your lordships have the petition of the landlord praying to put you into a new-washed room. Refuse." He was highly comical, and Robertson was an excellent hand
to laugh at his jokes. He had gotten his hair oiled. He said it was to
keep the dust out of it. Robertson laughed for near half an hour at this.
I was now become quite composed, and never spoke for speaking's
sake, or was uneasy because I was silent. The truth is I am now conscious of having attained to a superior character, and so rest satisfied.
Robertson had read my *Corsica* and could tell a good deal about it.
He sung pretty well, and in the chaise when he thought I was not
minding him, he hummed an amazing number of tunes. This morn-

[2] Perhaps "even."
[3] At Newark, Grantham, or Colesworth, depending on whether they drove two,
three, or four stages. See above, 17 March 1768, and below, 31 August 1769 and
1 September 1769. (Stilton was the fourth stage beyond Grantham.)

ing his music took an exceedingly droll turn. He sung "Blest as th' immortal gods is he" to the tune of *Black Joke*.[4] Much did I inwardly laugh. N.B. It will do nobly for Brigadier Bluster in my comedy.[5] We came at night to Biggleswade, having travelled this day 105 miles. We had an admirable supper. After my former sufferings from bad health and low spirits, I exulted in my present vigour and cheerfulness.

TUESDAY 22 MARCH. Mary began to fade.[6] I thought of marriage and was determined to have a good match, as I was become so agreeable and so happy a man. Miss Bosville my Yorkshire beauty, Mademoiselle de Zuylen my Utrecht *bel esprit* and friend,[7] were both before me. Yet still I had no determined purpose. About two we arrived at London and put up at the Star and Garter in Bond Street.[8] The streets and squares of the metropolis with all the hurry and variety struck me to a certain degree, but by no means as they had once done, and I contentedly felt myself an Edinburgh advocate. Our Lord President, who had made us live with economy upon the road, finding that of twenty-nine guineas set apart for our expenses there remained two, would needs conclude the session with a jovial repast. Accordingly, we had a cod with oyster and shrimp sauce, some other dishes, and three bottles of the best claret I ever drank. Prentice and Rowden, the two landlords, were called in to take a glass, and in short we were great men. Upon the whole, it was as good a journey

[4] "Blest as th' immortal gods is he" is Ambrose Philips's version of an ode by Sappho. *The Coal-black Joke* is an English air associated with very indecent words.

[5] So far as is known, this comedy was never written.

[6] On 10 June, Boswell wrote to John Johnston that he was distressed to find that there was "not a spark of virtue" in Mary.

[7] Boswell had written to Zélide as recently as 26 February to ask, "Whether do you think that you and I shall live happier: as distant correspondents, or as partners for life?" (*Boswell in Holland*, Correspondence with Belle de Zuylen).

[8] Not unheralded. On 1 March *The London Chronicle* printed the following notices: "Messrs. Herries and Co., merchants in this city, have received bills of loading from Leghorn of presents from General Paoli to Mr. Boswell." "James Boswell, Esquire, is expected in town." And under date of 24 March: "Yesterday James Boswell, Esquire, arrived from Scotland at his apartments in Half Moon Street, Piccadilly." Boswell's marked file of the *Chronicle* shows that he sent in these notices himself.

as ever was made; and, as in all other scenes, though words do but imperfectly preserve the ideas, yet such notes as I write are sufficient to make the impressions revive, with many associated ones. What should there be in this house but a club every Tuesday called the Roman Club, consisting of gentlemen who were at Rome the same year I was; and who should be upstairs alone but my friend Consul Dick. I sent to him, and he came down immediately. We embraced and in a few words renewed our covenant of cordiality. I then got into a hackney-coach and drove to Mr. Russel's, upholsterer, Half Moon Street, Piccadilly, where I had admirable lodgings. After unpacking my trunk, I sallied forth like a roaring lion after girls, blending philosophy and raking. I had a neat little lass *in armour*, at a tavern in the Strand. I then went to the Consul's and supped, and was quite hearty.

WEDNESDAY 23 MARCH. The Consul had provided me not only good lodgings, but a good servant. His name was Anthony Mudford, a Somersetshire lad who had served his time to a hairdresser. I gave him a guinea a week for everything. I called on Lord Mountstuart. But he was out of town. I waited on the Duke of Queensberry for ten minutes, as he had to dress to go to Court. He received me well, and assured me that Mr. Douglas would run no risk.[9]

I had this morning been at Tyburn seeing the execution of Mr. Gibson, the attorney, for forgery, and of Benjamin Payne for highway robbery. It is a curious turn, but I never can resist seeing executions. The Abbé du Bos ingeniously shows that we have all a strong desire of having our passions moved, and the interesting scene of a man with death before his eyes cannot but move us greatly. One of weak nerves is overpowered by such spectacles. But by thinking and accustoming myself to them, I can see them quite firmly, though I feel compassion. I was on a scaffold close by. Payne was a poor young man of nineteen. He was pale as death, and half a corpse before the rope was put round his neck. Mr. Gibson came in a coach with some of his friends, and I declare I cannot conceive a more perfect calmness and manly resolution than his behaviour. He was dressed in a full suit of black, wore his own hair cut round and a hat, was a man about fifty, and as he

[9] Charles Douglas, third Duke of Queensberry, famous as Gay's patron, was one of Archibald Douglas's guardians.

drove along it was impossible to perceive the least sign of dejection or gloom about him. He was helped up on the cart. The rope was put round his neck, and he stood with the mos. perfect composure, eat a sweet orange, and seemed rationally devout during prayers by Mr. Moore, the ordinary[1] of Newgate, who is really a good man and most earnest in the duties of his sad office, which I think a very important one. Stephen Roe, the last ordinary, was but a rough-spun blade. Never did I see death without some horror but in the case of Mr. Gibson. It seemed a very easy matter. I always use to compare the conduct of malefactors with what I suppose my conduct might be. I believe I confounded the people about me by my many reflections. I affected being shocked that punishment might have an effect on their minds, though it had none upon my own. I never saw a man hanged but I thought I could behave better than he did, except Mr. Gibson, who, I confess, exceeded all that I could ever hope to show of easy and steady resolution.[2]

I run about all the forenoon, and got to Mr. Dilly's about three. It was comfortable to find myself in the shop where my book was published, and, from the great connection between author and bookseller, I was very kindly received. Mr. Dilly made me acquainted with his brother, Mr. Charles, a good, tall, smartish, civil, bowing young man, quite of the city form, and to his sister, Miss Dilly, a neat, little, well-behaved young lady, smart too — not very pretty, but with a good air and a handsome headdress she appeared very well. Dinner was over, but I had some slices of good roast mutton and potatoes and excellent beer. Then we drank a glass of port and were like blood relations. A Mr. Clayton, a gentleman of £1500 a year and a good house about ten miles from London, was there. He lives at Messrs. Dillys' when he comes to town, and they go and visit him. Mr. Mayo, a dissenting clergyman, came in. I observed I was introduced with great ceremony, like one whose character was high.

[1] That is, the permanent chaplain.

[2] Boswell was sufficiently impressed by this execution to work up this portion of the Journal as a letter to *The Public Advertiser*, which he incorporated in a *Hypochondriack* essay (No. 68) fifteen years later. There he attempts to explain his lifelong interest in executions by saying that we have a natural anxiety to see how others face death, but he admits that a desire to see others suffer plays some part.

We went to Guildhall to see the poll for members. It was really grand. Harley (Lord Mayor), Beckford, Trecothick, Sir Richard Glyn, Mr. Deputy Paterson, and Mr. Wilkes[3] all stood upon the hustings, that is to say, a place raised by some steps at one end of the room. They had true London countenances. I cannot describe them. It was curious for me to look at Wilkes here and recollect my scenes with him at Rome, Naples, and Paris. The confusion and the noise of the mob roaring "Wilkes and Liberty" were prodigious. I met here Mr. Herries and Sir William Forbes,[4] and, after having had enough of the confusion, I went to them and drank a glass of claret. They showed me my Corsican gun and pistols. But the dog had broken loose and was running about town.[5] Thomas, Mr. Herries's servant, and Will, the butcher's man, and I went and patrolled an hour in the Borough,[6] but did not see him. I returned by Dilly's and drank tea. Doctors Saunders and Smith were there. I found it to be a very hospitable house. In the Strand I inquired at the girls for a Miss Simson whom I had known formerly. One of them very obligingly went with me to a Miss Simson's. But she was not the same. However, they both seemed good-natured, and I sat and drank some port with them, and then tossed up which I should make my sultana. Luckily the lot fell on my obliging conductress. I however was *armed*.

THURSDAY 24 MARCH. I patrolled the great metropolis the whole morning. I dined at the worthy Consul's; a lady and a gentleman were there. We were easy enough. At night I still patrolled, I cannot tell where. But about ten I came to Sir John Pringle's. He re-

[3] Whom Boswell had not seen since their parting in Paris in 1766. Still under sentence of outlawry, Wilkes had returned to England and had presented himself as candidate for London in the general elections. This was the last day of the poll. Though vociferously supported by the mob (many of whom were not entitled to vote), he finished last among the seven candidates for the four places. Wilkes thereupon declared himself a candidate for Middlesex, and on 28 March was chosen by a heavy majority (see p. 156 and p. 286 *n*.8).

[4] At that time a partner in the Edinburgh banking house where David Boswell had been employed. Forbes later became one of Boswell's closest friends and was named along with Temple and Edmond Malone as one of his literary executors.

[5] Paoli had presented Boswell with one dog, Jachone, while in Corsica, but Jachone had run away in France on the trip home. This was another dog sent by Paoli.

[6] Of Southwark.

ceived me with his usual grave, steady kindness. General Clerk was with him. The conversation turned on the wars of Venus. The General assured me that oil was an infallible shield. Sir John nodded assent; I resolved to try it fairly. After the General went away I talked to Sir John of Mademoiselle de Zuylen. I had just received a letter from Mr. Brown at Utrecht containing a very sensible proposal from her, that if I had any serious thoughts of her I should come to see her, and then we might judge whether we could live happily together or not. Sir John had opposed any such scheme. But I found him now better disposed to it, upon which I wrote to my father and begged permission to go to Utrecht.

FRIDAY 25 MARCH. I dined at my good kinsman Godfrey Bosville, Esquire's. Nobody was there, but just the family that I left. He received me with true kindness. Miss Bosville was now engaged to Sir Alexander Macdonald.[7] Godfrey had drawn up a very full account of his family. It entertained me a good deal and put some comfortable ideas in my mind.[8] I then went to Covent Garden and in one of the courts called for a young lady whom I had seen when formerly in London. I did not find her, but I found Kitty Brookes, as pretty a lively lass as youth need see. The oil was called and I played my part well. I never saw a girl more expert at it. I gave her only four shillings, to try her generosity. She never made the least sign of discontent, but was quite gay and obliging. Just as I was going away I turned back and again we loved. Then was the time for her to ask something. Yet she made not the smallest advance. I fell on my knees and kissed her hand: "My dear Kitty, you are a virtuous girl. I could marry you this moment."

I then came home, and Maconochie[9] and I went to Percy Coffee-

---

[7] Of Sleat, in the Hebrides. So, despite Lord Eglinton's opinion of its undesirability (p. 117), Miss Bosville did marry a Scotsman, and a Highlander at that. Sir Alexander and his wife entertained Boswell and Johnson on their tour of the Hebrides in 1773 in so miserly a fashion that Boswell complained of their lack of hospitality in his *Tour to the Hebrides*, 1785. Sir Alexander became very angry and a duel was barely avoided.

[8] At this point a leaf of the Journal has been removed, but the passage can be recovered from a typescript made at a time when this portion of the text was intact. This page of typescript is now printed for the first time.

[9] Alexander Maconochie, a "writer," was one of Douglas's chief legal agents.

house, Rathbone Place, to meet Mr. Guthrie, the historian and Critical
Reviewer, who had fought the battle of Douglas in the *Review*, and
had praised my *Account of Corsica*.[1] He was an old gentleman about
sixty, had on a white coat and a crimson satin waistcoat with broad
gold lace, and a bag-wig. We had port and madeira and a hearty supper. He had a great deal of the London author. He praised my book
much, and drank a bumper to Pascal Paoli, *omni titulo major*.[2] He
told me he and my father had been at the same class in the College,
and he talked of "little Robin Hunter." He said he did not wonder that
the Douglas cause was lost in Scotland, as it had against it all the interest of the families of Hamilton, Argyll, Hyndford, and the Dal-
rymples. As he had observed in the *Review* that it was a loss to us in
Scotland to have no jury in civil causes, I gave him Lord Hailes's argument that the lords of session made a jury, only a wiser and more en-
lightened jury than a number of tradesmen.[3] He answered this argument by observing that in England the jury is always changed for
every cause; that the jurymen are chosen by a sort of chance, as the
judges just take a pin and prick at random on the back of the paper
whereon their names are written, and wherever the holes happen to
be made these jurymen are chosen. "Whereas," said he, "the lords of
session form a *perpetual* jury, which is a very dangerous one."

He praised my *Account of Corsica* much, though he found some
faults with it. "You will see my opinion of it," said he. It was curious
to sit with the very person whom in a little I should look upon as an
awful reviewer. He talked very well (I mean very justly) of Wilkes.
Said that he wrote with vivacity, but that there was no political knowledge, no manliness, in his papers. "Ah," said he, "when Lord Bolingbroke and I wrote together, when the *Craftsman* came out, when *Old
England* by Jeffrey Broadbottom came out."[4] We took a very cheerful

[1] In conversation apparently, for his review had not yet been published in *The
Critical Review*. See later in this entry.

[2] "Greater than any title," that is, so great a man that no one used a title with
his name. Boswell is thinking of a passage in *Corsica* (3d ed., 1769, p. 154 *n.*) in
which he says that, at Lord Hailes's suggestion, he has avoided calling Paoli
"Signor" or "General." "You do not say King Alexander, but Alexander of
Macedon."

[3] Here the text is resumed in the manuscript.

[4] Guthrie himself was the principal writer of *Old England, or, The Constitu-*

glass of claret and madeira. He took me by the hand and said my con-versation exceeded my writing. "Well," said he, "you are a genius. A thousand people might have thought of making themselves famous before one would have thought of Corsica." He asked Maconochie and me to dine with him on the Sunday sennight. When the old man praised my book, I paid him a very genteel compliment. "Sir," said I, "amidst such historic oaks as yours, it is well if a little praise can be given to such a shrub as mine, growing on the rocky surface of Cor-sica." I gave him some curious anecdotes of Scotch antiquities which I had learnt from my father. Upon the whole, the evening went well off. We accompanied him home in our hackney-coach as far as Port-land Chapel, where he lived. Mr. Maconochie then set me down.

SATURDAY 26 MARCH. On my coming to London I had called on Mr. Samuel Johnson, but found he was gone to Oxford and was living at New Inn Hall. I was very anxious to see again my revered friend. I had written him many letters and had received none from him of a long time. I had published my *Account of Corsica*, in which I had spoken very highly of him, yet he had taken no notice of it. I had heard he was displeased at my having put into my book a part of one of his letters to me. In short, I was quite in the dark concerning him. But, be it as it would, I was determined to find him out, and if possible be well with him as usual. I therefore set out early this morning in the Oxford fly. Anthony had an outside place. My travelling companions were an old, red-faced, fat gentlewoman who lived in the borough of Southwark, and whose husband dealt in a wholesale trade of brandy and wine. Dr. Cockayne, a lecturer at one of the churches, lodged in her house, having his own maid-servant and a boy. But she would not board the Doctor. "No, no. I knows him too well. Why, he's the great-est epicure, perpetually minding his belly. I tells him, 'Why, Doctor, you do nothing else from morning to night. You sure have a false pocket.' And so I roasts him. But he's a good-natured creature, and would have everyone to share with him. He gets up my daughter: 'Come now, Miss, we'll have some tea and something very nice with it.' " Besides this good woman, there was a clergyman, a stiff divine, a

---

tional Journal, which was published under the pseudonym of Jeffrey Broad-bottom.

fellow of a college in Oxford. He was very wise and laughed at the old lady. The fourth in the coach was a little tailor who has often tripped over to France and Flanders, and who therefore had a right to talk as a travelled man. All the road was roaring with "Wilkes and Liberty," which, with "No. 45,"[5] was chalked on every coach and chaise. We breakfasted at Slough. We became very merry. We dined at Henley, and there we were as hearty as people could be. We had a good drive to Oxford, with always t'other joke on Dr. Cockayne. We stopped at the gate of Magdalen College, of which our clergyman was a fellow. He jumped out of the coach, and in a moment we saw what a great man he was; for he went into the barber's and got the key of his chambers, and two or three people followed him with his trunk, teathings, and I know not what all. The lady left us here too. The tailor and I put up at the Angel, where the coach inns; but we parted there.

I immediately had some coffee and then got a guide to show me New Inn Hall. Mr. Johnson lived in the house of Mr. Chambers, the head of that hall and Vinerian Professor at Oxford.[6] I supposed the professor would be very formal, and I apprehended but an awkward reception. However, I rung and was shown into the parlour. In a little, down came Mr. Chambers, a lively, easy, agreeable Newcastle man. I had sent up my name, "Mr. Boswell." After receiving me very politely, "Sir," said he, "you are Mr. Boswell of Auchinleck?" "Yes, Sir." "Mr. Johnson wrote to you yesterday. He dined abroad, but I expect him in every minute." "Oho!" thought I, "this is excellent." I was quite relieved. Mr. Chambers gave me tea, and by and by arrived the great man. He took me all in his arms and kissed me on both sides of the head, and was as cordial as ever I saw him. I told him all my perplexity on his account, and how I had come determined to fight him, or to do anything he pleased. "What," said he, "did you come

[5] The famous number of *The North Briton* in which Wilkes in 1763 had attacked the King and his ministers, and which had played a major part in his subsequent career. It was identified with popular as opposed to royal or aristocratic rule.

[6] A law professorship. In 1774 at about the age of thirty-seven, Robert (later Sir Robert) Chambers married Fanny Wilton, a fifteen-year old beauty, and went out to Bengal to serve on its supreme court. He subsequently became Chief Justice of this court and President of the Asiatic Society. Though Boswell does not seem to have known it, Johnson was visiting Chambers to help him write the lectures he was required to deliver.

here on purpose?" "Yes, indeed," said I. This gave him high satisfaction. I told him how I was settled as a lawyer and how I had made two hundred pounds by the law this year. He grumbled and laughed and was wonderfully pleased. "What, Bozzy? Two hundred pounds! A great deal."

I had longed much to see him as my great preceptor, to state to him some difficulties as a moralist with regard to the profession of the law, as it appeared to me that in some respects it hurt the principles of honesty; and I asked him if it did not. "Why, no, Sir," said he, "if you act properly. You are not to deceive your clients with false representations of your opinion. You are not to tell lies to a judge." "But," said I, "what do you think of pleading a cause which you know to be bad?" "Sir, you don't know it to be bad till the judge determines it. I have said that you are to state your facts fairly; so that your thinking, or what you call knowing, a cause to be bad must be from reasoning, must be from thinking your arguments weak and inconclusive. But, Sir, that is not enough. An argument which does not convince you yourself may convince the judge before whom you plead it; and if it does convince him, why, then, Sir, you are wrong and he is right. It is his business to judge, and you are not to be confident in your opinion, but to say all you can for your client and then hear the judge's opinion." "But, Sir," said I, "does not the putting on a warmth when you have no warmth, and appearing to be clearly of one opinion when you are in reality of another, does not such dissimulation hurt one's honesty? Is there not some danger that one may put on the same mask in common life, in the intercourse with one's friends?" "Why, no, Sir. Everybody knows you are paid for putting on a warmth for your client, and it is properly no dissimulation. The moment you come from the bar you resume your usual behaviour. Sir, a man will no more carry the artifice of the bar into the common intercourse of society than a man who is paid for tumbling upon his hands will continue tumbling upon his hands when he ought to be walking on his feet." Wonderful force and fancy. At once he satisfied me as to a thing which had often and often perplexed me. It was truly comfortable having him in his own old High-Church Oxford, and I had besides many good ideas of the Vinerian Professor, the head of a hall, &c. These halls were originally additions to colleges where there was not sufficient room. In time some of them became unnecessary as the number of students decreased. There are no students in New Inn Hall. But it is kept up and gives the rank of master to Mr. Chambers.

I told Mr. Johnson a story which I should have recorded before this time. The day before I left London, coming through Bloomsbury Square and being dressed in green and gold, I was actually taken for Wilkes by a Middlesex voter who came up to me. "Sir, I beg pardon, is not your name Wilkes?" "Yes, Sir." "I thought so. I saw you upon the hustings and I thought I knew you again. Sir, I'm your very good friend; I've got you five and twenty votes today." I bowed and grinned and thanked him, and talked of liberty and general warrants and I don't know what all. I told him too, between ourselves, that the King had a very good opinion of me. I ventured to ask him how he could be sure that I was a right man and acted from public spirit. He was a little puzzled. So I helped him out. "As to my private character, it would take a long time to explain it. But, Sir, if I were the devil, I have done good to the people of England, and they ought to support me." "Ay," said he. I am vexed I did not make more of this curious incident. After carrying my voter half-way down Long Acre, I stopped and looked him gravely in the face. "Sir, I must tell you a secret. I'm not Mr. Wilkes, and what's more, I'm a Scotsman." He stared not a little, and said, "Sir, I beg pardon for having given you so much trouble." "No, Sir," said I, "you have been very good company to me." I wonder he did not beat me. I said to Mr. Johnson that I never before knew that I was so ugly a fellow. He was angry at me that I did not borrow money from the voter. Indeed, it would have made a fine scene at Brentford when he demanded payment of the real Wilkes, and called him a rogue for denying the debt.

The conversation of Mr. Johnson, Mr. Chambers, and me then turned on the latest authors. Mr. Johnson would allow no *character* to *False Delicacy*. He praised Goldsmith's *Good-Natured Man*. He said it was the best comedy that has appeared since *The Provoked Husband*. "Sir," said he, "there has not been of late any such character exhibited on the stage as that of Croaker." I told him it was just the Suspirius of his *Rambler*. He said Goldsmith owned he had borrowed it from thence. "Sir," said he, "there is all the difference in the world between characters of nature and characters of manners. And there is the difference between those of Fielding and those of Richardson.

Characters of manners are very entertaining; but they are to be understood by a more superficial observer than characters of nature can
be, where a man must dive into the recesses of human nature. Even
Sir Francis Wronghead is a character of manners, though drawn with
great humour." He then repeated all Sir Francis's story to Manly of
his being with the great man and securing a place.[7] I asked him if
The Suspicious Husband did not furnish a well-drawn character, that
of Ranger. "No, Sir," said he, "Ranger is just a rake, a mere rake, and
a lively young fellow, but no *character*."

I asked him and Mr. Chambers to go and sup at my room. They
made me stay with them that night, and promised to come to me next
night. I brought on the subject of the Douglas cause. Mr. Johnson had
never studied it. He had just heard parts of it. He was of opinion that
positive, or what is called proof that admits of no doubt, should not
be required; but that judges should give the cause according as the
probability should preponderate, allowing, however, to Mr. Douglas
the general presumption of filiation as strong in his favour. He
thought a good deal of force should be allowed to the dying declarations for this reason, because they were voluntary and spontaneous;
for he observed that there is all the difference in the world between
what is said without our being pushed to it, and what is said from
a sort of compulsion. "If I praise a man's book without being asked
my opinion of it, that is honest praise and may be depended on. But
when an author asks me if I like his book and I give him something
like praise, it must not be taken as my real opinion." I thought within
myself I should not ask him about my book. He promised to read
my *Essence of the Douglas Cause.*

He told us he had not been plagued of a long time with authors
desiring his opinion of their works. He said he used once to be sadly
plagued with a man who wrote verses, but who had no other notion
of a verse but that it consisted of ten syllables. "Lay your knife and
your fork across your plate" was to him a verse:

Lay yóur knife ánd your fórk acróss your pláte.

[7] In Sir John Vanbrugh and Colley Cibber's *The Provoked Husband*, Sir Francis
Wronghead is a country squire who spends half his fortune to be elected to
Parliament, and at once brings his family up to London, all of whom hope to
make their fortune overnight. His kinsman, Manly, preserves them from their
folly by his secret intervention.

And, as he wrote a great number of verses, he sometimes by chance made good ones, though he did not know it.

He put me in mind of our journey to Harwich, and we recalled many a circumstance. He also renewed his promise of coming to Scotland and visiting with me some of the Western Isles. He was now to content himself with seeing one or two of the most curious. He said, "Macaulay, who writes the account of St. Kilda,[8] set out with a prejudice against prejudices, and wanted to be a smart modern thinker; and yet he affirms for a truth, that when a ship arrives all the inhabitants are seized with a cold." In this manner did our evening pass. When I got home I went to bed more comfortably than I had done for a good while past. But I was still apprehensive of some venereal mischief, and at any rate had the remains of an old one, though without infection.

SUNDAY 27 MARCH. I sent a card to Dr. Smith, the anatomy professor[9] and physician here, that if it was convenient I would come and breakfast with him. I was made welcome. So I went and found him just as he was in 1763 when poor Sir James Macdonald made me acquainted with him, only he was now become professor and had a very elegant house. Dr. Smith is a Maybole man. He had a sister who had come up two years ago and was our landlady. Various topics of conversation employed us. He is a great foe to Johnson and an admirer of Hume, but can bear my admiration of Mr. Johnson very well. After breakfast we went to Christ Church, where he introduced me to Frank Stewart, Lord Eglinton's nephew, a very pretty young man treading in the steps of Sir James Macdonald.[1]

[8] The Rev. Kenneth Macaulay, great-uncle of Lord Macaulay. ". . . who writes [for "wrote" or "who has written"] the account of St. Kilda . . ." is a Scotticism which Johnson could hardly have used. It escaped Malone and still stands in the *Life*.

[9] Officially, professor of geometry. Maybole, mentioned further on in this entry, is a town in Ayrshire.

[1] Sir James Macdonald, who had died in 1766, had been considered a young man of brilliant promise because he united scholarly attainments and the accomplishments of a man of the world. Frank Stewart was his first cousin, and like him died young. David Boswell admired Stewart extremely. "I never came into the room where he was," he wrote to Boswell (28 April 1767), "but I trembled as if some superior being had been present. I know you wonder that I should

I went to St. Mary's to hear *the sermon before the University of Oxford*, which has often filled me with a grand idea. But this institution is become a matter of mere form, and, although all the preachers in the university must have this office in their turns, they are allowed to employ others to officiate for them, to whom they give three guineas apiece, and it is generally performed by men who have no reputation to lose, and are indifferent how they are received. The show of vice-chancellor, proctors, masters of arts, &c., was well enough, but there were but few students there. A Dr. Blackstone, who had been a physician, preached. He gave us a good, sensible, common sermon.

After sermon, I went back to Mr. Stewart. He and I ordered dinner at the Golden Cross, and then went and walked in the venerable shade. I found he was a great admirer of my book, and was quite a Corsican. He resolved to visit that island, and I promised him a letter to Paoli. We talked of Mr. Johnson. He esteemed him highly for his learning and genius, but in the usual way of many people found fault with his language. He mentioned the ridicule of it, called *Lexiphanes*, written by one Campbell. "Sir," said I, "nothing can be more unfair. Mr. Johnson's language is suitable to his sentiment. He gives large words because he has large ideas. If Campbell clothes little paltry ideas with these big words, to be sure the effect must be ridiculous. The late King of Prussia's tall regiment looked very stately with their large grenadier caps. If Campbell had taken these caps and clapped them on the heads of a parcel of blackguard children in the street it would be highly ridiculous, but does that prove anything against the caps when properly applied?[2] No, Sir, Mr. Johnson has gigantic thoughts, and therefore he must be allowed gigantic words." This was quite in Mr. Johnson's own style. Mr. Stewart talked like a man of reflection and

---

rave so much about this young man, but I must say that I never did see one appear in my eyes to that advantage in conversation that he did the few times I was in company with him."

[2] This is so much like a passage in Longinus, *On the Sublime*, as to point to a conscious or unconscious adaption: "For dressing up a trifling subject in grand and exalted expressions makes the same ridiculous appearance as the enormous mask of a tragedian would do upon the diminutive face of an infant" (trans. William Smith, 2d ed., 1742, p. 71). Boswell read Longinus in the course in Logic taught by John Stevenson at the University of Edinburgh, 1756–1757.

principle. He approved of my sentiment, "Better occasional murders than frequent adulteries,"[3] and expatiated on the destruction of the nobler kinds of happiness, confidence, family affection, &c., which profligacy occasioned. We dined well at the Golden Cross, and had a serious and affecting conversation about Sir James Macdonald. We then adjourned to my inn, and had tea and coffee. I sent for Lord Dundonald's son, James, who was of Balliol College. He came and sat a while with us. Mr. Stewart was desirous to see Mr. Johnson. So I asked him to be of my party at supper, upon his promising to be very quiet and submissive. He left me a while to myself, when I indulged most agreeable thoughts of the good spirits and fortunate circumstances, in many respects, which were now my lot.

About nine Mr. Johnson, Mr. Chambers, and Mr. Stewart assembled. We had a good supper, and madeira and warm port negus. Mr. Johnson expatiated on the advantages of Oxford for learning, as there is there such a progressive emulation. "The tutors are anxious to have their pupils appear well in the college. The colleges are anxious to have their students appear well in the university. There are all opportunities of books and learned men; there are no avocations. There are excellent rules of discipline in every college." I objected that the rules and indeed the whole system is very ill observed. "Why, Sir," said he, "that is nothing against the institution. The members of an university may, for a season, be unmindful of their duty. I am arguing for the excellency of the institution." He was right. Indeed I can conceive nothing nobler in the way of learning and science than Oxford. If they who are there neglect the means, it is their own absurdity; it is their own loss. The means are always there for such as will use them. But the expense is great. No young man can do with less than £100 a year, and, if he takes the rank of a gentleman commoner, it will cost him £200 a year. But this rank is of no real service to his education, excepting that it puts him among young people of better fortune who may be of use to him afterwards.

I spoke of Guthrie. "Sir," said Mr. Johnson, "he has parts. He has no great regular fund of knowledge, but by reading so long and writ-

[3] In *Corsica*, p. 243. This "sentiment" was much ridiculed by the reviewers. Boswell's temporary separation from Mrs. Dodds at the time he wrote this section of the book probably added fervour to his denunciation of adultery.

ing so long, he no doubt has picked up a good deal." The great man still retained his prejudice against Scotland. The night before, he told us he had lately been a long while at Lichfield, but had wearied sadly. "I wonder at that," said I; "it is your native place." "Why," said he, "so is Scotland your native place." This night I talked of our advances in literature. "Sir," said he, "you have learnt a little from us, and you think yourselves very great men." Hume I knew he would abuse. "Sir," said he, "Hume would never have written history had not Voltaire written it before him. He is an echo of Voltaire." "But, Sir," said I, "we have Lord Kames." "You have Lord Kames," said he; "keep him, ha! ha! ha! We don't envy you him. Do you ever see Dr. Robertson?" BOSWELL. "Yes." JOHNSON. "Does the dog ever talk of me?" BOSWELL. "Indeed he does, and loves you." He said the severest thing of Robertson without intending it, for I pushed him to say what he thought of Robertson's *History*.[4] "Sir," said he, "I love Robertson, and I won't talk of his book." He was very hard on poor Dr. Blair, whom he holds wonderfully cheap for having written *A Dissertation on Ossian.* Talking of the future life of brutes, "Sir," said he, "if you allow Blair's soul to be immortal, why not allow a dog to be immortal?" I wanted much to defend the pleasing system of brutes existing in the other world. Mr. Johnson, who does not like to hear any ideas of futurity but what are in the Thirty-nine Articles, was out of humour with me, and watched his time to give me a blow. So when I, with a serious, metaphysical, pensive face, ventured to say, "But really, Sir, when we see a very sensible dog, we know not what to think of him," he turned about, and growling with joy replied, "No, Sir; and when we see a very foolish fellow, we don't know what to think of him." Then up he got, bounced along, and stood by the fire, laughing and exulting over me, while I took it to myself and had only to say, "Well, but you do not know what to think of a very sensible dog." About twelve they left me.

MONDAY 28 MARCH. I breakfasted with Mr. Stewart. Then he and I went to Mr. Chambers's and found him and Mr. Johnson drinking tea. I talked of the scorpion killing itself when encircled with hot coals. Mr. Johnson said that Maupertuis is of opinion that it does not

[4] William Robertson's *History of Scotland*, a very successful book, published in 1759.

kill itself, but dies of the heat, and that its clapping its tail to its head is merely a convulsion from the excessive pain, and it does not sting itself. I told him I had often tried the experiment, that it ran round and round, and finding no outlet retired to the centre, and, like a true Stoic philosopher, gave itself the fatal sting to free itself from its woes. "This will end 'em."[5] I said it was a curious fact, as it showed suicide in an insect. Mr. Johnson would not admit the fact. I said I would write to the great Morgagni, the anatomist, and get him to examine the head of one after the experiment, and to tell whether it was stung or not. Mr. Johnson said the report of Morgagni would convince him. I shall certainly try to get it. Mr. Johnson said that the woodcocks fly over to the northern countries, which is proved because they have been observed at sea. He said swallows certainly sleep all the winter; many of them conglobulate themselves by flying round and round, and then all in a heap throw themselves under water, and lie in the bed of a river. This appeared strange to me. I know not if Mr. Johnson was well founded in it. Our conversation was quite on natural philosophy. Mr. Johnson told us one of his first essays was a Latin poem on the glow-worm.

I then talked of law and of our courts of justice in Scotland, of which I gave them a very good account. I found that having been two years a lawyer in real business had given me great force. I could not be sensible of it, while living always with the same people. But I felt it when I was with Mr. Johnson.

Mr. Stewart went home with me. Riall, an honest Irishman who had studied civil law with me at Glasgow, came and saw me. He was now become a divine. We all three went to dine at Dr. Smith's. He had several more company; among the rest, Dr. Wilmot of Trinity, a pleasant, jovial parson who loves hunting and a glass dearly. He was well acquainted with Mr. Johnson, and said he submitted patiently to be bruised by him in order to enjoy his conversation. Dr. Smith was truly hospitable and civil. I had neglected in the morning to go and see the Bodleian Library, which I had not seen when formerly at Oxford. Dr. Smith got one of the under-keepers to show me it this afternoon, a Mr. Hall of Jesus, a Welshman. It is indeed a grand and venerable sight. I often repeated Mr. Johnson's line: "O'er Bodley's

[5] "This must end 'em," Addison, *Cato*, V. i. 20.

dome his future labours spread."[6] I was shown a few very fine old editions of books, and some rich manuscripts on vellum and illuminated. I must return and stay a month at Oxford some vacation, and enjoy it in calmness.

Mr. Stewart and I were invited to sup with Mr. Chambers. When we went, it was about eight. I had drank tea with Mr. Stewart in an Oxford coffee-house, while he listened to a wonderful variety of anecdotes which I gave him. Said he: "You are an extraordinary man, and have had extraordinary good fortune in meeting with such a singular variety. It has been said that Mr. Johnson is a walking library. You are a walking collection of men." Mr. Chambers was not come in when we came to his house. Mr. Johnson came and entertained us, bowed and said, "Your servant, gentlemen," and was really courteous. The house is a good one, and genteelly furnished. We talked of the Chinese and Russians. Mr. Johnson advised me to read Bell's *Travels.* I asked him if I should read Du Halde's *China.* "Why yes," said he, "as one reads such a book; that is to say, consult it." When Mr. Chambers came we had a good supper. Mr. Johnson was excellent company. He laughed a good deal. I really found him more cheerful and gay. His mixing more in society had dissipated much of that gloom which hung upon his mind when he lived much alone, when he brooded in the Temple.

I forgot to put down two things in former evenings: one, that he showed plainly that a general warrant *must* at times be granted by all governments, but they must do it at their peril; so that all the noise about Wilkes was idle, except as to some irregularities; the other thing was a fine specimen of his contriving always to have the superiority. When Mr. Chambers was getting the better of him in an argument, he said to him as to a boy, "My dear Chambers, take it to you, take it to you, since you will have it so," as if he made a concession to please him, when in reality he did not know how to answer him.

We talked of adultery. Mr. Johnson showed how highly criminal it was, because it broke the peace of families and introduced confusion of progeny. "These constitute the essence of the crime, and therefore a woman who breaks her marriage vows is so much more criminal

[6] *The Vanity of Human Wishes,* l. 139.

than a man. A man, to be sure, is criminal in the sight of God, but he does not do his wife a very material injury if he does not insult her; if, for instance, from mere wantonness of appetite, he steals privately to her chamber-maid. Sir, a wife ought not greatly to resent this. I should not receive home a daughter who had run away from her husband on that account. A wife should study to reclaim her husband by more attention to please him. Sir, a man will not once in a hundred instances leave his wife and go to a harlot, if his wife has not been negligent of pleasing." "Upon my word," said I, "he is grown liberal upon our hand." "But," said Mr. Chambers, "suppose a husband goes a-whoring, and then poxes his wife." "Why, Sir, if he poxes her, it is a bodily injury, and she may resent it as she pleases."

I asked him if it was not hard that one deviation from chastity should so absolutely ruin a woman. JOHNSON. "Why, no, Sir; the great principle which every woman is taught is to keep her legs together. When she has given up that principle, she has given up every notion of female honour and virtue, which are all included in chastity." I argued that virtue might be found even in a common street-walker. He laughed, and as I had told him of my Dutch lady, "Why," said he, "I shall have the Dutch lady; you can get a wife in the streets." I told him my objections to the Dutch lady were her superior talents. "O Sir," said he, "you need not be afraid, marry her; before a year goes about you'll find that reason much weaker, and that wit not near so bright." O admirable master of human nature!

He praised Baretti. "His *Account of Italy* is a very entertaining book; and, Sir, I know no man who carries his head higher in conversation than Baretti. There are strong powers in his mind. He has not indeed so many hooks as he might have had; but so far as his hooks reach, he lays hold of objects very forcibly." This was another good night. How different was I from what I was when I last saw Mr. Johnson in London, when I was still wavering and often clouded. I am now serene and steady. I took leave of the company, being to set out next morning.

TUESDAY 29 MARCH. I set out in the fly, or rather post-coach, all alone. I breakfasted at ———,[7] where to my astonishment I heard that Wilkes had been elected for Middlesex. So fascinating is success

[7] Probably Bensington, which was the stage between Oxford and Henley.

that I began to quit the determinations of my own reason, and to imagine him really a patriot and like a Roman whom

mobilium turba Quiritium
Certat tergeminis tollere honoribus.[8]

But a little reflection soon cured me of this. After breakfast I was joined by a jolly London justice who had lands in the neighbourhood. He and I were very hearty.

At Henley we came out and went and looked at the machine with which they are levelling a very steep hill on the London side, by digging it down and throwing the earth into the hollow at the bottom. This is done without horses, by two carts which are contrived to work as buckets in a well. There is a road cut down the hill, they having begun at the foot of it, and cut upwards as they removed the earth. A number of men dig the earth and throw it into the cart, to which a strong rope is fixed, which is wound upon a horizontal wheel above the face of the hill yet entire. The moment the cart is full, a bell is rung to warn the man at the bottom of the hill, who then lets go the cart which he has emptied into the hollow. Then two men go, one on each side of the loaded cart (or but one for each cart, I forget which. I now recollect the two men on each side of the loaded cart only set it a-going) for a little way and push it along; then one returns to his companions, and one goes along with the cart, guiding it till he gets to the brink of the deep bottom; then he has a long piece of wood fixed to the cart, but so as to be twisted about. This he twists till he fixes the end of it between two spokes of the left wheel, and so stops the cart.

In the mean time, the weight of the loaded cart going down the hill pulls up the empty cart, which is filled, and then pulls up the other. The wheel to which the rope is fixed is so made as not to turn too quickly; so it lets down the cart at a moderate pace. At three or four different places, there are across the road double horizontal trees, or long pieces of wood, which are fixed by swinging ligatures or insertions in notches to a post. Upon these trees the rope is put to preserve it from trailing and being rubbed on the hill. The man who guides

[8] "The crowd of fickle voters strives to exalt to the highest honours" (Horace, *Odes*, I. i. 7–8).

each cart runs now and then a little before it. He who goes down, runs to draw out the tree on one side to receive the rope. He who goes up runs to draw out the tree to receive the rope on the other side; and as the one side is drawn out, the other falls in, and it is so contrived that by these means the ropes are always kept at a proper elevation. This method was invented lately by a dissenting clergyman at Henley.[9] It is exceedingly useful, by making that be done by two men which would require a great number of horses and oxen.

When I came to Sandhill,[1] I quitted the coach and took a post-chaise and drove to Eton. I went into the college and walked about very agreeably, repeating Mr. Gray's verses, and as I looked at the statue of King Henry, I thought of

> grateful science still adores
> Her Henry's holy shade.

I then returned to my chaise and drove to Windsor. It was truly elevating to ascend that noble highth. When I enjoyed the prospect, I repeated Gray's lines:

> And ye, who from the lofty brow   .
> Of Windsor's highths th' expanse below, &c.[2]

I surveyed the rooms with solid ancient taste. When I was shown the armour of David King of Scotland my . . . [3]

Brentford, [then] home. Sallied [out in search of] Kitty. Borrowed [money] from Matthew; raged. Then Dun's, left watch and purse, and had [only a] crown. Wanted two [whores] like Bolingbroke. Got red-haired hussy; went to Bob Derry's, had brandy and water. She went for companion; found her not. Then once. Then home with her. Watchman lighted us, and she paid penny. Horrid room; no fire, no curtains, dirty sheets, &c. All night; three here.

WEDNESDAY 30 MARCH. About six in the morning I decamped. I was despicable in my own opinion for having been in the very sink of

[9] The Rev. Humphry Gainsborough, a brother of the painter.

[1] Probably Boswell meant Salthill.

[2] These, and the lines above, are slightly misquoted from Gray's "Ode on a Distant Prospect of Eton College," ll. 3–6.

[3] Here six pages have been torn from the Journal. The rest of this entry is supplied by the Notes for this day, which by chance have survived.

vice. I walked about a while and looked at the windows which had been broken by the mob.[4] I then came home, washed, shifted, and had my hair combed. Then called on Sir John Dick a moment. Then went to Giardini's in Queen Anne Street, Cavendish Square, and called for Signor Baretti. On my road to him I was a little faint, so I stepped into a chairman's public house and drank a glass of usquebaugh. Baretti was abed and bid the boy tell me he was not well. I made him be roused, and, when I had asked him all how he did, I found why he had been so restive. It seems one Mr. Bousfield lived in the same street with me. Baretti had called at his door, and met with a very rude reception, and all the time he supposed this Bousfield to be me; and so he had gone and abused me to all our common acquaintance. What confirmed him in this idea was that Davies[5] had told him that I was angry at a passage in his *Account of Italy* where he abuses the writers in the English newspapers in favour of Corsica.[6] However, I soon undeceived him, and then he gave me my breakfast in good humour. I found his manners exceedingly rough, which had not disgusted me when I saw him at Venice, because I was so happy to find there a great admirer of Mr. Samuel Johnson. He and I walked over the way to Mr. Wilton's and saw the noble monument . . . [7]

[Editorial Note: Great portions have been torn from the remainder of Boswell's Journal describing his stay in London, and no dates are given in what survives. Twelve pages have been torn away at this point, and the Memorandum for 30 March is very cryptic:

[4] On its return from Brentford after electing Wilkes on 28 March, the mob had compelled all householders to illuminate their windows on penalty of having them broken. They attempted to storm the Mansion House (the Lord Mayor's residence), and broke every pane of glass in Lord Bute's house. On the night of 29 March the disturbance was renewed, and many more windows broken.

[5] Thomas Davies, at whose bookshop Johnson and Boswell had met in 1763.

[6] Baretti had written to Boswell on 4 March to congratulate him on his "delightful book," but also to complain that he had been unfair to the Genoese. Baretti added that he hated to see them libelled, "especially in favour of the Corsicans, who upon the very face of your book do not appear to be anything better than bloody-minded savages."

[7] Probably the monument to General Wolfe, now in Westminster Abbey. Joseph Wilton, the father of Chambers's future wife (p. 146 *n*.6), did not complete it until 1772, but he had been at work on it for many years.

"Dined Great Piazza. Sent Matthew for Black. Down to Westminister. Two naked. 'Ah, 'tis the barber, he's a clever one.' " On 6 April, according to *The London Chronicle*, Boswell presided at a celebration honouring Paoli's birthday, which was so successful that "animated with universal ideas of liberty" and an extraordinary number of toasts the group formed itself into a Corsican Club to meet annually on that day. The remaining fragments of the fully written Journal follow.]

. . . He came to me this morning, and a terrible operation he had of it; and after all was obliged to leave so much of the nail in till he should get the proud flesh brought down.[8] He was an old, formal, lean man, pretty tall, in a brown coat and red waistcoat and long light-coloured bob-wig. He actually told me that he had always a turn for this profession, and when a boy used to get apples from the maids for cutting their nails. He was a Methodist, and whined grievously, giving one no comfort, but making the pain seem worse than it really was, though I do not think he had anything of a quack. But I shall know that when paying time comes.

I called this morning on Mrs. Macaulay.[9] She was denied, but her servant came running after me: "Sir, my mistress is at home to Mr.

[8] Boswell had had trouble with ingrown toe-nails since his trip to Corsica. They were probably acquired by walking along mountain trails in riding-boots.

[9] Catherine Macaulay, the Whig historian, whose footman Johnson invited to sit down with her at dinner to test her republican principles. She was a friend of the American cause and visited Washington at Mt. Vernon in 1785. This was Boswell's first meeting with her. In 1763, on the appearance of the first volume of her *History of England*, he had satirized her in his Ten-Lines-a-Day Verses (30 November 1763):

> Like a Dutch *vrouw*, all shapeless, pale, and fat,
> That hugs and slabbers her ungainly brat,
> Our Cath'rine sits sublime o'er steaming tea,
> And takes her dear Republic on her knee:
> Sings it all songs that ever yet were sung,
> And licks it fondly with her length of tongue.

This remained pretty much his private opinion of the lady, but he was now placed under the restraint of politeness, first by the fact that Dilly was their common publisher, and secondly by Mrs. Macaulay's having volunteered a constitution for Corsica, in the form of an open letter to Paoli.

Boswell." I was shown into her study where she was sitting in a kind of Spanish dress. Two gentlemen were with her, who went away. She was very complimentative to me, but formal and affected, and she whined about liberty as an old Puritan would whine about grace. In short, I was rather disgusted with her.

I then drove in a hackney-coach to Dilly's, where I was to dine. He had a company for me. He introduced me to Mr. Burgh, a Scotsman, master of an academy at Newington Green, who had written a very warm commendation of my *Account of Corsica* in a letter to *The London Chronicle* signed "Philopaolus." Mr. Burgh is the author of *The Dignity of Human Nature*, *Crito*, &c. He is a stiff, positive man, knowing, however, and shrewd. The next man I was introduced to was Mr. Ryland, master of an academy at Northampton, and a dissenting clergyman; a bold Briton with a very strong voice and much zeal. He has published a little book on mechanics, and is publishing packs of cards on all the sciences. The next was the Reverend Dr. Robertson, author of *An Attempt to Explain the Words, Reason, Person*, &c., who honestly resigned his living because he became convinced that several of the Articles to which he had subscribed were not true. Mr. Cumming, the Quaker, was there too;[1] and the Reverend Mr. Mayo, who I found was the person who had taken upon him to make some alterations in my language in the *Account of Corsica*, but which a violent letter from me to Dilly had prevented, all but one or two; and lucky was it, for sad alterations they were. After we were set down to dinner, Dr. Wayman, a physician in the city, also came. It was a most curious company. The most direct compliments were paid to me, without the least delicacy. "Dr. Wayman, this is Mr. Boswell, author of the *Account of Corsica*." WAYMAN. "Mr. Boswell is a very respectable character!" Such broad hints as these were thrown about. Dr. Robertson was also praised for his conduct. We had a good substantial dinner, after . . .[2]

. . . Another morning Willison the painter called upon me.[3] Mr.

[1] The *fighting* Quaker. He was a private merchant of London who persuaded the Government to allow him to lead an armed expedition into Senegal, which drove out the French and established British trading supremacy there.

[2] Fourteen pages have been torn out here. What remains was clearly not the record of a single day, but a "review."

[3] George Willison had painted Boswell's portrait at Rome in 1765.

Ryland of Northampton happened then to be with me. He and Willison began to dispute. Ryland was all enthusiasm, all in generals. Willison was slow, and wanted to bring him to particulars. Ryland boasted of his son Jack, his proficiency in learning, his excellent principles both in politics and morals.[4] "Well, but," said Willison, "what do you intend to make of him?" "Make of him?" cried Ryland, "I will make nothing of him. Would you have me cramp his inclinations, fetter the free-born mind? No, Sir!" "But," said Willison, "do you intend him for the Church or — " "Church!" roared Ryland. "No, Sir — to cringe to a despicable lord or duke, who has only the accidents of birth and fortune to recommend him, to be an utter sycophant, a fellow destitute of every noble sentiment?" "But, Sir," said Willison, "what profession, I say, what profession do you intend him for?" "Profession!" cried Ryland. "Why, Sir, a citizen of the world, a lover of his country, a friend of mankind. One who knows the dignity of human nature. Such a mind, Sir, such a soul, is beyond all that a painter can show." I all the while fanned the fire, sometimes joining Willison, sometimes Ryland, being like to burst out with a peal of laughter. Willison, with the Scotch sneer, snuffed at Ryland as at a great English fool, and Ryland strutted with the step of Costar Pearmain in *The Recruiting Officer*, despising Willison as a poor spiritless artist who knew nothing of sublime philosophy. Another morning I met Lord Mountstuart at Sir John Dick's . . . [5]

I was really put in a passion, and told them I was resolved to punish them, and would go immediately to Justice Fielding's.[6] I accordingly placed a ?watchman as sentry upon the house, and then actually went to the blind Justice's. A very decent, civil man came out to me; I suppose he was one of the clerks. I told him the trick that had

[4] John Ryland, though only fifteen years old, began about this time to teach in his father's academy. He is said to have learned Hebrew at the age of five, and Greek before he was nine. Like his father, he became a distinguished Baptist minister.

[5] The manuscript breaks off completely at this point, four pages having been torn out. The last page can be partly recovered from the "offset" on the blank page following. The dots indicate unrecoverable words, and the question marks doubtful readings.

[6] Sir John Fielding, half-brother to the novelist, and blind, apparently from birth. He served as a justice of the peace in Bow Street.

been put upon me. He said I could have no immediate redress, for, as I had given her the money out of my own hand, it was no theft. I had therefore no other method but to prosecute her for a debt in a . . . court of law, "which," said he . . . "I suppose you would not choose." I asked him what I ?owed him for his good advice. "Nothing at all, Sir," said he. This office of Fielding's is really an admirable institution. I ?posted home, and thought no more of it.

[EDITORIAL NOTE: Here the fully written Journal breaks off. For the remainder of Boswell's stay in London we have only two disjointed fragments of the condensed diary, the first covering 21 April to 16 May, and the other 20 to 22 May. The first fragment, though scrappy and obscure, is of the greatest interest and importance, as it probably records more meetings with famous men than any other portion of equal length in the whole Yale collection. Boswell's "roaring" having had its usual unhappy consequence, he was now confined to his room, "suffering severely for immorality" as he wrote to Temple on 26 April; and the great men of the literary and political world came to pay their respects to the author of *Corsica*, the book of the hour. Lord Lyttelton (an historian himself) called twice to discuss the possibility of aiding the Corsicans; old General Oglethorpe, Dr. Johnson, Baretti made their visits; and Sir John Pringle brought the most famous of Americans, Dr. Franklin, to dine.

[The cause of Corsican independence was in great danger at this time, London being filled with rumors, and true ones, that France was about to take over Genoa's claims to the Island and to subdue it. Boswell exerted himself on behalf of the Corsicans through his usual medium of newspaper "inventions," and also started to make a collection of essays by various hands, which was finally published in December 1768 as *British Essays in Favour of the Brave Corsicans*. His affair with Zélide came to an abrupt end when a stinging letter from her prompted Boswell to call them as incompatible as thunder and lightning.]

THURSDAY 21 APRIL. Lord Lyttelton sat an hour; talked much of Corsica. . . . Bid me be well informed; so I [would] show best my friendship [for Corsica]. Fine interview. In great pain, afternoon.

[Received *c.* 26 April, Johnson to Boswell][7]

Oxford, 23 March 1768

MY DEAR BOSWELL, — I have omitted a long time to write to you, without knowing very well why. I could now tell why I should not write; for who would write to men who publish letters of their friends without their leave?[8] Yet I write to you in spite of my caution to tell you that I shall be glad to see you, and that I wish you would empty your head of Corsica, which I think has filled it rather too long. But, at all events, I shall be glad, very glad to see you. I am, Sir, yours affectionately,

SAM. JOHNSON.

[Boswell to Johnson][9]

London, 26 April 1768

MY DEAR SIR, — I have received your last letter, which, though very short and by no means complimentary, yet gave me real pleasure, because it contains these words, "I shall be glad, very glad to see you." Surely you have no reason to complain of my publishing a single paragraph of one of your letters; the temptation to it was so strong. An irrevocable grant of your friendship, and your dignifying my desire of visiting Corsica with the epithet of "a wise and noble curiosity," are to me more valuable than many of the grants of kings.

But how can you bid me "empty my head of Corsica?" My noble-minded friend, do you not feel for an oppressed nation bravely struggling to be free? Consider fairly what is the case. The Corsicans never received any kindness from the Genoese. They never agreed to be subject to them. They owe them nothing; and when reduced to an abject state of slavery by force, shall they not rise in the great cause of liberty and break the galling yoke? And shall not every liberal soul be warm for them? Empty my head of Corsica! Empty it of honour, empty it of

[7] Boswell explains in printing this letter in *The Life of Johnson* (26 April 1768) that it had gone to Scotland, and had been sent on to him in London.

[8] See p. 145. In the *Life* (May 1768), Boswell mentions that he asked Johnson if it would be improper to publish his letters after his death, and Johnson replied: "Nay, Sir, when I am dead you may do as you will."

[9] Printed in *The Life of Johnson.*

humanity, empty it of friendship, empty it of piety. No! while I live, Corsica and the cause of the brave Islanders shall ever employ much of my attention, shall ever interest me in the sincerest manner. . . . I am, &c.

JAMES BOSWELL.

SUNDAY 1 MAY. Much better. Had written to Paoli and pledged honour no more vice, yet the scent of *eau sans pareille* would revive [thoughts of some] elegant Laïs. But I repressed [them]; I forfeit more healthy and worthy joys. I read Lord Lyttelton's *St. Paul*, and the Bible, and was well. Guthrie, Hamilton, and Maconochie dined. I was well. Guthrie said General Oglethorpe's mind and also Lord Elibank's [were] rich but like upholsterer's shop: carpets high up, glasses below, &c.[1] I talked of not writing till the very day a paper was needed; "because then," said I, "one runs downhill. Till then, one is labouring up the hill, but one is at the top the moment the point of necessity is reached. To write before that is double fatigue; but I must do so for my clients, lest running too quick downhill I miss something. Slowly going up, I take all." . . .

MONDAY 2 MAY. Morning, letter from Zélide; termagant![2] . . . Sent note to David Hume. He came, was most placid. Said it required great goodness of disposition to withstand baleful effects of Christianity.[3] . . . Just then entered Mr. Johnson. I jumped [up] and em-

[1] The simile may have been suggested by Boswell's surroundings: his landlord was an upholsterer. — James Edward Oglethorpe, full General in the British army, was a grand old man who had fought against the Turks under Prince Eugene and had founded the Colony of Georgia as a refuge for poor debtors. He had sought out Boswell of his own accord and had asked to be allowed to shake the author of the *Account of Corsica* by the hand. — Patrick Murray, fifth Lord Elibank, was a Scottish advocate and patron of literature. Johnson once wrote to him: "I never met you without going away a wiser man" (*Tour to the Hebrides*, 12 September 1773).

[2] Boswell enclosed her letter, which has not been recovered, in one to Temple (14 May 1768) and commented: "Could any actress at any of the theatres attack one with a keener — what is the word? not *fury*, something softer. The lightning that flashes with so much brilliance may scorch. And does not her *esprit* do so? Is she not a termagant, or at least will she not be one by the time she is forty?" (*Letters of James Boswell*, i. 159). Three years later, she married her brothers' former tutor, Monsieur de Charrière.

[3] Hume then left. In his letter to Temple of 14 May, Boswell remarked about

braced [him, crying] "Thou great man!" JOHNSON. "Don't call names." He would not dine; had bad spirits. I run on about the praise of my book. JOHNSON. "Sir, your book is very well. The *Account* may be had more from other books. But the *Tour* is extremely well. It entertains everybody. Sir, everybody who wishes you well [is] pleased." Asked him to review. JOHNSON. "No, one ass [should not] scratch [another]."[4] . . . [Talk of] liberty. JOHNSON. "Sir, they mistake [in ranting about] universal liberty without [considering] private. Political liberty is only as many private [persons] as can be happy. Liberty of press not much. Suppose you and I and two hundred more restrained: what then? What proportion?" BOSWELL. "Ay, but [suppose] ten thousand [restrained] from reading us?" JOHNSON. "Yes, they are the wretches [to be pitied.]" . . .[5]

TUESDAY 3 MAY . . . . Lord Lyttelton had been with Lord Hardwicke. Bid me not come to people's doors as minister [from Corsica]. Get introduced; speak as hinting, not as pointing out. Meantime, Corsican Club [would] make good blood. LYTTELTON. "Don't appear too hot-headed." . . .

FRIDAY 6 MAY. General Oglethorpe a little, morning; then Frank Stewart. Then Lord Drummond; eat eggs, sat till General Oglethorpe came, who said mob was now [the] best blood, [being] old families sunk: Mortimers sweeping streets. Coffee. Great Clarke, morning; who read *Corsica* believe you thus.[6]

---

him: "David is really amiable. I always regret to him his unlucky principles, and he smiles at my faith. But I have a hope which he has not, or pretends not to have" (*Letters of James Boswell*, i. 160).

[4] Johnson was remembering the Latin proverb, "Mutuum muli scabunt."

[5] This passage is expanded in *The Life of Johnson* as follows: "He talked in his usual style with a rough contempt for popular liberty. 'They make a rout about *universal* liberty without considering that all that is to be valued, or indeed can be enjoyed by individuals, is *private* liberty. Political liberty is good only so far as it produces private liberty. Now, Sir, there is the liberty of the press, which you know is a constant topic. Suppose you and I and two hundred more were restrained from printing our thoughts: what then? What proportion would that restraint upon us bear to the private happiness of the nation?' "

[6] Boswell was discovering that his chosen method of writing laid him open to the charge of personal fatuity (see Gray's comment, p. 91 *n*.8). He comforted himself all his life with the story of Dr. Clarke, the famous theologian, which

TUESDAY 10 MAY. The old General, Home of Billy, and Maconochie, forenoon. You was too eager with the worthy General and
raged on subjecting inferiors, and Home joined. You was sorry at
opposing too much the worthy man, so full of age and spirit. Maconochie stayed and eat a steak, and you and he studied President's
speech [on the Douglas cause]. No philosophy or wit today.

THURSDAY 12 MAY. Mr. Home of Billy [called]. Told me of
Percivall Pott.[7] Saw him; [was] quite firm. Read much.

SATURDAY 14 MAY. Mr. Kennedy, then Sir John Dick and Captain Meadows. I talked of some things though [they are] in my book.
I have observed Mr. Johnson do so. Almost every man you meet is,
either from not having read or [from] having forgotten, just as if he
had never seen a book. Sir John Pringle, Dr. Franklin, Mr. Rose,
[and] Mr. Burgh dined. All was elegant. You maintained [author
should] never correct [his] book. Sir John opposed. "But," said I,
"Lord Kames has made [his] *Elements of Criticism* so 'tis not the
same book." SIR JOHN. "Then it's another book" — very well. Burgh
[was] always saying, "Ah, that came off so fine and dry!" and Sir
John [sat] with leg crossed and [talked with] shrewd gravity and
satisfaction. You was quite happy and pleased *as a man.* Burgh and
Rose drank tea. Franklin asked whether infidels or Protestants had
done most to pull down Popery. We disputed the price of Robertson's
book,[8] [and] the good done by preaching; [agreed] the English tone
superior to Scotch, [possibly because there was] more music here,
except whistling.

SUNDAY 15 MAY. Mr. Bosville called and talked quite like one
of his letters.[9] Messrs. Dillys drank tea. All turned on Robertson's
book and *the trade.* At night Baretti came. He was pleasanter. Was for

---

he printed in the Dedication to *The Life of Johnson:* "It is related of the great
Dr. Clarke that when in one of his leisure hours he was unbending himself with
a few friends in the most playful and frolicsome manner he observed Beau Nash
approaching, upon which he suddenly stopped: 'My boys, (said he,) let us be
grave; here comes a fool.' The world, my friend, I have found to be a great fool."
[7] A famous surgeon, who helped to revise surgical practice of the day. Pott's
disease and Pott's fracture take their name from him.
[8] Robertson had just arrived in London with three large quarto volumes of his
History of the Reign of Charles V, for which he obtained £4500.
[9] That is, in a hearty, shrewd, amusing manner.

answering Kenrick. Had argued with Johnson: "As you expelled Lady Macclesfield from society, why not so bury Wilkes, Kenrick, Campbell, &c.? [If you succeeded] you would have done real service." JOHNSON. "Sir, I don't know but I've been wrong."[1] Baretti talked strongly against our liberty. BARETTI. "Had you been content like other nations to have just jogged on, with sometimes a good king, sometimes a worse, you'd have done very well, as other nations. But to please your mad notions of claims of right, you did an unjust and barbarous thing to turn away your king, and sacrificed four hundred of the best families, and by restraining the king's power so much you force him and his ministers to load you with taxes to purchase power which they ought to have."

He argued for the Italian ceremonies. "They are innocent," said he, "and our people are better so than yours, who get into taverns with whores and bottles and pots of beer." "But," said I, "the mind is hurt by that kind of idolatry, and drawn from just notions of God." "Nay," said he, "has any common people just notions of God?" "Yes," said I, "the people here." "No," said he, "they never think of God but with 'damn' joined to it." He was really well tonight.

MONDAY 16 MAY. Donaldson, morning, and Sir John Dick. Then Captain Bosville, not a bit spoiled. [In] afternoon [was] old John Frail a little; quite in love with opposite lady. She signed for a note.[2] I sent it; pretty answer. I have really strange fortune for adventures. But let's see ———.

FRIDAY 20 MAY. Called at Lord Mansfield's.[3] I was received. My Lord came forward and took [me] by the hand very courteously: "Mr. Boswell, your servant. I am glad I was at home. I should have been very sorry not to have seen you." I said, "My Lord, your Lord-

---

[1] William Kenrick had attacked Johnson through Boswell in a pamphlet on *Corsica*. Boswell first intended to answer it, but Johnson persuaded him that to do so would only keep the matter alive. Lady Macclesfield was charged with having treated her supposed son, the poet Richard Savage, with great cruelty; Johnson had excoriated her in his *Life of Savage*.

[2] That is, she made a sign for him to send her a note.

[3] William Murray, first Baron (later first Earl of) Mansfield, Lord Chief Justice of the King's Bench. One of the greatest of all English lawyers, he was also a fine orator, a Scotsman, a bitter rival of Chatham's, and unpopular with the masses for his juridical treatment of Wilkes.

ship never took any man by the hand who is more truly proud to
have the honour of waiting upon your Lordship than I am." After
talking of my having been ill, thus went the dialogue. MANSFIELD.
"You have travelled a great deal, Sir." BOSWELL. "Why, yes, my Lord,
I was very fond of seeing as much as I could, and travelled as much as
my father would allow me." MANSFIELD. "Pray, Sir, how did you
leave your father?" BOSWELL. "Very well, my Lord." MANSFIELD. "I
am glad of it; he is a very respectable man." BOSWELL. "Indeed, my
Lord, he is a very conscientious judge. He is content to do his duty.
He does not seek to be known beyond his own circle." MANSFIELD.
"Ay, but he is known here, especially among a certain class." BOS-
WELL. "Why, this great Douglas cause has made all our judges known
here by publishing their speeches." MANSFIELD. "I have not read a
word of it. But your father has been known in many other cases."
(Here he paid my father several compliments of which I do not re-
collect the precise terms.)

I was determined if possible to be at him on the great cause, so
began again. BOSWELL. "These speeches have been read over all
here." MANSFIELD. "If one thought them authentic, one would like to
look at them. Pray, how are they?" BOSWELL. "Why, my Lord, Almon
first published an edition, very imperfect indeed and so often nonsense, but very genuine so far as they went. After this, a writer's clerk
who had taken full notes sent each judge his own speech to look over
and make what corrections he pleased. Some of 'em have altered a
good deal. I may say there are thirteen looked over by them. Lord
Kames, who though I have a great regard for him, I must say made a
very poor speech — " MANSFIELD. "Ay?" BOSWELL. "Yes, my Lord, he
was taken at unawares. He was clear upon Mr. Douglas's side, and
he thought it would go without speaking — *cela va sans dire* — and
he would only vote. But, being called upon unprepared, he made
really a poor figure, which was a pity, as a man of my Lord Kames's
genius might have made a very fine speech." MANSFIELD. "Yes, indeed." BOSWELL. "Well, my Lord, being sensible that he had appeared so ill, he would not meddle with his speech, and I may say it is
now better than he made it, though a very poor one. Old Lord Strich-
en (Fraser), whom your Lordship may have heard of, would not
correct his speech. He said with great spirit, 'No. I have given accord-

ing to my conscience. I will not appeal to the world. If those who have given their opinions on the other side want a justification, let them publish. I want no justification.' Lord Strichen spoke like a plain country gentleman. Lord Alemoor (Pringle) made a very eloquent speech." MANSFIELD. "That's a very respectable character." BOSWELL. "My father made a solid, sensible speech: a few sound principles of law and a few reflections on the capital facts, without going into the wide field of circumstance, which is endless."

MANSFIELD. "I was sorry for the manner in which that cause was decided; so much time employed in a question of fact, when I should have decided it at a sitting. And such a division. It makes one suspect there was something more in that cause than the cause itself." BOSWELL. "Why, my Lord, that cause has done a great deal of harm. There was in particular the Lord President. A terrible outcry has been raised, though to be sure most unjustly, in regard of his giving an opinion contrary to his conscience; but, my Lord, it was not well in the president of a court to employ his supposed superior talents in making a violent harangue for the Pursuers. He even says in direct terms that he will not touch on the arguments on the other side. Now, my Lord, that is very dangerous. And we can prove one judge changed by this harangue. Old Charles Erskine, the Justice-Clerk, whom your Lordship must have known, his son, who has the title of Lord Barjarg, actually wrote a new speech. We can bring one clerk who wrote for him a speech for Mr. Douglas, and another who wrote for him one for Duke Hamilton. He took a cold and kept the house a day. I was surprised with Veitch (Lord Eliock), a sound-headed fellow. Burnett (Lord Monboddo) made an admirable speech, and with great dignity, after they had all spoken and it was in vain to try any more. It was just *victrix causa deis placuit, sed victa Catoni.*"[4]

MANSFIELD. "There are very respectable opinions on both sides." BOSWELL. "Yes, indeed. But the cause has done a great deal of harm. When the people of a country lose their confidence in their judges,

[4] Lucan, *Pharsalia*, i. 128:

> Victorious Caesar by the gods was crowned,
> The vanquished party was by Cato owned.
> > Nicholas Rowe.

and even hint anything against them, it is terrible. Now, there is Dundas, the President; a most dreadful outcry has been raised against him, though certainly most unjustly." MANSFIELD. "Ay, and does it continue?" BOSWELL. "Yes, my Lord. His manner was so violent; and then unluckily his whole speech from beginning to end is without the least foundation in the evidence. He has read it with very little attention and trusted to the Pursuers' memorial, which is a most unfair paper." MANSFIELD. "As I told you, I have not read a word of the cause." BOSWELL. "I dare say not, my Lord." MANSFIELD. "I have not, upon my honour." (He said this like one gentleman speaking to another. A man of curiosity would have looked at it.) "I have their great quartos lying here upon my table, but I have been so much employed with other things that I have not had time to open them." (I was highly pleased to find that he allowed me to talk so freely and even seemed very desirous to hear me, for when his servant came in and asked if his chariot should wait, and I rose up and was going away, he said, "Sit still, Mr. Boswell." So I thought I would do all the good I could.)

BOSWELL. "My Lord, the unhappy thing was that our judges spoke in so different a manner. Lord Lyttelton said their speeches were just pleadings on each side." MANSFIELD. "That's very bad. My Lord Lyttelton, I am sure, will determine very candidly; he is a very worthy man." BOSWELL. "I wish to God, my Lord, that everybody thought as Lord Lyttelton." (I then repeated his ideas, which seemed to please Lord Mansfield.) "But I fancy, my Lord, the peers in general will not interfere." MANSFIELD. "I don't know that. There never was a cause where they could do it better." BOSWELL. "I should be sorry to see the peers in general take upon them to judge in a cause of property." MANSFIELD. "To be sure." BOSWELL. "What made the judges on the Hamilton side so obnoxious was their maintaining that there was no law in the cause. Now, your Lordship sees that, although gentlemen without doors are not lawyers, they are still judges of that great principle of law — *filiation* — on which we all depend; and every man is alarmed at the danger of that principle being taken away. When a man is called, 'Sir, you must stand trial for your birthright,' [he replies,] 'Very well. I put myself upon my country. I rest upon my filiation.' [Then he is told] 'No, Sir, [there is] no law. You must bring proofs, and the plaintiffs must bring proofs; and then it will be judged whose proofs are strongest.' My Lord, when you thus deny a man the great privilege of filiation, you are taking the very pavement from under his feet. You are depriving him of half his cause." MANS-FIELD. "You are so." BOSWELL. "There was now poor Sir John Stewart; why, all the strange suggestions of his wild fancy must be made sus-picions against him."[5] MANSFIELD. "I did not know Sir John." BOS-WELL. "No, my Lord? Your Lordship knew Lady Jane?" MANSFIELD. "No, but I was once able to [do] her a piece of service"[6] BOSWELL. "I asked my father where I was born. He mentioned a house. I asked an old woman who was in the house at the birth, and she said another house. My Lord, if my birth had been scrutinized, my father and this old woman would have been declared perjured, as contradicting one another." MANSFIELD. "Very true." BOSWELL. "Every man must be alarmed. He runs back in his own mind and sees what difficulties must occur in such questions. We had a very busy winter with politi-cal causes." MANSFIELD. "The fewer political causes you have the better. They shake your court." BOSWELL. "They do so. I fear this great Douglas cause has been something of a political one." MANS-FIELD. "I imagine so. You are making great improvements at Edin-burgh." BOSWELL. "Yes. We have a Theatre Royal, too." MANSFIELD. "I believe you wrote the prologue at the opening of it. I assure you I admired it exceedingly." (BOSWELL. Here I told him all how Ross had applied to me, &c., &c.)[7] MANSFIELD. "Upon my word, it was a very pretty copy of verses, and I like the judicious style of it — so concilia-ting. I'm sure it must have done him a great deal of good."[8] I went home and felt myself in most admirable humour. N.B. Convinced him of importance of Corsica.[9]

[5] Douglas's father. The evidence he gave at various times was self-contradictory, and even Douglas partisans admitted that it looked as if he had forged certain important letters.

[6] He got her a pension of £300 from the Crown at a time when her fortunes were at a very low ebb.

[7] See p. 115 *n*.6.

[8] Boswell treasured this compliment, and quoted it years afterwards in the memoir of himself which he wrote for *The European Magazine*.

[9] Boswell was apparently mistaken here. Mansfield assured Choiseul, the French minister of war and foreign affairs, "that the English Ministry were too weak

SATURDAY 21 MAY. I dined at Lord Eglinton's, he and I and John Ross Mackye, very well. Evening, Lord Mountstuart's; much serious and open conversation. Our friendship quite renewed.

SUNDAY 22 MAY. Went in the morning to Lord Mountstuart's; saw his son; supposed him [one day] John Earl of Bute. I called at several places, and dined at Mr. Bosville's, quite easy and comfortable. Then drove about and called at doors. Between eight and nine at night went to Lord Mansfield's, being his levee. Found him alone; drank a dish of tea with him. He was quite easy with me. Told me the Anglesey cause was clearly shown to be an imposition by authentic papers.[1] The week before, he had had a cause of a horse before him. I pleaded Smith *contra* Steel.[2] He said there was no time fixed for *redhibition*,[3] but a jury would determine just by circumstances; and, to be sure, a man's having kept a horse two months without offering him back, and working him too, was virtually passing from his objection.

In a little, my Lord Oxford came. Then Lord Mansfield assumed all the state of a chief justice. Went to the opposite side of the room and sat by my Lord, and kept me down as I tried to speak. I was *étourdi*[4] enough to talk of Wilkes, which Lord Mansfield did *not* relish. When Lord Oxford went, Lord Mansfield became quite easy again. Came close to me and resumed his urbanity. I spoke again of the Douglas cause, but found I had exhausted it.

He spoke (or I did it first, I know not which) of Dempster's plea of privilege.[5] Said it was an absurd decision. I defended it. "Come,"

---

and the nation too wise to support them in entering on a war for the sake of Corsica" (*Autobiography of Augustus Henry, third Duke of Grafton*, ed. Sir William Anson, 1898, p. 204).

[1] The Anglesey cause was another famous eighteenth-century case of contested filiation. Smollett inserted an affecting *ex parte* account of it in *Peregrine Pickle*.

[2] A cause of Boswell's entered in his Consultation Book under the date of 2 February 1767. It concerned a horse.

[3] An action to annul the sale of an article and return it to the seller because of some material defect. Mansfield was mistaken; according to Scottish legal usage, the buyer had to offer the goods back to the seller within a few days of their purchase in order for such an action to be valid.

[4] Thoughtless or giddy.

[5] George Dempster, an old and close friend of Boswell's, was M.P. for the Perth

said he, "how, are they not to judge only by the statute and common law of Scotland? Well. Had the Scotch Parliament any privilege? No. How then are they to judge of the privilege of a British Parliament? Where do they find it?" BOSWELL. "Why, in Blackstone." MANSFIELD. "You may as well say that candle. He is no rule to them." (I then harangued, I forget how.) MANSFIELD. "Keep to the point. Answer me a plain question. Have they any other rule but statute and common law?" BOSWELL. "No." MANSFIELD. "Well, then, they had nothing to do with such a plea. They might as well have pleaded a statute of Paoli of Corsica. They should have said, 'We know nothing of this,' and so proceeded, or adjourned till they took advice. They had very near set the two houses of Parliament by the ears, and I can tell you the Speaker had thoughts of moving to have 'em brought up to answer for what they had done. And, what was most extraordinary, they not only decided, but they decided wrong; and I wonder Lord Justice-Clerk, who heard the debates in Parliament on that subject, could go so far wrong. They were to proceed, and let the prosecutor be answerable for what he did, as Mr. Dempster might call him before the House of Commons, the proper judges of privilege."

I asked him if it was advisable for a Scotch counsel to come to the English bar. "No," said he, "he has not the education for it. A man of very extraordinary parts may perhaps succeed." I had told him at my first visit that nothing would tempt me from being Laird of Auchinleck, &c., and he said, "A very laudable (or a very good) prejudice." He advised [me] to read Blackstone, and also Burrow's reports. He said he decided about seven hundred causes a year.

---

burghs. In 1767 he was charged with having resorted to bribery and corruption to assure himself a majority for the next election. To postpone his trial he pleaded privilege as a member of the House of Commons, and the Court of Justiciary sustained his plea, but the House of Lords, upon being appealed to, ordered the trial to proceed, in terms implying a rebuke to the Court. Dempster's defence was amusing: it was that no statute covered the alleged offence, and that bribery was not a crime at common law. The Court "repelled" this, but acquitted him on the ground that it had not been proved that he had been *successful* in his attempt to bribe the electors. Everyone knew, of course, that he had been successful, and that he had been forced to resort to bribery because his opponent, Lord Clive, had used the same tactic.

[7 June, Manuscript of *The Life of Johnson*][6]

Soon after this, he supped at the Crown and Anchor Tavern in the Strand with a company whom I collected to meet him. There were the Reverend Dr. Percy now Bishop of Dromore,[7] Dr. Douglas now Bishop of Carlisle, Mr. Langton, Dr. Robertson the historian, Dr. Hugh Blair, and Mr. Thomas Davies, who wished much to be introduced to these eminent Scotch *literati*; but on the present occasion he had very little opportunity of hearing them talk, for with much prudence, for which Johnson afterwards found fault with them, they hardly opened their lips, and that only to say something which they were certain would not expose them to animadversion; such was their anxiety for their fame when in the presence of Johnson. He was this evening in remarkable vigour of mind and eager to exert himself in conversation, which he did with great readiness and fluency, but I am sorry to find that I have preserved but a small part of what passed.

He allowed high praise to Thomson as a poet, but when a gentleman said he was also a very good man our moralist contested this with great warmth, accusing him of gross sensuality and licentiousness of manners. . . .

He was vehement against old Dr. Monsey of Chelsea College as "a fellow who swore and talked bawdy."[8] "I have been often in his company," said Dr. Percy, "and never heard him swear or talk bawdy." Mr. Davies, who sat next to Dr. Percy, having after this had

[6] The manuscript of *The Life of Johnson* now at Yale shows the book in all the stages of its composition. Boswell's first draft serves as the basic text for this and later passages, but certain additions and alterations have been retained. Reflective parts or general comments which appear to be afterthoughts are omitted. This supper is dated by an entry in Percy's Journal, now in the British Museum.
[7] Best remembered as the editor of the *Reliques of Ancient English Poetry*, which had appeared in 1765 and which did much to revive interest in older English literature.
[8] A famous eccentric, somewhat like Swift in temperament, who lived to be ninety-five. It is said that in old age he took savage delight in meeting younger physicians who were waiting for his appointment and in prophesying that they would die before he did, which proved to be true so far as most of them were concerned.

some conversation aside with him, made a discovery which in his zeal to please Dr. Johnson he eagerly proclaimed aloud from the foot of the table: "O Sir, I have found out a very good reason why Dr. Percy never heard Monsey swear or talk bawdy, for he tells me he never saw him but at the Duke of Northumberland's table." "And so, Sir," said Johnson loudly to Dr. Percy, "you would shield this fellow from the charge of swearing and talking bawdy because he did not do so at the Duke of Northumberland's table. Sir, you might as well say that you had seen him hold up his hand at the Old Bailey and he neither swore nor talked bawdy; or that you had seen him in the cart at Tyburn and he neither swore nor talked bawdy. And is it thus, Sir, that you presume to contradict what I have related?" Dr. Johnson's reprimand was uttered in such a manner that Dr. Percy was much hurt and soon afterwards left the company, of which Johnson did not take any notice at the time.

Swift having been mentioned, Johnson as usual treated him with little respect as an author. One or two of our number endeavoured to support the Dean of St. Patrick's by various arguments. One in particular praised his *Conduct of the Allies*. JOHNSON. "Sir, his *Conduct of the Allies* is a performance of very little merit." "I don't know, Sir," said the gentleman,[9] "you must allow it has strong facts." JOHNSON. "Why yes, Sir, but what has that to do with the merit of the composition? In the Sessions paper of the Old Bailey there are strong facts. Housebreaking is a strong fact, robbery is a strong fact, and murder is a *mighty* strong fact, but is great praise due to the historian of those strong facts? No, Sir. Swift has told what he had to tell distinctly enough, but that is all. He had to count ten, and he has counted it right."—Then recollecting that Mr. Davies by acting as an *informer* had been the occasion of his talking somewhat too harshly to his friend, Dr. Percy, for which probably when the first ebullition was over he felt some compunction, he took an opportunity to give him a hit; so added with a preparatory laugh, "Why, Sir, Tom Davies might have written *The Conduct of the Allies*." Poor Tom being thus suddenly dragged into ludicrous notice in presence of the Scottish doctors, to whom he was ambitious of appearing to advantage, was sadly mortified. Nor did the matter rest here; for upon after occasions

[9] Dr. Douglas.

whenever he, "statesman all over,"[1] assumed an over importance, I used to hail him "the author of *The Conduct of the Allies.*"

When I called upon Dr. Johnson next morning I found him highly satisfied with his colloquial prowess the preceding evening. "Well," said he, "we had good talk." BOSWELL. "Yes, Sir, you tossed and gored several persons."

The late Alexander Earl of Eglinton, who loved wit more than wine, and men of genius more than sycophants, had a great admiration of Johnson, but from the remarkable elegance of his own manners was perhaps too delicately sensible of the roughness which often appeared in Johnson's behaviour. One evening about this time, when his Lordship did me the honour to sup at my lodgings with Dr. Robertson and several other *literati*, he regretted that Johnson had not been educated with more refinement and lived more in polished society. "No, no, my Lord," said Signor Baretti, "do with him what you would, he would always have been a bear." "True," answered the Earl with a pleasing smile, "but he would have been a *dancing* bear." . . .

[EDITORIAL NOTE: On 9 June, Boswell left London to return to Edinburgh for the summer term of the Court of Session. He divided his time thereafter mainly between Edinburgh and Auchinleck until his jaunt to Ireland in the spring of 1769. No journal exists for the period.]

[Agreement between James Boswell and Margaret Montgomerie][2]

At Edinburgh, the eighth day of August one thousand seven hundred and sixty-eight years, I, Margaret Montgomerie, sister of the late James Montgomerie of Lainshaw, Esquire, considering that Mr.

[1] Churchill's description of Davies in *The Rosciad* (ll. 321–322):

> Statesman all over! — in plots famous grown! —
> He mouths a sentence as curs mouth a bone.

[2] This joking contract between Boswell and his impoverished first cousin, Margaret Montgomerie, is important as the first major indication of the ease and intimacy of their relationship, and also attests to the strength of feeling she was capable of arousing in him.

James Boswell, advocate, my cousin, is at present so much in love with me that I might certainly have him for my lawful husband if I choose it, and the said James being of a temper so inconstant that there is reason to fear that he would repent of his choice in a very short time, on which account he is unwilling to trust himself in my company; therefore, I, the said Margaret Montgomerie, hereby agree that in case I am married to the said James Boswell any time this year, or insist upon his promise thereto within the said time to take place any time thereafter, I shall submit to be banished out of Great Britain during all the days of my life. In witness whereof I have subscribed this paper written by the said James Boswell.

MARGT. MONTGOMERIE.

[Boswell to Temple]

Auchinleck, 24 August 1768

MY DEAR TEMPLE, — You have good reason to accuse me of neglect in being silent so long. My apology, I fear, is not sufficient; for, although I was a good deal taken up with the business of the summer session, had I not allowed myself to employ a great deal of time in gaming I need not have put off from day to day writing to my best friend. Some years ago I had the rage of gaming, and I lost more money than I was able to pay. Mr. Sheridan advanced me as much as cleared me, but took a promise from me that I should not play at all for three years.[3] When I was abroad he freed me from my promise, but restricted me not to lose above three guineas at a sitting. I thought my passion for gaming had been quite gone. But since I came last to Scotland, I began again to try a game of chance, and I found the fever still lurking in my veins. ⟨It⟩ seized me for a while, and I know not how much harm it might have done me had it continued. But after having recovered myself so as to have lost but about fourteen guineas, I have made a resolution never to play at a game of chance, and never at whist but for a trifle to make up a party.

My dear Temple, will you be so good as to pardon this last neglect,

[3] Thomas Sheridan was an actor and elocutionist, and father of Richard Brinsley Sheridan. The promise was made in the summer of 1761, when Sheridan was giving a series of lectures on English elocution in Edinburgh.

from which I am sure I suffer more than you do; and let us henceforth keep up a close correspondence, and so live together as much
as possible when at a distance. Your misfortune by the bankruptcy
of Mr. Fenwick Stow really afflicts me.[4] You have a noble spirit not to
be cast down by so many misfortunes. Are you in any immediate
want of money? If you are, I will send you all that I can command.
Do you remember how generous you was to me when I wanted to
purchase a commission in the Guards?[5] I hope Mrs. Temple is in a
good way. Let me know particularly about her.

I am exceedingly lucky in having escaped the insensible Miss
Blair and the furious Zélide, for I have now seen the finest creature
that ever was formed: *la belle Irlandaise*.[6] Figure to yourself, Temple,
a young lady just sixteen, formed like a Grecian nymph with the
sweetest countenance, full of sensibility, accomplished, with a Dublin
education, always half the year in the north of Ireland, her father a
counsellor-at-law with an estate of £1000 a year and above £10,000 in
ready money. Her mother a sensible, well-bred woman. She the
darling of her parents, and no other child but her sister. She is cousin
to some cousins of mine[7] in this county. I was at their house while she
and her father, mother, and aunt were over upon a visit just last week.
The Counsellor is as worthy a gentleman as ever I saw. Your friend
was a favourite with all of them. From morning to night I admired the
charming Mary Ann. Upon my honour, I never was so much in love.
I never was before in a situation to which there was not some objection. But "here every flower is united,"[8] and not a thorn to be found.
But how shall I manage it? They were in a hurry, and are gone home
to Ireland. They were sorry they could not come to see Auchinleck, of
which they had heard a great deal. Mary Ann wished much to be in
the grotto. It is a pity they did not come. This princely seat would have
had some effect.

I received the kindest invitation to come and see them in Ireland,

[4] The bankruptcy of Fenwick Stow, who was the grandfather of both Temple
and his wife, cost Temple £1100 of her marriage portion.

[5] Temple had offered to lend him £1000 towards the purchase of a commission,
probably in 1762.

[6] Mary Ann Boyd. See Introduction, p. xvii.

[7] The Montgomeries of Lainshaw.

[8] He had applied the same quotation to Miss Blair only a year before (see p. 81).

and I promised to be there in March. In the mean time both the father and the aunt write to me. What a fortunate fellow am I! What variety of adventures in all countries! I was allowed to walk a great deal with Miss. I repeated my fervent passion to her, again and again. She was pleased, and I could swear that her little heart beat. I carved the first letter of her name on a tree. I cut off a lock of her hair, *male pertinaci.*[9] She promised not to forget me, nor to marry a lord before March. Her aunt said to me, "Mr. Boswell, I tell you seriously there will be no fear of this succeeding, but from your own inconstancy. Stay till March." All the Scotch cousins too think I may be the happy man. Ah! my friend, I am now as I ought to be. No reserved, prudent, cautious conduct as with Miss Blair. No, all youthful, warm, natural; in short, all genuine love. Pray tell me what you think. I have a great confidence in your judgment. I mean not to ask what you think of my angelic girl. I am fixed beyond a possibility of doubt as to her. Believe me, she is like a part of my very soul. But will not the fond parents insist on having quality for their daughter, who is to have so large a fortune? Or do you think that the Baron of Auchinleck is great enough? Both father, mother, and aunt assured me of my high character in Ireland, where my book is printed, the "third" edition. That is no bad circumstance. I shall see in what style the Counsellor writes, and shall send some elegant present to my lovely mistress.

This is the most agreeable passion I ever felt. Sixteen, innocence, and gaiety make me quite a Sicilian swain. Before I left London, I made a vow in St. Paul's Church that I would not allow myself in licentious connections of any kind for six months. I am hitherto firm to my vow, and already feel myself a superior being. I have given up my criminal intercourse with Mrs. ———. In short, Maria[1] has me without any rival. I do hope the period of my perfect felicity as far as this state of being can afford is now in view.

The affairs of the brave Corsicans interest me exceedingly. Is it not shocking in France to send a great armament against such a noble little people?[2] I have had four letters from the General this summer.

[9] "Ill-defended" (Horace, *Odes,* I. ix. 24).

[1] Mary Ann.

[2] The French were now intent on making good their claim to Corsica, and were sending large numbers of troops into the Island.

He and his countrymen are resolved to stand to the last. I have hopes that our Government will interfere. In the mean time by a private subscription in Scotland, I am this week sending £700 worth of ordnance. The Carron Company has furnished me them very cheap. There are two 32 pounders, four 24's, four 18's, and twenty 9 pounders, with one hundred fifty ball to each. It is really a tolerable train of artillery. . . . [3]

And now, my dear friend, I trust that you will forgive my long silence and will be assured that I ever am with the warmest regard, your affectionate and faithful

JAMES BOSWELL.

[Boswell to Temple]

Edinburgh, 9 December 1768

MY DEAR TEMPLE, — I delay not a post to tell you that I have received your letter of the 27th November, and that I sincerely sympathize with the gloomy feelings which at present seem to distress you. Your long silence made me really uneasy. I did not know what to think, and I was just going to have written to Mrs. Temple or to Lord Lisburne to enquire if my best friend was alive. I thank God I have you still, for indeed, my dear Temple, I cannot be without you.

I trust that before this reaches you the clouds will be dispelled. Believe me, your imagination has suggested false terrors. Read Epictetus. Read Johnson. Let a manly and firm philosophy brace your mind, and you will be convinced that although you deserve a better situation, you have no reason to be dejected. After all your misfortunes, I believe you have £200 of your own, which with Mrs. Temple's 1300 is no inconsiderable fund. Your living is, I believe, £80 a year, which with what you have clear after paying your father's annuity may enable you to live very comfortably. Be not too anxious on account of your children. Educate them with good principles and active habits, and they will make their way through life. I wish you

[3] It was later decided to send fewer pieces of ordnance and a greater amount of ammunition. The shipment reached Leghorn safely, but it is not known whether Paoli ever received it. According to newspaper reports, almost £20,000 was raised by subscription and private gift for the Corsicans before their submission in the summer of 1769. Boswell was directly or indirectly responsible for all of this aid.

joy of your son, and I most heartily accept the office of being his god-father; I give you my solemn promise that I shall be in earnest to do my duty; and if my best friend shall leave the world before me, it may be a comfort to him to think that I am left some time longer to take care of his children. If taking a journey to Devonshire could be of any essential service to you, I should willingly come. But in this case, a proxy will do.

Mr. Hume is not to go to Paris. He is busy with the continuation of his *History*.[4] You admire our Scottish authors too much. But you know, my worthy friend, we differ just enough to enliven us and afford some exercise for our talents.

I cannot approve of your wishing to leave your family. It was a sudden wish while your mind was unhinged. Do not allow yourself to suppose that Lord Lisburne will do nothing more for you. He is your relation. Keep well with him, and things may come about. Let me beseech you, Temple, not to fix your desire on external greatness. Recollect how you and I flattered ourselves that we were to be the greatest men of our time.

> Rectius vives, Licini, neque altum
> Nimis urgendo.[5]

Do you know that in reality your uneasiness is owing to your allowing yourself to think too much of those who have superior degrees of the favour of fortune. Pardon me, my friend, if I write thus. I am sure I mean it well. I should like much to have you settled in the English Chapel here. But I believe the income is less than at your present residence. I shall, however, consider of it, and inquire as to particulars and when there will be an opening. Keep up your spirits, and pray let me know exactly the state of your affairs. Be assured that my friendship for you is unchangeable.

And now as to myself. What think you, my friend, Miss Blair is Miss Blair still. Her marriage with the Knight is not to be. I understand that when terms came to be considered, neither answered the expectations which they had formed of each other's circumstances,

[4] Of his *History of England*. Actually, Hume was engaged in revising rather than continuing it.

[5] Horace, *Odes*, II. x. 1–2 ("nimis" for "semper"): "You will steer your life's course better, Licinius, if you do not hazard yourself too often on the deep."

and so the match was broken off. After the departure of my *belle Irlandaise*, I was two or three times at Adamtown, and upon my word the old flame was kindled. The *wary mother*, as you called her, told me that it was my own fault that her daughter was not long ago my wife. But that after the young lady had shown me very particular marks of regard, corresponded with me, &c., I had made such a joke of *my love for the Heiress* in every company that she was piqued and did not believe that I had any serious intentions. That in the mean time, the Knight offered, and what could she do? Temple, to a man again in love this was engaging. I walked whole hours with the Princess. I kneeled; I became truly amorous. But she told me that "really she had a very great regard for me, but did not like me so as to marry me." You never saw such coldness. Yet the Nabob told me upon his honour and salvation that he had it from one who had it from Miss Blair's own mouth last year that she was truly in love with me, and reckoned upon having me for her husband.

My relapse into this fever lasted some weeks. I wrote to her as usual the most passionate letters. I said, "I shall not again have the galling reflection that my misery is owing to my own fault." Only think of this, Temple. She might have had me. But luckily for me she still affected the same coldness, and not a line would she write. Then came a kind letter from my amiable Aunt Boyd[6] in Ireland, and all the charms of sweet Marianne revived. Since that time I have been quite constant to her, and as indifferent towards Kate as if I never had thought of her. She is still in the country. Should I write to her and tell her that I am cured as she wished? Or is there more dignity in just letting the affair sleep? After her behaviour, do I, the candid, generous Boswell, owe her anything? Am I anyhow bound by passionate exclamations to which she did not even answer? Write to me immediately, my dear friend. She will be here soon. I am quite easy with her. What should I do? By all that's enchanting I go to Ireland in March. What should I say to Kate? You see I am still the old man. I have still need of your advice.[7] Write me without delay. I shall soon give you a more general epistle.

[6] Mary Ann's aunt, Mrs. Jane Boyd. She was probably a sister-in-law of Margaret Montgomerie's father, David Montgomerie.

[7] Here Kate Blair virtually disappears from the scene. She married her cousin,

Adieu, my dearest friend. My kind compliments to Mrs. Temple. Ever yours,

JAMES BOSWELL.

P.S. I am just now a good deal in debt. If you want any credit from me, let me know some weeks before. Excuse this. Whatever I can do you may always depend on.

Sir William Maxwell of Monreith in 1776, sold Adamtown in 1783, and died in 1798.

1769

[Boswell to George Dempster]

I

Edinburgh, 23 February 1769

DEAR DEMPSTER, — The fire was prepared,
    Your letter is burnt,
    Your sighs all consumed,
    A delicate show.
    Go on, undismayed,
    For love is a debt,
    A debt on demand,
    So she must not say no.

I would give the best horse in my stable to have you here just now. I would talk to you for seven hours without intermission — Dempster, you dog, why did you allow me to approach the mines? I went into the basket thinking to amuse myself by going down a little way, and looking at the spars, &c. But before I had time to recollect myself, away went the pulleys and I found myself two hundred fathoms below ground, where a candle would not burn and where I could hardly breathe. So it happened to me at John Tait's on Friday last. I had dined at Lord Glencairn's and was just mellow with claret. B. and Kate with Miss Gordon[8] and some more company supped at Mr. Tait's. I was there a little after eight. I got close to B. I never ceased conversation with her till supper. I told her, "You are in a noble situation. We

---

[8] Miss Gordon is probably Catherine Gordon of Stair, whom Boswell had briefly considered as a matrimonial possibility. Burns, who presented her with a manuscript collection of his poems, praised her "benevolence of temper and goodness of heart" (*Letters of Robert Burns*, i. 43). — B. remains a mysterious figure. As Boswell and Dempster's correspondence makes plain, she was Boswell's cousin, heiress to valuable mining properties, and much loved by Dempster. As early as July 1768 he had refused Boswell's offer to sound her out on his behalf.

all (except myself who am in Ireland) pass before you. You may choose whom you please." Said she, "Do you think that so great an advantage?" "Come," said I, "I know what you mean, you have the pain of refusing. Never mind that. It is all fancy. There is no doubt but you may prefer one man to another who you must own is a more respectable character. So no man can take it amiss." "But," said she, "everybody does not think as you do, and I should be sorry not to have it in my power to make a return to a man who thinks me essential to his happiness."

What think you of this? I gazed and admired. It is impossible to put in a letter the fiftieth part of our conversation. I got next her at supper, and she and I talked on and on together. I was the cousin and called her m. c.;[9] at last I felt myself absolutely in love. I am positive she saw it. I cried, "Ah! this is wrong, this is wrong." There was I, in torment before this divinity. In one corner, my sweet Marianne was chiding my inconstancy in her simple, lively way. *Malo me petit, lasciva puella.*[1] In another corner my friend like Banquo's ghost shook his gory locks at me. I endeavoured to rage about Ireland. But I faltered. I begged she would dance with me at next assembly. She agreed. Next day Peter Craufurd and Bob Chalmers dined at my father's. Bob joked about mines. I spoke strongly for you. He said, "She did not know you was Dempster's advocate." Yesterday I dined at Bob's: the President, Sinclair, and so many more jolly boys; B. and her sisters; I, next her again. Not as at Tait's in glowing spirits, but calm and placid, suffering real pain, and yet keeping conversation ever alive. I am sure I have said nothing amiss, and you may depend on an honesty which nothing can vary. This evening will try me severely. I wish from my soul that you had her. I know the feverish temperature of my soul, and I know I can cure it. But if I were sure that her fancy is wayward enough not to choose you, I would throw myself headlong into the awful abyss. May I ask her about you? May I tell her the whole truth?

The mistress of the Spuilhouse[2] said to me when I harangued on

[9] M. C. may well be initials for first names, as for Margaret Caroline.
[1] "The wanton girl flings an apple at me [and runs off, wishing first to be seen]" (altered from Virgil, *Eclogues*, iii. 64).
[2] Spuilhouse (properly spelled *speelhuis*) is Dutch; in the eighteenth century

Hibernia, "Ye're a great idiot." What could this mean? Plague on that disposition, be it vanity or be it idle fancy, which makes a man interpret everything for himself. When I asked B. to dance at this assembly, she said she made it a rule never to dance two nights together; and she was engaged to the Capillaire Ball on Friday.[3] "Madam," said I, "I beg you may do something more than common, something extraordinary for me." She waited a little, and then with that look and that soft voice which you know, said just — "Yes." I said, "I see you give your answer at once." Said she, "I always do, and that prevents me from being teased." She said she was very independent, and she was determined to (here she said something which meant that she was to make a very difficult choice; I forget the words). In short, Dempster, she is a perfect woman, and I think at this moment I could take her without a shilling. Such madness! However don't mind me. I can take care of myself. Where is the rock of Carrickfergus now?[4] It will soon appear again. Thus have I given you a most candid abstract. I shall write to you again tomorrow. Burn me as I burn you. I say there are few men who are capable of such a correspondence. Tell me what to do. Ever yours,

                                    J.B.

II

                        Edinburgh, 24 February 1769

DEAR DEMPSTER, — I did not send off my letter of last night. I waited till the Assembly should be over. I was worse than ever. I was in a delirium. But being dressed in sea-green and silver with a sword, I assumed spirits, and in a gay, smiling manner tried to find out how she would be courted. She said a man of sense might soon find out

---

it meant a low public dance hall (see *Boswell in Holland*, 26 May 1764). Boswell is presumably making a sarcastic reference to the Assembly of Edinburgh. The Mistress of the Spuilhouse would then be the Hon. Miss Nicholas Helen ("Nicky") Murray, who ruled over these dances for many years.

[3] The Capillaire Club was a convivial Edinburgh society (capillaire is a syrup used to flavour drinks). The Club's annual ball was one of the more brilliant social events of the year.

[4] The Irish seaport and fortress, celebrated in the song, *The Siege of Carrickfergus*, which served to remind Boswell of Mary Ann Boyd and his projected trip to Ireland.

whether he was a woman's choice, and that she would never be forced by perseverance to take a man she did not like at first, though she owned that perseverance in a real attachment might have some effect. But then she would be sure of his motives (no doubt she meant if *mines* or charms). "But," said I, "suppose a man loves you sincerely, and yet has always talked in a general style and has been afraid to address you particularly; what say you to that?" Said she, "That is a disagreeable situation, both for the man and the woman. And what can a woman do?" I said, "Oh, see him and give him an opportunity to open his mind." She said, "No — if you do not intend to have him." This was severe, for she certainly knew what I meant, as I had already said, "I had this morning a letter from a gentleman who I believe loves you as much as possible," and then expatiated on his character, as you know I can do.

I then asked her if sending a friend to inquire was a good way. She said, "Nothing can be more indelicate to a woman. If I even had some liking for a man, that would destroy it. If I had none, it would be a good reason to give for refusing him." Dempster, this made D. R.[5] alarming. I then asked her how comes it that a lady shall refuse a man whom all his friends love and esteem, who is worthy and amiable in every respect? Said she, "Perhaps the lady just thinks of him as all his friends do, who speak so much of him. But she has not that particular regard which you would have for one with whom you would spend your life." "Well," said I, "that is putting it in a light I never saw it before. I understand you. Perhaps we all like the man — but would any of us marry him? I see it."

Now, my friend, what say you to all this? Though my letter is dated on the 24 (Friday) I am writing this part of it on Saturday. I am rather warm with wine. But I would not delay another post. So you must take it as I can write. Yesterday (Friday) I called about twelve and found her in the coach waiting till her sisters should come down. She danced with young Pitfour at the Capillaire Ball last night, and this morning I found her at home just going out. By all that's sacred, *ut vidi, ut perii*.[6] I never in my life was so much in love.

For heaven's sake, Dempster, determine what you are to do. How pleasant is it to think that it is literally true that, although I now love

[5] Possibly David Rae, an advocate and later Lord Justice-Clerk.

[6] "I saw; I perished" (Virgil, *Eclogues*, viii. 41).

her to distraction, I would be sincerely happy at your getting her. This is upon honour the truth. Come over, or write to her, or give her up. And let me set myself at rest, one way or other. If she is for you, God bless you both. If not, I will ask her, and then we shall be *companions*. I will not see her again till I hear from you. For upon my conscience I am miserable in her company. I asked her if she would use a lover well who would candidly tell her all his mind. She said yes. Said I, "Would you endeavour to make him as easy as possible, and be a friend to him?" "Yes." O Dempster, write to me without delay, and instead of burning those frantic pages return them, that I may read them calmly. Pray do. Was there ever such a situation? Adieu, my excellent friend. What philosophy have I! What amazing command of human nature!

[Received ?6 March, Hailes to Boswell][7]

Edinburgh, 4 March 1769

Sir: — When I received that information which occasioned your letter, your father was just in my sight, and in my astonishment I relieved myself by telling him what I had heard.[8] What I said was from information, and did not consist with my own personal knowledge. Nor could it, for if all my friends had been at the door I might have

[7] On 27 February, the House of Lords had reversed the Court of Session's decision in the Douglas cause, and confirmed Archibald Douglas's position as lawful heir to the late Duke of Douglas. The news reached Edinburgh on the night of 2 March and the populace took over. They ordered among others all the judges, whether or not they had voted for Douglas, to illuminate, breaking windows and doing further mischief where they met opposition. On the second night of celebration, the military were called in to patrol the streets and protect certain judges' houses.

[8] Boswell's letter has not been recovered. From what Hailes writes, one would infer that Hailes had told Lord Auchinleck that Boswell was in the mob that attacked his house, and that Boswell had written to demand his authority: had he *seen* him there? It was commonly reported, probably correctly, that Boswell had not merely been one of the mob, but that he had headed it. John Ramsay says that his "behaviour on that occasion savoured so much of insanity that it was generally imputed to his Dutch blood" (*Scotland and Scotsmen*, 1888, i. 173). This letter of Hailes makes it appear either that Boswell was disguised or that he was confident that nobody except members of the mob had seen him while the assaults were being made.

been killed by going out to speak to them before I could be known. Had the mob satisfied themselves with breaking my windows and thrown in stones which might have murdered the family, I might have been less displeased when the first attack was over. But renewed attacks not at windows but at my door, in order to break it open; *these* are insults which every man of spirit and dignity must feel.

I am not at liberty to suppose that you had any hand in such things directly, and I wish that you may have an opportunity of letting me know that you did not countenance the mob when in my neighbourhood and just in the street where I live; I never could ask you any more particular question, for this reason which upon recollection will suggest itself to you, that had you in an unguarded hour forgot yourself and me, and had you acknowledged it, this would [have] been a circumstance for proving one of the greatest insults that has been committed, except those against the President.[9]

Had I been a private man I should have probably submitted to humour the mob in their fancy, but in my situation as a judge I thought that I could not submit to any commands but legal commands, unless in the case of necessity when the safety of an only child, and she too not in condition to be transported to a place of safety, might have prevailed over my sentiments of propriety. When I found that breaking my windows did not satisfy the populace, I had recourse to the last resort of civil order, a military force; a chairman whom I had not employed for many years came down to me and begged that I might call for instant assistance. I bless God, who enabled me to act according to my own opinion on Friday night. I did not call for any aid till the necessity urged, and if anything had happened, I should not have been answerable for the consequences. I am, Sir, your most obedient servant,

DAV. DALRYMPLE.

[Received *c.* 15 March, Dempster to Boswell]

[Dunnichen, *c.* 12 March 1769]

MY DEAR BOSWELL, — I thank you for both your letters. The contents of 'em were extremely acceptable to me. But my coat of mail is

[9] On his way to the Parliament House in his sedan chair, the President had been jostled by a mob crying, "Pull him down." Also his house was stoned.

all rust; neither sand nor files can give it the least polish. Even the soft breath of Melvina — stuff.[1] You have been rioting, you dog you, and have broke thy honest father's windows, as the story here tells.[2] Nobody suspects that you have thereby broke his heart. Nothing can be so strange as the present state of my affair. D.R. at my request waited of[3] B. and desired to know if I should take what I had got for a refusal, expressing in the strongest terms my resolution not to be a troublesome or impertinent suitor. He writes me he found B. ⟨so⟩ silent and reserved that he thought it indelicate ⟨to inquire⟩ farther, and is as little qualified to advise me now as before he spoke with B. on the subject. He recommends it to me to see her as I go to London, and doubts not but my own good sense and penetration will enable me to determine what is proper afterwards to be done.[4]

Your Irish plan is very prudently and properly concerted. By all means carry the approbation of the old gentleman along with you. Not that your interest would suffer by neglecting it, but that you may enjoy the exquisite satisfaction of gilding the evening of his life by every act of filial duty and attention. The public, whose faithful servant he has been so long, expect, nay exact, this of you. I am not much in the humour of writing today. The weather is fine, I have a

[1] Perhaps an allusion to Malvina in Book 4 of Macpherson's *Fingal*. Boswell, in a missing letter, had presumably urged Dempster to carry off B. like a hero of old.

[2] Lord Marischal wrote to Boswell (26 August 1769): "I am highly delighted with your behaviour in the Douglas cause. . . . You broke, I am told, your father's windows because they were not enough illuminate. Bravo, bravissimo!" According to Ramsay, Lord Auchinleck "entreated the President, with tears in his eyes, to put his son in the Tolbooth." Being asked by Sheriff Cockburn to tell what had happened in his own way Boswell is supposed to have said: "After I had communicated the glorious news to my father, who received them very coolly, I went to the Cross to see what was going on. There I overheard a group of fellows forming their plan of operations. One of them asked what sort of man the Sheriff was, and whether he was not to be dreaded. 'No, no,' answered another, 'he is a puppy of the President's making.' " On hearing this, the Sheriff went off and left Boswell to himself (*Scotland and Scotsmen,* i. 173 *n.*1). Boswell, of course, was not punished in any way.

[3] Scots for "waited on."

[4] Dempster later reported that he had called on B. twice in Edinburgh, but that she had refused even to see him.

guest who waits for me to ride out with him, my mind is distracted, but I could not restrain myself ⟨from⟩ sending you a letter. Write me ⟨? from the⟩ west, and believe me unalterably ⟨yours⟩.

[Boswell to John Johnston]

[Auchinleck, 31 March 1769]

DEAR SIR, — We had an agreeable journey west and a comfortable meeting with our cousins at Lainshaw, whom we found much better than we expected. We stayed six nights there. And now we are safe at Auchinleck, where is also my brother John.

I am endeavouring to acquire a taste for country affairs, and hope by degrees to do quite well. If you will give orders about the planting of the trees, I will fall on a method of getting them sent to Grange. But I would fain hope you may contrive matters so as to come here and stay a while, before you go home. My cousins of Lainshaw intend going to Ireland, so I shall have good company. We are to set out the last week of April or first of May. James Bruce tells me that the trees fit for sending you at present are the red fir of Hanover, the larix, and the different sorts of pines. I can get a parcel sent to Dumfries, from whence you can have them taken to Grange. Perhaps you have these kinds of trees already. If so, it is needless to send them. But if they will be an acceptable present to you, please let me know.

I have done nothing for my black friend these many weeks, which is very wrong. I therefore enclose you a draught for £10, which you may negotiate and deliver the money, together with my letter, to Mr. Hamilton, surgeon in the Back Stairs. If you think it needless for me to correspond with him about my black friend, you need not deliver the letter; but just at my desire inquire how all goes, and just say what I have said in the letter, and then inform me.[5] I think it would be proper to have as little interference as possible. If you would call yourself with Mr. Hamilton and deliver the money, it would be obliging. You will judge if any receipt is necessary.

I am now as calm and quiet as if I had not been from Auchinleck

---

[5] "Tell her," said Boswell in his letter to Alexander Hamilton, "that my reason for not seeing her for some time is my resolution to take no part, either one way or other, in a certain dispute." The matter of the dispute is unknown.

for years. Do come, my dear friend. Is it not very odd that one with whom I am in such intimacy should hardly ever be here? You ought never to be a year absent. I ever am, with most sincere regard, your affectionate friend,

JAMES BOSWELL.

TUESDAY 25 APRIL.[6] Miss Montgomerie and I set out from Auchinleck. My father was so averse to my Irish expedition that she had not resolution to agree to accompany me. Dr. Johnston took leave of me, and seemed most anxious for my safe return. My father walked out, and I did not take leave of him. It was a delightful day. We were calm and social. We came to Treesbank at four. Mr. Campbell[7] had been at a burial, so dinner was not begun. We were cordially entertained, and very merry here.

WEDNESDAY 26 APRIL. I gave up my place in the Lainshaw chaise to Lady Treesbank, and rode my mare. Miss Annie Cuninghame was with us.[8] We came to Lainshaw to dinner. The Captain[9] said he would fulfil his promise of going to Portpatrick with me. This left no objection to Miss Montgomerie's going, especially as both her sisters were clear for it. This was a great point gained to me. I felt myself quite at home at Lainshaw. Annie and her three eldest brothers were there. I gave them raisins and called this giving them *grocery*, a word which relished much. I sent Thomas to Glasgow to bring a chaise. My love for Marianne revived most beautifully.

THURSDAY 27 APRIL. The Captain, Mrs. Montgomerie-Cuninghame and Lady Treesbank, and I took a long walk. They were all of my opinion as to the Irish scheme, so right is it for a man to have perseverance. I stated to the Captain the process Brown against Parr, and was assisted by him. As there was no law in the case, his strong common sense was excellent for it. After dinner we drank pretty

---

[6] Here Boswell begins his Journal again. This section he endorsed: "Journal of the first part of my jaunt to Ireland in 1769 with Miss Peggie Montgomerie. I regret that I ceased when it would have been most interesting."

[7] See p. 55 *n.*6.

[8] Annie Cuninghame was the daughter of Captain and Mrs. Montgomerie-Cuninghame. "Lady Treesbank" was Mary (Montgomerie) Campbell, James Campbell's wife, sister to Mrs. Montgomerie-Cuninghame and Margaret Montgomerie.

[9] Captain Montgomerie-Cuninghame.

freely, and he gave me very good hopes of a scheme that will gratify my ambition in a very honourable way. The families of Auchinleck and Lainshaw and Corsehill and Treesbank united may do much, and we resolved they should be united to the end of time.[1] As we were much in the spirit of Douglas, I put a bottle of wine and a glass in my pocket, and he and I resolved to go and drink to Douglas under the old tower at Corsehill, which had formerly belonged to the illustrious family. We stopped at Oliver's in Stewarton and drank a little punch, and bottled up the rest of our bowl, and then, attended by Oliver and John Brown, one of the Captain's feuars,[2] we went to the ancient spot and did drink most happily, and huzzaed as boldly as if there had been a hundred of us. Drink makes men appear numerous. We feel double as well as see double. Mrs. Montgomerie-Cuninghame and Mrs. Campbell came out to us and brought us home. I was quite drunk. I am sorry for it. I behaved ill to Margaret, my own affectionate friend. Such terrible effects may intoxication have.

FRIDAY 28 APRIL. I rose with a headache and the disagreeable reflection that I had offended Margaret. When she came down I found her so much hurt that she would not have set out on our Irish jaunt, had she not been so kind that she would not assign the cause of her staying. I was very sorry, and resolved to make up to her for what she had suffered by my future good behaviour. We took some breakfast at Lainshaw; and then we and the Captain, Mrs. Montgomerie-Cuninghame, and Lady Treesbank all drove to Irvine, where Mr. Graham had breakfast ready for us at his house. On the road it was curious for me to think how different things in reality may be from what they appear. Margaret and I on bad terms were yet driving in one chaise, and going on a jaunt of pleasure all the way to Dublin. But the quarrels of friends never last.

At Irvine we had Dr. George Augustus Cuninghame to attend us. We left Mrs. Montgomerie-Cuninghame and Lady Treesbank, and the Captain and Mrs. Graham rode with us to Ayr. It was a charming day, and Margaret and I became gentle and complacent. My love of

[1] The scheme that would gratify Boswell's ambition was probably a union of the political interests of the families mentioned, which might help him to be elected to Parliament for Ayrshire.

[2] One who holds a piece of land on perpetual lease for a fixed rent.

making a show was gratified, for we had sent our servants on to order dinner, and it was a fair-day, and the streets were crowded with people; and honest James Gibson came forth and marched like a macer, clearing the way for us. After a cheerful welcome to each other to Ayr, James the waiter agreeably surprised me by delivering me my Roman ring, which I had lost. I also received a very handsome letter from Paoli, so that I was in noble spirits. We dined well and took a merry glass with our old landlord, who, having bought his house, was now *Laird* Gibson, and then we drank tea at Mrs. Kerr's, where was a whole drawing-room of people. Among others, who should be there but Balmuto's heiress and her Glasgow cousin![3] This was fine for show. I then paid a visit at Auchinskeith's, where I received a two-guinea consultation from a company at Glasgow, by the hands of Craigengillan. I next paid a visit at Mr. Duff's; and then returned to our inn, where we had Mrs. Kerr and her daughter, and Captain Ballantyne and Dr. Mackie, her attendants, and Miss Cuninghame of Auchinskeith to sup with us.

SATURDAY 29 APRIL. I breakfasted at Auchinskeith's, from whence we set out and drove all the length of the town of Ayr (a fine show, surely). We stopped a little at Rozelle.[4] There I put the Captain into the chaise, and I rode my mare. There was this day a meeting of the gentlemen of the shire, and so, besides shaking hands with Doon-side over one of his dykes, I had the satisfaction of *showing* to many of the Carrick gentlemen. It was fine to meet Sir Adam Fergusson after the glorious Douglas decision. I called out to him, " 'Sir Fletcher, Sir Fletcher, your servant.'[5] Well, Sir Adam, I never saw you with so much pleasure. We no longer meet as foes." I then showed him Paoli's letter, and we were classically companionable. I and my fellow travellers stopped at Maybole and got a pretty good dinner. The old Laird of Killantringan drank a glass with us.

[3] Claud Boswell of Balmuto married Anne Irvine, heiress of Kingcausie, but as the marriage did not take place until 1783 it is not probable that she is referred to here. Just possibly Balmuto is a slip for Adamtown.
[4] The seat of Robert Hamilton of Bourtreehill, and, after his death, of his daughter the Countess of Crawford, Margaret Montgomerie's dear friend.
[5] Sir Fletcher Norton had been one of Douglas's English counsel, and thus on the other side from Fergusson (see p. 27 *n.*5). Boswell appears to be recalling to Fergusson some joke about Sir Fletcher that they shared.

I felt myself in love with another woman than Marianne.[6] I spoke of it to Margaret. She is always my friend and comforter. She and I were now admirable company. I observed that there were few people but were mixed characters, like a candle: half wax, half tallow. But Sir Adam Fergusson was all wax, a pure taper, whom you may light and set upon any lady's table. I observed that she and I had more enlarged views, as we had fancy to look beyond what really is ours — like one whose house has a prospect not only of his own lands, but of many beautiful objects at a distance. That Balmuto saw nothing but what was solid, and substantially his own. That he had thick high stone walls built round that extent, and had that only in his view, except when I surprised him by sometimes taking a hammer and beating a hole in his walls so as to give him a peep of the fields of fancy, which made him caper; but his mother and sisters took care to build all up again directly. When I talked that Corsica was a very hilly country, Margaret observed that the French would have *uphill* work there.

We came at night to Ardmillan. Mr. Craufurd we had met going to Ayr, and he could not be home; but we found his mother, a fine old lady full of life, an Episcopal and a Jacobite, and his three sisters. We were most hospitably entertained, but my serious passion hung heavily on my mind. I feared that the lady was engaged, and I was in great uneasiness all night.

SUNDAY 30 APRIL. I was restless and rose at six, and walked to the top of the highest mountain, from whence I saw a great way. The sea and Ailsa pleased me. Ardmillan stands at the foot of a hill. There is little planting about it. But a good garden, some fields in excellent culture, and pretty green hills with a prospect as far as Ireland. The old lady and I were great friends. I read part of the service of the day to her, and took her prayer-book with me that I might get silver clasps put upon it at Dublin. No man ever understood the little arts of obliging better than I do, and the peculiar beauty in my case is that what others have done from designing views, I do from an amiable disposition to make people happy. No doubt, I have sometimes had my designs, too. But, in general, I have none.

[6] Margaret Montgomerie herself. Boswell continues to refer to her in this mysterious manner.

The Captain found himself fatigued, so Miss Montgomerie and I agreed that he should go no farther. We dined here, and at four we set out and took a Sabbath day's journey to Ballantrae. By the way, my serious passion came into my mind with more force than ever. I imagined that Miss Montgomerie knew the lady's mind, and from some things she said, I concluded that the lady was engaged. I was amazingly affected. I cried bitterly, and would not speak to my companion. I, who was on an expedition to court a pretty young lady at Dublin, and had with me a most agreeable companion, was miserable from love of another woman, and would not speak to my companion. Such a mind! I never was in greater torment, nor indulged gloomier schemes. We had a good inn at Ballantrae. For ten minutes I continued as bad as in the chaise, till Miss Montgomerie by chance discovered the cause of all my misery, and with her usual kindness assured me that I was mistaken. I then enjoyed the most delightful calm after a dismal storm. We drank tea comfortably after our journey, read part of the evening service, had some agreeable religious conversation, and then supped cheerfully. I was so much rejoiced that, after she went to bed, I got Mactaggart the landlord to drink with me till I staggered. Such wild transitions! A punster would say the landlord might be called *Macstaggered*.

MONDAY 1 MAY. My last night's riot hurt me a little. I begged my companion's pardon, we breakfasted, and set out in good humour. I entertained my companion with stories of Mr. Samuel Johnson, and we walked up the monstrous hill of Glen App very cleverly. We stopped at ——,[7] a place now Sir Thomas Wallace's, formerly a Colonel Agnew's. It is just a piece of low ground gradually descending from the bottom of a range of hills. There is a neat house, and the most is made of the space that ever I saw, there being a fine garden with variety of flowers and fruit both on standards and walls, fish-ponds, and a few pretty enclosures. The sea is just before it, and the avenue is in the old style. I had a great desire to buy this place. It was such a one as I had often fancied in a romantic mood, and I thought I and my companion could live at it most happily. We had a pretty drive along the shore and through Stranraer to Portpatrick, which has the oddest-like rocky shore I have seen. It is a poor town, and instead of appear-

[7] Lochryan.

ing a very public thoroughfare as it really is, it looks like a remote Highland sea-coast village. We dined here, and after dinner were visited by Mr. Fraser of the customs, formerly an attendant on the Earl of Cassillis, an obliging little man. He accompanied us to Craigbuy, the seat of Mr. Blair of Dunskey. There is little done about it. But there is a fine prospect to the sea. There was nobody at home but the two Miss Blairs. The eldest is a very pretty girl, and seems to have much goodness. I did not observe the other so much.

We drank tea, and then they walked down with us to the port, where we engaged a boat, the *James and* ———, Captain Cosh, commander, to carry us to the other side of the water. As we knew we would be sick, we determined to sail that night and try to sleep, as there was a good cabin. We had our company to sup with us, and were very well. Mr. Campbell of Airies, the collector of the customs here, arrived at home about eleven, and came to us. I had not seen him for seventeen years. We were very cordial. At twelve my companion and I went aboard. I tried to brave it out for a while, but grew very sick. She was better than I. Only I got some sleep, which she did not. Nothing can be severer than to be sick at sea, for one has no hope that immediate relief may come, as in other sicknesses. One grows quite weak. I thought my Irish jaunt madness, and that I would not try another. Such are our minds at times. It was a very moderate breeze. We got over in about five hours.

TUESDAY 2 MAY. It was pleasant to see the Irish shore, but from my distracted passions I had not the joy I had promised myself. We put up at the Hillsborough Arms, and drank a dish of tea. It was a bad house. Between seven and eight we went to Collector Boyd's.[8] We were met by our amiable friend Aunt Boyd, and in a little her husband came and we were received like relations and friends. We then saw Miss Boyd and the two youngest daughters, and my acquaintance Mr. Ponsonby Boyd, all their children then at home. We found here an admirable house, and took a good second breakfast. Then came Miss Macbride, a niece of Mr. Boyd's.

The Collector, Mr. Ponsonby, and I took horses from the stable, and rode out along the shore ———, which is every now and then agreeably varied with a fine strand on which a race might be run. I ob-

[8] Hugh, Aunt Boyd's husband. Ponsonby Boyd, mentioned below, was their second son.

served the ground naturally good and much enriched with marl, which covers it with daisies. The country here is, I may say, universally enclosed, though not in the best way, with mounds planted all over with whins, which do not look so well as thorns and are apt to spread. This may be much prevented by clearing the ditches and often ploughing the ground. And I observed a droll way of restraining their sheep, which was by putting them in couples just like dogs, which, however, they say prevents their feeding so well. I observed in the churchyards a kind of black stone like slate which was very becoming as gravestones, much more so than our white ones.

We went to Grey Abbey, where is one of the finest Gothic ruins I ever saw, though there are but small remains of it. There has been a noble church and a large convent. Of the convent little is left. But there is a good part of the church standing; in particular there is an end window with three divisions in it, exceedingly Gothic, and covered with a thicker ivy than I ever saw, which adds greatly to its appearance. There is also standing a side window just adjoining to this end. It is a lofty arch eight yards or more wide at the bottom. I measured seven lengths and a third of my cane.

While we were looking at this piece of antiquity, which belongs to Mr. Montgomery of Rosemount, his eldest son, a young officer, walking about with dogs and his gun, came up to us, asked Mr. Boyd and Ponsonby, whom he knew, how they were, and begged we might all go and see his father's house, which stands not far above where we were. We went with him and found it to be an excellent house of Mr. Montgomery's own planning, and not yet finished. He was not at home, but his lady and two daughters were very obliging, gave us bread and wine, and begged we would stay dinner. I already saw a specimen of an Irish gentleman's family in the country. We walked about the place, which is remarkable for a fine view of the sea, particularly of Strangford Bay. There is also a good deal planted. I saw here a singular thing, at least to me: a goldfinch's nest in a young pine. I believe birds never build in pines till they are well grown up, and then only large birds such as crows.

We rode another way from that which we had come. As we passed by ———,[9] Mr. Mathews, the gentleman to whom it belongs, met us as he was out riding, and begged we would take pot luck with him. So

[9] Probably Springvale, the seat of George Mathews.

hospitable is everybody here. We got home to dinner in good time. Aunt Boyd, as we call her, keeps a regular, genteel, good table as ever I saw, and the Collector and I took our bottle apiece of claret at dinner and supper every day.

WEDNESDAY 3 MAY. Mrs. Boyd carried Miss Montgomerie and me to wait of the Countess Dowager Mount Alexander, a French lady, who was first married to a peer of France, and afterwards to Lord Mount Alexander, by whom she has a great estate about Donaghadee.[1] She is a fine, lively old lady, has been much in the gay world, but lives now quite retired and dresses like a common farmer's wife. But as she has read a great deal, she is very good company. I should have mentioned that Mrs. Boyd and Miss Montgomerie had last night resolved not to go with me to Dublin. This vexed me much; and, although I said nothing, they saw me in such an humour that they this morning agreed to attend me. Our day passed very comfortably. We had with us at tea and supper a Mr. Sempill and his two daughters. I was really pleased to hear the Irish tone. But, being still sincerely in love with one whom I do not name, I was vastly uneasy in being distracted between that passion and my Irish schemes.

[Boswell to Temple][2]

Donaghadee, 3 May 1769

MY DEAR TEMPLE, — I am fairly landed in the kingdom of Ireland, and am tomorrow to proceed for Dublin to see my sweet Mary Ann. But my worthy friend, to whom my heart is ever open, and to whom I must apply for advice at all times, I must tell you that I am accompanied by my cousin Miss Montgomerie, whom I believe you saw at Edinburgh, and she perhaps may and perhaps ought to prevent my Hibernian nuptials. You must know that she and I have always been in the greatest intimacy. I have proved her on a thousand occasions, and found her sensible, agreeable, and generous. When I

[1] Boswell's information is unusually inaccurate. Lady Mount Alexander's father was a Huguenot refugee who served under William III, and she was a widow when she married Lord Mount Alexander, but her first husband cannot have been a "peer of France." She also outlived a third husband, whom Boswell does not mention.

[2] This letter is printed here for the first time. It was not sent until later (see entries for 5 May and 16 June 1769).

was not in love with some one or other of my numerous flames, I have been in love with her; and during the intervals of all my passions Margaret has been constantly my mistress as well as my friend. Allow me to add that her person is to me the most desirable that I ever saw. Often have I thought of marrying her, and often told her so. But we talked of my wonderful inconstancy, were merry, and perhaps in two days after the most ardent professions to her I came and told her that I was desperately in love with another woman. Then she smiled, was my confidante, and in time I returned to herself. She is with all this, Temple, the most honest, undesigning creature that ever existed.

Well, Sir, being my cousin german, she accompanies me on my Irish expedition. I found her both by sea and land the best companion I ever saw. I am exceedingly in love with her. I highly value her. If ever a man had his full choice of a wife, I would have it in her. But the objections are she is two years older than I. She has only a thousand pounds. My father would be violent against my marrying her, as she would bring neither money nor interest. I, from a desire to aggrandize my family, think somewhat in the same manner. And all my gay projects of bringing home some blooming young lady, and making an *éclat* with her brilliant fortune would be gone.

But, on the other hand, my cousin is of a fine, firm, lively temperament, and never can be old. She may have as many children as I wish, and from what she has already done as an aunt, I am sure she would make a very good mother. Would not my children be more obliged to me for such a mother than for many thousands? Then, she has much to say with my father, who could not reasonably be enraged at having his niece for daughter-in-law. She would live in such a manner that at my death my family may be richer than if I married a fortune; and for the gay projects of fancy, is there any doubt that they are nothing when compared with real happiness? Many men seek to form friendships with the great, the embroidered, the titled. If they succeed, are they as happy as I am in the friendship of Temple? I fear that if I marry any other woman, my love for my cousin may often distract me. And what weighs much with me, Temple, is that amidst all this merriment and scheming, I really imagine that she truly loves me, that by my courting her so often she is so attached to me, that she would silently suffer very severely if she saw me irrevocably fixed to another.

And yet my charming seraph, my Marianne, melts my heart. Her little bosom beats at the thoughts of seeing me — forgive my vanity — you know, strange as it may be, that women of all tempers and ages have been fond of me. Temple, you never failed me yet. What shall I do? This is the most delicate case of the many that I have laid before you. I must, however, tell you that my father is quite averse to Marianne, and declares he never will agree to it. But if *her* father gives me a round sum, I do not fear *mine*. But if I am certain that my cousin sincerely loves me, wishes to have me, and would be unhappy without me, what should I do? Should I be hard-hearted enough not to give happiness to *the woman I love, and the friend I can trust?* for such she literally is. And if I think of my own happiness, whether do you think that she or the seraph is most certain? And how shall I do not to hurt either of the two? Never did there live such a man as myself. I beseech you write to me without delay: Dublin is address enough for *Corsican Boswell.* Pray is not your wife about your own age? On the other hand, might I not by a couple of thousand pounds marry my cousin so as that both she and I may be more properly disposed of than if we went together?[3]

My dear Temple, I know both your heart and your understanding. Be so kind as immediately to exert them both for me. I shall just amuse myself at Dublin in an easy, general style till your letter arrives. I think I could give up my *certain* felicity with my cousin, and take my chance of the brilliant Irish scheme. But when I throw into the scale the concern that I believe my amiable, worthy, and desirable cousin has in it, what should preponderate? Let us ever be helpful to each other; and believe me to be, my dear Temple, your unalterable, affectionate friend,

JAMES BOSWELL.

THURSDAY 4 MAY. Mr. Ponsonby and I and a Mr. McMinn,[4] a young gentleman here, rode to Newtown, where I found the curate, Mr. Hugh Caldwell, brother to my old friend, Mr. Samuel Caldwell.[5]

[3] This sentence is heavily crossed out in an eighteenth-century ink.
[4] William McMinn later married Jane Charlotte, one of Collector Boyd's daughters.
[5] The Rev. Samuel Caldwell had been one of Boswell's confidants at the Hague in 1764.

He resembles him a good deal, but is bigger and jollier. Mr. Stewart[6] is proprietor of the place, having fourteen thousand a year estate round it. He is building some new streets, the town as yet being of no great extent. Caldwell was very happy to see his brother's friend. He showed me a very pretty chapel here which belonged to the Colville family, formerly lords of this manor. It is prettily stuccoed on the ceiling, and boxed, painted, and gilded on the walls. It stands at the end of the church, which is of no use, there being such a number of Dissenters[7] here that the chapel is sufficient to hold all those of the established communion; to the great concern of Mr. Hugh Caldwell, as I could well perceive from his manner of talking. We drank a glass of white wine at Tom Orr's, and then rode home by Bangor. When we came upon the shore we had a fine view of the bay and old Castle of Carrickfergus, that wonderful place of which I have thought and raved so much as the representative of all my Irish ideas. I sung the song with great violence and was quite the *Hawk*.[8]

After dinner Captain Murray of the old Highland regiment, brother to the Duke of Atholl, and a foreign engineer famous for directing many of the public works in Ireland, arrived in their way to Scotland. Mr. Boyd and I waited on them, and he asked them to his house. They drank tea with us, and showed us a raccoon, an American animal, which they had with them. Lady Mount Alexander drank tea with us. I accompanied her Ladyship home. She asked me in, and gave me a glass of good old claret, and talked of the wonderful works of nature, Fontenelle's *Plurality of Worlds*, and other such subjects. I amused my wild fancy for a moment with thinking how clever it would be for me to carry off the old lady and her great fortune, for which I might well spare a few years. We passed the evening at Mr. Boyd's at brag. The two strangers went away.

FRIDAY 5 MAY. I showed Miss Montgomerie a letter I had written to Temple to have his advice how to proceed in my distracted war

[6]Alexander Stewart, father of the first Marquess of Londonderry and grandfather of the second (better known to history as Viscount Castlereagh). He contributed £100 to the fund which Boswell raised for the Corsicans in Ireland.

[7] Emigrant Scots Presbyterians. The established church was Episcopalian.

[8] "Was quite the *Hawk*" probably means "realized all my spirited ideas of what a Boswell should be." The crest of the Boswells of Auchinleck is a falcon or hawk.

of passions. She would not allow me to send it. But convinced me that the other lady was of so generous a temper that I might marry anyone I liked best, or found most for my interest, and she would even help me to do so. I admired the other lady from the bottom of my heart, and all that Miss Montgomerie told me of her with intention to make me easy only served to distract me more, as it showed me more of her excellent character. We should have set out before now, but our chaises did not come from Belfast till this day.

SATURDAY 6 MAY. We set out for Dublin, Mrs. Boyd and I in one chaise, and Miss Montgomerie and Miss Macbride in another. We arrived safely at Belfast. We passed along a bridge over an arm of the sea. It is said to be an English mile in length. It is indeed amazingly long. It consists of above twenty arches. The town is beautifully situated, but it is not very pretty itself. We took a second breakfast here. Two Miss Pattersons of Comber visited Mrs. Boyd. They were both pretty girls. The eldest was clever and like an actress, and took my idle fancy. All this place belongs to Lord Donegall. I believe no subject in the three kingdoms has so large a town in property. There is a good mall to walk in, but there is some standing water in a ditch that is offensive, and spoils the pleasure of a grove of noble old trees. Miss Macbride and I next were companions. She was full of narrative and very obligingly told me the name of every place we saw, and gave me some account of every person. Between Belfast and Lisburn there is the finest country I ever saw, naturally rich, finely diversified, and improved to the utmost. I never saw such a verdure or such a quantity of grass and daisies upon ground. The linen manufacturers possess this country, and, as every one has but a few acres and pays a rent of four or five pounds an acre, everything is done to enrich the land, and there is plenty of marl in all corners here. It was very agreeable to see a number of bleach fields, the webs looking so white on the green grass, and the people looking so clean. A number of them are Quakers.

Lisburn is one of the prettiest towns I ever saw. The High Street is a good breadth, and consists of admirable brick houses, all inhabited by substantial people. We dined here. A Counsellor Smyth, formerly their Member, said to Miss Macbride that if I was come over to raise contributions for the Corsicans a considerable sum might be raised in Lisburn. I saw here a very odd sign: "Groceries, liquors, and coffins sold here." I made Miss Montgomerie look at it, lest my telling it should appear the report of a traveller. It seemed the man of the shop was resolved that his guests or customers should be in want of nothing, and, if the spirits conveyed them a little abruptly to their long home, coffins were ready for their reception.

I neglected to mention a curious epitaph in the church of New-town: "Here lies the body of one of Joseph Macowan's children, who died April 10, 1754." Epitaphs are usually intended to preserve the memory of the dead. My old professor at Utrecht, *doctissimus* Trot-zius, has written a book, *De memoria propaganda*, or the various methods which mankind have taken to preserve their memories. Amongst these, epitaphs are often mentioned. But this epitaph could only keep up Joseph Macowan's own memory, and assure posterity that he had more than one child. But as to the child, it could serve no purpose. It neither mentions its age, sex, nor even his or her name.

At Lisburn I visited my old acquaintance, Dr. Traill, Bishop of Down and Connor.[9] I was a very little while with him. He told me that, when he read in my *Tour to Corsica* that I had played to the brave Islanders on my flute, he thought how he had made me a present of it. We went at night to Hillsborough. Near to it I saw some of the largest silver firs that I ever beheld. There is at Hillsborough a magnificent inn built by the Earl.[1] But the landlord and landlady are rather too fine people for their business, for they had both their post-chaises away with themselves and friends on a party of pleasure. Miss Mac-bride and I walked round the Earl's improvements, and saw very rich fields, all kinds of trees and shrubs, a river formed into beautiful pieces of water, and an excellent kitchen garden. Mr. Atchison, from Duns in Scotland, my Lord's gardener, showed us everything. He was a sensible, understanding man. He had not been in Scotland for twenty years. He conducted us along a noble, broad walk, at the end of which we entered a place hedged round, and all at once found our-selves in the churchyard, which my Lord has taken into his place. It has a fine effect. There are in it many tombstones, a number of old trees, and the ruins of the burial-place of the Magennises to whom

[9] Boswell had met him in Florence in 1765.
[1] Wills Hill, first Earl of Hillsborough, noted for his improvement of his lands.

this domain anciently belonged. Atchison showed it to advantage, for he said he would take us the nearest way home; and, before we had any idea of it, we were on the solemn spot in the shade of night. Our evening passed pretty well.

SUNDAY 7 MAY. We set out early. Aunt Boyd and I were in one chaise. Our conversation was quiet, pleasing, and really sensible. We agreed that she should acquaint Mr. and Mrs. Boyd at Dublin that I had come contrary to my father's inclination; and that I should behave to Miss Boyd in such a manner as not to be particular while it was uncertain what could be done seriously. Aunt Boyd's observations on different characters and the conduct of life were exceedingly just and agreeable, and so were her notions of religion. We breakfasted at Banbridge, a very good house. We next stopped at Newry, where we saw at a window the three Miss McCammins who, for more gentility, call themselves Miss Cummins. Their father keeps a shop here. They are all pretty. But one of them is as beautiful a creature as I ever beheld. We then drove through the mountains of Newry. It pleased my Scottish soul to see mountains. The road here is as good as the military roads in the Highlands of Scotland. About two miles from Newry, the horse which the postilion rode before the chaise where Miss Montgomerie and Miss Macbride were lost his feet all at once, and the poor fellow fell on his neck and head, and was severely hurt. It was just by a little farmhouse, into which we went till the postilion and his horse recovered. It was a neat Highland house, and all the people spoke Irish, though they could speak English too. I gave the postilion half a crown, which proved an admirable medicine to him. We dined at Dundalk, a town pleasantly situated on the sea coast. But we . . .

[EDITORIAL NOTE. The Journal breaks off here "when it would have been most interesting," some four weeks before Boswell's return to Scotland, but it is possible to reconstruct in part the weak conclusion of his long contemplated attack on *la belle Irlandaise*. He came as a suitor, but as he drew nearer to Dublin his passion steadily evaporated, until, the goal of his longings reached, he ceased to be a suitor at all. Now believing that it was Peggie Montgomerie whom he really wished to marry, he conducted himself with such caution toward the heiress and her relatives (who apparently were very well disposed toward his advances) that they took offence. They perhaps saw little of his company. The scanty references which he himself made to his days in Dublin do not have to do with courtship, but with social dissipation and riot in the company of the Lord Lieutenant and the wits of the Irish metropolis, and with junketings to "beautiful country seats" in the County of Down. "One night of Irish extravagance" was to have serious consequences; he contracted a severe case of venereal disease. The humble lover recedes, and there emerges the more brilliant figure of the Corsican traveller and friend of Paoli, everywhere "treated with a distinction . . . very flattering to the blood of Auchinleck."[2] On 7 July there appeared in *The Public Advertiser* a paragraph dated "Dublin, June 8," written by Boswell and giving an account of his visit to Ireland. It ends with the information that the great man "is now set out on his return to Scotland." He made the crossing about 7 June, stopped briefly at Lainshaw, and arrived in Edinburgh on 12 June. One of the few surviving documents of his Irish trip illustrates the growth of his regard for Margaret Montgomerie.]

[Boswell to Margaret Montgomerie][3]

Belfast, 29 May 1769

My dear Peggie, — It gave me great concern that you got so bad an evening. I hope the rain has done you no harm. Pray take care of yourself. I solemnly assure you that my rash and most absurd passion at dinner has given me real uneasiness. And allow me to say, my dear friend, that your taxing me with indifference went to my very heart. I beseech you forget what is past that can anyhow offend you; and I promise you I shall for the future be so much on my guard that you never shall have any occasion to blame me. Oh, my dear Peggie, these few hours of separation have had a serious effect on me. Be sorry for

[2] So he wrote to Sir Alexander Dick, 29 May 1769 (*Letters of James Boswell,* i. 171).

[3] Addressed to Margaret Montgomerie at Hugh Boyd's in Donaghadee. Boswell set out from Donaghadee on this day for a jaunt to Lough Neagh and the Giant's Causeway. Apparently Miss Montgomerie accompanied him as far as Belfast, but returned to Donaghadee the same evening, possibly because of the display of anger towards her for which he is writing to apologize.

me, and let your friendship and affectionate temper have fair play. I drank tea at Mrs. Haliday's, where was a company to see me. I was surprisingly well. I supped with some of Captain Hoggan's corps, drank a single glass of wine, and a little wine and water.

We set out tomorrow by five o'clock, six of us in three chaises. By all I have seen, the Highland host did not strike you differently from what this corps does me. What an odds to read of a brave regiment in Germany or in America from what it is to dine or sup with the officers. But my old companion is exceedingly good. He is as careful as *my lady*[4] could wish. I said to him tonight, "Captain, I shall let Miss Montgomerie know." It will take us three days, so I cannot be with you till Friday to dinner. Believe me, the time seems dreary in prospect. I know not what a variety of curious objects may do to amuse my mind. In the mean time, my valuable friend, think of me, and for the sake of every good principle and *my real happiness* be kind enough to think no evil against an absent man. I am to sleep in the room where you and I were alone. You are present to my imagination in the liveliest manner. It is late and I am weary, not being well. Good night, my dearest. God bless and preserve you, and direct us. Make my best compliments to Aunt Boyd, Mr. Boyd, and all with you. Pray think of me as I wish and believe me to be while I have a being, your most sincerely affectionate

J.B.

MONDAY 12 JUNE.[5] Set out early from Lainshaw. Got to Glasgow to breakfast. Had Mr. Blair the hatter with me. Left Glasgow about eleven, Thomas in the chaise with me. Read newspapers all the way. Dined at Whitburn. Was grave and quite in the Auchinleck style. Thought of coming there with *my lady*. Young Samuel Mitchelson came in and sat a while with me. I arrived at Edinburgh about nine. Captain Erskine was at the Cross, and followed the chaise. He welcomed me to town, and asked me if I had not carried Miss Montgomerie to Ireland to compare her with Miss Boyd and take the one I liked best. Found my father and John quite well. Conversation slow and rather dry. In my own room thought of *my lady*.

TUESDAY 13 JUNE. Went to Parliament House; found it just as usual. Had many questions put to me as to my Irish jaunt, and where

[4] That is, Miss Montgomerie herself.

[5] A new Journal begins here, covering the summer term of the Court of Session.

was my heiress? I was prepared, and laughed them off with "My time's not come," or, "Aha, I'm just as I was." Mr. Claud and Miss Betty[6] dined with us. Claud and I drank tea at the Doctor's and saw Bob and his wife.[7] It was humbling and yet agreeable to see them all so happy. Came and sat a while with Mrs. Betty. Called for Lord Mountstuart.

WEDNESDAY 14 JUNE. Lord Mountstuart begged to see me in the morning. I went to him and found him as agreeable as ever. But I was in a different style from the gay, thoughtless way in which he and I used to be. Baron Mure and many more of the Bute train were with him. I dined at home quietly, and supped at Fortune's with Lord Mountstuart, &c.

THURSDAY 15 JUNE. Mrs. Fullarton and her son, Sandy Tait, Drs. Gregory and Austin, and Willy Wallace dined with us. I was not well, and in very bad spirits. At such times all the varnish of life is off, and I see it as it really is. Or why not may it be that there is a shade thrown over it which is merely ideal darkness? All my comfort was piety, my friends, and *my lady*.

FRIDAY 16 JUNE. I dined along with Lord Mountstuart at Fortune's. There was a great crowd there. I had little joy. Among others, Andrew Stuart[8] was there. I was very angry. "Why?" said Dr. Blair. "Because," said I, "there is no telling what he may do. He may bring a process to show my leg is not my own. In vain have I acknowledged it all my life long. He would insist it belonged to another person and should be cut off, and he would get a majority of the Court of Session for this, Doctor." My ludicrous indignation silenced the Doctor. "Ay," said Erskine, "it would be in proof that you had let the nail grow into your great toe, which no man would do were the leg his own!" I drank tea in comfortable quietness with Grange, whom I saw today for the first time this session. He and I had much conversation. He argued me quite out of my mercenary views for marriage, and was clear for *my lady* if I thought myself sure of happiness. But

[6] His father's cousin, Elizabeth Boswell. Boswell's evident liking for her ended abruptly when he learned that Lord Auchinleck had proposed marriage to her. She is also the Mrs. Betty mentioned further on in this entry.

[7] Dr. John Boswell and his son Robert, who had recently married a niece of Robert Sandeman, the Glassite sectary.

[8] Writer to the Signet, and the leading agent for the Hamiltons in the Douglas cause.

he wished to see Temple's answer to my letter, which I sent off. I supped at Mr. Moncrieffe's. The Club[9] was merry. Sandy Maxwell had some jokes on me. I said he was hard on me. He kept a close fire: *grape-shot* from a *wine-merchant*. This set me up. But I had only forced spirits.

SATURDAY 17 JUNE. The reports concerning the Corsicans were various. I was uneasy.[1] Grange brought me Mr. Macdonald, an obliging and clever surgeon, to take care of me. I passed part of the forenoon at Lord Mountstuart's, but was both ill and low-spirited. So sent an apology to Mr. David Ross, where I was engaged to dine, and stayed quietly at home. Was very gloomy. Wrote to *my lady*.

SUNDAY 18 JUNE. Lay quiet abed all day. Was calm. Sir George Preston, Dr. Webster, and Grange visited me.

MONDAY 19 JUNE. The Commissioner[2] dined. I had mentioned *my lady* by the by to many as a supposable case, if I had spirit to overcome my mercenary views. All approved. Even the Commissioner and Mr. Stobie were not against it. The Lieutenant[3] indeed was. I stayed at home all day and was rather better. Sir Alexander Dick drank tea, and ——.

TUESDAY 20 JUNE. The Dean of Faculty[4] showed me a letter from Colonel Lockhart of Carnwath, from Florence, confirming the defeat and destruction of the Corsicans. I was quite sunk. I thought of retiring to the country. I felt myself unable for the law. I saw I had parts to make a figure at times. But could not stand a constant trial. I received a most comforting letter from M. I just worshipped her. I was at home all day, except paying a short visit to Lord Mountstuart, and being at the Parliament House. The Doctor[5] was with me a while. He commended M. highly as a sensible woman, a fine woman. But seemed to have some extravagant idea of a wife for me.

[9] Nameless apparently, but composed of a convivial company of advocates who met on Fridays at David Stewart Moncrieffe's. Moncrieffe was noted for the quality of his dinners, for which his guests were expected to pay in flattery.
[1] On 8 May 1769 Paoli was defeated by the French in a decisive battle at Ponte Nuovo and fled to Leghorn.
[2] Basil Cochrane.
[3] Boswell's brother, John.
[4] Alexander Lockhart.
[5] Dr. John Boswell.

[Received 20 June, Margaret Montgomerie to Boswell]

Lainshaw, 17 June 1769[6]

How SINCERELY DID YOUR LETTER OBLIGE ME, but how sorry I was
to think by writing it you put a force on yourself. What is the reason
of your uneasiness? Why do you conceal from me what is the cause of
your unhappiness? Surely you forget how much I am interested in
what concerns you; otherwise you would not have left me in uncertainty. I was apprehensive you was not well, but you say you have
been oftener abroad than you would choose with Lord Mountstuart, so
that want of health cannot be the thing. Are you angry at me for keeping up a correspondence with one I could never view in the black
colours you do?[7] I am sensible amongst the number of her enemies
there are some who have the art of setting people's action in a very
bad light. She is now far removed from me and quite independent of
my friendship. It is therefore nothing wrong in me to say that, since
it gives offence to one whose good opinion I wish to preserve, I shall
give up all correspondence with her till I can convince him of his prejudice or he make me sensible of my weakness. Is not this sufficient? If
that will not do, I promise never to mention her name to you again.

How sorry I am for the poor Corsicans. I'm afraid the accounts of
their defeat is but too true.[8] I doubt not but you will see the General,
as it's said he is on his way to England. I am much distressed with a

[6] Dated 18 June in the typescript (see Introduction, p. xxii), and no doubt also in
the manuscript. But in her letter of 1 July, Miss Montgomerie says that she
never writes on Sunday, and she clearly plans to post this letter during the day
on which she is writing. Her reference later in the letter to Tuesday shows that
she can hardly be writing on Monday.

[7] To judge from a later letter, this refers to Margaret Stuart, wife of the Earl
of Bute's second son, Lieut-Col. James Archibald Stuart. (He later added the
names Wortley and Mackenzie.) Though the two saw little of each other after
Mrs. Stuart's marriage in 1767, they remained affectionate friends. The situation is amusing if Mrs. Stuart is meant, for Boswell later developed an extravagantly sentimental regard for her.

[8] "Accounts is" and similar expressions prove Miss Montgomerie Scotch rather
than illiterate. In the Scottish variety of English the ending for all persons and
numbers of the present is "s," except where the personal pronoun immediately
precedes. — Boswell himself was contributing some of the Corsican accounts in
the newspapers.

headache tonight, but could not think of missing this post, as I have not another opportunity till Tuesday.

May I once more entreat you to keep up your spirits, and do not keep the house too close. Exercise is absolutely necessary for your body, and society is a great relaxation to the mind. I approve much of your sober plan and hope you will continue it, and I am certain you will find it will make a great change on your sentiments; but is it necessary to be shut up to live sober? I hope not. Keep company with those who are so, and you will soon have a relish for that way of life.

I was very uneasy after I sent off your Irish packet and would have given anything I had sent them where you desired, but your goodness in forgiving me has reconciled me to my conduct. I am afraid I must lay aside thoughts of being in Edinburgh this summer, as our sacrament is not till the second Sunday of July, so that I would not have a fortnight to stay, as Mr. and Mrs. Boyd spoke of being here the beginning of August. It would not do for me to be from home; however, if you think I should perform my promise to Sir Alexander Dick's family, I shall not make my apology but endeavour to pay my visit, though it should be short.

It is now late, so I must bid you adieu, with wishing every happy thing to attend you, and assuring you how sincerely I am your affectionate and obliged

M.M.

I wish this long letter may not tire you, but I hope you will answer it and let me ⟨know⟩ particularly how you do.

WEDNESDAY 21 JUNE. I breakfasted at Sandy Gordon's tête-à-tête. He was for M. He and Claud and Miss Betty dined with us.

[Boswell to Dempster][9]

Edinburgh, [?21] June [1769]

I WAS RECEIVED AT DUBLIN with open arms by a numerous and creditable set of relations. But I give you my word, I found myself under no engagements. The young lady seemed the sweetest, loveliest

---

[9] This is the second portion of a letter to Dempster, of which the first part, dated 4 May at Donaghadee, covers much the same ground as Boswell's letter to Temple of 3 May (p. 200). This part is marked "sequel."

little creature that ever was born. But so young, so childish, so much *yes* and *no*, that (between ourselves) I was ashamed of having raved so much about her. I candidly told my situation: that I had come quite contrary to my father's inclination. That was enough for the present, and a genteel distance was the proper conduct. At the same time I found myself like a foreign prince to them, so much did I take; and I was assured of her having for certain £500 a year. You know me, Dempster. I was often carried by *fancy*, like a man on the finest race-horse; and, at all events, I would have her. But my cousin hung on my *heart*. Her most desirable person, like a heathen goddess painted alfresco on the ceiling of a palace at Rome, was compared with the delicate little Miss. Her admirable sense and vivacity were compared with the reserved quietness of the Heiress. I was tossed by waves and drawn by horses. I resolved to fix nothing. My cousin gave me that advice herself, for I had assurance enough to consult her deliberately. My journey to Scotland with her, during which I was a little indisposed and had occasion to see a new proof of her affectionate attention, has inclined me to her more and more.

Here then I am, my friend, at no loss to determine whom I really love and value of all women I have ever seen, but at a great loss to determine whom I should marry. No man knows the scene of human life better than you do. At least, no man gives me such clear views of it. Therefore, pray assist me. And whatever is the drawing of your reason, pray let me have it agreeably coloured by your fancy. An advice from you to a friend is singularly excellent for two reasons. First, because it is always at least ingenious; and secondly, because you are not a bit angry though he does not follow it. I depend on you, my worthy Dempster, and am your ever affectionate friend,

J.B.

Vraye Foi.[1]

THURSDAY 22 JUNE. Dupont and George Webster drank tea with us. I was quite fixed to a comfortable, quiet life. I paid a visit to Lord Barjarg.

FRIDAY 23 JUNE. I breakfasted at Sir George Preston's. My father dined abroad. I had Grange to dine with John and me. Grange

[1] The Boswell motto.

and Dr. Cairnie drank tea with me, and consulted as to my managing with economy that unlucky affair of Mrs. ———.[2] Dr. Cairnie's friendly activity pleased me.

SATURDAY 24 JUNE. Auchline and two daughters, a Mr. Mc-Intosh, and Miss Betty Boswell dined and drank tea. I was obtuse at night. My father talked to me of marriage. I avoided the subject. M. had my heart.

SUNDAY 25 JUNE. I lay quietly abed all day and read Tissot *On the Health of Literary Persons* and Strange's *Catalogue of Pictures*. The former gave me some curious thoughts. The latter cheered me with fine ideas of painting and the lives of painters. I felt the pleasures of taste to be exquisite. I thought of Margaret. But then, money would enable me to buy pictures, and my Irish connection make a pretty anecdote in my life. So I wavered. But then again, Margaret was like Raphael's mistress; and what real happiness all my life should I have with her![3] I was just calm. Sir George Preston and Dr. Webster visited me. At night I rose and read a good deal of the Bible. I was a Christian, but regretted my not being more devout, more regularly pious. This would make me happier.

MONDAY 26 JUNE. I have this summer session read and given my opinion both of a new tragedy and a new comedy by Scotch authors, the last by a lady.[4] Both pleased me. If every person would keep an exact list of all the books or parts of books he has read, it might be seen how a wit or a philosopher is gradually formed according to the

[2] Mrs. Dodds. Johnston and Dr. Cairnie had also helped Boswell manage the affair of his first illegitimate child, Charles, who died in 1764. (See *Boswell's London Journal*, 1950, p. 324.) With this entry Mrs. Dodds and Sally disappear for ever from Boswell's records. The complete absence of further references to Sally almost certainly means that she died an infant, for we know from the previous case of Charles that Boswell was not one to ignore his parental responsibilities. He would not have given an illegitimate daughter the advantages of a daughter of the house, but he would certainly have kept in touch with her, and would have made such provision for her care and upbringing as the gentlemanly code demanded.

[3] Raphaël deferred his marriage to his betrothed, Maria Bibiena, a lady of rank and fortune, and remained faithful to his mistress, who (according to tradition) bore the name Margherita.

[4] The tragedy, *Chateaubriant*, was by William Julius Mickle; the comedy was probably *Sir Harry Gaylove* by Jane Marshall. See pp. 275 and 285.

materials furnished to him. Lady Preston visited me this morning. I received a letter from M. which made me value her more and more, and one from Dempster in a gay, pleasant style which made me for a little lay marriage out of my mind, and so relieved me. Miss Betty Boswell, Professor Hunter, and M. Cauvin dined with us. I was quiet, but dispirited on account of Corsica. My views of life sunk very low. I wished merely for comfort. I drank tea at Crosbie's at a consultation, my fourth only for this session. There seems to be little business. I must study law.

TUESDAY 27 JUNE. The Reverend Mr. Foord, our housekeeper's brother, and Matthew Dickie dined with us. At seven I went to the Goldsmiths' Hall to the first night of a new society for speaking on different subjects. I was quite flat and had no ambition, yet I spoke with force and spirit on Britain's right to tax her colonies.

WEDNESDAY 28 JUNE. I breakfasted at Bob Boswell's. I saw his neat little house with satisfaction. Pope has a fine *Imitation of Horace:*

> What, and how great, the virtue and the art
> To live on little with a cheerful heart! &c.[5]

One may see this every day in many families, and learn contentment from example. I dined at Mr. John Chalmer's in company with two of his brothers-in-law: one a merchant in London, the other belonging to the sea.

THURSDAY 29 JUNE. I was called out of the Parliament House by Mr. Capper, who had been in Corsica. He sat some time with me, and gave me much interesting news of Paoli, and made me have better hopes. I dined at Lord Monboddo's. We were alone before dinner a while, and I talked to him of my marrying. He was first for the child, as a man may form such a one as he pleases. But when I assured him I had a bad temper, and he observed that it requires great patience to breed a wife, as it does to breed a horse, he was clear for one already formed, and for Margaret, saying, "How it will tell is nothing." We were interrupted. I was quiet at dinner. I drank tea at home. Dupont and George Webster were with us. My father and I supped at Balmuto's.

[5] *The Second Satire of the Second Book of Horace,* ll. 1–2.

FRIDAY 30 JUNE. Captain Lyon, an old schoolfellow who was just come from Berlin, Captain Charles Cochrane, David Stewart, Nairne, Balbarton,[6] and Mr. Stevenson, under clerk of session, dined with us; and the two captains and Stevenson drank tea with me. I was just resigned to my fate, and had no farther views. I had a most interesting letter from Margaret. I was much affected by it, and wrote a long letter to her. At night I was at Mr. Moncrieffe's, but finding brag run high, I calmly gave it up and looked on. I was quite dull, thinking that I had given up all gay and brilliant schemes of marriage. At supper they talked of the Duke of Kingston marrying Miss Chudleigh from principles of honour and gratitude.[7] I thought if he acted so towards a woman of her character, what ought I to do for a woman of real worth? I was resolved; and, what is really curious, as I considered that I was to make up for the want of £10,000 by frugality, my mind took the strongest bent that way, and I looked with aversion on a fine table and every piece of elegance then around me, wishing just for absolute plainness. I had, however, some suspicions that my father intended to *prendre encore une femme*,[8] and that soured me totally. But I had no certainty for this.

SATURDAY 1 JULY. I walked out early and met the Sixth Regiment of Foot and marched with my cousin, Captain Maxwell of Dalswinton, a captain in it, from about half a mile west from town, through the city, and till the Regiment was fairly out at the *Water Get* (gate). I have always had a great fondness for the army, at least for the show and parade of it, though I am fixed to the law. I am like a man who has married one woman while he is in love with another. Perhaps, indeed, if I had enjoyed my military mistress, I should have been heartily tired of her. Captain Maxwell returned to town, and he and his brother Hugh and Grange dined with us. The two former and I drank tea with Miss Webster.[9] At night my father hinted to me

[6] James Boswell, a distant cousin, a man well advanced in years. Captain Cochrane was also a relation.

[7] She had long been his mistress before marrying him on 8 March 1769. She was also, though unknown to the Duke, married to the Earl of Bristol. Her trial for bigamy in the House of Lords after the Duke's death was a *cause célèbre*.

[8] See p. 209 *n*.6.

[9] Anne Webster, Dr. Webster's daughter, and cousin to the Maxwells as well as to Boswell.

something of what I had suspected. I was amazed and hurt. It threw me quite into wild melancholy. It is many years since I, as it were, pulled myself up by the roots from the place where nature placed me; and though I have allowed myself to be brought back I have never taken firm root, but am like a tree sunk in a flowerpot that may be lifted at any time very easily. I must now endeavour to get matters settled so as to determine either on remaining where I am, or going somewhere else.

SUNDAY 2 JULY. I was at church all day decently. Between sermons I called on Grange and told him my uneasiness and wild schemes. He conjured me to lay aside such thoughts as would ruin me, and bid me consider how much it would please my enemies. I answered readily, "There is one comfort: it would not please them so much as it would me." So wild yet is my imagination. But my honest friend's advice weighed with me. Sir George, Lady Preston, and Miss Preston dined with us. I drank tea at Mrs. Scott's and spoke French, but was observed to look ill. I then called on Lady Crawford, who was not able to see company. But I sat a long time with Miss Macredie and had a very agreeable conversation with her, much indeed in praise of M. But she hurt me by saying she thought M. would do very well with the Irish doctor, and that she had a *hankering kindness* for Mr. C.[1] Strange that I, whose heart has been tossed about by all the winds, cannot bear to think that my friend has ever had a kindness for anybody, though I am sure she never thought of anyone as she does of me. I supped quietly with my father, and resolved to be prudent.

MONDAY 3 JULY. My father and I dined at Mr. Kincaid's where I drank tea. I then went to Mr. Charles Brown's and saw DOUGLAS,[2] who was just come to town. I had not seen him since the great decision. He was dressing and without coat or waistcoat when I came in. He expressed much joy on seeing me, and invited me to celebrate his birthday at Bothwell Castle. I was truly happy and easy. But wished I could feel the same joy I did on the glorious news.

[1] Jane Macredie was a sister of Campbell of Treesbank's first wife — a cousin by marriage. The Irish doctor and Mr. C. are unidentified.

[2] The names of Douglas and the Deity are frequently written large in Boswell's script.

TUESDAY 4 JULY. Whenever I do not mention my breakfasting, dining, drinking tea, or supping somewhere abroad, it is to be understood that I was at home. Business now began to look better. I walked in the Meadow with Lord Monboddo and talked of M. He said there was no question she was the woman for me, thought her being a little older nothing, and said she'd bring me children worth rearing, which is seldom the case nowadays. I mentioned to him my apprehensions concerning my father. He said it would be very foolish at his time of life — a terrible thing—a burthen on a family, &c. Bid me not delay getting a settlement made, which my marriage only would do. I saw Lord Monboddo's regard for me, and I was really happy with the scheme of *my lady*. I wrote to her at night and was in fine spirits. I drank tea at Mr. Thomas Boswall's.

[Received 4 July, Margaret Montgomerie to Boswell][3]

Lainshaw, Saturday night, 11 o'clock [1 July 1769]

I RECEIVED THE BOOK[4] you sent me last post, for which, and your friendly letter tonight, I return you my grateful thanks.

I shall read with attention the portions of Scripture you recommend, and hope I shall find great comfort and satisfaction in so doing. The pains you take to instruct me in what is of so much consequence gives me the strongest proof of the sincerity of your friendship. Prayers and wishes are all I have to offer in return for your goodness; if they are heard, I'm sure you will be happy.

I was very uneasy at your silence; fearful I had offended, or that want of health prevented you from writing. I own I am vastly too anxious, but I cannot help it; much I have endeavoured to be less so, but to no purpose.

I wish I had power to remove all uneasy thoughts from your mind — how happy would it make me! I would gladly recommend to you resignation to the Divine Will in everything, acknowledging that whatever He does is well and wisely ordered. I cannot see that, should

[3] The original of this letter, acquired separately from the Malahide collection, has survived.

[4] In later letters Miss Montgomerie refers to Andrew Michael Ramsay's *Les Voyages de Cyrus*, Johnson's *Rambler*, and Adam Smith's *Theory of Moral Sentiments*. The book here referred to might be any one of the three.

what you suspect take place, it could hurt you.[5] For God sake, do not therefore take any rash resolutions. You are warm, I know, but surely you will not allow any heat of passion to get the better of your good sense.

I will not allow the character you give of yourself to be just. If you are either sullen or discontented, it is your own fault. Naturally, you are quite the reverse. Allow your good principles once to get the better of bad habits, and you will be just as you could wish. Many times, though we are desirous to be cured of our faults, we are loath to part with them. Perhaps that may give you uneasiness without your being sensible of the cause; but persevere in your good resolutions, and you will find yourself quite a new man.

Captain Cuninghame speaks of being in Edinburgh in a fortnight. He asked me this day to put off my going till then, which I promised, but you know he sometimes changes his mind. I shall, however, endeavour to fix him one way or other and let you know what he determines on. You may believe the day you mention would be most agreeable to me could I possibly bring it about, but should I not have it in my power, I live in hopes of another opportunity.

Lady Crawford leaves Edinburgh in a week or two on account of bad health. Lady Cathcart, I hear, is still far from being well.

I thought to have finished my letter for this night post, but I could not possibly get it done; however, I shall end it tonight, as I lay it down for a rule never to write on Sunday. I was at Treesbank on Friday, where you was remembered by the Laird and Lady with great kindness. I saw Hugh Campbell there, and Bruce at Kilmarnock. I believe they are close on the wing.

Should MacNeil lose his lands, it will put a stop to his matrimonial affairs, which I'm told was to have been concluded immediately on the favourable decision of the Lords. Perhaps it was a story of his own inventing, but it gained credit here, as most reports of the kind does almost everywhere. The lady, I believe I mentioned to you formerly, is Miss Steuart of Steuart Hall.

I shall perhaps write again in a post or two and put it in some other post office, as the Stewarton stamp may give rise to suspicions when so often making its appearance. Good night, God bless you.

[5] Lord Auchinleck's possible marriage.

Remember me, if you think proper, to all with you, and believe me, my dear Jamie, your ever affectionate and obliged

M. MONTGOMERIE.

[Boswell to Margaret Montgomerie]

Edinburgh, 4 July 1769

YOU HAVE VERY WELL OBSERVED that you cannot write as you would speak. I am just in the same situation. It is impossible for me to put upon paper the sentiments which I have felt since we parted; and yet if we were together, I am very sure I could make you fully understand them. I read your letters with such feelings as I never before experienced. I have imagined such when I have thought of my grandfather receiving a letter from Lady Betty. I do not imagine it possible for a man to value and love at the same time a woman more than I do *my lady*. You remember you said at Donaghadee that it would be wonderful if I stood Dublin. You know what happened, and I believe both you and I thought more highly of my heart than we did before. Indeed, you have often said you was of opinion I had no heart. Is it so, think you? And do you intend to assume the merit of giving me what I had not before? Or is it that fancy has so prevailed that my heart could never appear? Methinks I may compare my heart to a rock in the sea. While the tempest of passions blew and the waves of vain folly beat, it could not be perceived. But now that these begin to subside, it shows itself as firm as any rock that ever existed. Now that I have told you all my history relative to yourself during such a number of years, you need not wonder at my present situation.

I thank you, my dearest friend, for your calm advice. I will try to compose myself. But what I hinted to you shocked me so much that I declare I was thrown into the wildest melancholy, and resolved to go and at once break off all connection for ever, that I might no longer struggle with uncertainty and a kind of unnaturality, if I may use the word. You alone distracted my mind. But I believe I could settle that, provided I myself was unhappy, for then nothing can be said. I am more composed now, as from some late hints I imagine any scheme to be concerning some other person whom I do not know. Believe me, such a step in a family is terrible, and I fairly own to you, that unless

I had an absolute security against what might be done, I would renounce all relation. The worst is that a wild, ruinous scheme in some measure pleases my gloomy temper, and there is not a man alive to whom poverty and obscurity would be easier. I shall, however, make no rash vows, and when you come to town we shall have a long conversation on the subject. In the mean time, be quite easy as to *my lady*. I am now better than at any time. I walked a long time with Lord Monboddo today, and, without giving you any share in it, talked to him fully. He was clear, and made me admire the scheme.

Is it not curious, my honest Margaret, to think how you and I are now together? Upon honour, I was uneasy that I did not hear from you yesterday. Are we not then pretty equal? You are, however, partial as to my character. I assure you, you are. But so much the more valuable are you to me. I have not yet heard from Ireland. I have written to Mrs. Sibthorpe and said many sincere pretty things in your name and mine.[6] I beg you may come for the race week, at least a part of it.[7] I wish to see you in a crowd at Edinburgh. You must undergo all trials. There is nothing in the Stewarton postmark appearing as often as you please.

This day poor Dr. MacNeil lost his cause. The Lords Barjarg, Pitfour, Monboddo, and Auchinleck were for him and all the rest against him, except one who did not vote and one who was absent. He may have a chance here yet, and I imagine a good one upon an appeal.

Adieu. Ever yours,

J.B.

WEDNESDAY 5 JULY. I was quite enamoured in the forenoon, and impatient to have M. for certain. I drank tea at Balmuto's. Mrs. Betty and I had much conversation about M. I was hurt by talking too much of her faults. It made me miserable. But I went home, read Tooke's *Pantheon*, wrote to her, and recovered all my fondness and really admiration.

[6] Mary Ann Sibthorpe was a maternal relation of Boswell's. Her husband, as Boswell remarks in his autobiographical memoir in *The European Magazine* (1791), was a gentleman of great consequence in the county of Down, and had introduced him into good society there.

[7] Race week started at Leith on 19 July.

THURSDAY 6 JULY. I heard a pleading in the case of the credi-tors of Auchinbreck, and really shuddered to think of the conse-quences of debt. I then waited on the Duke of Queensberry, who was just come to town, and was well received. I dined at Mr. Charles Brown's with Billy,[8] young Pitfour, Sir John Whitefoord, and Mr. Stewart of Blantyre. After dinner Mr. Charles read us a genuine copy of the Chancellor's speech on the Douglas cause.[9] I drank tea at home with my father and M. Dupont, and my father and I and John and Mr. Claud and Mrs. Betty all supped at Mr. Thomas Boswall's. I liked to see a good, open Scots wife, and a sensible, understanding man of business.

FRIDAY 7 JULY. Messieurs Baillie, Colquhoun, George Fergus-son, Blair, and Law, advocates, and William Macdonald and James Frazer, writers, dined with us. I was dull enough, but contented to be so. I had this day an answer from Temple, finely written, but prefer-ring interest and ambition to the heart.[1] I hoped easily to bring him into my opinion. Yet I considered what I owed to my family. But then again, insuring health, sense, and genius to my successor would be better than great riches. A man too rich is like a man too fat. Besides, I could save more than £10,000 portion by the manner in which I would live with M. So I continued firm, but was uneasy at not hear-ing from her for some days. At seven I was at Clerihue's at a consulta-tion for Douglas against Duke Hamilton and Lord Selkirk.[2] I felt myself weak and without much memory or application. I was hum-ble and modest. I consoled myself that M. thought so highly of me, and I hoped in time to acquire law and application. I rejoiced at being a regular counsel for the great Douglas, for whom I had done so much as a volunteer. Indeed, I received a handsome retaining fee, ten guin-

[8] That is, Patrick Home of Billy.

Lord Camden had performed the brilliant feat of recapitulating the entire cause from memory.

[1] Temple in his letter of 1 July paid high compliments to Miss Montgomerie's character, but insisted that the exalted position of Boswell's family made it impossible for him to marry from simple choice. "Your attachments of this sort, you know," he added, "are violent while they last, but like the hot fits of an ague of no long duration."

[2] Douglas's counsels were taking further steps to repel the Hamilton claims, con-sequent on the decision of the House of Lords.

eas. The news of Duke Hamilton's death struck us.[3] We all supped together.

SATURDAY 8 JULY. About noon Mr. Maconochie and I set out in a post-chaise for Bothwell Castle, to be present at the celebration of Douglas's birthday on Monday the 10 of July. We had a great deal of conversation. I wavered somewhat as to my plan of life still: whether to remain here, or go to the English bar. Maconochie showed himself a little man of admirable common sense, observation, activity, and really a good share of neat taste from having seen so much of the world. We dined at Whitburn, and got to Bothwell Castle to tea. I rejoiced to see the Duchess, now that all was well. Douglas and the Duke of Queensberry were there before us, as also Captain William Douglas of Kelhead and a Mr. Douglas of Fechil, somewhere in the North, a young gentleman just come from Vienna, having travelled several years.[4] He had much the foreign air, and brought my travels fresh into my mind. I then for a little disliked the thoughts of marriage. But then again, I thought it was time to settle and be comfortable; and my valuable M. had me all to herself.

SUNDAY 9 JULY. We sauntered about very agreeably. There is a fine bank of wood here. Douglas and I got by ourselves a while. We seemed great intimates. I told him I did not like to trust him abroad till he had a wife and a child. "Then," said he, "go along with me"; and described our travelling together, very agreeably. I told him it would take me quite out of the line of the Scotch law which I had taken, and I would not easily settle to it again. He argued that it might be made up to me. I was, for a while, very fond of the thought, which pleased my roving fancy and would furnish a good chapter in my life. But I thought warmly of Margaret. Douglas said a very good thing. "Boswell," said he, "you should now be just a worthy country gentleman, and not seek any more fame. You never can make yourself better known than you have done by your *Account of*

---

[3] James George, seventh Duke of Hamilton, the nominal plaintiff in the Douglas cause, was only fourteen years old when he died on this day.

[4] Sylvester Douglas; he married Lord North's daughter and in 1800 was created Baron Glenbervie. He was admitted to The Club in 1818. His *Diaries* (1793–1819) are a lively and valuable record of the times. — Captain William Douglas was a maternal relation of Boswell's.

Corsica. It is better known than Sir James Steuart's book. Be satisfied with it. You have just fallen upon a lucky thought." I was struck with this. We were very comfortable. The worthy Duke was very good company. I was deeply in love with M., and often wished to slip away and see her.

MONDAY 10 JULY. This was indeed a joyful day. The Duke assured me that he would be ready to do me any service in his power. We were busy in the morning concerting toasts and seeing that all was in good order. A numerous company came. We were about seventy at table. The Duke, Mr. Douglas, and I had each a copy of sixteen excellent toasts. Two engineers attended and took charge of a cannon and mortar. Whenever they were charged, they made a sign with a handkerchief to a servant who was placed at the door, and who gave notice to me. I then rose up and called with an audible voice, "Charged, all charged." Then a toast was given and I called "Fire!" to the servant, who made a sign to the engineers, and the artillery went off.[5] I was quite in my element, and had much satisfaction in philosophizing upon the Douglas cause and the grand period then before my eyes. I could not but drink pretty freely, but I was not drunk. We had fireworks, bonfires, and a ball, and a crowd of country people huzzaing. During the whole, I was constant to M. Mr. Maconochie and I set out half an hour after eleven and drove all night. It was very light, and I had a curious, agreeable, drowsy satisfaction.

TUESDAY 11 JULY. We came to Livingstone about three in the morning, and got some fried chicken and a bottle of madeira with Mr. Mackellar, the landlord, for company. I know not how it is, but I am very fond of the road between Edinburgh and Auchinleck. It brings a crowd of agreeable, family, sober ideas into my mind. However, travelling it as I now did seemed odd. It was like dancing in a church. I got to town just in time to throw off my laced coat and waistcoat, get on black clothes, and be ready at nine o'clock to attend some causes in the Parliament House. A thousand questions were put to me. I was sleepy all day, but stood it very well.

WEDNESDAY 12 JULY. I had received a letter from Sir John Dick informing me that Paoli was safe at Leghorn. This was great

[5] Boswell himself gave the last toast: "May fools become wise and knaves honest."

comfort to me. I was anxious and uneasy at having no letter from M. this week. I was apprehensive she was offended with me. Dempster was now in town. He came and saw me, and heard my anxious, irresolute situation with patience and complacency. He bid me treat it lightly. He said I was yet far from matrimony, and could easier return than advance. That supposing Glasgow to be marriage and Edinburgh the state of a bachelor, I was no farther on my road than Fountainbridge.[6] But, upon the whole, he was for M. Said she must have a noble mind, and that I would be happy. He put me in spirits. I told him of my reception in Ireland. "You know," said I, "how finely I can show away to strangers who see me for a little only. I can run the gauntlet very well, but cannot bear being tied up to the halberts" — a curious representation of my small degree of merit, or rather knowledge, that passes very well on a cursory view, but is found out to be very superficial if deliberately examined. I drank tea with worthy Johnston calmly and cordially.

THURSDAY 13 JULY. I received a letter from M. in a style that made me think she was angry, and had given up all love for me. She appeared to me so cool and indifferent that I was absolutely shocked. I thought with a kind of distraction of the world in which one whom I thought I knew so intimately could be so changeable. My head turned giddy, and I am positive no man was ever more severely tortured by love. Worthy Grange represented to me that it was all my own fault, for I had acknowledged to him that I had written to her with such censure that no woman of spirit could bear; and that I ought rather to be grateful to her for writing at all, and should make an apology for what I had written. He pacified me a little. But I have a wretched satisfaction in being surly. I, however, was much affected, and could for gleams of thought have almost cried; and, had she been near me, would have fallen at her feet. Yet my obstinate, unreasonable pride still rose again. I determined not to write till I was more moderate. Dempster was gone home, which I regretted.

After the House I had a walk with Lord Monboddo. He said I might be sure my father had thoughts *de se remarier,* and pushed me to think of marrying directly. He was clear and irresistible for M. I thought, "How curious is this compared with her last letter and its

[6] A western suburb of Edinburgh, now part of the city.

effects on me." Mr. Claud, Miss Betty, and Grange dined with us. I was quite thoughtful and vexed on a complication of accounts: my father, Margaret, and a very bad symptom of illness. I drank tea at Grange's along with Mr. Macdonald, the surgeon. But was really low. My heart was softened. I was all gratitude to M. But alas! what could I do for her? I was ready to give her myself, but was persuaded it would make her miserable.

At night I had a serious conversation with my father. He talked of my not minding affairs at home. That gave me a good opportunity to say that I really had no encouragement as I was in so incertain a way, and that he even talked *de se remarier*. He in a manner acknowledged his having such views. I spoke in the strongest terms, and fairly told him he should be no more troubled with me. I was really calm and determined. It is wonderful to think how he and I have differed to such a degree for so many years. I was somewhat hurt to find myself again thrown loose on the world. But my love of adventure and hope made me surprisingly easy. My great unhappiness was thinking of M. And yet in any way she could not but suffer, for I could not think of marriage when he exposed himself at his years and forgot my valuable mother. O unfeeling world! I declare I am not, nor ever could be, so much so. And yet, honest man! he talked of his affection for me and what he had suffered on my account with a tone that moved me, though I was quite irritated against him now. I am truly a composition of many opposite qualities.

[Received 13 July, Margaret Montgomerie to Boswell]

[Lainshaw,] Saturday [8 July 1769]
I AM MUCH OBLIGED TO YOU for both your letters,[7] and would have taken the very first opportunity of telling you so had I not recollected your intended visit to Bothwell Castle.

I heard of both the marriages. You ask me if I feel any regret when I hear of a good match going off. I answer, not the smallest when I have no attachment, notwithstanding the opinion a certain friend of mine entertains of me. I have not yet perceived such charms in the

---

[7] Boswell's letters of 4 and 5 July. Boswell's second letter, which is missing, must have taxed Miss Montgomerie with too great "frankness to gentlemen."

matrimonial state as to make me enter very deep into any plot to get myself a member of that society; however, this I know will gain but small credit, being inconsistent with female dependence. I must therefore be satisfied to lie under the general aspersion. I could not help being a little nettled at that part of your letter where you tax me with a too great degree of frankness to gentlemen. Without any regard to character, most men are more industrious to hide their faults than a friend of mine has ever shown himself to be; and, as I only meant civility, I see no reason why I should give myself the trouble to pry into the real worth of a common acquaintance. Do not imagine I mean by this to vindicate my behaviour; I am conscious I have been on many occasions too free. It is on that account I have often run out in praises of a prudent reserve which I'm afraid to a person of a frank disposition will border a little on disguise; but, believe me, most people will find this absolutely necessary to carry them through life. Experience has taught me under what disadvantages one labours who is totally free of it. I have often wished to follow the example of the lady you drank tea with in the many amiable and praiseworthy parts of her character, economy not excepted; but, though in some measure blinded by partiality to those I really like, my eyes are so far open to my own failings as to perceive I have been as yet very unsuccessful. But surely you cannot term it a weakness to be able to overlook the faults of our friends. I am so far from being of that opinion that I wish I could do it in a more extensive manner. To be able to separate the offender from the offence appears to me of some consequence; otherwise I'm afraid we shall run a risk of hating both, which would be a breach of that universal charity so often and strongly recommended by the great Pattern of all perfection.

I am most sincerely obliged to you for the friendly part you take in what concerns me. My debt will very soon be paid without the assistance of my board,[8] which you know is of some consequence to

[8] So in the typescript. Margaret had the income on £1000, and may well have paid board at Lainshaw. If the text is accurate, the passage perhaps means that she had got behind in her board and had gone further into debt to somebody for something — perhaps the expenses of the Irish jaunt. Boswell may have offered to ask Mrs. Montgomerie-Cuninghame to forgive the board bill. But it is perhaps

one of my way of thinking. I therefore beg you will not say a sentence on this subject. Most people wish to arrive at a state of independence; none likes the opposite situation worse than I. Why then shall I, by my own extravagance and folly, make myself unhappy? You seem to think the same frankness that has so great a share in my composition will secure me against the effects of inconstancy. I have never as yet been tried in that way, so cannot dispute your judgment. I have sentiments on this head perhaps peculiar to myself, but as silence cannot now be termed dissimulation, I beg to be indulged.

I have read your book and like it very much. I wish I could act up to the precepts it contains. I should then run little risk of being too deeply affected with any worldly concern. I am sorry you should find it difficult to preserve your good opinion of your friend. With me it is quite easy. You are therefore the less obliged, as it's generally according to the trouble we have in obtaining a thing that we affix a value to its possession.

I had wrote so far to be ready to send off tomorrow, when I received your letter dated the 7th.[9] I cannot imagine why you have not heard from me, as I wrote you an answer to your first letter that very post I received it. Surely it is in the possession of somebody or other.

So far from blaming your friend, I admire him for the part he has acted towards you.[1] I only think a supposition that I could take amiss his advice was owing to his not recollecting that the happiness of Miss Montgomerie was so much connected with his friend's that, in judging wisely for the one, they were certainly mutually obliged.

I am glad it will make you cautious. You know I recommended silence to you, both on my own account and yours. The instability of the human heart (not to fix it on either sex) should teach people to be a little prudent and leave to time to determine the sincerity of their affections. Why are you so gloomy? I cannot imagine what should make you so. Has these religious principles you recommend to me no influence over your own mind? Endeavour against it, I beg of you. It

---

more likely that the typist misread the manuscript, and that Margaret really wrote "assistance of any body."

[9] She is now writing on Monday 10 July.

[1] Boswell had retailed to her the substance of the letter from Temple which he had received on 7 July (see p. 222 *n.*1).

is really sinful to indulge melancholy and discontent when the Almighty has been so bountiful to you. Instead of allowing disagreeable ideas to take possession of your mind, think on what cannot fail to fill you with gratitude, and that will bring you to a cheerful, contented way. I'm sure I sincerely wish you happy and do not despair of seeing you so, if you yourself will but suffer it. Banish from your mind as much as possible that subject that has caused you so much uneasiness. You are secure and also free.[2]

My sister disapproves of my staying at Preston. I believe she is right; her arguments convince me. I must therefore lay aside all thoughts of being in Edinburgh without my sister or the Captain accompanies me.

I have many objections to the coming alone that I'm convinced you will approve of when I have an opportunity of communicating them to you. I must bid you adieu, with offering my duty to my uncle and best wishes to John, and begging you will believe me your sincerely affectionate and obliged

M.M.

I am very happy to hear your father is so well. I wish he could be prevailed on to come this way. My sister expects him.

FRIDAY 14 JULY. I continued most unhappy. Having sat up till four in the morning, I was very feverish. I loved M. from my soul, but saw myself to be incapable of any lasting connection. Grange and I walked down to Leith Links and saw a review of Cary's, the Forty-third Regiment. It entertained me somewhat. One of the Scots Greys, who stood as a sentinel to keep off the mob, did his duty so faithfully and yet with so much good nature that I gave him a shilling to drink. A little after this, I wanted to buy a bit of gingerbread. So, to make a trial of human nature, I came to my Grey and asked if he would give me some halfpence to buy some gingerbread. This was a pretty severe trial, for many fellows would have damned me and denied they had ever seen me. But my honest Grey said, "O yes, Sir,"

[2] As preserved in the typescript, this letter and one from Margaret Montgomerie to Boswell of 17 October 1769 (p. 334) contain near the end certain passages chronologically incompatible with what precedes. The simplest explanation is the most plausible: both letters occupied more than one sheet, and the typist assembled the sheets wrongly. The following paragraphs have been transferred.

and immediately pulled out a leathern purse. He had indeed but one halfpenny, but he gave me it very cheerfully; and, instead of buying gingerbread with it, I keep it with a piece of paper wrapped round it, on which I have written the anecdote.

I came home for a little. My father came into my room and spoke to me a little on indifferent subjects. But I shunned him. Grange and I dined comfortably at Purves's. He advised me strongly against any desperate scheme. But I was quite determined. Mr. Macdonald blooded me today to begin the cure of a severe symptom. It is hard for one night of Irish extravagance to suffer so much. I wrote a law paper this afternoon. But could hardly fix my attention. I then went to Mr. Moncrieffe's and played three rubbers at whist with him and Lord Galloway and David Kennedy, and then supped. I was observed to be very dull. It passed all to be on account of the fate of Corsica.

SATURDAY 15 JULY. I took a walk on the Castle Hill with Mr. Maconochie, and told him my dilemma. He was vexed, but advised me to be prudent. I became quite outrageous, and was mad enough to ask him if it would not be allowable to cut off ———, before he ruined his family? But this I certainly did not seriously mean for a moment. I went in the stage to Pinkie, to have talked with Commissioner Cochrane. But he was from home. My father and Miss Betty drove past in a chaise. I was quite chagrined. I hired a chaise and went to Sir Alexander Dick's. Amidst all my gloom the sweet place and amiable people soothed me. I told him my dilemma. He was vexed, and bid me do anything to prevent it. I was at home all the evening. My father sent for me to him. But I would not sit down. I just spoke a few sullen words. I was quite gone.

SUNDAY 16 JULY. After a wretched, feverish night I awaked in a dreadful state. I have no doubt that evil spirits, enemies to mankind, are permitted to tempt and torment them. "Damn him. Curse him," sounded somehow involuntarily in my ears perpetually. I was absolutely mad. I sent for worthy Grange, and was so furious and black-minded and uttered such horrid ideas that he could not help shedding tears, and even went so far as to say that if I talked so he would never see me again. I looked on my father's marrying again as the most ungrateful return to me for my having submitted so much to please him. I thought it an insult on the memory of my valuable mother. I thought it would totally estrange him from his children by her. In short, my wild imagination made it appear as terrible as can be conceived. I rose and took a little broth, and, in order to try if what I liked most could have any effect on me when in such a frame, I went to the chapel in Carrubber's Close, which has always made me fancy myself in heaven. I was really relieved. I thought of M., and loved her fervently. But I was still obstinate. A clergyman from Leith preached on these words, "I have learned, in whatever state I am, therewith to be content."[3] He said many good things on contentment, and that the text informed us it was to be *learnt*. I was averse to learn any good.

I then went and drank tea at the Miss Mackenzies'. M. again here in fancy. I am really constant. I wanted to be gloomy and like a man of such resolutions as I then had. But the agreeable company around me and my own gaiety insensibly made me otherwise. I then sat a while with Lady Crawford, with whom I have always a great deal of sentimental conversation. She made me love M. still more. I should have mentioned that in the forenoon my father wanted to speak to me, and I absolutely refused it by running away from him. I was very gloomy at night.

MONDAY 17 JULY. A kind letter from M., without taking any notice of our late quarrel, warmed my heart. I went and breakfasted with my uncle, the Doctor, who agreed with me in thinking my father would marry again, and said he had heard it. The family madness was kept up to a great pitch by the Doctor and me.[4] I was determined to throw myself on the wide world. I went and sat a while with Lady Crawford, and told her both my uneasiness and my love. She was

---

[3] Philippians 4. 11.

[4] Here is a clue to part of the secret of Boswell's "madness" overlooked by those who believe him to have been, at least at times, actually insane. There was undoubtedly insanity in the family. His brother John was sometimes violently insane and had to be locked up; his daughter Euphemia suffered from delusions of persecution and of grandeur. But Boswell's "madness" was partly posturing, partly the common depression of spirits suffered by all sensitive men who feel themselves thwarted in their ambitions. He rather liked to see himself in the role of madman, and in the Journal sometimes enacted that part with the same gusto with which he enacted the parts of traveller, lover, philosopher, or *littérateur*. Sometimes genuine "hypochondria" plunged him into despair and moral lethargy. In short, he was childish, unreasonable, above all melancholy; but not mad.

anxious to have me prevent the one, and clearly of opinion for the other. I took my clerk, Mr. Brown, to dine with me at Purves's. I had been with the Duchess and Douglas in the morning. At night I laboured at the law, but could hardly fix my attention at all. I wrote to Mrs. Montgomerie-Cuninghame to beg she would interpose in the unlucky affair. I also wrote to Margaret and to Temple.

[Boswell to Margaret Montgomerie]

Edinburgh, 17 July 1769

MY DEAREST PEGGIE, — The enclosed will account to you for my long silence.[5] It has been long in comparison of our frequent correspondence. Though your last letter but one made me imagine you had given me up, and I was for a while piqued and enraged, you see how humble I became, and how a true passion tears the heart. But my pride has made me keep the enclosed by me, and since I wrote it I have thought seriously that I am not fit for marriage with any woman. If I could behave so to such a valuable and affectionate woman as you, what a shocking temper must I have! The frankness for which I blamed you is really a perfection, for I never saw you improperly free.

My present situation is dreadful. What an infamous woman must she be who can impose on an old man worn out with business, and ruin the peace of a family! I am employing all prudent methods to prevent the ruinous scheme. If it shall go on, I am fixed in my resolutions. You must know that Douglas has pressed me to go abroad with him. This will be a very honourable employment for a year or two of my life. I shall not, however, determine hastily on anything.

What you tell me of my servant enrages me beyond measure.[6] Pray allow me to tell the rascal his villainy and turn him off. But you may depend on my doing nothing without your permission. Be not uneasy, my dear friend. Malicious reports against you can gain no credit. Your letter today has made me write this night. Be persuaded that my heart is wholly yours, though I am (perhaps madly) uneasy at what I formerly wrote to you about a certain gentleman. Adieu.

J.B.

[5] The enclosure, now missing, was apparently an apology, and possibly a further statement of his intentions toward her.

[6] The reference to Thomas is unexplained.

[EDITORIAL NOTE: The following essay, preserved among Boswell's miscellaneous papers, is undated but clearly was written during the summer of 1769 between the time when Boswell learned of his father's desire to remarry and the settlement of his own marital plans. The manuscript is at least a second draft, and very possibly was intended to serve as fair copy for the printer, though we have no evidence that it was ever published. "On Second Marriages" may be a reworking of an older narrative Boswell had come across, but it is more likely that "Queen Anne's Reign" and the English locale had their origin in the fancy that turned Douglas into Dorando and Edinburgh into Seville. The essay is a striking instance of how Boswell's imagination responded to the factual, when given a free rein, and provides as well a full and revealing account of his attitude towards his father and his father's prospective bride.]

ON SECOND MARRIAGES: A TRUE STORY
IN QUEEN ANNE'S REIGN

The duties which become essential to a man from the relation of family in the present state of society are most important and serious, and a neglect or transgression of them is often attended with such fatal consequences as I am now about to relate. A gentleman of distinction in Berkshire was at a proper age married to one of the best women that ever lived. He was one of those men of strong sense, prudence, and application to business, whose usefulness to society makes them generally respected. His lady brought him several children, all of whom she lived to see in a fair way of succeeding in the world, and then was carried off by a sudden illness. The gentleman's eldest son was then abroad upon his travels, but, being deeply affected with the loss of his valuable mother, and the distress into which his father was thrown, he returned home immediately. Though he had a distinguished genius, and a fire and impetuosity which could hardly brook the least control and disposed him to enjoy all the variety of life, regard for his father and for the family from which he was descended made him resolve to give up all the gay schemes of happiness which he had formed, and submit himself to a plan of living which he considered to be a perpetual succession of disgust. In order to this, he deadened his mind gradually, till he brought himself to a kind of state of indifference, forced himself to take a share in the dull employments and insipid society around him, and at length brought himself to be perfectly content. While the truly dutiful son conducted himself in this manner, the father, who had appeared almost inconsolable for the death of his wife and had been warned of mortality by a severe distemper, gave all the reason in the world to believe that he could have no other intention than to pass the rest of his days with a becoming gravity and abstraction, and would wish to see his heir assume in some measure the place which, in the course of nature, he was destined one day to fill. But instead of this, in little more than two years after the death of his wife, the father began to think of a second marriage. He communicated his design to his son with that awkward hesitation which generally shows itself when we are about to do anything of which we are ashamed. The young gentleman was shocked at the idea. He could hardly allow himself to believe such a thing of his father. Being of a melancholy temper, he began to doubt the reality of all apparent worth when he saw so shameful an instance of selfishness. His heart grew big, and he with difficulty could restrain himself from breaking out into sallies of indignation. He employed a prudent person to talk to the lady whom his father had in view, and to represent to her that if she complied with his proposals she would not only have the meanness to become the legal prostitute of libidinous old age, but would be the cause of destroying the peace of a family and ruining a young man of merit. He at the same time remonstrated to his father in the strongest terms, conjured him to remember his deceased spouse, and told him plainly that the keenness of his feelings were such that if his father put his scheme in execution, he would from that moment renounce him for ever. But vile interest in the one, and wretched appetite in the other of these parties prevailed over every proper sentiment, and produced a second marriage. The son, who was equally determined as he was warm, quitted his ungrateful father and retired to a distant country, where he indulged his gloomy reflections without restraint, and would upon no account listen to any terms of reconciliation. The father soon perceived that age and distemper are miserably suited for conjugal society, and for all the art of his new wife he saw her disgusted with his nauseous fondness. The respectable character which he had maintained was now sunk in folly and dotage. He became the subject of drunken jests, and *turpe senilis amor — peccet ad extremum ridendus*[7] were every day applied to him. None of his children would see a man who, for the selfish gratification of at most but a few years, had exposed himself, affronted the memory of their mother, driven from his country a son who did honour to it, and ruined a family which had supported itself for ages. He died in great agony both in body and mind, and may serve to teach decorum and generosity of conduct to those who come after him.

TUESDAY 18 JULY. I continued as bad as ever. I appeared before my father in some causes, and had a strange satisfaction in pleading calmly to a man with whom I could not have any intercourse in private. I felt a kind of regret to leave the Parliament House, to which I have a kind of family attachment. But I considered all attachments to be now at an end. I was really in a terrible state. Lord Monboddo desired to speak with me after the House. I accordingly took a walk with him, when he told me that he had just had a long and serious conversation with my father, who had complained to him of my behaviour, told him that it was my choosing to live in the irregular state of a bachelor which made him think of marrying again, and my Lord said if I would not alter my plan he was right. "But," said he, "will you let me negotiate between you? Yours is an estate and a family worth preserving." I said I could marry no other woman but Margaret. "Well," said he, "be serious and firm, and I hope to settle matters." This gave me quite a new set of thoughts.

I had told Douglas my uneasiness, and he promised to be my firm friend in all events. I went in the coach with the Duchess to Lord Chief Baron's, where we dined along with the Duke of Queensberry and Douglas. I was in perfect good spirits. The sight of grandeur made me for a second or two consider if I was not wrong to give up all schemes of marrying for ambition and wealth. But M. soon brought me back. I soon saw that my real happiness is not in such objects. That I only love sometimes to contemplate them, and that I would do it with double satisfaction when I have Margaret for my com-

[7] "An old man's love is shocking — ridiculous, he transgresses in his last years" (Ovid, *Amores*, I. ix. 4; Horace, *Epistles*, I. i. 9).

panion. Every different attempt to make me waver makes my love
steadier. The Duchess and I paid a visit to Lady Alva and the young
Countess of Sutherland,[8] and then returned to town, the mob huzzaing
and crying, "Douglas for ever!" I supped with my father. But Mr.
Brown was with us, as I wished to avoid particular conversation. We
were, however, tolerably well.

WEDNESDAY 19 JULY. Mr. Walter Campbell and his wife,
Mrs. Ritchie, Lord Monboddo, and Tilquhilly dined with us. I was
persuaded to go to the Assembly. There was a very fine company, and
I felt myself wonderfully calm and constant. I renewed my acquaintance with my old friend, Lady Colville. I was mad enough to dance
one country dance. Mrs. Walter Campbell was my partner, which
made me dance with violence. It did me much ill. I supped at Queensberry House with the Duke and the three Douglases. We were gay
and easy. I thought all the time how perhaps I should by and by be in
a company. Talking of the Hamilton Lords,[9] the Duke said, "Why,
the devil entered into them." "Yes," said I, "just as he did into the
swine."

THURSDAY 20 JULY. I was hurt by having danced. David Armstrong, Grange, and I took a chaise and saw a race at Leith. At night
I resolved to put M.'s affection to the strictest trial. I wrote to her,
taking no notice of any hopes of a compromise, but told her plainly
that if she would go off with me and live on my £100 a year, with the
interest of her £1000, I was ready to marry her. I bid her think fully,
and give me no reasoning but a direct answer. I wrote to Temple of
this, while I told him of the prospect of a compromise. This was truly
romantic, and perhaps too severe a trial of a woman of so much good
sense and so high a character.

[Boswell to Margaret Montgomerie]

[On the outside Boswell has written] Read this in your own room,
and think as long as you please. Only let me have a positive answer as
I am quite dependent on you.

---

[8] Very young; in fact, only four. "Lady Alva" was her grandmother.
[9] Either the five members of the House of Lords who had protested against the
Lords' decision in favour of Douglas, or the Lords of Session who had earlier
sustained the claim of the Hamilton side that he was a supposititious child.

Edinburgh, 20 July 1769

My dear Cousin, — I know I shall have a friendly and affectionate answer to the last letter which I wrote to you. But in the mean
time, I am going to write you a calm and determined epistle, in few
words but of infinite importance to us both.

You never knew till we were in Ireland that I had at different
periods of my life been deeply in love with you. That has, however,
been the case; and had not vanity or some other artificial motive made
me, from time to time, encourage my fancy in other schemes, the
genuine inclinations of my heart would ever have been constant to
my dear Peggie Montgomerie. As it was, you know how fond I have
been of you, and how I have at different times convinced you that my
love for you was truly sincere. While wavering in my resolutions, I
was always determined that if your happiness depended upon having
me, I would not hesitate a moment to make my best friend happy.
And I accordingly begged in a late letter that you would tell me
freely if that was the case.

I was at the Assembly last night, and saw a variety of beauties. I
was not inconstant to you for a moment. Indeed, after standing the
trial you did in Ireland, there could be little fear. Any other person
than you would be apt to disregard what I say in my present situation.
But I think I may trust to the generosity of a *noble-minded woman*,
as Dempster calls you. I therefore make you this proposal. You know
my unhappy temper. You know all my faults. It is painful to repeat
them. Will you, then, knowing me fully, accept of me for your husband as I now am; — not the heir of Auchinleck, but one who has
had his time of the world, and is henceforth to expect no more than
£100 a year? With that and the interest of your £1000, we can live in
an agreeable retirement in any part of Europe that you please. But
we are to bid adieu for ever to this country. All our happiness is to be
our society with each other, and our hopes of a better world. I confess
this scheme is so romantic that nothing but such love as you showed
at Donaghadee could make you listen to it. Nor ought I to be surprised
if a woman of your admirable sense and high character with all who
know you should refuse to comply with it, should refuse to sacrifice
every prudent consideration to me. But as I love you more than I can
express, you will excuse me for making this proposal. I am ready

upon these terms to marry you directly. And, upon my honour, I would not propose it now, were I not fully persuaded that I would share a kingdom with you if I had it. I also solemnly promise to do everything in my power to show my gratitude and make you happy. Think seriously of this. Give me any positive answer you honestly can. But I insist on no mediocrity, no reasoning, no hesitation. Think fully, and one way or other tell me your resolution. I am much yours,

JAMES BOSWELL.

FRIDAY 21 JULY. I dined at Lord Monboddo's with the Duke of Queensberry, Douglas, &c. All went on with politeness and most agreeable society. I passed the evening quietly at home.

SATURDAY 22 JULY. I breakfasted at Queensberry House with all the excellent friends there. Then Douglas carried me in his phaeton to the race at Leith. It was a handsome carriage with pretty mares, and he drove with great spirit among the crowd of company, always coming to pay his attentive duty to the worthy Duke. I was exceedingly happy. I exulted in reflecting that the author of the *Essence* had his charge so prosperous. As we drove home, I tried to make Douglas talk of immortality. He seemed to believe, and be animated with the idea of seeing the great who have appeared in the world. After the race, the Duke, Lord Monboddo, &c., and I went with Douglas to Willison's, and I made him fairly sit once to his picture, in order to begin it. I dined quietly at home with my brother. Grange drank tea with me. At night my father, having dined abroad and drank, cheerfully spoke to me of Lord Monboddo's telling him of my scheme as to M. I endeavoured to be as reserved as possible, but insensibly he and I fell into our usual bad humour. It is hard.

SUNDAY 23 JULY. I went to Mr. Erskine's church and heard Dr. Gibbons preach. This was an English clergyman recommended to me by Mr. Dilly.[10] In the morning I had been at the burial of John Mair, an extractor and the best formalist about the House, and then I breakfasted with Professor Wallace, who showed me a genealogy of the family of Fullarton vouched by papers for above five hundred years. It is curious how pleasing variety is. Mr. Wallace's style of conversation amused me much, and when I saw his law papers neatly

---

[10] It was Thomas Gibbons, a Nonconformist minister, whom Johnson invited to come "and dawdle over a dish of tea in an afternoon" (*Life of Johnson,* 3 June 1781).

bound up, with accurate indexes, and amongst them some of my own writing, the business of a Scotch lawyer acquired value in my mind, and I thought of continuing at it even in the worst event. But while I was in church, I thought that if M. gave me a prudent, cold, evasive answer, I would set sail for America and become a wild Indian. I had great thoughts of my acquiring strength and fortitude, and could not regret much leaving all I had known, as I should adore God and be happy hereafter. Between sermons, I called on Lady Preston and told her my dilemma. She was vastly hurt, and joined with me in rage. I then went to Queensberry House. I told my cousin, Willy Douglas, my dilemma. He was struck and said, "I sincerely commiserate you."

The worthy Duke had just a select company of us to dinner. He was very good company, and told us of a Scotch servant in London whom he turned off one day for drunkenness. Next day the fellow appeared at dinner. "How now!" said the Duke. Said the servant: "If ye dinna ken when ye hae a good servant, I ken when I hae a good master; and I'm no ga'in awa." All the company interceded, and he continued. Captain Douglas and I drank tea at the Miss Mackenzies' very agreeably. I then supped at the Duchess of Douglas's with the worthy Duke, Douglas, &c.

MONDAY 24 JULY. The Commissioner called on me a little. I told him my dilemma. He could not believe it. But when I raged, he stopped me and said, "No. You must make the best of it." His cool sense for a moment communicated itself to me. But I soon regained my usual warmth. I received a letter from my brother David, which pleased me much and gave me spirits. Dr. Gibbons and a young student of physic along with him, Mr. Harris a London dissenting clergyman, the Reverend Messrs. Walker and Erskine, and Mr. Andrew Hunter the preacher, dined with me, my father being at a Justiciary trial. I made myself excellent clerical company and was wonderfully well.

TUESDAY 25 JULY. The important answer from M. was brought to me in the Parliament House: "I accept of your terms." For a minute or two my habits of terror for marriage returned. I found myself at last fixed for ever; my heart beat and my head was giddy. But I soon recovered and felt the highest admiration and gratitude on a conduct so generous. Her letter was finely written, and did me more real honour than anything I have ever met with in life. I determined to make it my study to do all in my power to show my sense of her goodness. And I became calm and easy, thinking that as I was now fixed in the most important concern, everything else was but secondary. The Commissioner dined with us. At night I was at the Society, and spoke against repealing the Marriage Act.[1]

[Received 25 July, Margaret Montgomerie to Boswell]

[Enclosed in a wrapper endorsed by Boswell] The most valuable letter of my valuable friend, which does honour to both her and me. *Vraye Foi.*[2]

[Lainshaw] Saturday [22 July 1769]

I HAVE THOUGHT FULLY as you desired, and in answer to your letter I accept of your terms, and shall do everything in my power to make myself worthy of you. J.B. with £100 a year is every bit as valuable to me as if possessed of the estate of Auchinleck. I only regret the want of wealth on your account, not being certain if you can be happy without a proper share of it. Free of ambition, I prefer real happiness to the splendid appearance of it. I wish you could meet me at Glasgow on Saturday. Could you not come that length in the fly and return on Monday? Let me know and I'll be there any day you will appoint.

My heart determines my choice. May the Almighty grant His blessing and protection, and we need not be afraid; His providence extends over all the earth, so that wherever you go I shall willingly accompany you and hope to be happy. Had you been, as you mention, in your former prosperity, I should perhaps have indulged myself in female prudence, &c., but I think this is not now the time for dissimulation. I am therefore ready to meet you when you please and to join my fate to yours. Is not this as full an answer as you could wish? Say nothing of the affair to your father, as you are sure he will never consent; and to disobey after consulting is worse than doing it without saying a word.

[1] An Act passed in 1753 requiring that all marriages in England, with a few exceptions, had to be performed by an Anglican priest, or in Scotland by a Presbyterian minister, according to certain established rules.
[2] The original of this letter has survived.

Postscript to James Boswell's letter of proposal to Margaret Montgomerie (20 July 1769), and his endorsement on her letter of acceptance (22 July 1769). From the originals in the Yale University Library

My heart is more at ease than it has been of a long time, though still I feel for what I'm afraid you suffer. Be assured, my dear Jamie, you have a friend that would sacrifice everything for you, who never had a wish for wealth till now, to bestow it on the man of her heart.

I wrote two letters, one on Friday and one on Tuesday. I hope the contents of neither have offended you. My anxiety about your happiness made me use every argument in my power to prevail on you to stay at home. In hopes of meeting with you soon, I shall only add that I most sincerely am, my dear Jamie, your faithful and affectionate

M.M.

Sunday. I did not get this sent off yesterday, so have had one other night to think of it, and am still determined in my resolution to go with you where you please. Write me soon and let me know if you can meet me.

WEDNESDAY 26 JULY. I was in great uneasiness on account of my illness, but Macdonald and Dr. Cairnie, whom I also consulted, made me give over terrible apprehensions. I was this afternoon at a meeting of the late Mr. Adie's trustees. At night I wrote to M. She had proposed to meet me on Saturday at Glasgow. But I could not get so far, as the Duke was to dine with us. I begged to know if she could come to Whitburn. I was very desirous to see her.

THURSDAY 27 JULY. Cowhill, Skerrington, and Matthew Dickie dined with us. Dupont drank tea, and then he and I and my brother went and saw Willison's pictures.

FRIDAY 28 JULY. I was chancellor to the jury who served Horatius Cannan of Barlay heir to his father and grandfather. I liked a ceremony of this kind, and was pleased to think of my standing upon record in it. We all dined with the heir at Small's. It was quite a comfortable Edinburgh dinner, and I was neither better nor worse than my neighbours, but just plain and content. I supped at Mr. Moncrieffe's. It was a jovial meeting over a capercailye.[3]

SATURDAY 29 JULY. This has been a good week for me in the way of business. I have cleared twenty guineas, and have really been able to do very well. I am ready for whatever may happen. My dearest Margaret is my great object. The Duke of Queensberry, Douglas,

---

[3] A wood grouse from the Highlands.

Lords Pitfour and Monboddo, Mr. Stewart of Blantyre, Mr. Solicitor, Captain Douglas, Mr. Douglas of Fechil, and Lord Chief Baron dined with us. Things went on admirably. I then went with the Duke, Douglas, &c., to Lord Advocate's,[4] from whence Mrs. Montgomery, Lady Mary Hay, and her aunt, Miss Lockhart, were attended by us to Comely Garden. Lady Mary was a fine, good-humoured young lady of a noble carriage, stately person, and the daughter of the Lord High Constable of Scotland.[5] I was truly desirous to have a match between her and Douglas. We walked some time in the garden, then went in and drank tea, I in excellent spirits observing Douglas and Lady Mary taking to one another. They danced a country dance, and I stood with my black clothes and my cane, looking on as grave and anxious as if I had been their parent. There was a good company. I was quite constant to Margaret. I had once been with her here, and I had some conversation about her tonight with her correspondent, Miss Kitty Mackenzie, which pleased me more than I can tell. I was all affection and admiration. The Duke and Douglas and the Captain and I supped at the Duchess's, where we met my father, and my uncle the Doctor, and David Moncrieffe and Maconochie. We were all friends and very good company.

I find it is impossible to put upon paper an exact journal of the life of man. External circumstances may be marked. But the variations within, the workings of reason and passion, and, what perhaps influence happiness most, the colourings of fancy, are too fleeting to be recorded. In short, so it is that I defy any man to write down anything like a perfect account of what he has been conscious during one day of his life, if in any degree of spirits. However, what I put down has so far an effect that I can, by reading my Journal, recall a good deal of my life.

SUNDAY 30 JULY. I was at church all day. I fancied M. sitting beside me as she used to do. Sir George[6] and George Webster dined

---

[4] Chief prosecutor for the Crown in Scotland. The office was held at this time by James William Montgomery, later Lord Chief Baron of the Court of Exchequer and a baronet.

[5] The Earl of Erroll, in whose title the office is hereditary. Lady Mary (just fifteen when this was written) next year married General Scott of Balcomie, but before long ran off with Captain James Sutherland, later fifth Lord Duffus. She died in 1782, aged only twenty-seven.

[6] Preston.

with us. It was curious to observe how my father's manner awed and checked the freedom of conversation. This is really hard to bear. I went out with Ulbster to his house in a park off the Pleasance, and drank tea with Lady Janet. It pleased me to see his children coming so well on, and I found myself wonderfully regarded here.[7] Jamie Colquhoun was here. I applied to him, who is narrow and loves to stay at home, a droll story which George Webster told me of the late President Craigie's eldest son, who, when his father asked him to go abroad and offered him £400 a year, answered, "Very well; and wha'll that come off at the lang run?" Such a speech I think I never heard. I was in very good humour today. I recollected my former follies; I saw that my father had indulged and forgiven me more than I could a son of mine if I had one. I therefore would have no resentment against him, let him do as he pleased. I would just consider his marrying again as a fatality by which he was killed and his estate overwhelmed, and, without farther connection either with the one or the other, I would go and live as easily and agreeably as possible with my dearest M. I wished to tell him something like this at night. But I found myself kept back as usual.

MONDAY 31 JULY. The Commissioner carried me out in his chaise to Pinkie, where I dined with him most comfortably along with my brother John. The Commissioner did not seem very fond of my scheme with M. However, that will be got over. He spoke to me very seriously against being outrageous on my father's marrying again, and really his notions were rational. I came to town in the fly. A German was in it, and I spoke to him in his own language, but found myself much rusted. At night I was quiet at home.

[Received 31 July, Margaret Montgomerie to Boswell]

[Lainshaw] Saturday [29 July 1769]
I WAS SO HURRIED and had such a severe headache when I wrote my last letter, I had it only in my power to tell you I could not meet you at Whitburn. The Captain was so very ill I thought it was improper for me to leave my sister, but if he is tolerably well I shall be

---

[7] George Sinclair of Ulbster and Lady Janet, his wife. One of the children, John, was later a baronet, first president of the Board of Agriculture, and compiler of the *Statistical Account of Scotland.*

at Glasgow on Saturday, in case you think the journey will do you no harm; but I entreat you will not think of coming without you can do it safely, as a few weeks will soon pass over, when I hope to be happy with you here. You must, however, be punctual in writing, as your silence would now affect me very much. I hope nobody knows of my letter you received in the Parliament House. You must not mention it, as it would not be right anybody knew of it but yourself. I wonder you could ever imagine I would write you an evasive answer to yours. Have you not often experienced my sincerity? How could you, then, imagine me such a dissembling, mercenary being? Believe me, without the least hopes of a reconciliation, and with the prospect of setting out in a few weeks, perhaps in a few days, I wrote my letter. I had my uneasy reflections also, but they were quite different from yours. I was fearful you would have the feelings you describe, but I dreaded they would not so soon wear off. I was, however, satisfied that, notwithstanding my frankness in declaring my sentiments and resolutions, I would not take any advantage of the offer you made me if you was not perfectly convinced that, in making the proposal, you consulted your own happiness. I am much obliged to you for acting so honestly by me. You told me what was your situation when you read my letter; I have therefore no doubts of the sincerity of the declaration that follows. Believe me, I am perfectly satisfied of the reality of that affection you express, and shall make it my constant endeavour to be worthy of it. I neither fear for you nor myself. I am conscious my conduct will be such as you must approve, and I am likewise sensible your natural dispositions are good. I have therefore no doubts of our being constant friends. You must not indulge melancholy. You know it's what we may easily bring upon ourselves, but what is very hard to remove. Be therefore as cheerful as possible from this generous consideration: that the happiness of your friend depends on yours.

Did you not speak of buying some Holland for shirts? I wish you would get some female friend to choose it and send it to me. I'll get them made for you. Let it be pretty fine, as I hate to see you with coarse linens. Don't buy any stockings for me. I assure you I want nothing. I am determined to be a perfect economist now, so you must not put me out of my way.

The Captain is still very much distressed. He gets no sleep at nights, which makes the fever continue with him. Tell me if your father knows your resolutions with regard to me. If he does, and comes this way, I shall be frightened to face him. Have you heard from David? Poor man, I long to hear how he does. Pray, is the Lieutenant with you? Has he received his garters? This will reach you on Monday; I hope therefore to hear from you on Tuesday. You see I am selfish in some respects, for, notwithstanding your telling me how much you was busied, I scruple not to put you to additional trouble. Could you send me a few franks, as I never see Lord Eglinton now to ask them from him? I doubt you pay double postage for my letters. Write me if you do. You never mention the lady's name you suspect to be your father's favourite, but I imagine it must be B.B.[8] I believe I told you I had received a letter from Aunt Boyd. I had also one from her husband, but not a sentence of their coming to Scotland.

I see by the papers your friend General Paoli is on his way to England. He will surely visit Scotland also. The Captain has got your dog. I was obliged to write James Bruce to send him. I ought to have asked your liberty first, but he was so impatient I had not the time, but I know you will forgive me.

I must now bid you adieu in hopes of hearing from you soon that you was not angry at me for not being at Whitburn as you desired. I remain, my dear Jamie, your ever affectionate

M.M.

TUESDAY 1 AUGUST. Mr. John Chalmer, Mr. James Neill from Ayr, and Grange dined with us. At five I drank tea along with Maclaurin at Mr. John Swinton's, at a consultation. I really, for the most part, like the business of the law. There is a kind of entertainment in observing the progression of causes, and a great variety of ideas are made to work.

WEDNESDAY 2 AUGUST. Dempster was in town in his way to London. I had written him a letter while he was sick, which I said just came on its tiptoes to inquire how he was. I went now and found him at Peter Ramsay's, and observing him thin, "Dempster," said I, "your belly has been imitating the India stock of late — falling"; a very proper similitude for a director of the East India Company. I told him I was fixed to M. He said he was much pleased; that his only surprise

[8] Betty Boswell?

was how I could do so rational a thing. He said it was just as if either he or I could be transformed into a female, and the one marry the other. He was quite against my outrage, supposing my father to marry again. He said I had a title to remonstrate, and try to prevent it; but if my father insisted for it, it was my duty to submit. He said it was not an insult to the memory of a first wife to marry a second. "I suppose," said I, "you will say it is no more so than it is an insult upon boiled beef to eat afterwards of roast mutton." "Just so," said he, "when the first course is gone, why not take a second?" This lively argument would have some truth if a wife were looked upon with as little sentiment as a dish at one's table.

Dempster said that all schemes of flying one's country were bad, because the moment there is a variation in the sentiments of a person who does so he is miserable, because it is very difficult for him to return. Said I, "Would it not be noble for me to get among the wild Indians in America?" "What," said he, "would you give up for ever with me, with Miss Montgomerie?" I was sorry to part with him. I dined at Lord Monboddo's with the Duke of Queensberry and Douglas, and we were so well and cheerful that it was agreed we should all meet again at supper too. I was in admirable spirits, with perfect sobriety.

THURSDAY 3 AUGUST. I do not recollect this day.

FRIDAY 4 AUGUST. My father came into my room this morning and told me that although he thought my scheme of marriage improper and that Margaret and I would part in half a year, yet as I insisted for it he would agree. I was really very grateful to him, and hoped to be able to behave to his satisfaction.

SATURDAY 5 AUGUST. I had agreed to go to Lainshaw to see Margaret. I accordingly set out this morning in the fly. There was a very good company, and I was calm and just as I could wish. I was taking a glass of madeira at Graham's when Sir James Steuart sent to me that he was in the house and would be glad to see me. I went to him. I told him I had a companion whom I would wish to introduce. "Oh," said he, "bring him in by all means," "There he is," said I, pointing to my bottle of madeira, which I had made the waiter set upon the table. Sir James made it very welcome, and he and I were very social. He argued for prudent, interested marriages. I told him of mine. He opposed my scheme, "For," said he, "whenever you have enjoyed a woman you are in love with, love goes off." "No fear," said I, "my mistress and I are old friends; and surely our friendship will not be lessened because we enjoy happiness together? Do you think two friends will become less so by drinking a bottle of champagne together? I grant you that if the champagne is the only connection that brings two people together, their love will not last; but my situation is quite different." I really thought I had the better of Sir James when I argued for love. I received here a kind letter from Margaret. I was in the best frame imaginable.

I took a post-chaise and set out for Lainshaw. It pleased me to drive through Glasgow, and recall a variety of ideas. I got to Lainshaw before ten. The poor Captain was very ill. When I saw my valuable Margaret, I was in more agitation than I could have believed. Mrs. Cuninghame and I had a serious conversation, and all was now certainly fixed. It is impossible to write down all that M. and I said.

[Received 5 August, Margaret Montgomerie to Boswell]

[Lainshaw] Friday [4 August 1769]

IT MADE ME VERY UNEASY to be obliged to apologize for not coming to Glasgow, but I found it impossible for me to do otherwise, as the Captain continues so distressed, and Sandy is also very ill of a sore throat.[9]

I did not receive your letter till late last night; otherwise I would have told you how kind I thought you for remembering me so often. You may believe it hurts me to be obliged to act so ungratefully and inconsistently to one I am bound by the strongest ties to behave [to] in a different manner. But the opinion of those we live with must be attended to if we wish to have any satisfaction in life. You know I have often told you I am a coward, and in some measure a slave to public report. I never but in one instance got entirely the better of these two, and then I thought the affair of too great importance to me to be withheld by either.

I shall send this under cover to Mr. Graham's, lest my letter

---

[9] Alexander Cuninghame, one of the Captain's younger sons. He was at this time probably in his early teens.

should not reach you in time to inform you of the impossibility of my meeting you as you desired, and to beg you will come to Lainshaw if you can. I am not at all the housekeeper; I keep close in my own room except when called to the dining-room or to take a walk, and am never out of bed after eleven; so you see I follow all your prescriptions, and, what's more, I obey your commands in not writing to any disagreeable person.

I really wish above all things to see you, and, believe me, I am almost convinced you'll be here. If you do not come, figure what will be my disappointment. News I have none to entertain you with. I am accustomed to very little variety, and, I may say, with no conversation at all. The whole amusement I have is in reading my *friend's* letters and sometimes a paper of *The Spectator* or some serious book. As to my French, I have applied but little of late. A mind taken up with more important concerns is capable of making small progress in any piece of learning. But as you desire me to give attention to it, you may believe that is sufficient.

I will be much obliged to you for the picture. I often regret the one I have has no resemblance; the only thing makes it valuable is knowing who it was designed for, and remembering out of whose hands I received it. I shall walk at least a mile or two to meet you on Saturday evening; if you don't come, I shall go home not in good spirits.

You did not tell me if your father proposes coming this way. I should like to know, that I may be out of the way.

The Captain is still very feverish; he got no sleep last night, which has fretted him and makes him more uneasy today. I must now bid you farewell, with wishing every happy thing to attend you, and assuring you I am, with sincerity, my dear Jamie's ever affectionate and faithful friend,

M. MONTGOMERIE.

You are not angry at me for calling you by your name? Tell me and I will not do it again.[1]

SUNDAY 6 AUGUST. We did not go to church, but stayed quietly at home. I felt myself serene and happy, and I had infinite satisfaction

[1] Boswell intensely disliked being called "Jamie." He apparently made no protest at this time, but after marriage his wife seems to have addressed him invariably as "Mr. Boswell."

in seeing my dear M. as happy as I was. As I was to set out next morning at three to be in time for the fly I did not go to bed, but kept Mr. Grahames and Dr. Dean with me over a bowl of punch. M. went to bed early, as she was to go with me. During the night I became anxious and frightened that still I should not have her.

MONDAY 7 AUGUST. When she came down in the morning, I told her my uneasiness and insisted that we should take each other's hands and solemnly engage ourselves. We did so, and I was easy. We had an agreeable drive to Glasgow, where we breakfasted. I was happier than I can describe. It was curious to look back, and then to consider my present situation. It vexed me that I could not immediately marry. But I pleased myself that the scheme's being known for some time before would be more creditable, as it would show it to be no sudden flight. Captain Wood was in the fly with me, and some more good company. We were exceedingly merry. We took a mutton chop at Whitburn, and I pushed about madeira till four of us drank five bottles. I was hurt to find myself so inclined to intemperance. When I got to town, I went to the opera of *Artaxerxes*. Archie Stewart, my old Rotterdam friend, and Captain Erskine sat with me in a dark corner. I told them I was now fixed, and they rejoiced at my happiness, though they could not help hinting that they had apprehensions of my inconstancy. I was not afraid. My father was pretty kind when I came home.

TUESDAY 8 AUGUST. Sir Thomas Wentworth, Lady Macdonald's uncle, was now here in his way to Skye. I went and called for him, but he was abroad. In a little he came to me, and we were at once quite easy. My father and Balmuto and I dined along with him and the two Mr. Riddels and William Macdonald at Mr. Campbell of Ashnish's. I drank freely and then I went to Fortune's, where Mr. Moncrieffe's guests were entertaining him, and there I became outrageously jovial and intoxicated myself terribly, and was absurd and played at brag and was quarrelsome. How unhappy is this!

WEDNESDAY 9 AUGUST. I was quite gloomy and dejected. I wrote a long letter to Margaret. That valuable woman will make me the man I wish to be. The company who dined together yesterday, with the addition of Lord Hailes, dined at my father's. William Macdonald and I supped at Mr. Surgeon Macdonald's and drank bottles apiece of the finest old claret that I ever tasted. I consulted Dr. Gregory this afternoon. He thought me in no bad way and was of opinion I might be cured very well here, but as it would make my mind easy advised me to go to London and drink some of Kennedy's decoction.

THURSDAY 10 AUGUST. Mr. Riddel gave a dinner at Leith to Sir Thomas Wentworth and a number of others, amongst whom I was one. My spirits sparkled in an extraordinary degree. Lord Kellie was in high glee.[2] "Upon my soul," said he, "we are merry. We have said a devilish number of good things." "Why," said I, "my Lord, it is very natural for puns and rebuses, &c., to keep company with Riddels." My Lord abused his tailor for having given him a brown coat that made him look like a dean of guild. Said I, "It is very proper for you, my Lord, now that you are becoming a grave man: *Quid verum atque decens, curo et rogo.*"[3] "*Curo et rogo,*" said he; "I wish you would *cure* the *roguery* of the tailor." The Earl played his battery against me, and gave me many hard hits which I need not repeat. When he was in great triumph, I said, "My Lord, I can say nothing to you myself, but I'll tell you what Dictionary Johnson would say: 'Why, Sir, Kellie is a turf that burns for other people while he consumes himself.'" The whole company roared, and my Lord was foundered for some time. But he soon got up again and went on with immense spirit. I drank immensely and was so joyous that I was clearly of opinion that intoxication is a noble thing. Such is the effect of wine. And perhaps a good quantity of it may at times do well for many people. But I, who have so much extravagance and vice to subdue, must observe the strictest sobriety. Sir Thomas and William Macdonald and I walked up, and I was fit for business and wrote a law paper. I must mention that during all our excess of merriment, I was continually wafting my fervent vows to M., and rejoicing that I was at last so happily fixed.

FRIDAY 11 AUGUST. Lord Galloway carried Sir Thomas Wentworth and me in his coach out to St. Catherine's, Lord Gardenstone's country place.[4] By the way we were very pleasant. My Lord told us a

[2] Thomas Alexander Erskine, sixth Earl of Kellie, was a noted musician, humorist, and drinker.

[3] "What is right and seemly is my study and pursuit" (Horace, *Epistles,* I. i. 11).

[4] Francis Garden, a judge in the Court of Session with the style of Lord Gardenstone, was another able, literary, and eccentric judge. His eccentricity showed

repartee of Lord Hyndford's to the King of Prussia, who never had a child. He was laughing at the Emperor, and said, *"Il est bon à rien que pour bercer des enfants."* Replied Lord Hyndford, *"Et pour en faire. "*[5] My Lord did not relish much a joke of mine on the Hamilton tutors, who had about this time very serious meetings. "My Lord," said I, "you have had long *sederunts*[6] — a long *parliament;* and I believe a good many *bills* have been brought in." Mr. Lockhart and Mr. and Mrs. Macqueen were with us at dinner. I drank too much burgundy. I came to town in Mrs. Macqueen's chaise, with her and Sir Thomas. I supped at Charles Small's with Captain Erskine. I was in liquor, but good company. We drank bottles of claret apiece. Erskine would not let me call for any more.

[Received ? 11 August, Margaret Montgomerie to Boswell]

[Lainshaw] Thursday [10 August 1769]

WITH THE UTMOST IMPATIENCE I wait the arrival of the post in hopes he will bring me a letter from my dear friend. What an anxious, uneasy time have I spent since I received your last letter! I am fearful you are not well — your fatigue, hard drinking, and going to the opera all join to make me unhappy. I imagine you perhaps met some companion there who prevailed on you to sup abroad, and by that means finished the irregularities of the day. Oh, what would I give to be certain this was not the case, and to hear you had not suffered in the least by your journey! I can write no more till I see what accounts the post brings. I am just going to set off for Stewarton, so adieu for a little and God bless you, my best friend.

---

itself in a fondness for pigs, a visitor even having stumbled over one which slept in his bedroom according to report. He also successfully founded a large village.
[5] "He is only good for rocking children" . . . "And to beget them." John Carmichael, third Earl of Hyndford, acted as envoy extraordinary and plenipotentiary to mediate between Frederick II and Maria Theresa on Frederick's invasion of Silesia in 1741. He is the subject of one of Carlyle's best portraits (*History of Friedrich II*, Book xiii, Ch. 2). The "Emperor" alluded to was presumably Maria Theresa's husband, Francis of Lorraine, though he did not become Emperor until 1745.
[6] Sessions.

I am now returned and beg you will accept of my sincere, my grateful thanks for your kind letter. I have read your friend's epistle and admire him much, setting aside the partiality his goodness to me must naturally inspire me with.[7] His sentiments are beautiful, and his having so much vivacity is a convincing proof there is perfect peace within. I shall be happy to get acquainted with him, and hope our good opinion of each other will rather increase than diminish. How glad I am to see him of the same opinion I was with regard to your father.[8] I hope you and he shall always live in the strictest friendship, for such a companion, whose goodness you have experienced, is certainly valuable, and his advice will always be an unspeakable advantage.

I am happy to think your father treats you with so much kindness. It shall be my constant endeavour to behave so to him as that he shall have no cause to regret your choice. I am sensible of my faults, and very desirous to amend them. He shall ever find me dutiful to him, and extremely ready to follow his directions, as far as lies in my power.

I am sorry you met with Sir Thomas Wentworth, since it led you into a riot. It is on account of your health I am most uneasy, as I am not afraid but you will be very sober when you reflect that being otherwise will make a person unhappy who would sacrifice a great deal for your satisfaction.

As to your going to London, I cannot, will not, object if it's your interest to be there, but how will your father relish such an expedition? I'm afraid he will be greatly offended. In that case, I should be extremely uneasy. If your health is not in question, you could see Mr.

[7] Boswell's letter has not been recovered. He enclosed a letter from Temple (28 July) in which the latter says: "If you can obtain your father's approbation, you cannot be too soon united to so respectable, so amiable a woman. You have been tossed too long on the ocean of irregular desire, without compass, without real attachment, without real enjoyment. . . . I really now long to see you the *married man*. What a different turn will it give to your letters! No more venereal disasters, no more intrigues, no more Zélide, no more gardener's daughters. The volatile, the witty, the amorous Boswell will then write like any other grave, sensible man."

[8] Temple had argued that Lord Auchinleck had a right to remarry, to comfort his "cheerless solitude."

Johnson some other time, but you are surely the best judge yourself. I pretend not to dictate; I only wish you to act so as not to disoblige my uncle when he is so very good to you.

You are quite right as to my anxiety. I suffer as much from that as you can possibly imagine. I must surely see you before you set out for London. If you are determined to go, I'll endeavour to be in Edinburgh before you leave it. There's a great odds betwixt the distance of the two places to me; in the one I can see you in a day, but I would have no sort of excuse for setting out to London without the ceremony had been put over. I really think it should; it would have been much more satisfactory to me to think I had it in my power to see you without giving real cause for censure; and, when once people are determined, the sooner they put it over the better. I must have many promises of sobriety before I give my consent to your going to London.

The Captain, poor man, is extremely distressed; he seems to think himself, as he really is, in a dangerous way. Did you tell Archie Stewart, or was it his own supposition? I must surely write Lady Maxwell, as I was her confidante when she engaged herself, and I think I ought to act in the same manner by her, but I shall not do it till I hear from you. You are very good to allow me to correspond with Mrs. S.[9] I shall never abuse the confidence you put in me. I shall think it my duty to give up any acquaintance that is disagreeable to you, but I would willingly do it by degrees. I must once more entreat you will be sober. Consider, my dear Jamie, that my happiness is entirely in your power, and I'm sure your generosity will make you deny yourself an indulgence that may be hurtful to you as well as your friend. Lord Eglinton sent his compliments to me by Mr. Grahames today, and bid him tell me he heard for certain I was to be married to Mr. Boswell. How in the world does everybody know so well? It must surely be from you, for I declare it is not from me they know anything of the matter. I fancy you will have received my letter I wrote on Tuesday. I mentioned your keeping Thomas. It's on T. Bruce's[1] account I wish him continued, and, if you live with your father, he may do well enough; but I am doubtful he is not a servant where there is nobody to depend on but himself. I fancy you will have some conver-

[9] Mrs. Stuart? See p. 211 *n*.7.

[1] So in the typescript, but probably it should read "J. Bruce's."

sation with Lord Auchinleck before you part. Let me know what humour he is in with me.

I am obliged to make my letter shorter than I intended, as I was called down to entertain some of our neighbours while my sister was with the Captain. They are now gone, but I'm afraid I shall be too late for the post, and I should be sorry to lose the earliest opportunity of assuring you with what sincere gratitude and affection I ever shall be your faithful and affectionate

M.M.

SATURDAY 12 AUGUST. The session rose today. Lord Monboddo took leave of me, hoping to meet me next as a married man. My father was to have set out for Auchinleck today. But some business detained him. John went, and my father and I were easy and well. After dinner he talked of Margaret and me. Said we had both very good sense, but were thoughtless, and must become just different beings. I told him I was under a necessity to go to London for a little to clear my constitution. He acquiesced. The evening passed well.

SUNDAY 13 AUGUST. My illness was visibly decreasing, so I resolved to stay in and take care of it for a week or a fortnight, and be pretty well before I set out for London. My father and I had a warm dispute at night on male and female succession. I argued that a male alone could support a family, could represent his forefathers. That females, in a feudal light, were only vehicles for carrying down men to posterity, and that a man might as well entail his estate on his postchaise, and put one into it who should bear his name, as entail it upon his daughter and make her husband take his name. I told him that the principle of family, of supporting the race of Thomas Boswell of Auchinleck, was what supported my mind, and that, were it not for that, I would not submit to the burthen of life here, but would go and pass my days in a warm climate, easy and gay. I bid him consider that he held the estate of Auchinleck, at least the old stamen of it, in prejudice of no less than four females. That excluding females might at a time hurt a fond father who had daughters and no sons. "But what," said I, "is a sorry individual to the preservation of a family? Is there any comparison? Besides, in that view, why will you make the son whom you see miserable on account of some woman who may appear nobody knows when?" I saw he was quite positive in the

strange, delusive notion of *heirs whatsoever*, and I had the mortifi-
cation to be sensible that my dissipated and profligate conduct had
made him at all think of an entail, and made any arguments from me
of little force. I, however, hoped to get him prevented from ruining
his family. I was quite in a fever, for I declare that the family of
Auchinleck is my only constant object in this world. I should say, *has
been* so. For my dearest M. is now as firmly established. I determined
to leave the country if he made the settlement which shocked me. I
told him so, and I knew M. would not complain. Indeed I was too hot
for a son to a father. But I could not help it. I was like an old Roman
when his country was at stake.

I fell upon a most curious argument which diverted my own
fancy so much that it was with difficulty I could preserve my gravity
when uttering it. "If," said I, "you believe the Bible, you must allow
male succession. Turn to the first chapter of Matthew: 'Abraham
begat Isaac, Isaac begat Jacob,' &c. If you are not an infidel, if you do
not renounce Christianity, you must be for males." Worthy man! he
had patience with me. I am quite firm in my opinion on this point. It
will not do to say a grandson by a daughter is as near as a grandson by
a son. It leads into a nice disquisition in natural philosophy. I say the
stamen is derived from the *man*. The woman is only like the ground
where a tree is planted. A grandson by a daughter has no connection
with my original stock. A new race is begun by a father of another
name. It is true a child partakes of the constitution of his mother, gets
some of his mother's blood in his veins. But so does he as to his nurse,
so does he as to the ox whose beef he eats. The most of the particles of
the human frame are changed in a few years' rotation. The stamen
only continues the same. Let females be well portioned. Let them enjoy liberally what is naturally intended for them: dowries as virgins,
a share of what their husbands have while wives, jointures when
widows. But for goodness' sake, let us not make feudal lords, let us not
make barons of them. As well might we equip them with breeches,
swords, and gold-laced hats.

In every age some instances of folly have occurred to humble the
pride of human nature. Of these, the idea of female succession is one
of the most striking. A foolish fondness for daughters has introduced
it, when fathers thought they could not do enough for them. Like the

ancient Scottish clergy, who became so very fond of the Virgin Mary that, not satisfied with *Aves* and other acknowledgments, they gravely disputed in a synod at St. Andrews whether they should not say *Pater Noster,* "Our Father which art in heaven," to her. Spottiswood relates this as a most monstrous absurdity. To make a woman a feudal lord is much such another. If it be said that remote heirs male may be in the lowest ranks, surely remote heirs female may be so too. I love the late Earl of Cassillis, who, when settling his estate, being told by his man of business that he had called all the heirs male, "Then," said he, "give it to the devil." This was the true spirit and dignity of the ancient peer.[2]

MONDAY 14 AUGUST. The Commissioner and I had a serious conversation in which he gave me hopes that by patience, calmness, attention, and good behaviour, I would get all matters made easy with my father. This cheered me. My father was quite in good humour again, and took a kind leave of me as he set out for Auchinleck. I was now left quiet, and hoped to get away soon to London.

TUESDAY 15 AUGUST. I wrote law papers and stayed close at home. I should have mentioned that I received some time ago an admirable letter from Temple, approving much of my marriage with M. and putting it in the most agreeable light.

Having from this day till Thursday the 24 omitted to mark what passed every day, it is enough to say that I have been close keeping the house, that Dr. Cairnie has attended me now and then, and Mr. Macdonald constantly. That my distemper has been gradually melting away. That I have written a great many pages of law papers, and been employed several hours for several evenings in sorting a large mass of session papers belonging to my father and selecting such as are worth binding; and, to show the force of custom, I have been very fond of this business. I have been visited by Sir George Preston very frequently, by M. Dupont every Thursday, by worthy Grange often. One day Mr. David Hume came and sat a while with me. I said that Dr. Robertson from the first part of his Spanish history had drawn the

[2] Here begins the long and wearisome contest between Boswell and his father over the Auchinleck entail, not ended until 1776, and then by a compromise satisfactory to neither. By that time, Boswell had two daughters himself, and his "old Gothic Salic male enthusiasm" had so far abated that he wished them "called" in the entail after the male heirs of Lord Auchinleck's own body.

riches of Peru, of which the second is to treat. Mr. Balfour of Pilrig
was with me one morning. I thanked him for his *Philosophical Essays*, particularly for the one on liberty and necessity. "You have
smoothed it finely, Sir," said I. "You have put a good swaird[3] upon it."
M. Dupont and Surgeon Macdonald drank tea with me today.

[Boswell to Margaret Montgomerie]

Edinburgh, 21 August 1769

I HOPE MY LETTER OF SATURDAY has prevented you from being uneasy till this arrives. Be assured that it shall ever be my constant study
to ward off pain from my dearest friend, and to make her as happy as
I can. You have been kind enough to accept of me with all my faults.
I am sure I have told you everything bad about myself: my melancholy, my jealousy, every unhappy feeling to which I am subject.
You are prepared to bear with them all, or to prevent them by your
kindness. You may just keep in mind that a disposition to melancholy
and the most violent passion for the family of Auchinleck make a part
of my very existence. So you are not to wonder at their effects. I indeed hope that neither the one nor the other shall trouble you much.
If I am at times unhappy, I trust I shall not make you so. To see my
dearest Peggie well is enough to comfort me. But enough of this at
present, when I am as contented and cheerful as you could wish me to
be. I am recovering my health very fast, and pleasing myself with the
most agreeable prospect of our mutual happiness.

I do not wonder at your panic and reluctance to go to Auchinleck.
Nobody but such as know my father's way perfectly can imagine how
hard it must be upon you. For the truth is that his manner of keeping
people in awe, joined with his peculiar talent of putting what he
pleases in a contemptible light, is galling beyond expression to a feeling mind. The best remedy which I have found against the effects of
this has been to prepare myself calmly for it, as for a piece of *caricatura*, which I am certain is unjust but which may entertain me. A
great part of the happiness of lovers and friends consists in the high
opinion which they entertain of each other. In what particular way
you think of me, I cannot know; but am convinced that you have a

[3] An obsolete form of "sward," surface.

value for me, as I have for you, as much as ever man had for woman, and for which I have often given you the best reasons. Now how terrible must it be for any one of us to have the other represented as a very inconsiderable being. However, allowance must be made. No other person can think equally high of us as we do of each other, and my father less so perhaps than anybody else. Let us bear it patiently, and hope to make him by degrees think better of us.

I approve of your not being in too great a hurry to go to Auchinleck. I have written to my father telling him that, as I now look upon you as my *wife*, it will be very obliging to me if he will send his chaise for you, or at least write to you, and behave to you with kindness as his daughter-in-law. My letter will be with him this afternoon. You may wait a day or two, and see what effect it produces. As this is our sacrament week at Auchinleck, he may put off sending for you till next week. But if you do not hear from him by Friday, I would have you send your letter to him. You will observe that I have shortened it considerably and have struck out the paragraph justifying yourself as to our marriage. I think you have no need of a justification. Are not you my equal? Are not you his own niece? Keep in mind your own value, my dearest. Keep in mind that you are my spouse, the woman whom I have preferred to all others for her real merit. Will you forgive me for rejoicing in my reformation? and let me add the woman whom I have preferred to the temptations of fortune? for so you know to be true. On my account, as well as your own, I will not suffer you to write to my father as if you were a milliner or a tenant's daughter whom his son had married in a foolish fit of love. Remember you are *my lady*. I have also thought it best to keep out the paragraph as to some of your relations having contributed to prejudice him against you. Let all these things be forgotten. My life for it, we shall hear no more of them now. I have taken the same liberty with the expression, "If you admit me into your family," because I wish if possible that he should invite us rather than that we should propose it. With the alterations I have made, I am of opinion your letter will be of service to prepare him for receiving you.

I do really believe that the reason of his asking you to come to him is to talk with you calmly, and judge how far it will be proper for him to have us to live in family with him. Do not suspect him of attempting to make you give up your marriage with me. Let us not, amidst many unhappy differences, forget his real worth. It was from him that I derived that strict regard to truth and to honour which I have ever preserved. He has already plainly given his consent to the match. He has said so to myself; and he knows that I went to Lainshaw the day after, and that I am positively engaged to you. No, no, my dearest life, you wrong him when you carry your apprehensions so far. All you have to fear is a kind of chilling and dispiriting method in which he may talk to you.

I should not imagine he will, like the Doctor,[4] be inquisitive as to when I made my proposals, and all the circumstances of our attachment. If it should so happen, you must tell him that, in the very time of my schemes for heiresses, I used often to make strong professions of love to you, to tell you that I would marry you rather than any other woman, were it not that I was resolved to have £10,000 with a wife. That, at the same time, I bid you not mind me; and that accordingly you considered all I said to be words of course. That when you was at Auchinleck last spring, I paid you more than ordinary attention. That before you was aware, this made some impression on you. That you concealed your sentiments, as you knew I was upon another scheme, and besides imagined that he would not approve of a match for me by which I got neither money nor any new connections that could be of use to me. That you wished much to avoid going to Ireland, but that I insisted on it, and got your sister and the Captain to join their influence. That on the journey to Ireland, I became unusually thoughtful and uneasy, told you that you was the woman on earth whom I really loved, that I had been in love with you in my earliest years and twenty times since, that you was my friend whom I valued, and that I was miserable to think that I was going to marry another, which was at the same time not honourable, considering my love for you. That you then began to think me serious, but still resolved to keep your mind to yourself, and, though you should be unhappy, let me do what was most for my interest. That at Donaghadee, I put myself in such a passion with you at your declining to go to Dublin, that you was so much affected as to let me know the impression I had made upon your mind, though you at the same time continued

4 Dr. Boswell.

your resolution to keep both our secrets. That in Dublin I saw everything fair for me; but confessed to you that although I was distracted between gay views of fortune and real attachment, the latter would prevent me at that time from making any advances to the Heiress.

That my passion continued in the same way till we returned to Lainshaw. But you did not allow yourself to reckon on me as yours, though we corresponded very frequently this summer. That you received a letter from me, telling you that my father was going to marry again, which hurt me so much that I was to leave Scotland for ever, and that I then owned to you that I durst not see you, because I had been indulging hopes of getting his consent to marry you, and that to see you in view of parting for ever would almost turn me mad. That you was shocked with this letter, wrote to me in the most earnest terms and used every argument to reconcile me to my father's scheme; but in vain. That your affection for me was such that you wished to let me know that you would go with me. That while you was in that situation, you received a letter from me, telling you that if I were not conscious I would share a crown with you if I had it, I would not make the proposal I was going to make; which was that if you chose to join the interest of your £1000 to my £100 a year, and would go with me to some agreeable retirement, I was ready to marry you directly. That you readily accepted my proposal, trusting to God's providence which extends over all the earth. That I was most grateful for this; I informed you that I had hopes of a mediation by means of Lord Monboddo. That this having accordingly taken place, and my father having kindly told me that he would give his consent to our marriage, I came to you at Lainshaw, and then we solemnly engaged ourselves *as we should answer to God.*

This, my dear Peggie, is, I think, a just and true abstract of our story. It does you great honour, and I appear a better man than people have imagined. Take courage, and tell this slowly to my father, and I am almost sure it will please him. Take care, at the same time, to let him know that as you have always been my confidante, and are therefore the best judge of me, you can assure him I never was before in the style in which you now know me to be. Do as I direct you, and there will be no room for dissimulation. Be rather silent and reserved, and let him take the lead. What a comfort would it be if you and I could make him happy, and prevent his doing a very improper thing which would lessen his character and estrange him from me. The Commissioner was with me this forenoon. He again repeated what I formerly wrote to you, and said he was persuaded that if you and I humour my father, and behave properly, he never will marry again. So let us be much in earnest. I give you full liberty to come under all engagements for me as to sobriety, application, and every part of my behaviour. Be not hurt by what my father may throw out either against you or me. Just let it blow over and by your gravity and cheerful composure of manners conciliate his affection. I cannot help indulging hopes that before two years are over he may be perfectly satisfied with us, and that we may be living together in the greatest harmony. Assure him of my sincere wishes for this. How comfortable, how respectable would it be for all of us!

Nothing more occurs to me as necessary to be remembered. Your own admirable sense can be at no loss. I am clear for your taking Mrs. Campbell with you, though she should stay but a single night. The meeting with my father must be awkward. All meetings between people who have anything of importance upon their minds are awkward. When I was last at Lainshaw, I was quite uneasy and in the strangest palpitation when you came into the room; and, do you know, for all the anxious wishes that I have for our meeting again, I think of the very moment in the same manner. There is no help for such sensibility. It carries its superior joys along with its pains. What would I give to have you just sitting by me at present!

You was right to own so far to Lady Crawford. I wonder how Lord Eglinton said that he had it from myself. It is true I have told him that I loved you better than any other woman. But I have never told him that we were to be married. Shall I write him a pleasant letter, as my old governor in the gay world, and tell him that I am at last happily fixed? I think you may allow me. I shall keep within proper bounds. For your entertainment, I enclose you the copy of a letter to M. van Sommelsdyck, our grand Dutch relation and my very good friend. You will see how I make you appear abroad.[5] M. Dupont could

[5] Boswell, in his letter (18 August), described Miss Montgomerie as follows: "She is not what is called a beauty, but she is well built, has a very agreeable countenance, and, without boasting of being a *bel esprit*, has a great deal of good

not find one fault in the French of it. I beg you may return it to me, with a translation. It will please me to see how well you understand it.

I wish you would allow me to let Aunt Boyd know what is fixed. I am to write to her and worthy Mr. Hugh this week. I have only one frank for her, which I shall send to you along with my letter. I wish to keep a good understanding with our Irish friends, and, if I have your permission, I will write from London to Dublin Mrs. Boyd, inform her politely of my situation, and return her the *paper*.[6]

Mr. David Hume was with me this morning, and gave a philosophical opinion that our marriage must be a happy one. Were it not for his infidel writings, everybody would love him. He is a plain, obliging, kind-hearted man. By the by, as a tax for the privilege of keeping Mr. Temple's letter, I must put you to the trouble of sending me a copy of that part of it where he desires me to put some questions to Mr. Hume on the study of history. You must know my friend Temple is a man of much reading, especially since he was married. He says to me in a late letter, "You will be surprised and vexed to find how much knowledge I have acquired."[7] This is a delicate reproof to me for my idleness and dissipation.

I wish Mrs. Montgomerie-Cuninghame would not interfere at all. My father is not to be *managed*. He must have his own way.[8] I hope we shall recommend ourselves to him.

I have now fixed Monday next for setting out on my London journey. You may depend on my writing to you very often. All letters to me must be sent under cover "To George Dempster, Esq., M.P., London," and they will come safe. I am quite satisfied with the way in which you account for your having been so much abroad when here. My kind compliments to all at Lainshaw. Adieu, my dearest.

J.B.

---

sense and the most engaging vivacity. . . . Besides having the most affectionate heart, my cousin has also the best principles of religion."

[6] An obscure item, variously described as a paper, letter, and picture, which had caused hard feelings between Boswell and the Dublin Boyds.

[7] Boswell somewhat alters a sentence in Temple's letter of 1 July.

[8] But on 17 July Boswell had written to Mrs. Montgomerie-Cuninghame asking her to interpose in the tangled affairs of the family.

FRIDAY 25 AUGUST. The day passed on with a variety of business. Dr. Boswell was a while with me. I told him he and I had frequent flows of high spirits: we had bottles of champagne in our heads which were every now and then poured out. It will do better in French: "Nous avons des bouteilles du vin de champagne à la tête qui se versent de temps à autre," or "de temps en temps." M. Dupont says of me, "Vous êtes né pour le francais." I must make my dear Margaret a good French scholar.

SATURDAY 26 AUGUST. I took a chaise and carried George Webster with me to dine at the Commissioner's. We were very comfortable. I relished much being again in life after a fortnight's confinement and starving. The Commissioner gave me some more good advice. George and I went and saw a singular curiosity, a playhouse in Musselburgh. Fisher's strolling company were there; the play was *The Provoked Husband*. We just saw the beginning of it. We supped at Sir George Preston's.

SUNDAY 27 AUGUST. I was at home, calm and comfortable, having fixed next day for setting out. Horatius Cannan and young Mr. Hair, his governor, and Dr. Cairnie drank tea with me. Captain James Webster was arrived. I went and sat a while with him, his sister, and George. He was in prodigious spirits. He pleased me highly. George was merry. He was impatient for his Sunday's supper, for his sheep-head broth. He cried, "Bring in the sheep-head, bring in Scipio Africanus."[9] Such ludicrous nonsense as this will entertain one surprisingly. Miss Webster said of my marriage, "It's in every drawing-room in town." "Ay," said George, "but it is not in a bedroom yet." A real *bon mot*, upon honour — by an Edinburgh cloth merchant. I supped at worthy Dr. Boswell's. Talking of Johnson, he said he was a Herculean genius, just born[1] to grapple with whole libraries. The Hon. James Cochrane was there. My marriage was talked of, and I was quite easy and cheerful.[2]

[9] Give it the Italian pronunciation. "Scott used to *take off* [William Coulter, Lord Provost of Edinburgh in 1810] as saying at some public meeting, 'Gentlemen, though doomed to the trade of a stocking weaver, I was born with the soul of a *Sheepio!*' " (Lockhart, *Life of Scott*, Ch. xix).

[1] The manuscript has the alternative, "made."

[2] The Journal, which has been on loose sheets, now shifts to a quarto notebook which Boswell provided with an elaborate title-page that promises more than it

MONDAY 28 AUGUST. As I had full time to prepare for setting out on this jaunt, I thought for once to have everything quite ready a day before. But I find leaving a place where one has been for some time is like dying and so leaving the world, in this respect: that something is always forgotten. Last night I recollected owing a number of letters. So in order to get them dispatched, I was obliged to sit up till five this morning. I was called before seven, so was a little feverish and uneasy. However, my constitution is now so much changed for the better that this did not disconcert me, and I rose in good spirits. My worthy friend Grange came to me, and we had some kind, cordial conversation. Mr. Surgeon Macdonald and he breakfasted with me, and then came Mr. Farquhar Kinloch, merchant in London, my companion for the journey, with his brother and Mr. John Chalmer, his brother-in-law, who saw us to our chaise.

It was a fine day. My companion was a man between forty and fifty, dressed in black, with buckskin breeches and boots and a queue-wig. He had been many years a merchant in London, and was acquainted with various branches of trade. I made our conversation turn upon it, and learned a good deal from him as to some mercantile causes in which I am concerned. I have heard my father say that the old Earl of Aberdeen was continually asking questions at everybody he met, by which means he was always picking up knowledge of one kind or other. This is sometimes a good rule. But if too often applied I should think it would be ridiculous. A great deal of the knowledge to be casually picked up from those we meet is hardly worth having. I would dig for a golden treasure or look for diamonds with as much attention as any man. But I would not toil to get at a lump of copper, nor hang my head anxiously and search every seam in my chamber-floor in order to find pins. As I was determined to make this a jaunt of perfect economy, just to take care of my health and have my blood thoroughly purified, I took nothing with me but a suit of black clothes in my portmanteau, and an old suit of the same colour which I wore. I was entertained and pleased to find Mr. Kinloch fond of ancient families. Though he was but the son of James Farquhar, *merchant* (as

---

performs: "Journal of my jaunt to London, the Jubilee at Stratford upon Avon in memory and honour of Shakespeare, and to visit my old and most intimate friend, the Reverend Mr. Temple in Devonshire, &c., &c., &c. Autumn 1769."

we say in Scotland, but truly just *hardwareman*) at the sign of the
Red Lion, he seemed to love noble blood as if he had been a true *lion's
whelp*, as the poets talk. I gave him a history of our family. I was quite
in my element.

We eat an egg at Norton, and drank a dish of tea at Cornhill, and
got at night to Wooler Haugh Head. Mr. Kinloch proved a knowing
man in his profession, spoke very slow but very distinctly, and was
extremely obliging and really careful of me, as he knew I had not
been well.

TUESDAY 29 AUGUST. We set out by five o'clock, three hours
sooner than we did yesterday. When I made the comparison between
leaving home and finally leaving the world, I might have observed
that when one forgets anything in the first case it may be remedied
by writing back. But in the last, that cannot be done. Nothing but a
permission to revisit the world can do. That such permissions have
been granted I firmly believe.

We breakfasted at Morpeth. I went here and paid a visit to Mrs.
Collingwood, a widow, lady of a gentleman in the neighbourhood
and aunt to Mrs. Temple. She has a fine family of daughters. I
was made acquainted with this family by my last companion from
London, Captain Dickson, whose brother is married to one of her
daughters. I was in fine spirits, and charmed to hear English so
prettily spoken. My dearest love was ever present to my mind, and
every happy moment I felt, I wished she was with me to partake of it.

We got to Newcastle to dinner. Here my companion met two
London acquaintances: Mr. Phipps, a young lawyer, a clever con-
veyancer, and a kind of buck in vacation time, as I thought; and Mr.
Sitwell, an old bachelor, a comely old gentleman with a grey coat,
large white wig, fair complexion, and linen remarkably well got up.
He was formerly an ironmonger, but was now worth £200,000, partly
in money, partly in landed estates. We dined all together and were
very hearty. It was curious to observe in old Sitwell the true littleness
of a London cit.[3] There was a bottle of port on the table untouched,
when my companion and I were going away to visit some people.
"Come," said he, "gentlemen, you shall pay no part of this bottle";
and violently did he battle it. A *just* idea, no doubt. But a very *mean*

[3] Johnson defines cit as "a pert, low townsman."

one. I introduced Mr. Kinloch at Dr. Wilson's, where we drank tea, and then the Doctor and I went and sat a while with Mr. Aitken, the dissenting clergyman. I wrote from this to my love, and thought a lively letter might do her spirits good and dissipate too much thoughtfulness in my absence.

We took tickets in the fly here as far as Grantham, when we could judge whether to travel in that manner any farther. But, in order to get a sound sleep, we took a post-chaise and went on at night to Durham. Having seen in the papers that Sir John Pringle was arrived from Paris, I wrote to him tonight, informed him of my whole situation, and prepared him for receiving me in London, so as that I should not have the awkward task of telling him all about myself. I was not at all fatigued, and my spirits were admirable.

WEDNESDAY 30 AUGUST. There came up to us this morning about seven in the fly, Mr. Dodds, a little, fat woollen-draper in Newcastle, a cheerful old gentlewoman, and her daughter Mrs. Topham, wife to one of Sir Francis Delaval's tenants. We all breakfasted together, and then set out. We were exceedingly chatty, and well entertained with that kind of broken conversation that leaves no trace behind it. I told them I was to be married so soon as I returned from London. Being free with absolute strangers is really and truly no freedom. For when you say, "I am to do so and so," to people who know nothing about you, it is the same thing as if you said A or B are to do it, and you are amused with their remarks and sometimes even helped by their advice. I said my great study at present was to get a proper posy or motto for my spouse's wedding-ring: "With this ring I thee wed." Mrs. Topham had none on hers. But her mother had a very good one: "Love and live happily." I took a memorandum of it in my pocket-book, and said I questioned if I should find a better.[4]

The good gentlewoman treated us with some excellent cake, and when we came to Darlington we made her and her daughter take a glass of white wine from us. How pleasant is it to live well with our fellow creatures, and interchange civilities. Here our ladies left us. But a younger and genteeler one than either came in, Lord Darling-

---

[4] Margaret Montgomerie's wedding ring is now owned by Mrs. Joyce T. McCombe, who has kindly described it for us as 'gold, plain, very thin, and for a very slight finger.' It bears no inscription.

ton's gardener's daughter, the wife of a shopkeeper here. She was smart and could talk incessantly. Mr. Kinloch and she kept up a close conversation on all sorts of provisions. We took up here, too, Mr. Howell, a farmer of this country, very little removed from a brute. He was not ill natured. But he was monstrously big, had the coarsest dress and manners, and spoke a language that could hardly be understood. We dined at Northallerton, where our lady parted from us, and we got to Wetherby at night.

THURSDAY 31 AUGUST. We set out at four. I slept very soundly in the fly. Mr. Dodds told us he was from Scotland, and had a pretty estate of £40 a year at Melrose, to which he intended to retire. He had travelled to London and back again very often, and was prodigiously knowing as to everything upon the road.

We breakfasted at Ferrybridge. The joy of an English breakfast in a clean, handsome inn, after having travelled a couple of stages, is great. We took up here another good old woman, a Yorkshire farmer's wife. I was in a droll humour, and, seeing rich clover fields, I started a scheme of feeding the human race upon them. I was for bringing up a young child with a calf, giving it a little milk for so long, keeping it in a cowhouse at night, and, in the daytime, making the calf and it feed in a clover field. There is no describing the rage of the worthy farmer's wife at this doctrine. "You are little better than an atheist!" said she. "I don't believe you fears either God or man." I persisted with great composure and gravity to enforce my system, and I thought my other companions would have died of laughing. Mr. Dodds was quite overcome. It is, however, really a bad thing to joke in that manner. How are people to be sure that a man is in earnest, when they have seen him, with the earnest and serious appearance of truth, maintaining what is farthest from his mind?

We dined very well at Barnby Moor, and instead of waiting near an hour, as we did yesterday at Northallerton, we had dinner immediately. The farmer's wife left us at Tuxford, not a little regretted by Mr. Howell, to whom she very cordially communicated a brandy bottle which she had in her pocket.

We got into Grantham before eight. I went and called on my acquaintance, the Reverend Mr. Palmer, chaplain to Sir John Cust, the Speaker of the House of Commons, a sensible, knowing man who improves much on acquaintance. He insisted I should sup with him, and he entertained me in a plain, friendly manner. His lady was indisposed; but he introduced to me his children, a daughter and two sons, saying before his eldest son that he was glad he would have it to say that he had taken by the hand the friend of the great Paoli. It is amazing how much and how universally I have made myself admired. This is an absolute fact. I am certain of it, and with an honest pride I will rejoice in it. Mr. Heron, another clergyman here, supped with us. We talked of Johnson, and particularly of his wonderful knowledge of the world, which I observed was most extraordinary, as he had lived so much in the retirement of Oxford and the Temple. Mr. Palmer remarked very justly that to know the world really well one must not be too much in it. One will see better what is going on, and be able to trace the springs of action better by standing sometimes at a side. I pursued the thought. "One," said I, "should not be too early in the world, otherwise he will never know it fully; that is to say, in a philosophical sense. If he goes into it early, he becomes so insensibly accustomed to everything that he never inquires into its causes. Let him first study human nature in speculation, and form to himself a habit of examining it as exerted in active life, and then every scene he sees will be an experiment, and he will in time acquire much knowledge of the world. Though perhaps being late of entering upon it may make one's manners somewhat awkward. But that is but of inferior consequence." I went to my inn and had a few hours' sleep.

FRIDAY 1 SEPTEMBER. We set out at three o'clock, breakfasted at Stilton, dined at Biggleswade, and got to London between eight and nine. The sights of London again put me in high spirits. I cannot well account how it has had so strong an effect upon me since I can remember anything. Both before I saw it and since, my ideas of it have been very high. Messrs. Howell and Dodds were set down in Gray's Inn Lane. Mr. Kinloch and I took a hackney-coach in Holborn and drove to Mr. Dilly's. There was nobody in the house at this time but the two brothers, who received me with a most lively joy. I introduced Mr. Kinloch to them, and he stayed and supped with us. I was quite at home. I liked to see the effects of being an author. Upon the strength of that, here were two booksellers who thought they could not do enough for me.

At eleven I walked down to my revered friend Mr. Samuel Johnson's to see if he was in town. But Miss Williams, the blind old lady who lives with him, told me he was down at Brighton. I sat some little time with her, and was rejoiced just to sit in Mr. Johnson's parlour, and see his inkhorn standing on the table. Miss Williams advised me to go to the Jubilee in honour of Shakespeare, at Stratford upon Avon.[5] Indeed, when I left Scotland I was resolved not to go. But as I approached the capital I felt my inclination increase, and when arrived in London I found myself within the whirlpool of curiosity, which could not fail to carry me down.

Mr. Dilly insisted that I should live at his house, where I should be quite at home. I accepted of his kind invitation; and was pleased to be lodged in the house of my bookseller in the Poultry, in one of the most frequented streets of the city of London, where coaches pass at all hours. I was calm and well.

SATURDAY 2 SEPTEMBER. I went immediately and waited on Sir John Pringle. My principal intention in coming to London now was to put myself under the care of the famous Dr. Kennedy, to purify my blood from every remain of vicious poison. Sir John received me with his usual reserved kindness. He was not for my applying to Kennedy, but just taking Mr. Forbes, a regular surgeon, as the phrase is. However, he allowed me to please myself. It is amazing to see a man of Sir John's character so impregnated with partiality as to refuse its just credit to a medicine which has undoubtedly done wonders.

[5] An elaborate publicity stunt of Garrick's, flamboyantly designed and poorly executed. The first day, Wednesday 6 September, began with an oratorio in the church. Then the company marched in procession to the amphitheatre erected for the occasion, where it dined and various songs, such as *Sweet Willy O,* composed for the Jubilee were sung. A ball was held in the evening. The next morning Garrick recited his *Dedication Ode* with a musical accompaniment. During this performance benches gave way in various parts of the amphitheatre, injuring several people. At night there were fireworks, and the masquerade ball took place. On the third and final day, despite the continued unfavorable weather, a horse race (with the horses knee deep in water) for the jubilee cup was held, but a grand procession in Shakespearian costume had to be cancelled. Those who had not escaped from Stratford by that evening attended a ball which closed the Jubilee. Between the weather and inadequate arrangements it was hardly a full success, and the general vulgarization of Shakespeare which characterized it was widely satirized in the next few months.

I tried him formerly as to Keyser's pills,[6] and found him equally prejudiced. As Sir John has witnessed many of my weaknesses and follies, and been always like a parent to me, I cannot help standing much in awe of him. He would insist that I was not yet in earnest to marry. I told him that I could not show him the inside of my mind as one does a watch, but that I was certainly conscious that my wheels now went calmly and constantly. He said, "Vous avez encore un peu de vertige." I was slightly angry and a good deal diverted, as I was sure of my being quite a different man from what he had formerly known me.

I breakfasted at the Smyrna Coffee-house, now removed to St. James's Street. When it was in Pall Mall, it was one of my first resorts in London, in the days when Derrick, the late Master of the Ceremonies at Bath, was a kind of governor to me.[7] I thought its being removed a striking instance of the instability of human affairs. Such consequence do objects acquire which have entered our minds early. They are like people who come to the play when the doors open, and take up more room in the pit than others who come in late and are obliged to squeeze themselves into any little space they can find. I went to Greek Street, Soho, and called on my friend Dempster. We were rejoiced to meet. He had a letter for me from my dearest Margaret, as all my letters come under his cover. It was a kind, sensible, admirable one. I showed him her noble and generous letter.[8] He said it was the finest he had ever seen. "And," said he, "she gets an honest and honourable man." He and I agreed to dine together and parted.

I went to Lincoln's Inn Fields and called on Dr. Kennedy. I had a letter for him from my uncle the Doctor, but would not deliver it till I saw how I liked him. He was a very old gentleman, large and formal and tedious, but seemingly worthy.[9] After talking over my case with him, I told him who I was and gave him my uncle's letter. He allowed

[6] An extensively advertised nostrum presented to the public with certificates of "ambassadors, ministers of state, and other noblemen of the first rank" as an efficacious and mild cure for a "certain disorder, without the least trouble or confinement." It also cured "scorbutic eruptions, leprosies, white swellings, stiff joints, gout, and rheumatic disorders" (*Public Advertiser*, 4 February 1768).

[7] Derrick, who had died in March 1769, introduced Boswell to the sensual pleasures of London in 1760.

[8] Her letter accepting his proposal (see p. 240).

[9] He was supposed to be nearly ninety and was probably seventy-seven. For a

me to go to Shakespeare's Jubilee before I began my course of his medicine. I then went to a Mr. Dalemaine, an embroiderer in Bow Street, Covent Garden; gave him, cut out in paper as well as I could, the form of a Corsican cap, and ordered *Viva la Libertà* to be embroidered on the front of it in letters of gold.

Dempster and I dined at the Crown and Anchor Tavern in the Strand. He had just come from Orme who wrote the history of Hindustan. Dempster found him reading Euripides in Greek. He said, "I know not how it is. But my mind does not relish anything very easy. I must have something hard to chew, like one who has got the toothache." His house was pretty. He said, "I have been several years gradually making this an agreeable habitation for myself, like an insect making its nest." Over one door a drawing of a boy painting. Over the opposite door, a boy playing on a flute. "There," said he, "is my notion of poetry: beautiful images and fine sounds." There is a famous *bon mot* of his on Lord Clive. When somebody said his Lordship neglected his old friends, Orme answered, "Lord Clive is a man who rides post through life and changes his horses at every stage." This may be applied to most ambitious rising men.

Dempster said he was happy I had escaped being made the matrimonial prey of a certain junto.[1] "That is true," said I. "It would have been putting an ortolan on the same spit with a parcel of dunghill fowls, while one turnspit dog served to roast them all." "Yes," said he, "it would have been putting a goldfish into the same basket with skate." We both talked how much *bons mots* were relished by everybody. Plutarch has collected a number of ancient ones, and Ménage, of modern ones. Dempster said a man who publishes such a collection will be more a favourite of the public than one who publishes some able work of his own. When Dempster lived at Kensington, he one day asked his sister if *currants* and *raisins* could be bought there. "O yes," said she, "as *currently* and *reasonably* as in London."[2]

We went and took a survey of Blackfriars Bridge, and were agree-

---

quack he had good credentials, being M.D. of Rheims and Oxford, and Fellow of the Royal Society.

[1] Probably a reference to the proposed match with Mary Ann Boyd, but possibly a reference to Miss Blair and her connections. See p. 126.

[2] Walker's *Pronouncing Dictionary* (1791) defends the pronunciation "reezon" for "raisin."

ably struck with its grandeur and beauty. We walked upon it first, and then took a boat and sailed a little up and down the Thames to see it perfectly. We then drank tea at the Somerset Coffee-house. I asked Dempster if I should go to the Stratford Jubilee. He said that belonged to the chapter of whims, as to which no advice should ever be given. He made me happy by saying that my dearest Margaret might be quite sure of me, for that the idea of my drawing back from my solemn engagement was just the same as the idea that Blackfriars Bridge should walk from its foundation.

We argued on newspaper fame. He was against it, because he thought that he who is pleased with that kind of praise will be hurt by censure of the same kind. I maintained that it was not so. For I said that I did not allow anything written against me to make an impression, while I enjoyed fully anything written for me. I did like one eating cherries. While I get good sweet ones, I hold them in my mouth and have all their relish. When a bad one comes in my way, I spit it out without chewing. I declare I have attained to this happy art. This was really a very agreeable day. I came home quietly, supped genteelly, and was comfortable.

SUNDAY 3 SEPTEMBER. I employed a Scots barber called Gall. I called him the *perfidious Gaul*, a term very proper to denote him when he does not come at the time he promises. I went to St. Paul's, but was too late. I then went to the Temple Church. The idea of the Knights Templars lying in the church was solemn and pleasing. The noble music raised my soul to heaven, though it was not Stanley's day, who officiates as organist every other Sunday. A Dr. Morell preached on these words: "For neither circumcision availeth anything nor uncircumcision, but faith which worketh by love."[3] He argued against a formal shadow of religion, and against Methodists with simple faith, and just recommended plain, rational, calm piety. I was much pleased with him. It was very agreeable to find myself in so good a frame. I thought much on my dearest Peggie. She and I were very happy together in Dublin at different places of worship; I wished to have had her here with me. After this I shall not mention my dearest in my Journal, unless when something extraordinary occurs. To say that I love her and wish to have her with me is like saying my pulse beats and my blood circulates. It is to be always understood.

[3] Author of the libretti for several of Handel's oratorios. His text is Galatians 5. 6.

I dined at Sir John Pringle's. There was nobody with him but Sir John Mitchell from Shetland, a quiet, genteel man to appearance. He had been in the army. Sir John kept his authority *ut semper.* He talked of Shakespeare as a barbarous writer, and run out in praise of the French tragedies. He said if he was a *savant* about town, he would read Corneille with Voltaire's notes and observations, and was sure he would make a figure, as dramatic excellence was there reduced to a system which a man may learn. He spoke of the inconveniency of the old town of Edinburgh. I told him I would never leave it, for I preferred our good old house in the Parliament Close to all the elegance of the new buildings.[4] I made him almost angry by maintaining this. At last I finished the dispute with a droll application of a passage in Cicero, where he says that Ulysses preferred his old wife to immortality. "Ay, ay," said I, "I love my old house. *Vetulam suam praetulit immortalitati.*"[5]

We went and walked round St. James' Park, taking the Green Park in our circuit. It was fine to see such crowds of well-dressed people, without being known to one of them. Sir John Pringle observed that the manners of Edinburgh are very bad. That the people there have a familiarity, an inquisitiveness, a way of looking through one, that is extremely disagreeable. He is very right. But how can a man do who is to live amongst them? He must be exceedingly reserved, for, if he allows his vivacity to play, the sarcastical rogues will attack him; and should he, with the politeness well known abroad, show his displeasure, they would raise a hoarse laugh and never mind him. So that nothing less than a downright quarrel can make them understand that they have hurt him. I drank coffee at the Smyrna, and then came home to supper.

MONDAY 4 SEPTEMBER. I breakfasted with Mr. Dempster. He had company with him, so nothing material passed. In one of the streets of Soho I met Mr. Sheridan, whom I had not seen for many

---

[4] Boswell is referring to the northern extension of Edinburgh known as the New Town, which was begun in 1767.

[5] Boswell's Latin is really from Bacon's *Advancement of Learning* (I. viii. 7) or the essay, "Of Marriage and Single Life." Cicero (*De oratore,* i. 196; *De legibus,* ii. 3) says Ulysses preferred *Ithaca* to immortality, and his language is quite different. Boswell had probably read an edition of Bacon's *Essays* in which the editor had pointed to the parallel in Cicero.

years.[6] I lie under many obligations to him, as he took a great concern about me when I was a very idle, impetuous young fellow, and had me often in his house in the kindest manner. So I was happy to meet with him, and promised to come and dine with him without ceremony, when I was not engaged. I then called on Mr. Thomas Davies, bookseller, whom I must always remember as the man who made me acquainted with Mr. Samuel Johnson. He is a very good kind of man himself, and has been long my acquaintance. He told me that Mr. Berenger, the Master of Horse, who it seems is mighty delicate and polite, said that Mr. Johnson was, in a genteel company, like an ox in a china-shop. He overturns everything. I dined at home, and after dinner Mr. Dilly and I walked about searching all over the town for my necessary accoutrements as a Corsican for the Stratford Jubilee. Some I had made on purpose. Others I borrowed.[7] But at last I got everything in order, and everything that I wanted went into such small bounds that I could carry the whole in my travelling-bag, except my musket and staff. I met by chance with a most curious staff in a shop in Cheapside: a very handsome vine with the root uppermost, and upon it a bird, very well carved. I paid six shillings for it. After I had bought it, I told the master of the shop, "Why, Sir, this vine is worth any money. It is a Jubilee staff. That bird is the bird of Avon." I supped quietly at home.[8]

TUESDAY 5 SEPTEMBER. I set out at seven in the Oxford fly, having for my companions a tradesman of Oxford, brother to Fletcher the bookseller in St. Paul's Churchyard, a cook-maid going home to Lord Harcourt, and the nurse of some nobleman's child, carrying it in her lap. We were all quiet, obliging, good-humoured people. We breakfasted at Slough. At Maidenhead the nurse left us. We jogged along. But I cannot say anything either instructive or entertaining passed. We dined at Henley, where we were joined as messmate by a brisk lawyer's clerk. We got to Oxford about six. I put up at the Angel Inn.

[6] Probably not since the spring of 1763.

[7] He had brought a native costume back with him, as he says in *Corsica*, but had left it in Edinburgh.

[8] The Memorandum for this date adds: "M. the guardian angel — to heaven in her arms."

The grandeur and solemnity of Oxford as a literary retreat always fills me with agreeable reverence. But it makes my heart sore too, for it recalls the memory of Sir James Macdonald. I may add, too, the memory of Frank Stewart.[9] Last time I was at Oxford he supped with me, along with Mr. Samuel Johnson and Mr. Chambers, the Vinerian Professor, in the very room where I now sat. My intention was to go on a stage or two this night towards Stratford, to be ready to get up to the Jubilee next morning. But finding myself in remarkably good spirits, I sat down and wrote letters to my dearest love, to Mr. Samuel Johnson at Brighton, and to my cousin, Mr. Bosville of Yorkshire. I drank some coffee, and then sent for Mr. Mickle, corrector of the Clarendon Press, author of *The Concubine, a Poem in the Manner of Spenser*, beautifully describing the fatal effects of licentious passion, as also author of *Chateaubriant, a Tragedy*, which he sent to me to read, and which I had recommended to Mr. Garrick.[1] I found myself appearing to great advantage before this poet, who, though of a superior genius in my opinion as a bard, was awkward in conversation. It however pleased me to find him a sincere believer in religion.

I had a fine thought in a letter to Miss Montgomerie tonight. "Let us not," said I, "have much concern about settlements. In contracting and binding two lovers, the elegant passion is often destroyed; just as we have seen a bunch of flowers, of roses, jessamine, and honeysuckle, lose their flavour in being tied together." The thought is pretty, and is better expressed in my letter, if I could recollect it. It is amazing how much of sentiment consists in expression. Nothing but hard science remains the same when put in different words.

Mr. Mickle supped with me, and a little before twelve I set out in a post-chaise alone for Stratford, not having been able to find an idle scholar in all the university to accompany me. They were all gone already. It was very dark, and I was afraid both of being robbed and being overturned, so could not sleep.[2]

[9] Frank Stewart had died at Rheims in October 1768.

[1] Garrick rejected it, to Mickle's rage, and it was never produced. It was printed in 1794, after Mickle's death, under the title, *The Siege of Marseilles*.

[2] Half a leaf of the manuscript has been cut away. When the narrative is resumed Boswell has digressed to give an account of a visit to "an old dallying companion," Miss Reynolds, who during one of his earlier sojourns in the metropolis had impressed him by her generosity.

. . . for, after having given her genteelly for some amorous interviews, I pretended that I had spent all my money. "My dear," said I,
"such is my situation. I gave you when I had money. Now, when I
have none, will you favour me with your company? I can hardly ask
such a ⟨thing, much as⟩ I ⟨wish⟩ to try." She . . . [3]

. . . tints of delight, I allowed myself no other liberty than once
drawing my hand gently along her yellow locks. I had my valuable
spouse ever present before me, and not only my reason but my heart
and every feeling were even at that moment sensible of her superiority. I was wholly hers. I told Miss Reynolds with a most engaging
address, "You are not made for this way of life. You have not the
qualifications for it, except, indeed, being very pretty and very agreeable. You have not the avarice, the falseness, which is requisite. I
wish to have you out of it." She promised to me that she would go into
the millinery business and behave properly. It was curious to see her
drink. "Sir, I vish" ("wish," according to the true London pronunciation) "I vish you all happiness in your new state of life." She asked
me to come and see her again. But I was determined to let this be my
last visit.

And now let me return to my journey to Stratford. Before I got
to Woodstock I had, from an over-caution, put my watch in one pocket
of the chaise, my purse in another, and my pocket-book in another. I
thought I had taken them all out again. But when I was three miles
beyond Chapel House, the next stage, I missed my pocket-book, in
which I had several papers, particularly *the most valuable letter of
my valuable friend.* I was in great uneasiness. First I thought of sending back an express for it. But my anxiety made me take fresh chaise
and horses and return myself. I thought most fervently of my dearest
all the way, which kept up my spirits. I imagined I should be obliged
to go all the way to Oxford, as the chaise from that place, in which
was my pocket-book, must be gone back. I was beginning to fret. But
at once I turned my mind to philosophical resolution. I know from
experience how much power we have over our minds.

[3] Two and a half pages of the manuscript have been removed.

[Boswell to Margaret Montgomerie]

Oxford, 5 September 1769

MY DEAREST LIFE, — My last was not half an answer to yours. You quite overpower me with goodness. What return can I make for the beautiful sentiments of sincere regard which your last contains? Indeed, my dear friend, my only uneasiness now proceeds from melancholy fears, at times, that this happiness is too great to last long in human life, and an anxiety lest you should *really* imagine that I am not sufficiently sensible of what I owe to you. There is the most refined delicacy in your manner of expressing a doubt that my affection is not so strong as yours, because I can go at such a distance from you with so much ease. This would strike most people. But be assured, my dear Peggie, it is not a just conclusion. Consider that it was absolutely necessary for me to go to London, and a journey which appears long to you cannot affect in the same manner one who has travelled so much as I have done. And, since I am upon this subject, believe me, my going to Shakespeare's Jubilee, and wishing to see many friends and enjoy many amusements, ought not to be interpreted as marks of indifference. I am forwarding the recovery of my health; I am acquiring an additional stock of ideas with which to entertain you. I am dissipating melancholy clouds, and filling my mind with fine, cheerful spirits.

You are, however, my constant object. What we read in the old romances is realized in me. Upon honour, my dearest life, I just adore you. I doubt if the style in which you found me when last at Lainshaw be altogether natural to me. I hope it shall be so from custom. I am at present the most sober, amiable, polite man that you can imagine. I am quite pleased with myself, and see the justness of your being raised in your own opinion, by thinking that you are the person whom such a man prefers to all the world besides. I give you my word, your attachment has that effect upon me. Let us be mutually happy in thinking how much each contributes to make the other so. You have no occasion to fear Yorkshire.[4] I am positive — absolutely certain —

[4] Not clear. Elizabeth Diana Bosville had married Sir Alexander Macdonald more than a year before this. Godfrey Bosville had another daughter, Julia (later Lady Dudley and Ward), but she was only fifteen at the time, and is nowhere mentioned in the Journal as a matrimonial possibility.

that my constancy to you is invariable. I now believe the doctrine I have often heard, that we can be in love but once; for I never before felt what I feel now. I took the liberty to show my friend Dempster your noble, generous letter *accepting of my terms*. He said it was the finest letter he had ever read, and with the greatest warmth he rejoices at our being to be united. He gives me franks for you, and he says very pleasantly that, next to seeing my face, you will be happy to see his hand.

I left London this morning and came in the post-coach to this venerable seat of learning, on my road to Stratford. The Jubilee begins tomorrow. I have forty miles yet to go. So I take a post-chaise at every stage, and well wrapped up in a greatcoat I travel all night asleep; and shall be at Shakespeare's birth-place tomorrow morning early, and put myself under the tuition of Mr. Garrick, who is steward of the Jubilee. I believe you and I differ as to shows and grand occasions. This Jubilee, which makes all my veins glow, will make little impression on you. I shall not therefore insist much upon that topic, but leave you to the newspapers for information. I have engaged to Dempster not to describe myself there, and yet I could hold any sum that other people will; for I assure you my Corsican dress will make a fine, striking appearance.[5] My gun slung across my shoulder, my pistol at one side and stiletto at another, with my bonnet or kind of short grenadier cap, black, with *Viva la Libertà* (that is, "Long live liberty," or, as the English say, "Liberty for ever") embroidered upon its front in letters of gold, will attract much notice. I have that kind of weakness that, when I looked at myself in the glass last night in my Corsican dress, I could not help thinking your opinion of yourself might be still more raised: "She has secured the constant affection and admiration of so fine a fellow." Do you know, I cannot think there is any harm in such a kind of weakness or vanity, when a man is sensible of it and it has no great effect upon him. It enlivens me and increases my good humour.

Donaldson, who was formerly at Edinburgh, is now an esteemed miniature painter in London. I was fairly set down to him since I came up. But difficulties occurred which your ladyship must be pleased to settle. Do you choose the size to be for a bracelet or for

[5] He broke his promise — or got Dempster to release him from it.

hanging at your watch? What clothes do you choose? Shall my hair be powdered or not?

I beg to know if I should not get Lady Margaret Macdonald to choose a marriage gown for you. Might you not have a silver stuff? You know it must be white. Or do you really prefer a plain white? Write me as to this. You know you and I are not to be tied down to the ordinary rules and ceremonies.

I am delighted with the pious strain of your letters. I hope we shall be truly happy together in devotion. I bless the memory of my valuable mother, who gave me impressions of religion which I shall ever retain, and which I flatter myself shall henceforth have a constant influence on my conduct. Between ourselves, the Church of England worship is infinitely superior to our Presbyterian method. I at present have my mind raised to heaven by the grand churches, noble organs, and solemn service of the churches around me. Our Jubilee tomorrow begins with an oratorio in the church, which will give me great satisfaction. I am just now expecting a very ingenious gentleman, here, the author of a tragedy which I have recommended to Mr. Garrick. I never saw the gentleman, but he corresponds with me. I must entertain him for an hour, and then set out. So, my dear, dear Peggie, farewell for this night, and may God bless and preserve you to your ever grateful, affectionate, and *constant*

JAMES BOSWELL.

My compliments to all at Lainshaw. What says the Captain to us? I cannot omit giving you a simile which occurred to me when travelling in the coach this afternoon. Love such as ours is of a most delicate nature. In treating and settling and binding, it might be destroyed, just as you have observed a fine bunch of flowers — roses, jessamine, and honeysuckle — lose their flavour by being handled too much in tying them together.

WEDNESDAY 6 SEPTEMBER. When I arrived at Woodstock, the landlord had my pocket-book for me. I was comforted and happy. I took breakfast, it being near six in the morning. But I was now in a new difficulty. Such crowds had passed that there was no post-chaise to be had. Here then was I, on the very morning of the Jubilee, in danger of not getting to it in time. I became very impatient, so hired a couple of horses and off I set, the postilion carrying part of my baggage and myself the rest. I had no boots, and only a short greatcoat which I had borrowed of a postilion, and it rained pretty thick. I was really distressed, and the fear that my health would suffer made me worse. However, at the end of six miles, I found a post-chaise into which I got directly, and partly by threatenings, partly by promises, prevailed on the post-boys to drive fast, and arrived at Stratford between twelve and one. The first view of the Avon and of the town where Shakespeare was born gave me those feelings which men of enthusiasm have on seeing remarkable places. Cicero had them when he walked at Athens.[6]

I went to Mr. Payton's at the Red Lion, the great inn here.[7] There was no room, but one of the maids pointed me out an old woman called Mrs. Harris, who had a house just by, directly opposite to Shakespeare's house; and she let me have a tolerable old-fashioned room with a neat, clean bed at a guinea a night, the stated Jubilee price for beds.

Having fixed this point, I went immediately to the great church.[8] It was surrounded by a crowd of people; and, as objects anyhow similar call up similar circumstances, I could not help thinking of the Monday's meeting after giving the sacrament in a country church in Scotland. I was exceedingly dirty; my hair hung wet about my ears; my black suit and the postilion's grey duffle above it, several inches too short every way, made a very strange appearance. I could observe people getting together and whispering about me, for the church was full of well-dressed people. At last Mr. Garrick observed me. We first made an attitude to each other and then cordially shook hands. I gave him a line I had written to let him know I was incognito, as I wished to appear in the Corsican dress for the first time they should know me. Many of those who had stared, seeing that I was intimate with the steward of the Jubilee, came up to him and asked who I was. He answered, "A clergyman in disguise." To see a noble band of the first musicians from London with Dr. Arne at their head, Mr. Garrick, a

[6] Probably Boswell refers to *De finibus*, v. 1.

[7] Rather the White Lion. Payton became notorious for his exorbitant charges during the Jubilee. It cost those resident in the inn a shilling to use the outhouse, and those who were not resident eighteen pence.

[8] Dr. Arne's oratorio, *Judith*, was being given there.

David Garrick (1717–1779) as Steward of the Stratford Jubilee, September 1769, from a mezzotint in the Theatre Collection of the Harvard College Library, by Joseph Saunders after Benjamin Van der Gucht

number of nobility and gentry and of the learned and ingenious assembled to do honour to Shakespeare in his native place, gave me
much satisfaction.

As for a description of the Jubilee, I must refer to a letter which
I have written upon the subject in *The Public Advertiser* of Saturday,
September 16th.[9] I here mention what was particular to myself. I met
several acquaintances before I was aware: two Mr. Swintons from
Scotland, Mr. Love, Mr. Lee, Mr. Victor, Mr. Richardson, printer. At
dinner in the amphitheatre, I found my old brother soaper,[1] Dr. Ber-
keley, who introduced me into a party where he was. It consisted of
several ladies and gentlemen. A Mrs. Sheldon, an Irish lady, wife of
Captain Sheldon, a most agreeable little woman, pleased me most. I
got into great spirits. I paid her particular attention. I began to imagine that she was stealing me from my valuable spouse. I was most
unhappy from this imagination. I rose and went near the orchestra,
and looked steadfastly at that beautiful, insinuating creature, Mrs.
Baddeley of Drury Lane,[2] and in an instant Mrs. Sheldon was effaced.
I then saw that what I feared was love was in reality nothing more
than transient liking. It had no interference with my noble attachment. It was such a momentary diversion from it as the sound of a
flageolet in my ear, a gay colour glancing from a prism before my
eye, or any other pleasing sensation. However, the fear I had put myself in made me melancholy. I had been like a timorous man in a post-
chaise, who, when a wagon is passing near it, imagines that it is to
crush it; and I did not soon recover the shock. My having had no
sleep all night, travelled in the rain, and suffered anxiety on account
of my pocket-book, no doubt contributed to my uneasiness. I recollected my former inconstancy, my vicious profligacy, my feverish

[9] It is more accessible in *The London Magazine* for September 1769, which
reprinted it together with "an account of the armed Corsican chief at the
masquerade at Shakespeare's Jubilee."

[1] That is, a member of the Soaping Club, a jovial Edinburgh society founded by
Boswell on his return from London in 1760.

[2] Actress and singer, she was the rage of fashionable London. Her acting of
Fanny in Garrick and Colman's *Clandestine Marriage* so delighted George III
and Queen Charlotte that they ordered her painted by Zoffany in the character.
In later years she became addicted to laudanum, and died poor and wretched in
Edinburgh in 1786.

gallantry, and I was terrified that I might lose my divine passion for Margaret, in which case I am sure I would suffer more than she. I prayed devoutly to heaven to preserve me from such a misfortune, and became easier.

My friend, Mr. Ross of the Edinburgh Theatre, was here. He and Mrs. Ross had come up on purpose. I drank tea with them, and there I got acquainted with Mr. King, the comedian, and his wife. King seemed a genteel, agreeable man. I went to the ball tonight just to see how the company looked when dressed, and to be able to tell that I had been there. I was so sleepy that I could hardly stand upon my feet, so I went home and went to bed immediately. My landlady got me warm negus, and seemed to be a good, motherly woman. I told her that perhaps I might retire from the world and just come and live in my room at Stratford.

THURSDAY 7 SEPTEMBER. I dined with Messrs. Ross and King quietly and comfortably. After dinner in came Mr. Richard Baldwin of London, bookseller, in immense spirits. He told us that he would soon have *The Public Advertiser* worth £2000 a year, and was quite heroic as a publisher. Mr. and Mrs. Ross and I went to his lodgings to drink tea. His wife was really a grave, sensible, well-behaved woman, and his daughter took after the mother.

This was the night of the ball in mask, when I was to appear as a Corsican chief. I had begun some verses for the Jubilee in that character but could not finish them. I was quite impatient. I went home and forced myself to exertion, and at last finished what I intended. I then ran to Garrick, read them to him, and found him much pleased. He said the passage as to himself:

> Had Garrick, who Dame Nature's pencil stole,
> Just where old Shakespeare dropped it, &c.,

was both a fine poetical image and a fine compliment. There was a fellow called Fulke Weale here, who advertised "printing at an hour's notice," I suppose taking it for granted that Stratford would produce a general poetical inspiration, which would exert itself every hour. To him I went. But Mr. Angelo's fireworks turned his head, and made him idle. He preferred them to all poetical fire. I then went to the bookseller and printer of the place, Mr. Keating. He had a lad from

Baskerville's at Birmingham, of Scots extraction, his name Shank. I found him a clever, active fellow, and set him to work directly. He brought me a proof to the masquerade ball about two in the morning. But could not get my verses thrown off in time for me to give them about in my Corsican dress.

I was quite happy at the masquerade. I had been at a public breakfast in the town hall, and had tea made for me by my pretty Irish lady, who no longer disturbed me. Tonight she did me the favour to dance with me a minuet while I was in complete armour,[3] and, when I laid aside my arms, a country dance. I got acquainted with Mr. Murphy, Mr. Colman, Mr. Kelly, Mr. Foote at this Jubilee;[4] also with Mr. Solicitor Dagge and many others. My Corsican dress attracted everybody. I was as much a favourite as I could desire.[5] I had been in the morning to wait on Mr. Garrick. He lived at Mr. Hunt's, the town clerk, to whom he introduced me. Mr. Hunt seemed a jolly, sagacious lawyer, and had an admirable house. I pleased myself with a variety of ideas with regard to the Jubilee, peculiar to my own mind. I was like a Frenchman at an ordinary, who takes out of his pocket a box of pepper and other spices, and seasons a dish in his own way.

FRIDAY 8 SEPTEMBER. We did not get home, many of us, till past six in the morning. I got about three hours' sleep. Then rose and called at Baldwin's, where I had some breakfast. The true nature of human life began now to appear. After the joy of the Jubilee came the uneasy reflection that I was in a little village in wet weather and knew not how to get away, for all the post-chaises were bespoke, I don't know how many times over, by different companies. We were like a crowd in a theatre. It was impossible we could all go at a time. I first thought of going to Birmingham with Ross, which, though above twenty miles out of my way, was the speediest, if not the shortest, way to London, as I could there get carriages enough. But Baldwin found for me a gentleman originally from Scotland, a kind of genius and patriot. Sir Andrew Chadwick designs him in his will *"honest Scott,"*

[3] That is, with his musket, stiletto, and pistols.
[4] All these men were well-known dramatists; Foote was also a celebrated mimic.
[5] As Boswell modestly reported in *The London Magazine,* "The novelty of the Corsican dress, its becoming appearance, and the character of that brave nation concurred to distinguish the armed Corsican chief."

and leaves him three thousand pounds. He had here a chaise from London to himself, and politely offered me a seat in it next morning.

I sauntered about till about two, when I went into Payton's public room to have some dinner. At a table by themselves sat two gentlemen who seemed to know me. I asked them if I could have anything to eat. They asked me to sit down with them; I did so. They were both Lichfield men. The one, Mr. Bailye, a middle-aged gentleman who had been at school with Garrick and knew Mr. Samuel Johnson well. The other, Lieutenant Vyse of Sir Joseph Yorke's Dragoons, who also knew Mr. Johnson, being the son of a clergyman in Lichfield in whose family my revered friend is intimate. They both named me, and we dined very agreeably together. It is fine to have such a character as I have. I enjoy it much.

I then took the parish clerk and went into the great church, and viewed calmly and solemnly the tomb of Shakespeare. His wife lies buried beside him. I observed with pleasure that she was seven years older than he, for it has been objected that my valuable spouse is a little older than I am. I read with much satisfaction a monumental inscription to the memory of Samuel Walford (I think, as I had neither pen nor pencil), "who, after many years spent in trade, retired to think of eternity."[6] This is just my system. I have mentioned it in my *Account of Corsica* on the subject of convents.

I began to think that *honest Scott*, who seemed to be very dissipated, would not be the best travelling companion for me. Mr. Richardson, the printer, and a Captain Johnston of an Indiaman, had also a chaise. I drank tea with them, and we agreed to go all three together, which was a more comfortable plan for me. I went to Mr. Garrick and gave him a parcel of my *Verses*.[7] He read them to me in such a manner that I was quite elated. They seemed admirable. My money had run short. So I asked him to let me have five guineas. He told me his brother George had taken almost all he had from him. "Come, come," said I, "that won't do. Five guineas I must have, and you must find them for me." I saw very well that he was not making any serious

[6] A good opportunity to test Boswell's memory. Samuel Walford, "after many years *employed* in trade, retired to *prepare for* eternity." Boswell was writing at least eight days later (see the reference to *The Public Advertiser* of 16 September in the entry for 6 September).

[7] His *Verses in the Character of a Corsican*. They are printed in Appendix A.

difficulty. "Well," said he, "you are right, you are a stranger. I must get you them." So he run to Mrs. Garrick, and brought me them. I went to bed in good time.

SATURDAY 9 SEPTEMBER. I left an apology to *honest Scott* that, as I was in a hurry to get to town, I had set out. About five o'clock we left Stratford, much consoled by comparing our situation with that of such as were left. We had a London chaise which had come down here, and we agreed to take it all the way. It seemed very tedious. But luckily for us, the chaise was in such bad condition that we had a just plea to get rid of it at Oxford. The driver too was a surly dog. He stopped us at a village near half an hour to get a wheel mended, and then swore we had not been kept above five minutes. My companions scolded him to good purpose. Richardson said his meas-urement of time was such that he might make hour-glasses to the Patagonians, a droll fancy, as if the time of these people were in pro-portion to the size of their bodies. We breakfasted at Chapel House, and got to Oxford to dinner. I sent for Mr. Mickle, who came and sat a while with me; and then he and I paid a visit to Dr. Smith, my old acquaintance. It was very agreeable to see a Maybole man a professor at Oxford. We took a post-chaise and drove to Benson, where we stayed all night.

SUNDAY 10 SEPTEMBER. We reposed well here, and after tak-ing a comfortable breakfast drove on. It is not right to travel on Sun-day. I very seldom do it. We were amused with Captain Johnston speaking such broken English as the Chinese do. He told us a China-man at Canton showed him Wilkes's head in china, and said, "He knockifar your king. Your king fooly king. Do so here, cutty head. Inglis no love your king; Cots (Scots) love your king." It is curious that people at such a distance can understand so much of the minutiae of Britain. We dined at Salthill.

Colman and Lacy of Drury Lane were there. I walked a little with Colman in the garden, and asked him if he would bring on a comedy written in Scotland which I had read, and which was then lying with him. He said no. It would not do. There was very good sense in it. But it would not bear representation. He said it was with writers of plays as with players: many of lesser sense will please when those of greater sense fail. There is a particular knack necessary.

We stopped at Hounslow and had coffee and tea. Captain Johnston was born at Dumfries, but had not been in Scotland for a vast many years, and had acquired the true English oddity. He said he should find nobody in London on a Sunday, and therefore he would stay a couple of hours at Hounslow, and take a chaise and drive in at night. A true John Bull scheme. Surely he would tire as much at Hounslow, one should think, as in London. We persuaded him off his project, and came all to town together. I found at Mr. Dilly's two French translations of my *Account of Corsica*. One of them had come consigned to Mr. Wilkes, who sent me many compliments. I had a desire to visit the pleasant fellow, but thought it might hurt me essentially.[8] The translations of my book flattered my vanity. It is a curious sensation one has from reading one's own composition when put in a foreign dress.[9]

MONDAY 11 SEPTEMBER. I hastened to my friend Dempster's, and found excellent letters from my valuable friend. We breakfasted agreeably. I was finding fault with John Home, and regretting that an ingenious and really a good man should be such a coxcomb.[1] Dempster said it was not to be regretted. It was John's distinguishing characteristic. "Every man," said he, "carries his flag, like the ships of different nations. Foppery is John Home's flag." A lively thought. He and I went and called on Sir John Pringle. I cannot say anything passed but the weather and the Russian fleet.[2]

I called on Dr. Kennedy, and this night I began to take the Lisbon Diet Drink.[3] I called on my fellow-traveller, Mr. Kinloch, but did not

[8] Wilkes was in jail. After his election from Middlesex, he surrendered on the decree against him of outlawry that had been passed in 1764, and was committed to prison. The Court of King's Bench reversed the outlawry, but fined him £1000 and sentenced him to nearly two years' imprisonment on his prior convictions. The House of Commons expelled him three times, and finally declared a Court tool elected in his place. He remained in prison until 17 April 1770.

[9] On 4 October he made a note to "write letter against" one of them (that by J. P. I. Dubois), probably because he had found that it was an abridgement.

[1] Author of the noted neo-classical tragedy, *Douglas*. Formerly a minister in the Church of Scotland, he had been secretary to Lord Bute and tutor to George III while Prince of Wales.

[2] Russia and Turkey were at war. A Russian fleet headed for Constantinople was expected at Spithead, where it arrived near the end of the month.

[3] Dr. Kennedy's nostrum. (He had been for many years physician to the British Factory at Lisbon.) Its virtues are thus extolled in a contemporary advertise-

find him. I received a noble letter from Mr. Samuel Johnson, then at Brighton, containing both warmth of friendship and admirable praise of my *Tour to Corsica.* It set me high. I dined at Mr. Dilly's. Dr. Dawson, a physician, a great man for the reigning notions of liberty and for the dissenting kind of religion, dined with us. I went to Foote's theatre in the Haymarket, and saw Sheridan play Brutus. One of the players, I forget his name, I shall call him Carey, was always laughing. Many people around me grumbled, but did no more. "Come," said I, "I'll stop him." So, as he was going off, I called quite out, "Carey, you rascal, what do you laugh for?" This made him as grave and serious as a bishop. The people around thought me a great man. "I'll tell you," said I, "if he had continued to laugh, I would have catched hold of the spikes, jumped upon the stage, and beat him with my stick before the audience." This made me appear as great as Brutus himself. So easily is momentary admiration to be gained, and so wonderfully inclined am I to be a London playhouse buck.

[Received 11 September, Johnson to Boswell][4]

Brighton, 9 September 1769

DEAR SIR, — Why do you charge me with unkindness? I have omitted nothing that could do you good or give you pleasure, unless it be that I have forborne to tell you my opinion of your *Account of Corsica.*[5] I believe my opinion, if you think well of my judgment,

---

ment (*Public Advertiser,* 7 October 1769): "The Lisbon Diet Drink, so well known to people of the highest rank for many years in curing every species of the scurvy, even to that of a leprosy. It acts as an alterative, and answers every intention of a benign salivation, without the least confinement or hurt to the most delicate constitution. Also those who have been injured by a certain disorder, and brought almost to a total weakness, will find this the greatest restorative in nature. . . . This solution is more pleasant to the taste, will keep longer, and may be sent to any part of the kingdom put up in pint bottles, with printed directions, at half a guinea each. To be had at Mr. Woodcock's, perfumer, in Orange Street, Red Lion Square, and nowhere else."

[4] Printed in *The Life of Johnson.*

[5] Actually Johnson had already expressed his opinion of *Corsica* (see entry for 2 May 1768). Geoffrey Scott suggested that Boswell suppressed this earlier conversation in *The Life of Johnson* because he wanted Johnson's later written praise to appear with the greatest possible effect.

might have given you pleasure; but when it is considered how much vanity is excited by praise, I am not sure that it would have done you good. Your *History* is like other histories, but your *Journal* is in a very high degree curious and delightful. There is between the *History* and the *Journal* that difference which there will always be found between notions borrowed from without and notions generated within. Your *History* was copied from books; your *Journal* rose out of your own experience and observation. You express images which operated strongly upon yourself, and you have impressed them with great force upon your readers. I know not whether I could name any narrative by which curiosity is better excited or better gratified.

I am glad that you are going to be married; and as I wish you well in things of less importance, wish you well with proportionate ardour in this crisis of your life. What I can contribute to your happiness, I should be very unwilling to withhold; for I have always loved and valued you, and shall love you and value you still more as you become more regular and useful: effects which a happy marriage will hardly fail to produce.

I do not find that I am likely to come back very soon from this place. I shall, perhaps, stay a fortnight longer; and a fortnight is a long time to a lover absent from his mistress. Would a fortnight ever have an end? I am, dear Sir, your most affectionate, humble servant,

SAM. JOHNSON.

TUESDAY 12 SEPTEMBER. I dined at Mr. Harris's. I observed that the petitioners to His Majesty at this season of opposition, when they tried to appear sensible amidst their madness, were like a drunken man trying to seem very grave and rational.[6] Between five and six I came home and stood to have a drawing of me, as the armed Corsican chief at Stratford, taken by Mr. Wale.[7] It was pleasing to

[6] The controversy over Wilkes's status had given rise to numerous petitions listing grievances against the Ministry and urging the dissolution of Parliament.
[7] Wale's sketch (which may have been a work of some distinction) is not known to have survived. An uninspired engraving from it by J. Miller (see the entry for 23 September) appeared in *The London Magazine* for this month accompanying Boswell's letter and essay (see p. 281 *n*.9). It is not a good likeness, and has been so much hackneyed by reproduction that we have ventured to exclude it from our list of illustrations. A re-drawn version of it appears on the spine of the dust jacket.

think that I was at that moment getting my figure done in London, to be engraved for four thousand *London Magazines.*

WEDNESDAY 13 SEPTEMBER. I breakfasted with Dempster. He was reading Carter's Epictetus, and he spoke much in praise of Stoicism. I said, "We should only have a little of it." "True," said he, "a man should have it like a box of Cayenne pepper. It is the best seasoner in the world." Mr. Kinloch went with me to the Old Bailey, where I heard two women tried for theft and found guilty. Justice is administered here very quickly, but I believe very fairly. I dined at Mr. Dilly's, and after dinner he and I went and saw the Bank of England, the grandeur and elegance of which filled me with noble ideas. The number, too, of the books and papers gave me great satisfaction, to see with what order and exactness the greatest multiplicity of affairs may be conducted.

Mr. Samuel Vaughan, who had been one of the most zealous friends of the Corsicans in promoting the contribution for them, had called several times on me, and I on him at his town house.[8] Mr. Dilly and I this afternoon took the Hackney stage and went to see him there. He was at this time under a cloud, having offered £5000 to the Duke of Grafton to procure a place to his son. He was writing his defence. So we found him in his nightcap. He chanced to let it fall. I lifted it. He made an apology. "Sir," said I, smiling, "it is the cap of liberty." He lived in noble apartments in the house which formerly belonged to the noted Ward, mentioned by Pope:

To Ward, to Waters, Chartres, or the Devil.[9]

(Sir John Pringle sarcastically observed that the house had good luck as to inhabitants; and when I said I had heard that Mr. Vaughan was truly a worthy, generous man, "True," said Dr. Franklin, "he was very generous to the Duke of Grafton.")[1] Mr. Vaughan seemed not a little confused and awkward. He was engaged to tea at Dr. Dawson's

[8] Vaughan, a wealthy West-Indian merchant, was an ardent Wilkesite and "American": in 1785 he presented Washington with the elaborately carved Italian mantelpiece still to be seen in the banquet room at Mount Vernon.
[9] *Moral Essays*, iii. 20 ("or" for "and").
[1] Benjamin Franklin. These remarks were probably made on 15 September (see end of entry for that day).

just by. So we went there. It was tiresome enough. But it did not last long. Mr. Dilly and I returned quietly home.

THURSDAY 14 SEPTEMBER. Dempster called on me and carried me with him to the India House, where I heard some debates on sending the supervisors to India, and felt that I could debate there too if I were a proprietor. I was happy to hear Dempster doing very well. I was here till near five. It was grand to think that these people here in London had power over immense countries at so great a distance. I eat a beefsteak at Dolly's.

I then called on Dr. Kennedy. Found he was a gaping babbler. I had no trust to his head, but made use of him as an engine to play upon and extinguish fire, which his decoction certainly does. I was uneasy, and already impatient to see some effect. I had heard that Colin Campbell, the advocate, who was now going to Grenada, had received much benefit from Kennedy. I called on him at his lodgings in Devereux Court. But he was in the Temple at Mr. Irving's, late of Auchinbedrig, a solicitor here. I went there and was introduced to Mr. Irving, whom I found to be an agreeable and a sensible man, who brought Scotch ideas fully into London. Colin assured me that after spending above £300 on his cure at Edinburgh in vain, Kennedy had cured him in a very few weeks; and he told me Duncan Forbes, surgeon to the Horse Guards, had gone with him to Kennedy. This comforted me. For it makes a great odds when one has the aid of a regular practitioner whom one knows.

FRIDAY 15 SEPTEMBER. I breakfasted with Mr. Forbes. His firm tone and rough animal spirits raised mine. He was very candid. He said different kinds of medicines would be effectual on different constitutions and at different times. That it was needless to argue against facts. That he had known very desperate cases cured by Kennedy's Diet Drink. That I was pursuing a very safe course; that he approved of it, would superintend my cure, and would go with me to Kennedy's. This made me very easy.

I called on Mr. Sheridan. His astonishing vanity made me wonder. But his knowledge and talents pleased me. He complained that our present system of education is too general, and does not fit a young man for any one state of life. That it was as if people should read lectures upon the human frame to a young man, and then bid him go and make a statue. I met Mr. Forbes at Mr. Colin Campbell's, and he and I went to Kennedy's and had the form of a consultation.

I then dined quietly at home with Mr. Charles Dilly, after which I went to call on my cousin, Mr. Charles Boswell. He is a younger son of the late David Boswell of Craigston, whose father was Mungo Boswell, son to John Boswell of Auchinleck by a second marriage with the daughter of Stewart, Lord Ochiltree.[2] Charles was upon the expedition to Cartagena with Lord Cathcart, as a surgeon.[3] On his return he was very poor, and his relations in Scotland were not kind to him. He then went to Jamaica, and afterwards was a lieutenant in a regiment in Britain for several years. He went back again to Jamaica, got the care of several plantations, and made a great deal of money. He had not been in Scotland for thirty years. He came to England above a year ago. His relations, who had heard nothing certain of him for many years, were extremely curious to know all about him when it appeared that he was very rich. His brother John, and his nephews Hallglenmuir and Knockroon, came up and saw him.[4] I wrote to him on hearing that he was a zealous friend both to the Corsicans and to Douglas. His answer to my letter showed a proper feeling of the neglect he had formerly experienced, and a strong regard for me. "My heart warms to such a man," were his words. He had called on me this forenoon. I wished to show him my eagerness to meet him. So went, as soon as I could, to his house in Newman Street, Oxford Road. He was not at home. So I left a card with my name. The maid ran after me, and told me that her mistress was at home and begged to see me. I knew he had a lady who had lived with him for several

[2] This genealogy is far from accurate. The Boswells of Craigston derived from the first marriage of John Boswell of Auchinleck, and there was at least one more generation in the descent. Though loyalty to the Family of Auchinleck was one of the main passions of Boswell's being, he was always very vague and hazy as to the details of his family history. His father and grandfather, though less enthusiastic in their professions, were both precise genealogists.

[3] The British attacked this Spanish possession on the Caribbean in 1741. The attack was a miserable failure, owing chiefly to poor medical and sanitary arrangements. Smollett also served on this expedition, and drew on his experiences in writing *Roderick Random*.

[4] John Boswell, younger brother to Charles, had married the heiress of Knockroon, which explains why his son was Knockroon and he was not.

years. I returned, and found her to be a comely, sensible, agreeable woman, with a modesty and decency of behaviour very different from that of a kept mistress. I drank tea with her, and was pleased to find that she knew so much of our family. She told me what age I was. It gave me concern to think she was not my cousin's wife. It was also out of character for a son of Auchinleck to be living in a licentious style.[5] I promised to return to breakfast next morning.

I called at Sir John Pringle's. I found him and his travelling companion, Dr. Franklin, sitting playing at chess.[6] Sir John, though a most worthy man, has a peculiar, sour manner. Franklin again is all jollity and pleasantry. I said to myself, "Here is a fine contrast: acid and alkali." I took the warm bath in Newgate Street.

SATURDAY 16 SEPTEMBER. I walked out betimes to visit my cousin Charles. I was impatient, curious, and agitated to think of meeting for the first time with him. He received me in the passage, and I at once saw him to be a son of Thomas Boswell of Auchinleck.[7] Each of us could perceive a family likeness in the other. He proved to be a sensible, plain, well-bred gentleman, very cordial, and very good company. I cannot describe what satisfaction I had from seeing a descendant of our ancient family. We were just like brothers. I told him a great deal about Scotland, and he entertained me with telling me a great deal about Jamaica. "Come," said he, "will you take pot luck with us?" And turning to his mistress, "We are not," said he, "in order yet, as we are just got into this house. But I see he's an easy man." I was engaged to dinner, but promised to come back and drink tea.

I observe continually how imperfectly, upon most occasions, words preserve our ideas. This interview is but faintly seen in my Journal. And all I have said of the Stratford Jubilee is very dim in comparison of the scene itself. In description we omit insensibly many little touches which give life to objects. With how small a speck does a painter give life to an eye! The vivid glances of Garrick's features, which cannot be copied in words, will illuminate an extent of sensa-

[5] Charles Boswell married his mistress later in the autumn, perhaps partly through Boswell's urging.

[6] Pringle had travelled with Franklin on the Continent.

[7] First laird of Auchinleck, who died at Flodden Field in 1513.

tion, if that term may be used, as a spark from a flint will throw a lustre in a dark night for a considerable space around it.[8] Certain looks of my dearest life and certain tones of her voice, which I defy all the masters of language to show upon paper, have engaged my soul in an angelic manner. I find myself ready to write unintelligibly when I attempt to give any kind of idea of such subjects.

I called on Lady Margaret Macdonald, but did not find her at home. I then called on Signor Baretti, who had been on a tour through Spain, and was employed in preparing for the press four octavo volumes of his travels, for which he got £500. He was so full of himself, and so assuming and really ferocious in his manner, that he disgusted me not a little. I then called on Dempster, with whom I sauntered about through the new streets round Soho till dinner time.

I dined with Mr. Sheridan. He had nobody with him but his two daughters and two sons, who were surprisingly grown since I saw them in 1763, and seemed to be a fine family.[9] Sheridan said he thought Dr. Reid of Glasgow's *Essay on the Human Mind on the Principles of Common Sense* a standard book. It gave me satisfaction to hear this. For my Lord Marischal lent me it at Berlin soon after it came out, and it settled my mind, which had been very uneasy from speculations in the abstruse and sceptical style. Sheridan said that Reid's book was the most correct of any that North Britain had produced, for that he had not found one Scotticism in it. I am amazed this book is so little known. Hume has spoiled the taste of this age. Men do not wish to be taught sound wisdom and morality. I observed to Mr. Sheridan that although my father and I differed a good deal, yet upon

[8] Garrick's powers of expression were famous. Boswell reported in his description of the Jubilee in *The London Magazine* that after Garrick had recited his *Dedication Ode*, Lord Grosvenor "told Mr. Garrick that he had affected his whole frame, showing him his veins and nerves still quivering with agitation."

[9] The younger of the sons was the statesman and dramatist, at this time not quite eighteen. Anne Elizabeth, the youngest daughter, aged eleven, remembered this day and told her daughter about it: "In the year 1769, Mrs. H. Lefanu, then a child, remembers a thin, eager-looking young man in black who talked a great deal about General Paoli. Mr. Sheridan said to him in his good-humoured way, 'I suppose you are in mourning for Corsica?' to which he answered in the affirmative. This was James Boswell" (Alicia Lefanu, *Memoirs of the Life and Writings of Mrs. Frances Sheridan*, 1824, pp. 336–337).

the whole our system was much the same. That we were like two men on horseback who set out from a post at one part of a circle in order to reach a post at an opposite part. My father $|\overset{N}{\underset{S}{O}}|$ takes the northern and rugged side. I again take the southern, gay side. He is very angry to see me taking what is seemingly the direct contrary road to his. But if he will have patience, he will find us both at the same ending post. In the mean time, however, he cries, "It is a strange thing you will not come with me," and is very ill pleased. While I cry, "Never mind. Let me take my own way. I shall do well enough."

I called for a quarter of an hour on Dempster, and he and I talked of the sarcastical temper of the Scots: how it checked all endeavours at excellence, and made people very uneasy. I then drank tea at Charles Boswell's. I informed him of my being to be married, and he was very glad to hear that I was to be so happy. I then marched home to the Poultry.

SUNDAY 17 SEPTEMBER. My illness seemed to go off very slowly. I was anxious and uneasy. I breakfasted with Mr. Forbes, and he gave me encouragement.[1] I then called on Sir John Pringle, and strolled a little with him towards Golden Square. I then went to the Bavarian Minister's Roman Catholic Chapel to revive in my mind former days when, in that very place, I was so solemnly happy in thinking myself united to the grand and only true church. But it had little effect upon me. I could not have so much devotion there as in the Churches of England. Mrs. Bellamy, the actress, was there. I just bowed to her and went out, without any farther intercourse.

I dined at Dr. Kennedy's. His sister was a great, fat woman, a kind of greasy wit. There was a curious company, and strange formality. A Dr. Sutherland from Bath, who had just come from a tour in Germany, was there. He was the most determined talker I ever heard. He hardly ever looked at the company, but keeping his eyes on the table he would go on as a boy says his lesson. He seemed to be a jolly, sensi-

---

[1] In the Memorandum for this day, Boswell advised himself to "breakfast, Mr. Forbes. Consult as to plaster and camphorated friction." The plaster almost certainly contained a mercuric ointment. "Camphorated friction" probably refers to the use of camphor liniment, which was applied externally as a mild stimulant or counter-irritant. See p. 317 *n.*9.

ble fellow. We had here, too, Shirley, the author of *The Black Prince*, a tragedy. Mr. Garrick had kindly brought on that play at Drury Lane, and so put a considerable sum in Shirley's pocket. But, because he did not bring on another for him, Shirley most ungratefully became his mortal enemy. He attacked our Stratford Jubilee and Garrick's *Ode* with virulence, and I defended both with keenness. I did not know till he was gone that my antagonist was Shirley. Had I known it, he should have had enough from me. I would have trimmed him.

After coffee, Dr. Kennedy and Dr. Sutherland and I went to Dr. Campbell's in Queen Square, when I was introduced to that voluminous author. I found him to be a fat, pleasant man, full of knowledge and of entertaining stories. He had a rosy countenance, a large wig, a brown coat, with a scarlet waistcoat with broad gold lace. He had no rust of authorship upon him, and looked more like an admiral himself than like one who had written the *Lives of the Admirals*. He had been a great favourite of the Duke of Argyll's, and he revived to me my ideas of the Duke in my younger years.[2] He told me that Wilkes said to him one day, "Dr. Campbell, I have seen a miracle this morning"; to which he answered, "Miracles are now very rare, and, if there was to be one, I doubt if you would believe it." "But," said Wilkes, "I really have seen a miracle: a Scotsman in a post-chaise going home — with a smile upon his countenance." This happened to be Mr. Veitch, now Lord Eliock, who has always a kind of smile or grin. I should have mentioned that I called before dinner on George Lewis Scott, whom I found hearty and well. I observed to him that there should be half a dozen of Ménages in every age to preserve the remarkable sayings which are often lost. Dr. Campbell said Mr. Johnson was a very great man. In short he pleased me much.

I made an experiment to see if I could go home without asking the way at all. So I walked from street to street a long time. At last I found myself in the fields near to the Foundling Hospital. This was not so safe. So I just turned back, was happy to get again into a crowded street, and then asked my way and got to my quarters in good time.

[2] It was the Duke who remarked when Boswell wanted a commission in the Guards in 1760: "That boy must not be shot at for three and sixpence a day" (*Boswelliana*, ed. Rev. Charles Rogers, 1874, p. 229).

I was very well at Mr. Dilly's. Mrs. Jedd, his housekeeper, was a governess to me. James, his footman, was most obsequious, and my linen were washed and dressed by a city laundress to do one's heart good to see them.

MONDAY 18 SEPTEMBER. I had promised to pay a visit to my old friend Mr. Love, and see him in his greatness as manager of the Theatre Royal on Richmond Green. So I this morning set out in the Richmond stage. Among the passengers was one who, I believe, was a German old lady. She spoke broken English. But, knowing the antipathy of the people of this country to foreigners, she thought to persuade us that her manner of speaking was owing only to loss of teeth. We had a fine, hale old gentleman, a Tory, who took care to remind us that the title which his present Majesty has to the British throne is his being a descendant of the House of Stuart; and he gave it as his opinion that the mad Lascar who some days before that had disfigured Queen Anne's statue in St. Paul's Churchyard, was not so very mad, but was in fact set on by the violent Whigs.[3]

It was a most delightful day. Richmond seemed delicious. Mr. Love's theatre is a very handsome one, having everything in miniature. He and I, after seeing it, took a walk on the banks of the Thames, and recalled our having walked together on Arthur's Seat. Mrs. Love looked very well, though verging on fifty; and Billy was grown a surprising musician. He played to me on the pianoforte.[4] I tried to analyse the operation, and saw how mechanical music is when a boy of thirteen can do so much in that art. I know not how it is, but we fancy we feel a kind of soul in music, a kind of expression which speaks to us. We respect the performer of a noble piece. But I believe that the performer is often less sensible than the people who hear him.

Miss Radley, apprentice to Mr. Love, a fine little young actress, a very good singer and a very modest girl, dined with us, as did Mrs.

[3] Not "some days before" but on the previous morning. The Lascar broke off both the arms, with the globe and sceptre, and disfigured the emblematic figures surrounding the pedestal. When apprehended he drew a knife on one of the constable's men.

[4] William Dance (Love was his father's stage name) became eminent in his profession, and in 1813 was made a director and treasurer of the newly formed Philharmonic Society.

Moffat, a Carlisle woman, cousin german to Mr. David Armstrong the advocate, and dresser to Mrs. Barry of Drury Lane Theatre. My old friend treated me with old hock, and I was really well, thinking of the ideas of players which we find in Addison, and many other ideas which please such a fancy as mine. When Mr. and Mrs. Love went to the theatre to dress, Miss Radley made tea for me, and went with me to one of the high boxes, and was like a little daughter to me. Mr. Love played Richard the Third very well in some of the kind of comic scenes, but he is not a good tragedian. Mrs. Love as Catherine, and Keaseberry, whom we had formerly at Edinburgh, as Petruchio, played very well in the farce, as did Waldron, also one of our Edinburgh performers.[5] I had my Kennedy's bottle by the afternoon stage and was quite regular, and I had a neat little room at Mr. Love's (I fancy Miss Radley's), with bandboxes and laced caps and I know not how many pleasing objects all about me.

TUESDAY 19 SEPTEMBER. Between eight and nine I had a comfortable breakfast, and at nine took the stage to town, but had no company except some idle women. My cousin Captain Bosville, then on duty in the Tower, called for me at Mr. Dilly's and engaged me to dine in the Tower next day.[6]

Mr. Sheridan, Dr. Dawson, and a Captain Clunie, formerly a very rich man, dined with us at Mr. Dilly's. Mr. Sheridan in his usual style lamented the depravity of the age, and maintained that there was little religion. "Oh," said I, "when they who seem most thoughtless are dying, they have all serious apprehensions." Mr. Sheridan upon this made a curious observation. "Very few now die," said he. "Physicians take care to conceal people's danger from them. So that they are carried off, properly without dying; that is to say, without being sensible of it." Clunie had commanded a merchant ship, and made many voyages. He had just published a book called *The American Traveller*.[7] He talked incessantly, and put an end to all reciprocation of converse. He would make us hear his many projects. At first we were angry with him, till we saw him to be what is called a

---

[5] The farce was David Garrick's alteration of *The Taming of the Shrew* entitled *Catherine and Petruchio*.

[6] William, eldest son of Godfrey Bosville, a lieutenant in the Coldstream Guards.

[7] Through Dilly; hence his presence at the dinner.

character, and then he entertained us. He insisted on our dining with him on Saturday.

Mr. Sheridan and I walked to Soho, and I informed him of my marriage. I drank tea with Dempster. I said the Outer House of the Court of Session was a good house for me, but it required a garden, and the amusement of London was my garden. We were very cheerful and happy.

WEDNESDAY 20 SEPTEMBER. I breakfasted with Mr. Forbes. I found myself in such a state that it would be necessary for me to have lodgings nearer him than in the City. I tried to get lodgings in Boswell's Court near Red Lion Square, or in Boswell's Court, Lincoln's Inn Fields. But could get none.[8] I however met with a very good habitation, just opposite to the latter, at the house of Mr. Careless. I saw the name upon a door in Carey Street. It took my fancy. There was a bill, "Lodgings to be let." So I went in and found very pretty ones. I asked Mrs. Careless what was Mr. Careless's profession. Her answer was, "No particular profession." This was quite in character for *Careless*. I took the lodgings for a week.

I dined at the Tower with Captain Bosville and several of his brother officers of the Guards, some of whom were really very sensible, agreeable company. Colonel Wright and Bosville fell a-disputing about something. Bosville would not give up his argument. The Colonel said he put him in mind of a young man who was once under his care, and, while he thought he was profiting by a serious lecture he was giving him, the young man looked up to a flock of crows flying over their heads and bid the Colonel look, who therefore gave him up as incorrigible. How the story was to apply to Bosville, I cannot say. But I called to him, "Come, Captain. Don't give up your argument to the Colonel. Don't let him *crow* over you."

THURSDAY 21 SEPTEMBER. I breakfasted with Mr. John Donaldson, the bookseller, and then he carried me over the way to Marr's, the hatter, in whose house was lodged a Chinese. Mr. Marr took me into his back parlour and there he introduced me to the Chinese, who was not a man of fashion but an ingenious artist in taking likenesses

[8] He was trying to imitate Johnson, who at this time lived in Johnson's Court. When he was in Scotland in 1773, Johnson referred to himself as "Johnson of that ilk."

in terracotta (fine earth), which he works very neatly. He spoke some imperfect English. He was precisely such a figure as we see on an Indian screen. I got him to read a little to me from a fan with Chinese characters. It was just what Mr. Johnson told me of another Chinese: a sound like the ringing of a small bell.

I then called at Mr. Thomas Davies's, the bookseller. Dr. Goldsmith was there. I had not seen him for near three years. We met quite frankly. He pleased me by telling me that he had supped the night before in a company where I was highly spoken of, and that Mr. Colman had very justly observed that my character was simplicity: not in a sense of weakness, but of being plain and unaffected. Rose, Matthew Henderson's old governor, who keeps an academy at Chiswick, came in. He is a bold, honest fellow, and a man of coarse abilities. We talked of the celebrated political writer, Junius. Goldsmith would not allow him great merit. He said he was like a flower upon a dunghill. He appeared in a newspaper in which the writing is so bad that his seems very good. I said he was a keen writer; that his pen was a caustic, and like a caustic burnt a sound part as well as a corrupted. Rose said writing for the stage was the most profitable. Goldsmith said, "No"; writing for Davies was the most profitable. "Why, now," said he, "I am just now writing a natural history for which I get a thousand pounds. That kind of writing is sure, whereas writing plays is difficult and their profits uncertain."[9] He recounted to us all the disagreeable circumstances attending a dramatic author.

I dined at Mr. Dilly's. We had with us the Reverend Mr. Stretch, who has compiled a book in which he praises my *Account of Corsica* very much.[1] I said I was afraid he had *stretched* a point. But I said this only to Mr. Dilly. I called at Dempster's, and finding no letter from my dearest was uneasy. It was not a post day from Scotland. So Dempster cheered me with hopes for next day. He and I had a dissertation on my plan of life. We agreed that I might be happy with a

[9] This is somewhat misleading. Goldsmith was not writing the "natural history" for Davies, but for Griffin. He was to receive 800 guineas for it. In June of this year, however, he had interrupted the work on that project to write *The History of England* for Davies, a four-volume work, for £500.

[1] *The Beauties of History, or Pictures of Virtue and Vice drawn from Real Life,* 2 vols., published by Dilly. It ran through fifteen editions between 1769 and 1815.

seven years' seat in Parliament, if it could be had easily. But, in the mean time, I was very well with the law in Scotland.

I went to a club to which I belong.[2] It meets every other Thursday at St. Paul's Coffee-house. It consists of clergymen, physicians, and several other professions. There are of it: Dr. Franklin, Rose of Chiswick, Burgh of Newington Green, Mr. Price who writes on morals, Dr. Jeffries, a keen Supporter of the Bill of Rights,[3] and a good many more. We have wine and punch upon the table. Some of us smoke a pipe, conversation goes on pretty formally, sometimes sensibly and sometimes furiously. At nine there is a sideboard with Welsh rabbits and apple-puffs, porter and beer. Our reckoning is about 18d. a head. Much was said this night against the Parliament. I said that, as it seemed to be agreed that all Members of Parliament became corrupted, it was better to choose men already bad, and so save good men. Dr. Franklin informed me that Paoli was actually arrived in London, for he had seen Mr. Wood, the Under-Secretary of State, who had been with him. This was noble news to me. I went this night to my lodgings at Mr. Careless's. I said I was now the *Philosophe de Sans Souci.*[4] The very name of the maid was uncommon. She was called Phoebe. I liked my lodgings much.

FRIDAY 22 SEPTEMBER. I breakfasted with Mr. Forbes, who has the best breakfast in London, having marmalade made him by his nieces in Scotland. I then went to Old Bond Street and called on Paoli. A footman who opened the door said he was not well and could not see company, and made a great many difficulties. "Stay," said I. "Get me a bit of paper and pen and ink, and I'll write a note to him." His *valet de chambre* came down. Seeing something about him like what I had been used to see in Corsica, I asked him in Italian if he was a Corsican. He answered, "Yes, Sir," "Oh, then," said I, "there is no occasion to write. My name is Boswell." No sooner had I said this,

[2] Essentially a group of Benjamin Franklin's friends called by him "The Honest Whigs." Boswell seems out of place in a club of honest Whigs and dissenting clergymen, and a few years later would certainly have felt uncomfortable in that company. He was now united to them by his love of "liberty," the first word and recurring theme of *Corsica.*

[3] The "Supporters of the Bill of Rights" were a group of Wilkes's friends.

[4] Frederick the Great was the "philosopher of Sans Souci," the name of his retreat in Potsdam. It means "Careless."

than Giuseppe (for that was his name) gave a jump, catched hold of my hand and kissed it, and clapped his hand several times upon my shoulders with such a natural joy and fondness as flattered me exceedingly. Then he ran upstairs before me like an Italian harlequin, being a very little fellow, and opening the door of the General's bedchamber, called out, "Mr. Boswell." I heard the General give a shout before I saw him. When I entered he was in his night-gown and nightcap. He ran to me, took me all in his arms, and held me there for some time. I cannot describe my feelings on meeting him again. We sat down, and instantly were just as when we parted. I found myself much rusted in my Italian. The General made a fine observation upon a man's being in want of language. "'When," said he, "I came over to Italy, and was obliged there and in Germany to speak French, in which I had not a fluency from want of practice, *je trouvais mon âme renfermée comme dans un cachot*."[5] An admirable metaphor. The more it is considered, the better it appears. How well does it show the soul shut up, and ideas struggling to get out! He had a number of newspapers on his table. He was struck with the daring style of the political writings in them. Said he: "I am come here to a northern country, and I find the newspapers all on fire."

In came Count Gentili, a Corsican, who had a company in the Imperial service but left it from a zeal to serve his country, and had been about a year with Paoli. He was a lean, beak-nosed gentleman between thirty and forty, much Germanized in his manner, no extraordinary genius but good-natured and enterprising. He was very happy to see me. The General had also with him his secretary, the Abbé Guelfucci, whom I have painted in my Corsican *Tour*.[6] He and I were glad to meet again. Here was also Mr. Burnaby, chaplain to the British factory at Leghorn. Though I had corresponded with him frequently, I had never seen him till now.[7] He did not answer my idea at all. He seemed a worthy, sensible, and knowing man. But he had a

[5] "I found my soul shut up as if in a cell."

[6] "A man whose talents and virtues, united with a singular decency and sweetness of manners, have raised him to the honourable station of secretary to the General" (*Corsica*, p. 338).

[7] Burnaby, who had visited Paoli in 1766, had allowed Boswell to quote at length from his Journal in *Corsica*.

curious, lank countenance, and a reserve and closeness that I sometimes laughed at and sometimes was angry at. The General had his
hair dressed and then appeared in a blue frock suit, plain cloth with a
white silk lining. He looked very well, having recruited wonderfully
upon his journey. He told me he would have written to me, had he
not expected to see me soon. He said, "This country ought to renew
its alliance with Austria, the real advantageous alliance for the rival
of France. Great Britain and Austria," said he, "are like two lovers
who have quarrelled. Both wish to make it up. But neither will make
the first advance." He insisted on my dining with him, ill dressed as
I was.

I left him a little to go and look at the company going to and
coming from Court, to please my monarchical genius. I met the
worthy Duke of Queensberry in his chair in St. James's Street. He
made his chairmen set him down, and shook hands with me cordially.
I told him of Paoli's arrival, and asked him if he would not go and see
him. He said he should be very happy. "But where," said he, "and
how shall I find him?" "Just now," said I, "my Lord. Follow me,
chairmen." So I just walked back to his lodgings, and introduced the
Duke. His Grace seemed much struck. He said, "Je rencontrais mon
ami, Monsieur Boswell. Il vous dira combien j'ai été intéressé pour
vous."[8] The General behaved with the utmost ease and politeness.
I sat by with joy in my heart and a cheerful smile on my countenance
to see my illustrious friend and the worthy Duke together.

Paoli's lodgings were in the house where the Duchess of Douglas
had lived. They were the most magnificent, I suppose, to be hired in
all London. I dined with Paoli; Count Gentili and Abbé Guelfucci
were with us. I felt myself just as when at Sollacarò.[9] As I hardly
hoped to meet Paoli in this world again, I had a curious imagination
as if I had passed through death and was really in Elysium. This idea
made me not afraid of actual death, of which I think so often, just
as my grandfather Mr. James Boswell did. I was filled with admiration whenever the General spoke. I said that after every sentence
spoken by him I felt an inclination to sing *Te Deum*. Indeed, when he

[8] "I met my friend, Mr. Boswell. He will tell you how interested I have been in
your cause."
[9] The Corsican town where Boswell had visited Paoli.

speaks it is a triumph to human nature and to my friendship. He said the Russian fleet was moving up the Mediterranean like the mother of Proserpine, with a torch in each hand to kindle a fire all the way she advanced. (I might say *it* of a fleet. But, as we say *she* of a single ship, why not say so also of a large fleet?) He said he believed that, in a course of years, perhaps moral events would be calculated just as physical ones are. That, as there is a gradual progress in states, it might be calculated such a year will be a war, just as we see in the almanac that there will be an eclipse. I fear this is too curious. General events of a moral nature may be prognosticated. But particular events depend so much on circumstances for the time of their happening, that I fancy it cannot be calculated with any precision.

I then went to Dempster's, and finding no letter from my dearest Peggie, I was really uneasy. I sat down and wrote to her, which did me good. The General's arrival obliged me to alter my retired, frugal system. It was my duty to attend upon him, and be genteelly dressed accordingly. So I ordered a genteel, plain, slate-blue frock suit, and a full suit of a kind of purple cloth with rich gold buttons, and Mr. Dilly supplied me with a silver-hilted sword. Paoli said he was sorry he had not room for me in the house with himself. I could have wished it. But I did my best, and immediately took very handsome lodgings within a few doors of his, at a M. Renaud's, an old Swiss, whose wife kept a milliner's shop. She was a well-behaved, obliging woman. The Bishop of Peterborough had been her lodger many years. Indeed the apartments were excellent. I had a large dining-room with three windows to Old Bond Street, a bedchamber, and a dressing-room, both looking into Burlington Gardens. So that I saw a pretty large extent of green ground and stately trees in the very centre of the court end of the town.

I took a coach to Carey Street about eleven. Mrs. Careless was in bed with her husband, whom I had never seen. Phoebe called her up. She seemed amazed when she heard that I was to leave my lodgings in her house after sleeping there only one night. And I dare say she had a shrewd suspicion that I was about no good, when I shifted so suddenly. It looked somewhat like a highwayman. However, I told her the reason of it, paid her five and twenty shillings, the whole week's money, and left my new address. And thus did I quit *Sans*

Souci, though it sounded like the seat of the King of Prussia, and the maid Phoebe, though a song in *The Spectator* says:

> My time, O ye Muses, was happily spent,
> When *Phoebe* went with me wherever I went.[1]

Such nonsense. But I may now and then play myself with ideas. I paid for my apartments in Old Bond Street a guinea and a half a week, only the half of what they bring in winter. I found there a pretty little Yorkshire maid called Mary. I determined however to get a servant who could speak Italian. It seemed pleasant thus to move from lodging to lodging.

SATURDAY 23 SEPTEMBER. I went this morning and sat for above an hour to Mr. Miller, who was engraving a print of me in the Corsican dress; and while I am sitting to him, I may bring in a bit of Journal omitted, I think, on Thursday. I called on Dr. Armstrong, whom I found as worthy, as lively in his way, and as splenetic as ever. He is a violent Scotsman. He said the only advantage the English had over us was the *recitativo*, the tone of speaking. He said Drummond of Hawthornden's verses were equal to Waller's, and that the style of his *History* was excellent. He owned indeed he had never read it through, which led me to talk of the little which most people read. I said I had read very little. He owned to me he had never read Virgil through. "Nay," said I, "that is too much."

I dined this Saturday at Captain Clunie's, the strange mortal whom I have mentioned as dining at Mr. Dilly's. Mr. Sheridan, Dr. Dawson, and Mr. Charles Dilly were there. Clunie was more moderate this day. He had lost a great part of his fortune, but had spirits and projects to make him not mind it. The conversation turned on Admiral Byng[2] and some such old topics, which, like old brass candlesticks, required a great deal of scouring to make them fit to be presented to company. Sheridan, Dr. Dawson, and I drank coffee at Dilly's. I then called at Dempster's, and found an agreeable letter from Margaret, which cheered me. I know not how the evening passed. I had called

---

[1] No. 603; John Byrom's pastoral, *Colin and Phoebe*.

[2] Byng's fleet had been defeated by the French off Minorca in 1755. Accused and found guilty of misconduct, he was shot in 1757. His execution prompted Voltaire's famous remark in *Candide* that in England it is thought good to execute an admiral from time to time "to encourage the others."

at the General's in the morning and he was not up, and when I called at night he was gone to bed.

SUNDAY 24 SEPTEMBER. I breakfasted with Mr. Forbes. He thought me much better, and so gave me spirits. I then waited on Paoli. Frederick, natural son to King Theodore, was with him.[3] He seemed to be a low-lifed being, though well dressed. He was explaining to the General a court calendar with the names of all the principal officers in Great Britain. Sir Edward Hawke drew his Excellency's attention, as having been the admiral on whom the fate of this nation once depended; and also as he had last winter strongly opposed Great Britain's assisting Corsica, by which he had done an essential service to France, which has now that Island. Frederick, pointing out Hawke, said, "È quello che ha battuto i francesi" (It is he who beat the French). The General answered, "Non, è quello che non ha battuto i francesi" (It is he who did *not* beat the French), meaning in not preventing them from obtaining Corsica.

I went to the Temple Church. Dr. Morell preached on this text: "Thou hast made him a little lower than the angels."[4] I dined at Dr. Campbell's. He had with him a Dr. Archer, much like one of Sir John Douglas's family in appearance, and a mild, genteel man in his behaviour; and a Mr. Briscoe, who belonged to some of the public offices, a very well-dressed young man, who spoke with wonderful keenness without any meaning, or such as every human being had without his speaking. Last time I was with Dr. Campbell, he told me that he was beginning to agree with Mr. Johnson about the colonists. "Sir," said Johnson, "they are a parcel of convicts, and if they get anything short of hanging they ought to be content." The Doctor entertains very hospitably. His wife is a notable woman,[5] and his son is all the children he has that I know of, except a daughter married in Scotland.

---

[3] Theodore, Baron von Neuhoff, was a Westphalian adventurer who in 1736 persuaded the Corsicans to proclaim him King, on the strength of the promises of support he said he could procure. Not long afterwards he fled from Corsica and died in a London debtor's prison in 1756. Frederick was probably an impostor.

[4] Psalms 8. 5.

[5] She was supposed to have been a printer's devil before marriage. Johnson once described her in company as having "a bottom of good sense," and when he observed that "bottom" provoked tittering and laughing, sternly continued: "I say the *woman* was *fundamentally* sensible" (*Life of Johnson*, 20 April 1781).

The Doctor seemed very fond of me. He said, "I look upon it as one of the white days of my life that brought you here." I stayed a long time here.

I then called for the General. He was just gone to bed. But he desired that I would walk up. I was afraid to see him in bed, lest it might lessen his dignity and diminish my grand idea of him. But it had no such effect. Though his hands and arms were under the clothes and he showed his countenance only, he appeared with superior lustre. His eyes alone expressed the vivacity of his mind. He talked of the political heats of this country and of his own incertain situation with ease and cheerful manliness.

MONDAY 25 SEPTEMBER. While I was sitting at breakfast, I was agreeably surprised with the arrival of Mr. George Frazer, who was just returned with his wife and daughter, with whom he had been in France on a visit to his son Andrew, the commissary at Dunkirk. As Andrew is a great engineer, I borrowed a simile from his art to make his father eat a hearty breakfast. "You must consider, Sir," said I, "that a breakfast in London is a fortification which is to stand the attack of so many hours till dinner comes to its relief. It never can hold out unless it have a proper degree of strength. So you must make ravelins of muffins, and other works accordingly."

The General carried me, Mr. Burnaby, and the Abbé Guelfucci an airing in his coach. A crowd followed him in the streets. He graciously smiled and bowed, while they paid him what honours they could. We drove to Putney and then down the river, and returned by Westminster Bridge. It was a delightful day, and the country round London appeared to great advantage. He was charmed with it. He seemed to be an accurate observer of the beauties of nature. After we returned, I called on Mr. Burnaby Greene, a gentleman of fine fortune, author of *Corsica, an Ode*, in which he has paid me a very genteel compliment. Talking of the influence of truth in Corsica, he says,

And grace a classic isle with Boswells of her own.[6]

I found him a genteel man about thirty, very polite and easy. He had translated Anacreon. He said there was something peculiar in the style of that poet which would always distinguish his compositions.

[6] Boswell reviewed the poem in *The London Chronicle* for 31 October, and quoted the passage in which this line occurs.

I dined at Paoli's. He had a good table, having dinner at a crown
a head from the Brawn's Head Tavern in Bond Street. Mr. Sheridan
had expressed the strongest desire to see the General. I obtained leave,
and in the evening introduced him. He was exceedingly struck, and
although he spoke French very ill and understood little or no Italian,
I contrived to have some conversation kept up between the General
and him. Paoli, being informed by me of Mr. Sheridan's study of
language, entered immediately on that subject. He said a great
language, or a noble language, was a language in which great men
have written; for it is by being moulded and animated by superior
souls that a language becomes superior. He told us he had said to the
Emperor[7] that he would either ruin or aggrandize the House of
Austria. His opinion was that the latter would be the case. "Consider,"
said he, "a young man, very hardy, very enterprising, with the true
spirit of a soldier, at the head of 250,000 troops including hussars and
other irregulars, and consider the state of Europe by and by: France
under a minority; Spain having an idiot for her king; the King of
Prussia sunk into the dotage of old age, or succeeded by a very weak
prince." This was well drawn. It is disagreeable to think he might
have added, "Great Britain deprived of her colonies, and her trade
gone."

After Mr. Sheridan went away, I sat with the General and gave
him a lesson on the English language by reading newspapers with
him. He and I reclined upon a couch, and his vivacity, nobleness of
thought, and engaging manners raised my ideas and made me truly
happy. I then told him how the thoughts of my father's marrying
again had agitated me, and from that I introduced an account of my
dearest spouse's generous behaviour. In a cursory way, he seemed to
approve my warm resentment of my father's conduct. But we soon
passed from it to the beautiful subject of Miss Montgomerie. I took
out her *most valuable letter*. Paoli read it, and translated it with
elegant spirit into Italian. "Free of ambition, I prefer real happiness
to the splendid appearance of it," struck him much. He read it over
again and again, and repeated it, saying, "Questo è sublime" (this is
sublime). He with much cordiality wished me all happiness. This
was a rich evening.

[7] Joseph II, son of Maria Theresa. He was twenty-eight at this time.

TUESDAY 26 SEPTEMBER. Mr. and Mrs. and Miss Frazer, having come from the country somewhere, took an early breakfast with me. Edinburgh ideas and sounds afforded a variety to me in the midst of London. I took this visit very kind, and I was a plain, hospitable, hearty landlord for tea and bread and butter. After they were gone, Mr. Burnaby came and breakfasted with me at the usual hour. His closeness and most anxious concern to observe the strictest propriety in every trifle diverted me not a little. I could see that the Ministry had employed him to consult with respect to Paoli; and that this, joined with his natural disposition, produced the behaviour which appeared to me so curious. He seemed, however, to be a man of worth, knowledge, and good understanding. I sat at home and wrote this my Journal all the forenoon. I was calm and cheerful from living with perfect sobriety. I dined with Dr. . . . .

[EDITORIAL NOTE. Here the Journal stops. Had Boswell continued, the next word would have been "Goldsmith"; it was at this dinner that he first met Sir Joshua Reynolds, who was to be his loyal and affectionate friend for more than twenty years. The remainder of Boswell's stay in London is covered by two overlapping series of Journal Notes and Memoranda, which are interwoven here with passages from the manuscript of *The Life of Johnson* and letters.]

TUESDAY 26 SEPTEMBER . . . . Dined Dr. Goldsmith's. Mark company. Colman said Sir John Vanbrugh our best comic writer. His wit flows; Congreve's, in artificial jet d'eaus. Congreve's may apply anyhow, Vanbrugh's in character. Sir John Brute's admirable.[8] Chambers maintained him architect of much fancy. Dispute as to Garrick's vanity. Baretti said he wondered he was not more vain. GOLDSMITH. "How can he more, unless [he wears] real caps and bells?" COLMAN. "He is not more vain than others, but has this, that he must have frequent drams to his vanity." I was happy; looked at Colman as comic writer to be talked of in future. Full feeling of London society of wits. Colman said yours the truest book.

WEDNESDAY 27 SEPTEMBER. Breakfast, Forbes. Then home, dressed. Court. The sentries happy. Waited with impatience. Fine to

[8] A character in Vanbrugh's *The Provoked Wife*.

see presentation, Paoli and King of Britain.[9] Hervey told me King said [Paoli had] the most sensible and spirited countenance. . . .

[Boswell to Margaret Montgomerie][1]

[London, ?2 October 1769]

. . . LORD LYTTELTON'S LETTER ABOUT YOU. It never entered into my head.[2] I am going to write to my father tonight. I shall not take any notice of having heard that he was angry. I shall write to him in my usual style. But you may depend upon it, I never will make him any apology for warning him of what he is to expect. It is lucky I have contrived to enjoy so much of the estate of Auchinleck while I was abroad. By what I can see, I shall have little more of it. I am obliged to Mrs. Montgomerie-Cuninghame for her kindness. But still I heartily wish she would not interfere. If she writes to me, I will tell her so again. I hate absurd consultations. Soften my father! What nonsense would it appear to any rational being who does not know

[9] Boswell repeated an anecdote of this meeting in a letter to Sir Alexander Dick. "The King said, 'I have read Boswell's book, which is well written (*scritto con spirito*). May I depend upon it as an authentic account?' The General answered, 'Your Majesty may be assured that everything in that book is true, except the compliments which Mr. Boswell has been pleased to pay to his friend' " (*Letters of James Boswell*, i. 174). The original of this letter is in the Manuscript Division: Miscellaneous Papers (Boswell, James) of the New York Public Library.

[1] A fragment, probably lacking at least four pages at the beginning. The Notes for what appear to be this letter survive, dated 2 October: "Letter to M. Explain to her your keen feelings, and say SHE has no reason to be uneasy — if having her friend invariably attached be enough. Say you must take time to recover yourself after her unhappy letters, that she should have recollected into what a fever I was formerly thrown. That Father seems a selfish and really a bad man." After having persuaded himself that the scheme was given up, Boswell seems to have heard that his father intended to marry a second time, and wrote to him "in very strong terms" (Boswell to John Johnston, 16 October 1769). Lord Auchinleck was very angry, but communicated his wrath to the blameless Miss Montgomerie, not to his son. It may have been, however, in response to this letter that Lord Auchinleck said, "James, my estate is not entailed" (John Ramsay, *Scotland and Scotsmen*, i. 173).

[2] What never entered his head is not clear. Lord Lyttelton had written Boswell a note of congratulation on hearing of his approaching marriage, but there appears to be nothing in it that should have offended Lord Auchinleck.

him, should he be told what are the offences for which it is necessary to plead as if a man had been upon the highway! Mr. Johnson settled my mind fully this afternoon as to my father. "Sir," said he, "the disputes between you and him are matters of sensation not of judgment. So it is in vain to reason with him. He grumbles because you come to London. He cannot understand why it is very right you should from time to time enjoy London. There is no help for it. Let him grumble."

Mr. Johnson is of opinion that when a man marries and becomes the head of a family, he ought to have his own house, and cannot possibly be happy under his father's roof, more especially if circumstances are such, from temper or anything else, that a man and his father cannot live well together even while the son is unmarried. He advises me strongly to have my own house. He says my father will treat you and me much better when we have our own home and leave him at night. As to my father's marrying again, he thinks it had much better not happen. But he is of opinion that I would be *a fool* (there he goes) should I give up *with everything and everybody* on that account. His feelings are not such as mine, you see. I am supported by enthusiasm, and would care little for existence did I not, like Zoroastre (was it not?), hope for *everlasting love.*[3] So cannot bear what I need not repeat. If there is not love, let there be at least a decent regard. But that vile subject haunts me. Down with it! Mr. Johnson says that if you and I live near my father and are often with him, it will be as effectual in preventing his marrying again as living with him would be. Be not uneasy. I shall do nothing rashly, nor take any hasty resolutions. I again beg you may just think of me as your friend and lover. Leave everything else to time. Perhaps I may bring myself to try to live in Scotland. But in the mean time, I positively insist on your having no intercourse whatever with the infamous wretch.[4] I am not for Robert.[5] But I thank you for your attention.

Now, my dear Peggie, be so good as excuse the freedom with which

[3] A reference to Andrew Michael Ramsay, *Les Voyages de Cyrus*, Book 2, end of the story of Selima: "Those who love each other purely will love thus forever; true love is immortal."

[4] Probably Elizabeth Boswell, the prospective second Lady Auchinleck.

[5] Someone whom she had suggested as a servant?

I have written. You may be certain that you see the worst of me; and I can assure you beforehand that no paragraph in any of my letters, or insinuation of my father's, ought to make you unhappy. I have erased from your letter the sentence which shocked me more than I can express. "Good God," said I, "is this her idea of love? Let me return to abandoned profligacy." So mad did you make me.[6] Adieu, my dearest. Ever yours,

J.B.

[Manuscript of *The Life of Johnson*]

On the 30 September we[7] dined together at the Mitre. I attempted to argue for the superior happiness of the savage life, upon the usual fanciful topics. He said, "Sir, there can be nothing more false. The savages have no bodily advantages beyond those of civilized men. They have not better health; and as to care or mental uneasiness they are not above it but below it, like bears. No, Sir, you are not to talk such paradox; let me have no more on't. It cannot entertain, it cannot instruct. Lord Monboddo, one of your Scotch judges, talked a great deal of such nonsense. I suffered *him*, but I will not suffer *you*." — BOSWELL. "But, Sir, does not Rousseau talk such nonsense?" JOHNSON. "True, Sir, but Rousseau *knows* he is talking nonsense, and laughs at the world for staring at him." BOSWELL. "How so, Sir?" JOHNSON. "Why, Sir, a man who talks nonsense so well must know that he is talking nonsense. But I am *afraid* (chuckling and laughing) Monboddo does *not* know that he is talking nonsense." BOSWELL. "Is it wrong then, Sir, to affect singularity in order to make people stare?"[8] JOHNSON. "Yes, if you do it by propagating error; and, indeed, it is wrong in every way. There is in human nature a general inclination to make people stare, and every wise man has himself to cure of it, and does cure himself. If you wish to make people stare by doing better than others, why, make them stare till they stare their eyes out. But consider how easy it is to make people stare by being absurd. I may do it by going into a drawing-room without my shoes. You remember

[6] Miss Montgomerie's shocking observation, so far as one can gather, amounted to no more than that she found nothing repugnant in second marriages.
[7] Johnson and Boswell.
[8] Perhaps Boswell was thinking of his masquerade appearance at the Jubilee.

the gentleman in *The Spectator* who had a commission of lunacy taken out against him for his extreme singularity, such as never wearing a wig but a nightcap. Now, Sir, abstractly the nightcap was best; but relatively the advantage was overbalanced by his making the boys run after him."[9]

Talking of a London life[1] he said, "The happiness of London is not to be conceived but by those who have been in it. I will venture to say there is more learning and science within the circumference of ten miles from where we now sit than in all the rest of the kingdom." BOSWELL. "The only disadvantage is the great distance at which people live from one another." JOHNSON. "Yes, Sir, but that is occasioned by the largeness of it, which is the cause of all the other advantages."[2] BOSWELL. "Sometimes I have been in the humour of wishing to retire to a desert." JOHNSON. "Sir, you have desert enough in Scotland."

Although I had proposed to myself a great deal of good conversation from him on the conduct of the married state, of which I had then a near prospect, he did not say much upon that topic. . . .

When I found fault with a gentleman of my acquaintance for entering into a second marriage,[3] as it showed a disregard of his first wife, he said, "Not at all, Sir. On the contrary, were he never to marry again, it might be concluded that his first wife had made him heartily sick of marriage; but by taking a second wife he pays the highest compliment to the first, by proving that she made him so happy as a married man that he has a mind to be so a second time." . . .

We drank tea with Mrs. Williams. I had last year had the pleasure of seeing Mrs. Thrale at Dr. Johnson's for a short while in a morning, and had conversation enough with her to admire her talents and to show her that I was as Johnsonian as herself. Dr. Johnson had prob-

---

[9] Johnson is recalling, somewhat inaccurately, *Spectator*, No. 576.

[1] As the Notes show, Boswell raised this topic by asking how Johnson could describe life when he had lived in Oxford and the Temple rather than in the world (see entry for 31 August 1769). Johnson replied, "Sir, I was in [the] world," and went on to say that one could "live and appear genteel" in London on £30 a year (see *Life*, under 1737).

[2] The Notes add: "BOSWELL. 'Is it not hurtful?' JOHNSON. 'No, Sir, health [is] as good [here as elsewhere].' "

[3] Lord Auchinleck, of course.

ably praised me, for this evening he delivered me the following card from Mr. Thrale and his *Thralia dulcis*,[4] in the fair handwriting of that lady. I preserve it as my first ticket to a great deal of most agreeable society: "Mr. and Mrs. Thrale present their best compliments to Mr. Boswell, and should think themselves highly favoured in his company to dinner at Streatham."

On the 6 of October I complied with this obliging invitation, and found, at a charming villa six miles from town, every circumstance that can make society valuable. Johnson, though quite at home, was yet looked up to with an awe tempered by affection, and seemed to be equally venerated by his host and hostess in their different ways. I rejoiced at seeing him so happy.

He played off his wit against Scotland with a good-humoured pleasantry, as giving me, though no bigot to national prejudices, an opportunity for a little contest with him. I having said that England was obliged to us for gardeners, almost all their good gardeners being Scotchmen; — JOHNSON. "Why, Sir, that is because gardening is much more necessary amongst you than with us, which makes so many of your people learn it. It is *all* gardening with you. Things which grow wild here must be cultivated with great care in Scotland. Pray now (throwing himself back in his chair and laughing), are you ever able to bring the *sloe* to perfection?"

I boasted that we had the honour of being the first to abolish the unhospitable and troublesome and ungracious custom of giving vails to servants. JOHNSON. "Sir, you abolished vails because you were too poor to be able to give them."

Mrs. Thrale disputed with him on the merit of Prior. He attacked him powerfully; said he wrote of love like a man who had never felt it. His love verses were college verses, and he repeated the song, "Alexis shunned his fellows swains," so ludicrously, that he made us laugh very heartily and wonder how anybody could have been seriously pleased with such fantastical stuff. Mrs. Thrale stood to her guns with great courage in defence of amorous ditties which Johnson despised, till he at last silenced her by saying, "My dear lady, talk no more of this. Nonsense can be defended but by nonsense."

[4] So Johnson had called Mrs. Thrale in a Latin ode to her, written on his tour to the Hebrides with Boswell in 1773.

Mrs. Thrale then praised Garrick's talent for light, gay, lively poetry, and, as a specimen, repeated his song in *Florizel and Perdita*, and dwelt with peculiar pleasure on this line:

I'd smile with the simple, and feed with the poor.

JOHNSON. "Nay, my dear lady, this will never do. Poor David! Smile with the simple! What folly is that! And who would feed with the poor that can help it? No, no, let me smile with the wise, and feed with the rich." I repeated this sally to Garrick, and wondered to find his sensibility as a writer much irritated by it. To console him, I observed that Johnson at times spared none of his friends; and I quoted the passage in Horace, *foenum habet in cornu*, where he represents one who attacks his friends for the sake of a laugh to be avoided as a pushing ox that is marked by a bunch of hay put upon his horns. "Ay," said Garrick vehemently, "he has a whole *mow* of it."

Talking of history Johnson said, "We may know historical facts to be true, as we may know facts in common life to be true. Motives are generally uncertain. We cannot trust to the characters which we find in history, unless when they are drawn by those who knew the persons: as those, for instance, by Sallust or by Lord Clarendon."

He would not allow much merit to Whitefield's oratory. "His popularity, Sir," said he, "is chiefly owing to the strangeness of his manner. He would be followed by crowds were he to wear a nightcap in the pulpit, or were he to preach from a tree."

I know not from what spirit of contradiction he burst out into a violent declamation against the Corsicans, of whose heroism I talked in high terms. "Sir," said he, "what is all this rout about the Corsicans? They have been at war with the Genoese for upwards of twenty years, and have never yet taken their fortified towns. They might have battered down the walls and reduced them to powder in twenty years. They might have pulled the walls in pieces, and cracked the stones with their teeth in twenty years." It was in vain to argue with him upon the want of artillery: his powerful imagination was not to be resisted for the moment.

On the evening of the 10 October, I presented Dr. Johnson to General Paoli.[5] I had greatly wished that two men for whom I had

[5] This appears to be a mistake. Boswell makes no mention in the Memorandum

the highest value should meet. They met with a manly ease, mutually conscious of their own abilities and of the abilities one of each other. The General spoke Italian and Dr. Johnson English, and understood one another very well with a little aid of interpretation from me, in which I compared myself to an isthmus which joins two great continents. Upon Johnson's entering the room the General said, "From what I have read of your works, Sir, and from what Mr. Boswell has told me of you, I have long had you in great esteem and veneration." The General talked of language being formed on the particular ideas and manners of a country, without knowing which we cannot know the language. We may know the direct signification of single words, but by these no beauty of expression, no sally of genius, no wit is conveyed to the mind. All this must be by allusion to other ideas. "Sir," said Johnson, "you talk of language as if you had never done anything else but study it, instead of governing a nation." The General said, *"Questo è un troppo gran complimento"* (this is too great a compliment). Johnson answered, "I should have thought so, Sir, if I had not heard you talk." The General asked him what he thought of the spirit of infidelity which was so prevalent. JOHNSON. "Sir, this gloom of infidelity, I hope, is only a transient cloud passing through the hemisphere which will soon be dissipated and the sun break forth with his usual splendour." "You think then," said the General, "that they will change their principles like their clothes." JOHNSON. "Why, Sir, if they bestow no more thought on principles than on dress, it must be so." The General said that "a great part of the fashionable infidelity was owing to a desire of showing courage. Men who have no opportunities of showing it in real life take death and futurity as objects on which to display it." JOHNSON. "That is mighty foolish affectation. Fear is one of the passions of human nature, of which it is impossible to divest it. You remember that the Emperor Charles V, when he read upon the tombstone of a Spanish nobleman, 'Here lies one who never knew fear,' wittily said, 'Then he has never snuffed a candle with his fingers.' "

He talked a few words of French to the General, but finding he did

covering this day that he had brought Paoli and Johnson together, and *The London Chronicle* (2 November 1769) declared that Boswell introduced Johnson to Paoli on 31 October.

not do it with facility, he asked for pen, ink, and paper, and wrote the following note:[6]

"I have read in the geography of Lucas de Linda a *Pater Noster* written in a language completely different from Italian and from all others which derive from Latin. The author calls it *linguam Corsicae rusticam*. It has perhaps been extinguished little by little, but it certainly once prevailed in the mountains and in the country. The same author says the same thing in talking of Sardinia: that there are two languages in the island, one of the cities, the other of the country."

The General immediately informed him that the *lingua rustica* was only in Sardinia.

Dr. Johnson went home with me, and drank tea till late in the night. He said General Paoli had the loftiest port of any man he had ever seen. He denied that military men were in general the most genteel, for "Perfect good breeding," he observed, "consists in having no particular mark of any profession, but a general elegant smoothness of manners; whereas in a military man you can commonly distinguish the marks of a soldier, *l'homme d'épée*."

He shunned tonight any discussion of the perplexed question of fate and free will, which I attempted to agitate: "Sir," said he, "we *know* our will is free, and *there's* an end on't."

SATURDAY 14 OCTOBER. Yesterday I breakfasted with Tom King, genteel, easy, and lively. Said he loved and respected Sheridan, but that he was mad on oratory and would persuade you that a man could not be a good gingerbread baker without it. Then Davies's a little. Heard from him that all Baretti's friends had been to see him, so you called at Newgate. But he was bailed. Then to Poultry; met Dilly and Baldwin and Rivington, and settled *London Magazine*.[7] Then Cleland; curious figure. Thought how 'twould have struck you some years ago. . . . [8]

[6] In French, which Boswell prints.

[7] Boswell became a part proprietor in the magazine, buying probably a one-fifth or sixth share. Later he published his *Hypochondriack* essays in it.

[8] John Cleland, whose *Fanny Hill, or, Memoirs of a Woman of Pleasure*, has often been called the most obscene book in English literature, though there is not a dirty word in it.

SUNDAY 15 OCTOBER. Yesterday breakfast, Forbes. He saw that incision was to be performed. Then strolled about. Called Kennedy; he frightened you. But no matter. Dined Charles Boswell, very well. Told him of Father's scheme. He said it amazed him. Said I, "One would have laid one hundred to one against it." "One hundred," said he; "ten thousand. I should have thought the chance was not upon the dice. It is enough to give one misanthropical ideas. Ay, to see what we may come to. I profess I am afraid to live till sixty." . . .

MONDAY 16 OCTOBER. Yesterday morning Duncan Forbes came, and with kindness to save dire forebodings *cut*. . . . Then called Kennedy; nonsense. Then Pott; sensible, neat, and fine.[9] . . . Journal all evening.

[Manuscript of *The Life of Johnson*]

He[1] honoured me with his company at dinner on the 16 of October at my lodgings in Old Bond Street, with Sir Joshua Reynolds, Mr. Garrick, Dr. Goldsmith, Mr. Murphy, Mr. Bickerstaff, and Mr. Thomas Davies. Garrick played round him with a fond vivacity, taking hold of the breasts of his coat, and, looking up in his face with a lively archness, talking how well he now was; while the Sage, shaking his head, beheld him with a gentle complacency. One of the company was late in coming. I started the usual question upon such occasions if I should not order dinner to be served, and said, "Ought six people to be kept waiting for one?" "Why, yes," answered Johnson, "if the one will suffer more by your sitting down than the six will do by waiting." There was a delicate humanity in this observation. Goldsmith, to divert the tedious minutes, strutted about bragging of his dress, and I believe was seriously vain of it, for his mind was wonderfully prone to that passion. "Come, come," said Garrick, "talk no more of that. You are, perhaps, the worst — eh, eh!" Goldsmith was

[9] Boswell wrote to John Johnston on 16 October: "My illness has taken various turns. At last I see a prospect of being soon perfectly well, and you may believe I am very much relieved, for I have been under sad anxiety. The knife has been absolutely necessary, and you know I am a very bad bearer of pain. However, the thoughts of being made well once for all cannot fail to cheer me." Dr. Harry Keil suggests that the incision was probably made to relieve a paraphimosis, though it is possible that some form of local infection was in question.
[1] Johnson.

eagerly breaking in, when Garrick went on, laughing ironically, "Nay, you will always *look* like a gentleman, but I am talking of being well or ill *dressed*." "Well, let me tell you," said Goldsmith, "when my tailor brought home my bloom-coloured coat, he said, 'Sir, I have a favour to beg of you. When anybody asks you who made your clothes, say John Filby at the Harrow in Water Lane.' " JOHNSON. "Why, Sir, that was because he knew the strange colour would attract crowds to gaze at it, and thus they might hear of him and see how well he might make a coat even of so absurd a colour."

When we were set down[2] our conversation first turned upon Pope. Johnson said his characters of men were admirably drawn, those of women not so well. He repeated to us, in his forcible, melodious manner, the character of Moore[3] and the concluding lines of *The Dunciad*. While the company were loud in praise of the lines, I ventured to say, "Too fine for such a poem: a poem on what?" JOHNSON (with a disdainful look), "Why, on *dunces*. It was worth while being a dunce then. Ah, Sir, hadst *thou* lived in those days! It is not worth while being a dunce now, when there are no wits." Bickerstaff observed, as a peculiar circumstance, that Pope's fame was higher when he was alive than now. Johnson said his *Pastorals* were poor things, though the versification was fine. He told us with high satisfaction the anecdote of Pope's inquiring who was the author of *London, a Satire*, and saying, he will be soon *déterré*.[4] He said that in Dryden's poetry there were passages drawn from a profundity which Pope could never reach. He repeated his lines on love (gentle, tempestuous, &c.; *look for them*),[5] and gave great applause to the character of Zimri. Goldsmith said that Pope's character of Addison was drawn deep from feeling and knowledge of the human heart. Johnson said that the description of the temple in *The Mourning Bride* was the finest poetical passage he had ever read; he recollected none in Shakespeare equal to it. "But," said Garrick (all alarmed for "the god of his idolatry"),[6] "we know not the extent and variety of

[2] "After dinner" according to the printed version of the *Life*.

[3] Probably the lines on James Moore Smythe (*Dunciad*, ii. 35–50).

[4] Unearthed. *London* was Johnson's first major poem.

[5] The parenthesis in the printed *Life* reads, "which I have now forgotten." The lines in question are probably those from *Tyrannic Love* which Johnson later quoted in his *Life of Dryden*.

[6] See *Romeo and Juliet*, II. ii. 114.

his powers. We are to suppose there are such passages in his works. Shakespeare must not suffer from the badness of our memories." Johnson, diverted by this enthusiastic jealousy, went on with greater keenness: "No, Sir. Congreve has *nature*" (smiling on the tragic eagerness of Garrick); but composing himself he added, "Sir, this is not comparing Congreve on the whole with Shakespeare on the whole, but only saying that Congreve has one finer passage than any that can be found in Shakespeare. Sir, a man may have no more than ten guineas in the world, but he may have those ten guineas in one piece; and so may have a finer piece than a man who has ten thousand pounds: but then he has but one ten-guinea piece. What I mean is that you can show me no passage equal to this where moral ideas are not mingled and there is simply a description of material objects, which produces such an effect." Mr. Murphy mentioned Shakespeare's description of the night before the Battle of Agincourt, but it was observed it had *men* in it. Mr. Davies suggested the speech of Juliet imaging what she should feel if she awaked in the tomb. Somebody mentioned the description of Dover Cliff. JOHNSON. "No, Sir, it should be all precipice — all vacuum. The crows impede your fall. The diminished appearance of the boats and the other circumstances may be all very good description, but do not at once affect the mind with the horrible idea of immense highth. The impression is divided; you pass on by computation from one stage of the tremendous space to another. Had the girl in *The Mourning Bride* said she could not cast her shoe to the top of one of the pillars in the temple, it would not have aided the idea, but on the contrary weakened it."

Talking of a barrister who had a bad utterance, some one (to rouse Johnson) wickedly said that it was a loss to him that he had not been taught oratory by Sheridan. JOHNSON. "Nay, Sir, if he had been taught by Sheridan he would have cleared the room." GARRICK. "Sheridan has too much vanity to be a good man." Now mark Johnson's mode of *defending* a man; taking him into his own hands, and discriminating. JOHNSON. "No, Sir. There is, to be sure, in Sheridan something to reprehend, and everything to laugh at; but, Sir, he is not a bad man. No, Sir, were mankind to be divided into good and bad, he would stand considerably within the ranks of good. And, Sir, it must be allowed that Sheridan excels in plain declamation, but he can exhibit no character." . . .

Mrs. Montagu, as the author of an *Essay on Shakespeare*, being mentioned; — REYNOLDS. "I think that *Essay* does her honour." JOHNSON. "Yes, Sir, it does *her* honour, but it would do nobody else honour. I have, indeed, not read it all. But when I take up the end of a web and find it packthread, I do not expect by looking farther to find embroidery. Sir, I will venture to say there is not a sentence of true criticism in it." GARRICK. "But, Sir, surely it shows how much Voltaire has mistaken the English, which nobody else has done." JOHNSON. "Sir, nobody else has thought it worth while. But what merit is there in that? You may as well talk of a schoolmaster whipping a boy for construing ill. No, Sir, there is no real criticism in it: none showing the beauty of thought, as coming from the human heart, from certain dispositions of the mind." . . .

Johnson went on with his notion of true criticism: "It is what the Scotchman[7] has attempted in his *Elements of Criticism*. I don't mean that he has taught us anything, but he has told us old things in a new way." MURPHY. "He seems to have read a great deal of French criticism and wants to make it his own, as if he had been for years anatomizing the heart of man and peeping into every cranny of it." GOLDSMITH. "It is easier to write that book than to read it." JOHNSON. "As an example of true criticism there is Burke's *Essay on the Sublime and Beautiful*; and, if I recollect, there is also Du Bos and Bouhours, who shows all beauty to depend on truth. There is no great merit in telling how many plays have ghosts in them, and how this ghost is better than that. You must show how terror is impressed on the human heart. In the description of night in *Macbeth*, the beetle and the bat detract from the general idea of darkness — inspissated gloom."

Politics being mentioned he said, "This petitioning is a new mode of distressing government, and a mighty easy one. I will undertake to get petitions either against quarter-guineas or half-guineas with the help of a little hot wine. There must be no yielding to encourage this. The object is not important enough. We are not to blow up half a dozen palaces because one cottage is burning."

The conversation then took another turn. JOHNSON. "It is amazing what ignorance of certain points one sometimes finds in men of

[7] Lord Kames.

eminence. A wit about town, who wrote Latin bawdy verses, asked me how England and Scotland, which were once two kingdoms, were now one; and a great barrister[8] did not seem to know that there were such publications as the Reviews.

"The ballad of *Hardyknute* is nothing extraordinary if it be really ancient.[9] People talk much of nature. But mere obvious nature may be shown with very little power of mind."

TUESDAY 17 OCTOBER. Donaldson the painter breakfasted with you; continued your miniature. He had fallen into the absurd practice of sneering at what is universally established: Pope, &c. Poor being then; so made him use hands and eyes only.

Called Mr. Johnson.[1] Talked of suicide, if a crime. He said, "Yes. Thought so by all Christians. Saul forsaken of God. Cut off leg to preserve life." BOSWELL. "But may it not be done to save many lives, if you can't bear torture and would discover?" JOHNSON. "Why, Sir, there's no end of arguing on improbable suppositions. And after all, you do not make out that what you allow is not vicious. Only this, that in a supposable case, a smaller vice is to be chosen rather than a greater." I instanced Turenne.[2] BOSWELL. "If you promise to a highwayman £100, should you keep it?" JOHNSON. "Why, yes. It is binding not as an obligation with respect to the highwayman but with respect to society, which has an interest that promises be kept and men do not explain them away." BOSWELL. "But, Sir, if £10,000?" JOHNSON. "Why, then, Sir, a man is to balance the circumstances. If himself alone concerned, 'tis binding." BOSWELL. "But he has perhaps a wife and family." JOHNSON. "Why, then, their claim in justice may be preferable. But, Sir, that kind of casuistical reasoning is very per-

[8] Sir Fletcher Norton.

[9] *Hardyknute* was published in 1719 as an ancient poem, but is generally believed to have been the composition of Lady Wardlaw of Pitreavie, who died in 1727. Percy, who had introduced the poem in the famous *Reliques* (1765), had cast doubt on its antiquity.

[1] The following conversation between Boswell and Johnson was overlooked when Boswell was writing the *Life*, and is printed here for the first time.

[2] The person instanced is undoubtedly the great seventeenth-century French general, the Vicomte de Turenne, but just what he is brought in to illustrate is not clear.

nicious. Rules cannot be given for improbable cases. One must judge when they happen. There may be with the temptation a way to escape not allowable but on necessity. Y'are not to stand forth and do wrong for good. Otherwise, there'd be no security, as the man who acts judges of the good." Dined London Tavern, &c. . . . Then *Jubilee* in Drury Lane.[3]

[Manuscript of *The Life of Johnson*]

On Thursday 19 October, I had a long evening with him[4] at his house by ourselves. He advised me to complete a Dictionary of words peculiar to Scotland, of which I showed him a specimen. "Sir," said he, "Ray has made a collection of North Country words. By collecting those of your country, you will do a useful thing towards the history of the language." He bade me also go on with collections which I was making upon the antiquities of Scotland. "Make a large book, a folio." BOSWELL. "But of what use will it be, Sir?" JOHNSON. "Never mind the use; do it."

I complained that he had never mentioned Garrick in his *Preface to Shakespeare*, and asked if he did not admire him. JOHNSON. "Yes, as 'a poor player, who frets and struts his hour upon the stage' — as a shadow."[5] BOSWELL. "But has he not brought Shakespeare into notice?" JOHNSON. "Sir, to allow that would be to lampoon the age. Many of Shakespeare's plays are the worse for being acted: *Macbeth*, for instance." BOSWELL. "What, Sir, with the advantages of decoration and action? No, I do wish that you had mentioned Garrick." JOHNSON. "My dear Sir, had I mentioned him, I must have mentioned many more: Mrs. Pritchard, Mrs. Cibber, — nay, and Mr. Cibber too; he too altered Shakespeare." BOSWELL. "You have read his *Apology*, Sir?" JOHNSON. "Yes, it is very entertaining. But as for Cibber himself, if you took from his conversation all that he ought not to have said, he was a poor creature. He was in earnest with his odes. I

[3] Garrick presented a stage version of the Stratford Jubilee as an afterpiece at the Drury Lane Theatre, in which Boswell saw himself (no doubt to his great satisfaction) impersonated by an actor. He seems, indeed, to have lent Garrick his costume so that the impersonation might be more apt.

[4] Johnson.

[5] See *Macbeth*, V. v. 24–25.

remember he brought me one to have my opinion of it, in which was this stanza:

> Perched on the eagle's soaring wing
> The lowly linnet loves to sing.

I could not bear such nonsense, and would not let him read his ode out; so little respect had I for *that great man!* (laughing). Yet I remember Richardson wondering that I could treat him with familiarity."

I mentioned to him that I had seen the execution of several convicts at Tyburn two days before, and that none of them seemed to be under any concern.[6] JOHNSON. "Most of them, Sir, have never thought at all." BOSWELL. "But is not the fear of death natural to us all?" JOHNSON. "So much so, Sir, that the whole of life is but keeping away the thoughts of it." He then, in a low and earnest tone, talked of his meditating upon the awful hour of his own dissolution, and in what manner he should behave upon that occasion: "I am uncertain," said he, "whether I should wish to have a friend by me, or have it all between God and myself."

Talking of our feeling for the distresses of others: — JOHNSON. "Why, Sir, there is much noise made about it, but it is not true. No, Sir, you have a decent feeling to prompt you to do good: more than that Providence does not intend. It would be misery to no purpose." BOSWELL. "But now if I were in danger of being hanged?" JOHNSON. "I should do what I could to bail you, but when you were once fairly hanged I should not suffer for you." BOSWELL. "Would you eat your dinner that day, Sir?" JOHNSON. "Yes, Sir, and eat it as if you were eating it with me. Why, there's Baretti who is to be tried for his life tomorrow; friends have risen up for him on every side, but if he should be hanged, none of those friends will eat a slice of plum pudding the less. Sir, that sympathetic feeling goes a very little way in depressing the mind."

[6] *The London Chronicle* printed Boswell's own report of the incident on 24 October: "As a strong instance of strange curiosity, James Boswell, Esquire, was observed last Wednesday at Tyburn when six men were executed. And in order to be as near as possible, where did he sit but on the top of the hearse which waited to carry away the body of George Low, one of the malefactors. 'A man so various,' &c."

I told him that I had dined lately at Foote's, who showed me a letter to him from Tom Davies, telling him that he had not been able to sleep from the concern which he felt on account of *this sad affair of Baretti*, begging of him to think if he could suggest anything that would be of service to Baretti; and, at the same time, recommending to him an industrious young man who kept a pickle shop. JOHNSON. "Ay, Sir, here you have a true specimen of human sympathy: a friend hanged, or a cucumber pickled. We know not whether Baretti or the pickle man has kept Davies from sleep, nor does he know himself. But, Sir, as to his not sleeping, Tom Davies is a very great man; Tom has been upon the stage, and knows how to do these things. I have not been upon the stage, and cannot do these things." BOSWELL. "I have blamed myself for not feeling for others in the keen manner that others say they do." JOHNSON. "Why, Sir, don't be duped by them any more, and, Sir, you will find these very feeling people are not very ready to do you good. They pay you by feeling." BOSWELL. "But I am uneasy that I do not feel enough." JOHNSON. "Why then, keep better company, and read melancholy stories."

BOSWELL. "Foote has a great deal of humour?" JOHNSON. "Yes, Sir." BOSWELL. "He has a singular talent of exhibiting character." JOHNSON. "Sir, it is not a talent, it is a vice; it is what others abstain from. It is not comedy, which exhibits the character of a species, as that of a miser gathered from many misers; it is farce, which gives individuals." BOSWELL. "Did not he think of exhibiting you, Sir?" JOHNSON. "Sir, fear restrained him; he knew I'd break his bones. I would have saved him the trouble of cutting off a leg; I would not have left him a leg to cut off."[7] BOSWELL. "Pray, Sir, is not Foote an infidel?" JOHNSON. "I do not know, Sir, that he is an infidel. But if he be an infidel, he is an infidel as a dog is an infidel; that is to say, he has never thought upon the subject." BOSWELL. "I suppose, Sir, he has thought superficially, and seized the first notions which occurred to his mind." JOHNSON. "Why, then, Sir, still he is like a dog that snatches the piece next him. Did you never observe that dogs have not the power of comparing? A dog will take a small bit of meat as soon as a big, when both are before him.

[7] Foote had lost a leg in 1766 through a fall from a high-spirited horse on which he had been mounted as a practical joke.

"Buchanan has fewer centos[8] than any modern Latin poet. He not only had great knowledge of the Latin language, but was a great poet. Both the Scaligers praise him."

He again talked of the passage in Congreve with high commendation, and said, "Shakespeare never has six lines together without a fault. Perhaps you may find seven, but this is not against my general assertion. If I come to an orchard and say there's no fruit here, and then comes a poring man and finds two apples and two pears, and says, 'Sir, you are mistaken; I have found both apples and pears,' I should laugh at him: what would that be to the purpose?"

BOSWELL. "What do you think of Dr. Young's *Night Thoughts*, Sir?" JOHNSON. "Why, there are very fine things in them." BOSWELL. "Is there not less religion in the nation now, Sir, than there was formerly?" JOHNSON. "Why, I don't know not." BOSWELL. "For instance, there used to be a chaplain in every great family, which is not the case now." JOHNSON. "Neither do you find many of the state servants which great families used formerly to have. There is a change of modes in the whole deportment of life."

Next day, 20 October, he appeared, for the only time I suppose in his life, as a witness in a court of justice, being called to give evidence to the character of Signor Baretti, who had stabbed a man in the street, and was arraigned at the Old Bailey for murder.[9] Never did such a constellation of genius enlighten the awful Sessions House: Mr. Burke, Mr. Garrick, Mr. Beauclerk, and Dr. Johnson; and undoubtedly their favourable testimony had much weight with the court and jury.[1] Johnson gave his evidence in a slow, deliberate, and distinct manner, and with a minuteness of circumstance which was uncommonly impressive. It is well known that Mr. Baretti was acquitted.

On the 26 of October, we dined together at the Mitre Tavern. I found fault with Foote for making a fool of his company. JOHNSON. "Why, Sir, when you go to see Foote, you do not go to see a saint: you

---

[8] Compositions made up of bits from other authors.

[9] Baretti was accosted in the street by two prostitutes, and drove one off with a blow of the hand. Three bullies, friends of the women, then attacked him, and in self-defence he stabbed one of them mortally with a pocket fruit knife.

[1] Goldsmith and Reynolds were also witnesses.

go to see a man who will live at your house and then bring you on a public stage; who will have you at his house for the very purpose of bringing you on a public stage. Sir, he does not make fools of his company; they whom he exposes are fools already; he only brings them into action."

Talking of trade, he observed, "It is a mistaken notion that a great deal of money is brought into the nation by trade. It is not so. Commodities come for commodities, but trade produces no capital accession of wealth. But, though there should be little profit in money, there is a considerable profit in pleasure, as it gives to one nation the productions of another; as we have wines and fruits and many other foreign articles brought to us." BOSWELL. "Yes, Sir, and there is a profit in pleasure, by its procuring occupation to mankind." JOHNSON. "Why, Sir, you cannot call that pleasure to which all are averse, and which none begin but with the hopes to be idle; a thing which men dislike before they have tried it, and when they have tried it." BOSWELL. "But, Sir, the mind must be employed, and we grow weary if idle." JOHNSON. "That is, Sir, because others are busy, and we want company; but if we were all idle, there would be no wearying; we should all entertain one another. There is, indeed, this in trade: it gives an opportunity for change of situation amongst men. If there were no trade, those who are poor would always remain poor. But no man loves labour for itself." BOSWELL. "Yes, Sir, my father does. He is a very laborious judge, and he loves the labour." JOHNSON. "Sir, that is because he loves respect and distinction. Could he have them without labour, he would like it better." BOSWELL. "He tells me he likes it for itself." JOHNSON. "Why, Sir, he fancies so, because he is not accustomed to abstract."

We went home to his house to tea. Mrs. Williams made it with sufficient dexterity notwithstanding her blindness, though her manner of satisfying herself that the cups were full enough was a little awkward. She put her finger down a certain way till she felt the tea touch it.[2] In my first elation at being allowed the privilege of attend-

[2] Boswell toned down this account of Mrs. Williams's manner of pouring tea in the printed *Life*, saying rather that such *seemed* to be her method; he added in a footnote in the second edition that he had since been given reason to think that she could estimate the amount of tea in a cup by feeling its outside.

ing Dr. Johnson at his late visits to this lady, which was like being *e secretioribus consiliis*,[3] I willingly drank cup after cup, as if it had been the Heliconian spring. But as the charm of novelty went off, I grew more fastidious; and besides I discovered that she was of a peevish temper.

There was a pretty large circle this evening. Dr. Johnson was in very good humor, lively, and ready to talk upon all subjects. Mr. Ferguson, the astronomer, told him of a new-invented machine which went without horses. A man who sat in it turned a handle which worked a spring that drove it forward. "Then, Sir," said Johnson, "what is gained is, the man has his choice whether he will move himself alone, or himself and the machine too." Dominiceti being mentioned, he was violent against him, and said, "There is nothing in all this boasted system. No, Sir, medicated baths can be no better than warm water: their only effect can be that of tepid moisture." One of the company[4] took the other side, very keenly maintaining that medicines of various sorts, and some too of most powerful effect, are introduced into the human frame by the medium of the pores; and, therefore, when warm water is impregnated with salutiferous substances it may produce great effects as a bath. This appeared to me very satisfactory. Johnson did not answer it; but talking for victory, and determined to be master of the field, he had recourse to the device which Goldsmith imputed to him in the witty words of one of Cibber's comedies: "There is no arguing with Johnson, for 'when his pistol misses fire, he knocks you down with the butt end of it.' "[5] He turned to the gentleman, "Well, Sir, go to Dominiceti, and get thyself fumigated; and let the steam be directed to thy *head*, for *there's* the *peccant part*."[6] This produced a triumphant roar of laughter from the motley assembly of philosophers, printers, and dependents, male and female.

I know not how I came to introduce so wild a supposition, but I

[3] One of the inner circle.
[4] Probably Boswell himself.
[5] Altered from *The Refusal*, act 1.
[6] Pope, *Essay on Man*, ii. 143–144:

> Imagination plies her dangerous art,
> And pours it all upon the peccant part.

ventured to say, "If, Sir, you were shut up in a castle, and a new-born child with you, what should you do?" JOHNSON. "Why, Sir, I should not much like my company." BOSWELL. "But would you bring it up?" He seemed, as may well be supposed, unwilling to pursue the subject; but, upon my persevering in my question, replied, "Why yes, Sir, I would; but I must have all conveniencies. If I had no garden, I would make a shed on the roof, and take it there for fresh air. I should feed it, and wash it much, and with warm water to please it, not with cold water to give it pain." BOSWELL. "But, Sir, does not heat relax?" JOHN-SON. "Sir, you are not to suppose the water is to be very hot. I would not *coddle* the child.[7] No, Sir, the hardy method of breeding up children does no good. I'll take you five children from London, who shall cuff five Highland children. Sir, a man bred in London will carry a burthen or run or wrestle as well as one brought up in the hardiest manner in the country." BOSWELL. "Good living, I suppose, makes the Londoners strong." JOHNSON. "Why, Sir, I don't know that it does. Our chairmen from Ireland, who are as strong men as any, have been brought up upon potatoes. Quantity makes up for quality." BOSWELL. "Would you teach your child anything?" JOHNSON. "No, I should not be apt to teach it." BOSWELL. "Would not you have a pleasure in teaching it?" JOHNSON. "No, Sir, I should *not* have a pleasure in teaching it." BOSWELL. "Have you not a pleasure in teaching men? — *there* I have you. You have the same pleasure in teaching men that I should have in teaching children." JOHNSON. "Why, something about that."

BOSWELL. "Do you think, Sir, that what is called natural affection is born with us? It appears to me to be the effect of habit, or of gratitude for kindness. No child has it for a parent whom it has not seen." JOHNSON. "Why, Sir, I think there is an instinctive natural affection in parents towards their children."

Russia being mentioned as likely to become a great nation by the rapid increase of population: — JOHNSON. "Why, Sir, I see no prospect of their propagating more. They can have no more children than they can get. I know of no way to make them breed more than they do. It is not from reason and prudence that people marry, but from inclination. A man is poor; he thinks, 'I cannot be worse, and so I'll

[7] By "relax" Boswell means "enfeeble." And by "coddle" Johnson means "parboil" (as in the expression "a coddled egg"), not "pamper."

e'en take Peggie.' " BOSWELL. "But have not nations been more popu-
lous at one period than another?" JOHNSON. "Yes, Sir, but that has
been owing to the people being less thinned at one period than another, whether by emigrations, war, or pestilence, not by their being
more or less prolific. Births at all times bear the same proportion to
the same number of people." BOSWELL. "But to consider the state of
our own country; does not throwing a number of farms into one hand
hurt population?" JOHNSON. "Why no, Sir, the same quantity of food
being produced will be consumed by the same number of mouths,
though the people may be disposed of in different ways. We see now if
corn be dear and butchers' meat cheap, the farmers all apply themselves to the raising of corn till it becomes plentiful and cheap, and
then butchers' meat becomes dear; so that an equality is always preserved. No, Sir, let fanciful men do as they will, depend upon it, it
is difficult to spoil the system of life." BOSWELL. "But, Sir, is it not a
very bad thing for landlords to oppress their tenants by raising their
rents?" JOHNSON. "Very bad. Why, Sir, it never can have any general
influence. It may distress some individuals. But consider this: landlords cannot do without tenants. Now tenants will not give more for
land than it is worth. If they can make more of their money by keeping a shop or any other way they'll do it, and so oblige landlords to
let land come back to a reasonable rent, in order that they may get
tenants. Land in England is an article of commerce. A tenant who
pays his landlord his rent thinks himself no more obliged to him than
you think yourself obliged to a man in whose shop you buy a piece of
goods. He knows the landlord lets him have his land for no less than
he can get from others, in the same manner as the shopkeeper sells
his goods. No shopkeeper sells a yard of riband for sixpence when
sevenpence is offered for it." BOSWELL. "But, Sir, is it not better that
tenants should be dependant on landlords?" JOHNSON. "Why, Sir, as
there are many more tenants than landlords, and a state of dependence is not a desirable state, we should wish not. But, if you please,
you may let your lands cheap, and so get the value, part in money,
part in homage. I should agree with you in that." BOSWELL. "So, Sir,
you laugh at schemes of political improvement?" JOHNSON. "Why,
Sir, most schemes of political improvement are very laughable
things."

He observed, "Providence has wisely ordered that the more numerous men are the more difficult it is for them to agree in anything, and so they are governed. There is no doubt that if the poor should reason, 'We'll be the poor no longer, we'll make the rich take their turn,' they could easily do it, only that they could not agree. So the common soldiers, though so much more numerous than their officers, are governed by them for the same reason."

He said, "Mankind have a strong attachment to the habitations to which they have been accustomed. You see the inhabitants of Norway do not with one consent leave it and go to some country in America where there is a mild climate and where they may have the same produce from land with the tenth part of the labour. No, Sir, the attachment to their accustomed dwellings and the terror of a general change keep them at home. So we see many of the finest spots in the world thinly inhabited and many rugged spots well inhabited."

The London Chronicle, which was the only newspaper he constantly took in since I was acquainted with him, being brought, the office of reading it aloud was assigned to me. I was diverted by his impatience. He made me pass over so many parts of it that my task was very easy. He would not suffer one of the petitions to the King about the Middlesex election to be read.

I had hired a Bohemian as my servant while I remained in London, and being much pleased with him, I asked Dr. Johnson if his being a Roman Catholic should prevent my taking him home to my family. JOHNSON. "Why no, Sir. If *he* has no objection, you can have no objection." BOSWELL. "So, Sir, you are no great enemy to the Popish religion." JOHNSON. "No more, Sir, than to the Presbyterian religion." BOSWELL. "You are joking." JOHNSON. "No, Sir, upon honour I think so. Nay, Sir, of the two, I prefer the Popish." BOSWELL. "How so, Sir?" JOHNSON. "Why, Sir, the Presbyterians have no church, no apostolical ordination." BOSWELL. "And do you think that absolutely essential, Sir?" JOHNSON. "Why, Sir, as it was an apostolical institution, I think it is dangerous to be without it. And, Sir, the Presbyterians have no public worship: they have no form of prayer in which they know they can join. They go to hear a man pray, and are to judge whether they will join with him." BOSWELL. "But, Sir, their doctrine is the same with that of the Church of England. Their Confession of Faith and the Thirty-nine Articles contain the same points, even the doctrine of predestination." JOHNSON. "Why yes, Sir, predestination was a part of the clamour of the times, so it is mentioned in our Articles, but as little positively as could be." BOSWELL. "Is it necessary, Sir, to believe all the Thirty-nine Articles?" JOHNSON. "Why, Sir, that is a question which has been much agitated. Some have thought it necessary that they should all be believed; others have considered them to be only articles of peace; that is to say, you are not to preach against them." BOSWELL. "It appears to me, Sir, that predestination, or what is equivalent to it, cannot be avoided, if we hold an universal prescience in God." JOHNSON. "Why, Sir, does not God every day see things going on and does not prevent them?" BOSWELL. "True, Sir, but if a thing be *certainly* foreseen, it must be fixed, and cannot happen otherwise; and if we apply this consideration to the human mind, there is no free will, nor do I see how prayer can be of any avail." He mentioned Dr. Clarke, and Bishop Bramhall on liberty and necessity, and bid me read South's sermons on prayer, but avoided the question which has excruciated philosophers and divines beyond any other. I did not press it farther when I perceived that he was displeased and shrunk from any abridgement of an attribute usually ascribed to the Divinity, however irreconcilable in its full extent with the grand system of moral government. His supposed orthodoxy here cramped the vigorous powers of his understanding. He was confined by a chain which early imagination and long habit made him think massy and strong, but which, had he ventured to try, he could at once have snapped asunder.

I proceeded: "What do you think, Sir, of the doctrine of purgatory, as believed by the Roman Catholics?" JOHNSON. "Why, Sir, it is a very harmless doctrine. They are of opinion that the generality of mankind are neither so obstinately wicked as to deserve everlasting punishment, nor so good as to deserve to be admitted into the society of blessed spirits; and therefore that God is graciously pleased to allow of a middle state, where they may be purified by certain degrees of suffering. You see, Sir, there is nothing unreasonable in this." BOSWELL. "But then, Sir, their masses for the dead?" JOHNSON. "Why, Sir, if it be once established that there are souls in purgatory, it is as proper to pray for *them* as for our brethren of mankind who are yet alive." BOSWELL. "But the idolatry of the mass?" JOHNSON. "Sir, there is no idolatry in the mass. They believe God to be there, and they adore him." BOSWELL. "The worship of saints?" JOHNSON. "Sir, they do not worship saints, they invoke them; they only ask their prayers. I am talking all this time of the *doctrines* of the Church of Rome. I grant you that in *practice*, purgatory is made a lucrative imposition, and that the people do become idolatrous as they recommend themselves to the tutelary protection of particular saints. I think their giving the sacrament only in one kind is criminal, because it is contrary to the express institution of Christ, and I wonder how the Council of Trent admitted it." BOSWELL. "Confession?" JOHNSON. "Why, I don't know but that is a good thing. The Scripture says, 'Confess your faults one to another,' and the priests confess as well as the laity. Then it must be considered that their absolution is only upon repentance, and often upon penance also. You think your sins may be forgiven without penance, upon repentance alone." . . . [8]

When we were alone I introduced the subject of death, and endeavoured to maintain that the fear of it might be got over. I told him that David Hume said he was no more uneasy to think he should *not be* after this life than that he *had not been* before he began to exist. JOHNSON. "Sir, if a man really thinks so his perceptions are disturbed, he is mad; if he does not think so, he lies. Hume knows he lies. He may tell you he holds his finger in the flame of a candle without feeling pain; would you believe him? When he dies, he at least gives up all he has." BOSWELL. "Foote, Sir, told me that when he was very ill he was not afraid to die." JOHNSON. "It is not true, Sir. Hold a pistol to Foote's breast or to Hume's breast and threaten to kill them, and you'll see how they behave." BOSWELL. "But may we not calm our minds for the approach of death?" — Here I am sensible I was in the wrong to bring before his view what he ever looked upon with horror; for, although when in a celestial frame in his *Vanity of Human Wishes* he can suppose death to be "kind Nature's signal for retreat" from this state of being to "a happier seat," the general state of his thoughts upon this awful transition was dismally apprehensive. Garrick told me that he believed him to be harassed with doubts. I

[8] Boswell goes on to remark in the printed *Life* that this is an accurate account of what Johnson had said, but if someone "had taken the other side he might have reasoned differently."

agreed, and said his mind resembled the vast amphitheatre, the Colosseum at Rome. In the centre stands his judgment like a mighty gladiator, which combats doubts that like the wild beasts are all around in cells ready to be let out upon him. He grumbles and growls while they foam and roar. They fight, and he drives them back into their dens, but never kills them, so that they are always coming out again upon him. To my question, if we might not calm our minds for the approach of death, he answered in passion, "No, Sir, let it alone. It matters not how a man dies, but how he lives. The act of dying is not of importance, it lasts so short a time." He added, with an earnest look, "A man knows it must be, and submits. It will do him no good to whine."

I attempted to continue the conversation. He was so provoked that he said, "Give us no more of this," and was thrown into such a state of tumult that he expressed himself in a way that alarmed and distressed me; showed an impatience to have me leave him, and, when I was going away, said, "Don't let us meet tomorrow."

I went home exceedingly uneasy. All the harsh observations which I had ever heard made upon his character crowded into my mind; and I seemed to myself like the man who had put his head into a lion's mouth a great many times with perfect safety, but at last had it bit off.

Next morning I sent him a note acknowledging that I might have been in the wrong, but it was not intentionally; he was therefore, I could not help thinking, too severe upon me. That notwithstanding our agreement not to meet today, I would call in my way to the City, and stay five minutes by my watch. "You are," said I, "in my mind since last night surrounded with cloud and storm. Let me have a glimpse of sunshine, and go about my affairs in serenity and cheerfulness."

Upon entering his study I was glad that he was not alone, which would have made our meeting more awkward. There were with him Mr. Steevens and Mr. Tyers, both of whom I now saw for the first time. My note had, or[9] his own reflection, softened his ferocity, for he

---

[9] Since Boswell's *r*'s and *n*'s are ordinarily identical, this might be read "on" as it is printed in the *Life*. Nevertheless, in this case, it looks much more like "or," as Hill conjectured it might be. The phrase, "or his own reflection," is inserted

received me very complacently; so that I unexpectedly found myself at ease, and joined in the conversation.

He said the critics had done too much honour to Sir Richard Blackmore in writing so much against him. That his *Creation* had been helped by various wits, a line by Philips and a line by Tickell; so that by their aid and that of others the poem had been made out.

I defended Blackmore's lines, which have been celebrated for absolute nonsense:

> A painted vest Prince Voltiger had on,
> Which from a naked Pict his grandsire won.[1]

I maintained it to be a poetical conceit. A Pict being painted, if he is slain in battle and a vest is made of his skin, it is a painted vest won from him, though he was naked.

Johnson spoke unfavourably of a certain pretty voluminous author, saying, "He used to write anonymous books and then other books commending those books, in which there was something of rascality."

I whispered him, "Well, Sir, you are now in good humour." JOHNSON. "Yes, Sir." I was going to leave him, and had got as far as the staircase. He stopped me, and smiling said, "Get you gone — *in*"; a curious mode of inviting me to stay, which I accordingly did for some time longer. . . .

[Received ?23 October, Margaret Montgomerie to Boswell]

Lainshaw, 17 October 1769

ON SATURDAY YOU WILL RECEIVE MY LETTER OF THE 15TH with the paragraph on friendship which I transcribed from *Cyrus*. I thought it applicable, as like Araspes I have had my fears, whilst you, with a generosity equal to the Persian monarch, removed them by your assurance of unalterable regard and affection.[2] I likewise thought it

---

above the line in the manuscript, and perhaps Boswell actually meant to put it before rather than after "had." If so, the printer may have read "on" because it made more sense considering where the phrase is inserted.

[1] Actually, as Boswell pointed out in a note to the second edition of the *Life*, these lines are a parody of a passage in *The British Princes* by the Hon. Edward Howard.

[2] *Les Voyages de Cyrus*, in the middle of the third book.

would please you to see I was paying some attention to a language which you wish me to understand. I hope with your assistance I shall make some proficience, but at present my mind is too much taken up to apply to what requires a good deal of study.

I have read your *Tour to Corsica* with great pleasure and shall read the *History* also.

We had a meeting today about settling the turnpike road from Stewarton to Kilmarnock. Lord Eglinton and Captain Montgomerie-Cuninghame are on opposite sides. There has no great friendship subsisted between them for some years, and any difference in opinion or interest augments a disgust which is at best only smothered. It's a most disagreeable thing to live at variance with one's neighbours; at least it appears so to me, whose wish it is to live in peace with all the world. But I cannot answer for myself if I was as wealthy as some people. Riches often brings such a spirit of independence that its possessors are apt to forget they have superiors. I mean those who acquire the advantages of fortune at a time of life when the love of the world begins to take root in their minds; with such, in the Apocryphal style, "according to their riches, so is their anger."[3]

The Rambler has a very good paper on foolish passion. He has drawn a most natural picture of a domestic tyrant.[4] It appears pretty much the character of an acquaintance of yours: rough at the best, his passion seems to gather strength as his body decays. Don't tell me of your being hot tempered. Where a man has sense and any degree of politeness, I never think there's any fear of his allowing himself to be transported beyond the bounds of good nature. If you are angry at me at times I shall always suppose myself in the wrong, as I'm positive I must be; but I shall likewise trust to your generosity for pardon when I acknowledge my fault. I have ever met with this indulgence from you, and I fear not that you will deny me when you have me, if possible, more in your power.

I flatter myself my temper is much calmed of late. I am sure I can bear a great deal from one I really like, and also am positive that your advice and opinion will have its due weight with me.

I have sent you inclosed a brass ring as a measure. It is fully wide,

[3] Altered from Ecclesiasticus 28. 10.

[4] No. 11. Apparently Lord Auchinleck is meant.

but I could get nothing that fitted so well except the one I have with my brother and sisters' hair; however, you will order it a very little less.

I wish to see your friend the General; at the same time I am afraid I should make a very awkward figure.[5] Consider me living at Lainshaw, unaccustomed to see the face of a creature except our own family, and you will not wonder at my being apprehensive of appearing greatly to the disadvantage before so great a man. I cannot think he will leave London before the meeting of Parliament, as the favourable reception he has met with from our good King will, I hope, assist him to make friends amongst the people in power, who may in some period, I hope not far distant, be helpful in restoring him to his beloved Corsica.[6]

My anxiety is certainly too great. I went to the post-office, and, because there was no letters, which I might reasonably have expected would be the case, I was uneasy and disappointed. Perhaps you will be in Devonshire before this reaches London. I wish you safely there, and that you may find your deservedly esteemed friend happy and well. Ask him if he thinks you had cause for being as angry at me as you say you was for what I formerly wrote. Do you recollect a book you gave me, of which I remember nothing more than the name (Smith on *The Theory of Moral Sentiment*), except one observation, to wit: that a person is much more displeased when their friend does not enter warmly into their sentiments than when they appear insensible of the merit and good qualities of those they love?[7] It's perhaps not expressed in this manner, but it runs in my mind that it's something to the same purpose. I wish I had a memory equal to Paoli's, but I find myself very different as to that. I trust I shall hear from you tomorrow. I beg you will observe this is the third letter I have wrote without once enquiring when you propose being home. I saw Mr. Montgomerie, Coilsfield and Mr. Hamilton, Sundrum. They joked me a good deal, but were pleased to signify how much they rejoiced at the prospect of having me for a near neighbour.

We have Treesbank and Hugh Campbell tonight. I must draw my

[5] Boswell wrote to John Johnston on 16 October that the General "has promised me that he will go to Scotland, and I have hopes that he will go down the beginning of next month and be present at my marriage."

[6] For what follows, see p. 229 *n*.2.

[7] See Part I, Section i, Ch. 2, entitled, "Of the Pleasure of Mutual Sympathy."

letter to a conclusion, as I scruple to trouble you with such long, stupid scrawls. I shall therefore, though unwillingly, bid my dear friend adieu, after assuring him that I sincerely am his ever faithful and affectionate

M.M.

[Received ?30 October, Margaret Montgomerie to Boswell]

Lainshaw, 24 October 1769

I AM JUST RETURNED FROM THE POST-OFFICE quite disappointed at not receiving a letter from my dear friend. I was not well and very low spirited, and therefore stood in need of comfort, but your former goodness to me puts it out of my power to complain. I have just now had very melancholy accounts of poor Lord Eglinton. He was on his way to Lord Glasgow's and met an excise officer amongst his enclosure at Ardrossan; as he is a notorious poacher, my Lord ordered him to deliver his gun, which he positively refused, adding he would part[8] with it and life together. My Lord upon this jumped out of his coach, and the fellow presented his piece to him, warning him to keep off; in the mean time Campbell's foot struck a stone and he fell back into a furrow; when, seeing Lord Eglinton advancing towards him, he fired and shot him through the body. Expresses are gone every way for assistance, but, by the accounts I have received, I'm afraid all is over with him. I have sent off to get the particulars from Charles Crookshanks,[9] and shall be able to give you distinct information about this unhappy affair as soon as the express returns.

The man has just arrived and has brought me a letter from one of the surgeons, which I inclose to you. Oh, what a melancholy thing it is to lose one's friend in such a shocking, barbarous manner! The fellow is put in jail, and was examined before the magistrates of Irvine. He confessed he shot my Lord, but insists that he was in the way of his duty and therefore not culpable. He had information of smugglers coming that way, if one can credit his method of telling the story. But surely the law was open to him; if my Lord did an unwarrantable thing, he therefore ought to have sought his redress in that way.

What an afflicted family! Poor Lady Eglinton[1] parted with him in

[8] Typescript, "hunt."
[9] Lord Eglinton's steward in England.
[1] His mother. Eglinton never married, but is said at the time of his death to have

great health and spirits, and in a few hours after had him brought. back a woeful, bloody spectacle.

How vain, how transitory, is every earthly enjoyment! O that such a striking instance of mortality may teach us to keep in mind our latter end, and so to number our days as to apply our hearts unto wisdom.[2]

I cannot write anything else, I am so distressed with this sad accident. I really hardly know what I am doing. Write me soon, my dear Jamie, and tell me how you do. I am more and more anxious about you. When I feel so much for the danger an old and intimate acquaintance is in, what must I not suffer for the man I prefer to every earthly being, when I consider that he is not well, and, for aught I know, may at present be under the greatest distress?

I suppose next letter I write will inform you that your old friend is now no more. I was told so this moment, but as it was not from certain authority I do not assert it for a truth, though Mr. Fleming's account makes it extremely probable.[3]

Adieu, my dearest friend. May the Almighty bless and preserve you to your ever faithful and affectionate

M.M.

[Boswell to Margaret Montgomerie]

Mamhead, Sunday evening [5 November] 1769

MY DEAREST LOVE, — Times and places have much influence on souls so happily enthusiastic as mine. You know this, and therefore you will easily conceive what are my calm, agreeable feelings on a Sunday evening at the parsonage of Temple, my old and most intimate friend. I got here to breakfast on Friday morning, and had the pleasure to find Mr. and Mrs. Temple very well. The parsonage is a small thatched house. But it contains several very tolerable rooms, which are neatly fitted up so that one may live in them comfortably enough.

---

been engaged to Mrs. Jean Montgomerie, Margaret Montgomerie's widowed sister-in-law.

[2] See Psalms 90. 12.

[3] Eglinton did, in fact, die that night. Fleming was the surgeon referred to earlier. His letter has not been recovered.

We passed the day on Friday very happily. I found myself quite at home. Mrs. Temple is an amiable, well-behaved young woman, and is interested about me as if I had been her friend as long as I have been that of her husband. My friend has a fine boy about fourteen months old. He was privately baptized long ago. But yesterday we had him solemnly admitted a Christian in the church, where I stood as godfather to him. Mr. Harington, a clergyman in the neighbourhood, who stood for the other godfather, a gentleman now in London, dined with us. He is a man of an ancient family and a high Tory, so was an admirable companion for me. Yesterday passed away in conversation and friendly sentiment more valuable than I can describe without appearing to exaggerate.

I have been today at the parish church. It is a small, old building, but like every church in England, even the smallest, has something venerable and ornamental about it. There is a ring of five bells. Some pillars in the church. Some curious painted glass in the windows, and some inscriptions on the walls. Over the door is, "To him that knocketh it shall be opened." On one side fronting the pulpit is, "Wherewith shall I come before the Lord," &c., from Micah — "To do justly, love mercy, and walk humbly with thy God" — and over the communion table in a little chancel railed in with Gothic carving in wood, "But let a man examine himself, and so let him eat of this bread and drink of this cup."[4] My friend preached on II Timothy, chapter 1, verse 10: "Our Saviour Jesus Christ hath brought life and immortality to light by the gospel." He gave us an excellent consolatory discourse on the immortality of the soul. He has a very small congregation, not above fifty people. I was in the best frame imaginable, full of present contentment and future hope.

I wish you was here with me. We all flatter ourselves with that prospect. Devonshire is a delightful country. This parsonage has a good glebe, and a charming prospect both of land and sea. Mr. Temple is to accompany me this evening to Exeter, from whence I set out tomorrow morning at one in the post-coach for London. This visit to my friend has fully answered my expectations. Adieu, my dearest love. I am ever your faithful and affectionate

　　　　　　　　　　　　　　　　　　　　　　　　　　　J.B.

[4] Luke 11. 10; Micah 6. 6, 6. 8; I Corinthians 11. 28.

[Received ?8 November, Margaret Montgomerie to Boswell]

Lainshaw, 31 October 1769

AFTER INFORMING YOU THAT I HAVE RECEIVED BOTH YOUR AGREE-ABLE LETTERS,[5] it is almost unnecessary to say how happy they made me, as you must ere now be persuaded that every proof of your affection and remembrance confers an obligation on your grateful friend. I shall say nothing of the one dated the second of October; only you are sensible I am not without feeling, so can easily imagine I could not read it without pain.

Though you may believe I wished and likewise expected to have seen you sooner than I now can; yet, as you tell me your absence is necessary, I submit. I cannot help being uneasy at the thoughts of General Paoli's being witness to the ceremony. It's at any rate an awful affair, and would be doubly so in the presence of so great a man. To be sure, I ought to carry my views much higher and consider myself before the Supreme Being, but sensible objects have too great an effect on our minds, and are apt to draw them off from things of greater importance. I sincerely wish he may not come, but if he does, and you signify to me your desire to have him, you may believe I shall agree, whatever it should cost me. Do not again take a disgust at me and think me a weak, awkward, spiritless being. Remember, with advantages vastly superior to mine, you yourself was uneasy in the presence of the illustrious Chief. You bid me tell you every thought of my heart and have no other confidant but you. I really have none, and do fairly acknowledge to you that I wish you could steal out of Edinburgh when nobody can suspect where you are going, and let the ceremony be put over as privately as possible, as I would like to remain in the country till you thought it necessary for me to come to town; however, determine on whatever is most agreeable and convenient for yourself, and be assured I shall willingly comply with whatever you judge right.

You would be greatly shocked with the accounts of poor Lord Eglinton's death. His murderer is nephew to Netherplace. I doubt not but they will apply to you to be his counsel, but I am likewise certain their application will be in vain. It was put in the newspapers that it was accidental, but my Lord expressed himself in a very different

[5] These letters have not been recovered.

manner, and his servants were witnesses to its being designed. I forgot if I told you Lord Eglinton settled £100 a year on Charles Crookshanks and two hundred a year on Mrs. Brown.[6]

My sister talks of being in Edinburgh in ten days to settle her eldest son at the college, and secure a house for herself and family. I wish you could come west while she remains in town. I am clearly of opinion you should continue your servant, and I don't believe that his wages are higher than Thomas's were; but you may try if he will agree to the same terms, as it will not sound so ill to the Commissioner and some more of your economical friends.

I hope you will not be angry at me for objecting to the presence of Paoli. I am only telling you my uneasiness, at the same time assuring you that I shall do all in my power to get the better of it. This will not reach you till after your return from Devonshire, but I hope I shall hear from you while there. I must now conclude with assuring you that I sincerely am my dear Jamie's ever faithful and affectionate

M.M.

[Received ?8 November, Margaret Montgomerie to Boswell]

Lainshaw, 2 November 1769

I HOPE THIS WILL FIND MY DEAR FRIEND IN PERFECT HEALTH and safely returned from his Devonshire excursion.

I wrote you last night, and am now sorry that I expressed myself as I did on a certain subject. I wish you may not blame me also, but remember I am willing to be entirely guided by you; so you must forget as much as possible what is weak and foolish, and consider that when we meet I shall not only act as you think proper, but I hope through time to acquire a manner of thinking agreeable to you.

I am not in spirits for writing at present. This is poor Lord Eglinton's burial day. I am something of an Episcopal in my heart, and often read the Book of Prayer with great satisfaction. Their form of burying their dead pleases me much; it is so decent and solemn. How differently do they go about it in the Presbyterian way: talking without any concern about their business, or perhaps the most trifling sub-

[6] Lord Eglinton's kept mistress. Boswell considered her good looking, and was agreeably impressed by her quietness and good nature upon first acquaintance, but afterwards thought her "a low censorious Scots lass" (*Boswell's London Journal,* 14 May 1763).

jects that can occupy the thoughts of reasonable beings. My Lord begged he might be privately interred, and above all things recommended sobriety. On most occasions this advice might be very necessary ⟨to⟩ the Colonel, but he is in such real distress about his brother's death that I believe he has little relish for his bottle.[7]

The wife and sister of the unhappy murderer went to Lord Loudoun, but my Lord would have nothing to say to them. He desired they might apply to some other person, for he never would interest himself in such a cause. Campbell is one of the most worthless of the human race. He twice attempted to murder before ⟨he⟩ deprived poor Lord Eglinton of life. What can be expected from a creature who, without the principles of what the world calls honour, denies the existence of a God?[8] I am called downstairs, so must bid my dear friend good night, but I shall write soon again. Adieu, and may the Almighty bless and preserve you is the sincere prayers of your affectionate and faithful

M.M.

[Manuscript of *The Life of Johnson*]

Being to set out for Scotland on the 10 of November, I wrote to him at Streatham begging that he would meet me in town on the 9th; but if this should be very inconvenient to him I would come out to him. He answered:

9 November 1769

DEAR SIR, — Upon balancing the inconveniencies of both parties, I find it will less incommode you to spend your night here, than me to come to town. I wish to see you, and am ordered by the lady of this house to invite you hither. Whether you can come or not, I shall not have any occasion of writing to you again before your marriage, and therefore tell you now that with great sincerity I wish you happiness. I am, dear Sir, your most affectionate, humble servant,

SAM. JOHNSON.[9]

[7] Archibald Montgomerie, who succeeded his brother as eleventh Earl, was notorious for his hard drinking.

[8] Campbell was found guilty of murder and condemned to death, but he hanged himself in prison.

[9] This letter is missing in the manuscript, and is supplied from the printed *Life*.

I was detained in town till it was too late on the 9th, so went out to him early in the morning of the 10th November. "Now," said he, "that you are going to marry, do not expect more from life than life will afford. You may often find yourself out of humour, and you may often think your wife not studious enough to please you, and yet you may have reason enough to consider yourself as upon the whole very happily married."

Talking of marriage in general he observed, "Our marriage service is too refined. It is calculated only for the best kind of marriages, whereas we should have a form for matches of convenience, of which there are many." He agreed with me that there was no absolute necessity for having the marriage ceremony performed by a regular clergyman, for this was not commanded in scripture.

I was volatile enough to repeat to him a little epigrammatic song of mine on matrimony, which Mr. Garrick had a few days before procured to be set to music.

A Matrimonial Thought

> In the blithe days of honeymoon,
> With Kate's allurements smitten,
> I loved her late, I loved her soon,
> And called her dearest kitten.
>
> But now my kitten's grown a cat,
> And cross like other wives,
> Oh! by my soul, my honest Mat,
> I fear she has nine lives.

My illustrious friend said, "Mighty well, Sir, but don't swear." Upon which I altered, "Oh! by my soul" to "alas, alas!"

He was good enough to accompany me to London, and see me into the post-chaise which was to carry me on my road to Scotland.

[Received ?12 November, Margaret Montgomerie to Boswell]

Lainshaw, 5 November 1769

I WAS THIS NIGHT FAVOURED WITH TWO KIND LETTERS from my dear friend, for which I beg leave to offer my sincere and grateful thanks. The one dated the 30th had by the stupidity of some of the clerks to the post-office been missent, which made me a day longer of receiving it and of consequence a sufferer. I am truly sorry to think you have been melancholy, but I know it's in vain to argue against it. To the Almighty I put up my earnest request that he may remove far from your mind every gloomy, every discontented thought. In His mercy I trust that you will have few returns of such a disagreeable complaint. Do not be uneasy at the thought of your being ill to live with, when you can have the satisfaction to think you have never deceived me; on the contrary have always made yourself worse than you really are. Be that as it will, I have no right to believe you free of the faults and imperfections you charge yourself with, and therefore am prepared to bear with them. Be not therefore distressed about what ought never to give you pain. You have plainly told me what is your real temper. It will be my duty to study your happiness; otherwise I shall be much more faulty than you.

I am very unhappy to think you are complaining of a bad cold. Oh, be careful of yourself, and consider how dangerous it is to neglect it, how fatal it has been to many by laying the foundation of long and tedious disorders. I wrote you last night, as I thought there was a chance my letter might reach you, but I fancy Mr. Dempster will send it after you, though it's of no great consequence whether or not. As to our meeting, you may believe I earnestly wish it may be soon, but not till you have recovered the fatigue of your journey and find yourself better of your cold, as I would not wish to see you at the expense of your health. I really think it would be more proper for you to come this length; it would have a much better appearance, and that, you know, should be considered. You are, I dare say, perfectly convinced that my inclination would lead me to do what you desire, but for your sake I wish to behave with prudence and propriety. I hope you will write me from Newcastle in case you stay a day on the road. I know I shall hear upon your arrival in Edinburgh. May God bless you and return you in safety is my sincere and fervent prayer. I am under a necessity to make this letter shorter than I could wish, as I have no frank.

All here are pretty well; the Captain complains of a rheumatic disorder. My sister had a letter from your father, who has been distressed with the same complaint. He is better, but was not so well as to be able to do the last sad office to poor Lord Eglinton's remains. Adieu, my dearest friend, and that you may be at all times directed by infinite wisdom to what is for your happiness here and hereafter is the earnest wish of your ever faithful and affectionate

M.M.

[Received ?16 November, Margaret Montgomerie to Boswell]

Lainshaw, 15 November 1769

SINCE YOUR ARRIVAL IN SCOTLAND I have received no less than five letters: one from Mr. Temple's, one from London, and one from Musselburgh last night, and this post brought me a letter from Exeter, and another from Edinburgh.[1] Words cannot give you a just idea of the grateful sense I have of your goodness. I can only at present offer you my thanks, but trust that you shall be convinced by my conduct that I am truly sensible of the obligations I owe you for your friendly attention. My heart is greatly at ease now that you are safely arrived in Edinburgh, and the prospect I have of seeing you so soon is most agreeable to me, but yet I'm afraid it may fatigue you too much. I reflect with uneasiness on your travelling so far without sleep, and am fearful that you may still feel the bad effects of it.

It is my sincere wish that you and your father may be on a friendly footing. I know it is a matter of consequence to you. Independent of any prudent motives, the affection of a parent, even in an humble station, is necessary to promote the happiness of one of your principles. This I am positive you will find to be the case, and therefore hope you will have great satisfaction to think you have in some measure yielded to him.

I sent you by the carrier a little black jelly[2] for your cold, as I could get no honey. It was made by your friend, the Lady Treesbank.

The Captain, poor man, has been more distressed than usual, which has determined Mrs. Montgomerie-Cuninghame to put off coming to Edinburgh for some time. Her sons and their governor are to be in town Saturday night.

If you tell me you are determined to be here, I'll meet you on the

---

[1] Only the letter from Temple's (printed p. 338) has been recovered.

[2] Probably black currant jelly.

road if in health; but if not, you must just come up to my room, where I shall be alone to receive my dear friend. But if you are in the least degree complaining, or imagine your father will disapprove of your coming, do not think of it; for, believe me, I shall not misconstruct the delay. Will you take the trouble to tell Dr. Boswell to send out the picture he took to get framed, as the Captain is impatient to have it. I shall not lose hopes of seeing you on Saturday till I hear from you that you are not to be here, so you see by this that it is no small sacrifice to give up a point of that kind. Adieu, and believe me your faithful and affectionate

M.M.

I have only one frank for you, which I keep till I have a longer letter to write.

[Received ?17 November, Margaret Montgomerie to Boswell]

Lainshaw, 16 November 1769

I WROTE YOU A LETTER LAST NIGHT begging you would not think of coming here without you was in perfect health and found it would not disoblige your father. By yours tonight I am happy to see you are quite well, and would gladly hope there can be no objections made to your coming out, as I am extremely anxious to see you, having a thousand things to tell you which I cannot write. Believe me, I almost repent my writing last night, as I think it may have prevented you from coming, which will be a very great disappointment to me; but I am sure it will not happen without a good cause, so I ought to be quite submissive. I am extremely happy to think home is so agreeable to you. I hope you will always find it so. I shall enclose this to Bob Boswell, in case you are set out before it arrives.

I see the Captain and my sister expect you, and from some things I have heard, though not from themselves, they will think it odd if you are not here soon. The Captain keeps the fatted calf for your arrival. Poor man, he has not been well for some time past; his rheumatic disorder has increased, as also his stomachic complaints. I shall hear from you on Saturday what time you think of being here, that I may know when I should set out to meet you. You see I will have it that you are to come, notwithstanding what I wrote on Wednesday.

You don't say anything about your father's want of health, so I would gladly hope he is now perfectly well. I believe the children will not be in Edinburgh till the beginning of next week. They are gone to Treesbank to take leave of their friends there. All here join in best wishes to you. My prayers are more fervent for your happiness than my own. Adieu, and believe me, my dearest friend, your ever faithful and affectionate

M.M.

[Boswell to Margaret Montgomerie]

Edinburgh, Thursday 23 November 1769

MY DEAR PEGGIE, — This is probably the last letter which I shall have an opportunity to write to *Miss Peggie Montgomerie*. Your kind favour (your last, too, as a young lady), which I received this morning, is another proof of your admirable heart and spirit. I went to your friend Lord Eglinton and delivered your polite message, which he received in the best manner. A favour is making for him, and he is to appear with it on Sunday. I cannot think of our coming to my father's house. It would be mixing gall with my honey. We shall concert what to do when we meet. I like your saying, "Be you positive to take me with you." Only think: *the day after tomorrow* we are to be *married*. Pray look back and recollect all our former scenes. I have some bitter oranges for the Captain. I am so earnestly invited to Bothwell Castle that I cannot refuse. So I shall be there tomorrow night. Your gown comes with me. You can soon put it on. Let dinner be late. We shall both dress in white before it. I ever am your faithful and affectionate

J.B.

This is written from worthy Grange's room. He offers you his best compliments.

[*Scots Magazine*]

25 [NOVEMBER].[3] At Edinburgh, Alexander Boswell, Esquire, of Auchinleck, one of the Lords of Session and Justiciary, to Miss Betty

[3] The Edinburgh Marriage Register gives the date of Lord Auchinleck's marriage as 19 November, which is more likely the correct date.

Boswell, second daughter of John Boswell, Esquire, of Balmuto, deceased.

25 [NOVEMBER]. At Lainshaw, in the shire of Ayr, James Boswell, Esquire, of Auchinleck, advocate, to Miss Peggie Montgomerie, daughter of the late David Montgomerie of Lainshaw, Esquire.

[EDITORIAL NOTE. Boswell, always keenly sensitive to symbolism, summed up in his marriage contract all the major enthusiasms of his life for the three years immediately preceding his marriage: love, Corsica, Dr. Johnson, and the Douglas cause. It is a contract with the woman of his choice, drawn by himself as an advocate; it is witnessed by General Paoli, Dr. Johnson, and Archibald Douglas. He has folded it in the usual style of a legal paper, and endorsed it, *Marriage Contract between James Boswell, Esq. and Miss Peggie Montgomerie, 1769*.]

This is the marriage contract between James Boswell, Esquire, eldest son to the Right Honourable Alexander Boswell, Esquire, of Auchinleck, one of the Lords of Session and Justiciary in Scotland, and Miss Peggie Montgomerie, daughter to the late David Montgomerie of Lainshaw, Esquire.

The said parties do hereby agree that, in consideration of the sincerest mutual love and regard, they will, on or before the holy festival of Christmas next to come, be united to each other by marriage.

They solemnly engage to be faithful spouses, to bear with one another's faults, and to contribute as much as possible to each other's happiness in this world; hoping through the merits of their blessed Saviour, Jesus Christ, for eternal happiness in the world which is to come.

In faith of which, this paper, written by the said James Boswell, Esquire, is subscribed by him at London on the thirty-first day of October in the year of our Lord one thousand seven hundred and sixty-nine, before these witnesses: Pascal Paoli, General of the Corsicans, and Samuel Johnson, Doctor of Laws, and author of *The Rambler* and other works.

JAMES BOSWELL.

The Marriage Contract between James Boswell and Margaret Montgomerie, 31 October 1769, signed by Miss Montgomerie on 25 November 1769; with endorsements by Pasquale de Paoli, Samuel Johnson, and Archibald Douglas. From the original in the Yale University Library

This is the Marriage Contract
between James Boswell Esquire
Eldest Son to The Right Honourable
Alexander Boswell Esquire of
Auchinleck, one of the Lords of
Session and Justiciary in Scotland
and Miss Peggie Montgomerie
Daughter to the late David
Montgomerie of Lainshaw Esquire.

The said Parties do hereby
agree, that in consideration
of the sincerest mutual love
and regard, they will on or
before the holy Festival of
Christmas next to come, be
united to each other by marriage.

They solemnly engage to be
faithful Spouses, to bear with
one anothers faults, and to
contribute as much as possible
to each others happiness in
this World, hoping through
the merits of their blessed
Saviour Jesus Christ, for
eternal happiness in the
World which is to come.

In faith of which, this
James Boswell.   Paper

Paper written by the said
James Boswell Esquire, is
subscribed by him at London,
on the Thirty First day
of October in the year of
our Lord one Thousand
Seven Hundred and Sixty
nine, before these Witnesses
Pascal Paoli General of
the Corsicans and
Samuel Johnson Doctour
of Laws and Authour of
The Rambler and other Works.

James Boswell.

Io sottoscritto ho veduto e sono stato presente quando
il Sig. Giacomo Boswel ha detto scritto questo
foglio — Pasquale de Paoli

Sam: Johnson Witness.

and by the said Miss Peggy Montgomerie
at Lainshaw on the twenty fifth of
November in the year of our Lord one
thousand seven hundred & sixty nine before
these witnesses the honourable Archibald
Douglas of Douglas Esquire & the said
James Boswell Esquire

Douglas Witness   Margaret Montgomerie

Io sottoscritto ho veduto, e sono stato presente, quando il Signore Giacomo Boswell ha sottoscritto questo foglio.[4]

PASQUALE DE PAOLI.

SAM. JOHNSON, Witness.

And by the said Miss Peggie Montgomerie at Lainshaw, on the twenty-fifth of November in the year of our Lord one thousand seven hundred and sixty-nine, before these witnesses: the Honourable Archibald Douglas of Douglas, Esquire, and the said James Boswell, Esquire.

MARGARET MONTGOMERIE.

A. DOUGLAS, Witness.

[4] "I, the undersigned, was present and saw James Boswell, Esquire, subscribe this document." Paoli did not come to Scotland for the marriage.

APPENDIX A

*Verses in the Character of a Corsican at Shakespeare's
Jubilee, at Stratford-upon-Avon, Sept. 6, 1769.*

BY JAMES BOSWELL, ESQ.

From the rude banks of Golo's rapid flood,
Alas! too deeply tinged with patriot blood;
O'er which, dejected, injured freedom bends,
And sighs indignant o'er all Europe sends:
Behold a Corsican! — in better days,
Eager I sought my country's fame to raise;
When o'er our camp Paoli's banners waved,
And all the threats of hostile France we braved,
Till unassisted, a small nation failed,
And our invaders' tenfold force prevailed.

Now when I'm exiled from my native land,
I come to join this classic festal band,
To soothe my soul on Avon's sacred stream,
And from your joy to catch a cheering gleam.
To celebrate great Shakespeare's wond'rous fame,
And add new trophies to the honoured name
Of nature's bard, whom though your country bore,
His influence spreads to ev'ry distant shore:
Wherever genuine feeling souls are found,
His "wood notes wild" with ecstasy resound.

Had Shakespeare lived our story to relate,
And hold his torch o'er our unhappy fate;
Lived with majestic energy to tell
How long we fought, what heroes nobly fell!
Had Garrick, who Dame Nature's pencil stole,

Just where old Shakespeare dropped it, when his soul
Broke from its earthy cage aloft to fly,
To the eternal world of harmony —
Had Garrick shown us on the tragic scene,
With fame embalmed our deeds of death had been;
If from his eyes had flashed the Corsic fire,
Men less had gazed to pity — than admire.

O happy Britons! on whose favoured isle,
Propitious freedom ever deigns to smile,
Whose fame is wafted on triumphant gales,
Where thunders war, or commerce spreads her sails,
I come not hither sadly to complain,
Or damp your mirth with melancholy strain;
In man's firm breast concealed the grief should lie,
Which melts with grace in woman's gentle eye;
But let me plead for liberty distressed,
And warm for her each sympathetic breast:
Amidst the splendid honours which you bear,
To save a sister island be your care!
With generous ardour make us also free;
And give to Corsica a noble jubilee!

A MAP OF ENGLAND

locating many of the places mentioned in the text

A MAP OF SCOTLAND AND IRELAND
locating many of the places mentioned in the text

Scale of Miles

0   10   20   30   40   50

HIGHLANDS

BEN LOMOND

Dunnichen

Valleyfield

Glasgow
Pollok
Bothwell Castle
Whitburn
Livingstone
Edinburgh
Arniston
Haddington
Old Cambu

SCOTLAND

Lainshaw
Ardrossan
Stewarton
Strathaven
Irvine
Newmilns
Kilmarnock
Mauchline
Ayr
Auchinleck
Dalblair
Moffat
Norton

JURA
ISLAY
ARRAN

Maybole

Ailsa Crag

Ardmillan

Ballintrae

Dumfries

CHEVIOT HILLS

GIANT'S CAUSEWAY

Lochryan
Stranraer

Portpatrick

ENGLAND

Carrickfergus

LOUGH NEAGH
Belfast
Bangor
Donaghadee
Lisburn
Grey Abbey
Hillsborough
Newtown
Banbridge
STRANGFORD BAY

IRELAND

Newry

Dundalk

IRISH   SEA

ISLE OF MAN

DETAILED MAP

Edinburgh
Leith
Musselburgh
Haddingto
Prestonfield
Pinkie
Newbattle
Whitburn
Livingstone
Arniston
Bothwell Castle
Norton

Dublin

Kilmaurs
Kilmarnock
Loudoun
Strathaven
Irvine
Newmilns
Galston
Treesbank
Coilsfield
Mauchline
Adamton
Auchinleck
Ayr
Auchinleck Place
Ochiltree
Wardlaw
Cumnock
Dalblair

AUCHINLECK
TO EDINBURGH

Scale of Miles

0   5   10   15   20   25

DRAWN BY HAROLD K. FAY

APPENDIX B

Genealogical Tables

Chart I—Boswell's Paternal Line

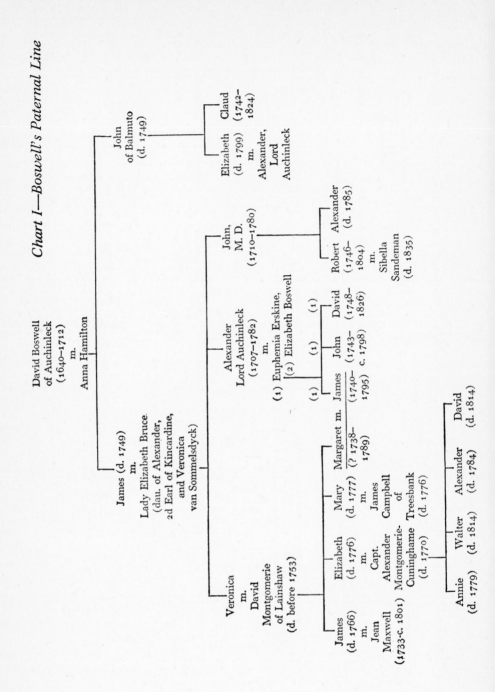

Chart II—Boswell's Maternal Line

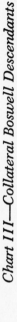

Chart III—Collateral Boswell Descendants

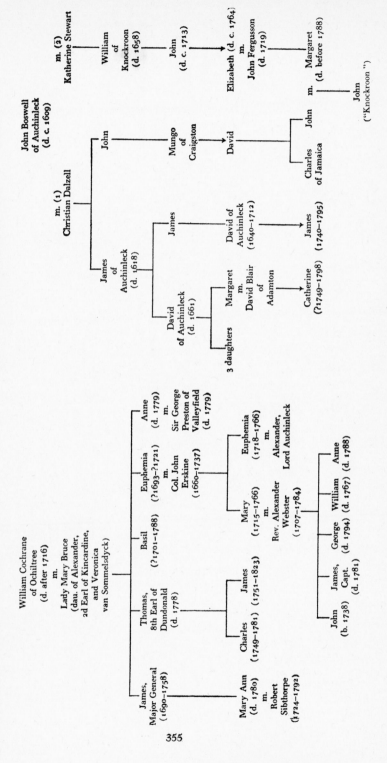

INDEX

This is in the main an index of proper names, but Part I of the article, Bos-WELL, JAMES, collects and digests under general headings Boswell's references to his states of mind, traits of character, opinions, feelings, &c. There is a brief analysed article, SCOTLAND, and general subjects which Johnson happened to discuss are fully reported in Part III of the article, JOHNSON, SAMUEL. Observations on specified persons and places are ordinarily entered under the person or place in question; for example, Boswell's opinions of Lord Auchinleck will be found under Lord Auchinleck and not under Boswell. Churches, streets, inns, mountains, &c. are given separate articles in the main alphabet, except for those in London and Edinburgh, which will be found under those entries. Place names, if no country is specified, are in Great Britain and Ireland, or are so well known that to add the name of a country would be an impertinence. Emperors and kings are entered under their Christian names; other sovereign princes under either Christian name or title, according to which is the better known; noblemen and lords of session and their wives under their titles. The styles chosen are usually those proper to 1766–1769. Well-known names (e.g., Eugene, Prince of Savoy) have been anglicized in cases where it was thought that English-speaking readers would be more accustomed to the English forms. Maiden names of married women are given in parentheses. Titles of books are listed under the name of the author, except where the author has not been identified in the text or notes, in which case a cross reference is given from the title to the author. The following abbreviations are employed: D. (Duke), M. (Marquess), E. (Earl), V. (Viscount), B. (Baron), JB (James Boswell), SJ (Samuel Johnson).

why we suffer from what no longer exists, 33; on savage and civilized life, 22, 311; sympathizes more with poor than genteel, 26, 118*n*.4; sees contemptible people vain of being satirical, 39; feels existence unreal, 39–40; sees everything is only practice, 52; thinks impetuosity better than bashfulness, 69; finds appearances often deceitful, 84, 194; resolves to take men as he finds them, 114; sees no difficulties in life, 114; on preconceptions of future, 68; on remorse, 80; talks on fear, 130; thinks eating, drinking, and sleeping important, 136; on suicide of scorpion, 153–154; finds success fascinating, 156–157; on shop sign, 205; on epitaph, 205; on churchyard, 205–206; admires the military, 208, 216; sees military review, 229; on effects of variety of objects, 208, 297; compares a man too rich to a man too fat, 222; thinks it curious how pleasing variety is, 238; feels all important meetings awkward, 261; on joy of English breakfast, 267; compares breakfast to fortification, 306; on activity and retirement, 284; on true English oddity, 286; on music, 296; London his amusement, 298; thinks Chinese sounds like tinkling of bell, 299; asks if promise to highwayman should be kept, 321; would have pleasure in teaching children, 328; on tenants and landlords, 329; Corsican Boswell, 202

II. *Writings, Mainly between 1766 and 1769.* 1. *Account of Corsica,* &c., 1768, Walpole first suggests writing, 132; purpose of, xv; translations of, xv, 286; influence of, xv; JB's little monument, xv, 108; JB hopes to arouse interest in Corsica through, 11; JB intends to write, 10, 35; JB collects material for, 12–13, 54; JB obliged to write like egotist in, 11; JB undecided about title and epigraph for, 11; JB writes, 44, 45, 46, 47, 52, 55, 56, 57, 58, 63, 70, 88; Johnson's opinion of, 15, 145, 149, 164, 166, 287–288; Hume agrees to manage publication of, 28, 35, 46; Pringle advises on, 30, 107–108; described to Chatham, 53–54; Hailes as critic of, 13–14, 73, 75, 93, 104; Temple to revise, 73, 91, 93–94, 98; Temple's

opinion of, 75, 100, 103, 104, 108; Gray's opinion of asked, 11, 91; Gray's comment on, 91*n*.8; Wyvill as critic of, 84, 91, 93–94; JB thinks he is writing for Europe, 45; writing of elevates JB's soul, 51; dates of completion and publication predicted, 46, 51; JB revises, 83, 90; JB sells to Dilly, 83, 85; printing of, 88, 105; JB hopes for applause from, 90; JB thinks *Journal* most valuable part of, 91; JB thinks will give him character to support, 104, will do him credit, 112; on publication of, 129, 133; has many curious readers, 137; JB honoured and flattered for, 141, 163, 165*n*.1, 207, 268; JB's language in, slightly altered by Dr. Mayo, 161; praised, 134, 137, 144, 151, 159*n*.6, 161, 166, 223–224, 299, 308, 309*n*.9, 335; attacked, 152*n*.3, 159*n*.6, 168*n*.1; JB criticized for method of writing, 166 *and n*.6; Irish edition of, 180; mentioned, xiv*n*.4, 18*n*.1, 119, 122, 138, 144*n*.2, 152, 167, 205, 300*n*.2

2. Journal, bibliography of, xx–xxi, xxii–xxiii, xxiv, xxv, 19, 69, 160, 163, 206, 308; JB writes, 304, 308, 317; JB records ideas and scenes imperfectly in, 292; JB finds it impossible to record life fully in, 140, 242; JB reads London Journal aloud, 32; Holland Journal lost, 64; *quoted or referred to in footnotes on pp.* 20, 31, 32, 38, 113, 128, 141, 143, 144, 158, 161, 162, 208, 231, 263, 275, 276; mentioned, 1, 73, 177

3. Memoranda and Notes, bibliography of, xxi, xxii–xxiii, xxiv, xxv, 163, 308; *extracts quoted in text on pp.* 158, 160, 163, 165–174, 308–309, 316–317, 321–322; *quoted or referred to in footnotes on pp.* 158, 274, 294, 312, 314; mentioned, 159

4. Letters, bibliography of, xxii, xxiii, xxiv; JB writes, 31, 264; JB writes extravagant epistle, 5; JB thinks his letters genuine effusions, 6; JB writes strange sultanic letter, 100–101; *specimens appear in the text on pp.* 3–11, 16–18, 21–24, 31–32, 32–35, 36–38, 45–46, 49–51, 52–54, 71–72, 73–74, 75–76, 80–81, 82–84, 85–87, 89–92, 93–94, 95–96, 100–105, 108–112, 125–128, 132, 164–165, 178–189, 192–193, 200–202, 207–208, 211–213, 220–

Herries, Robert, *later* Sir Robert, Kt., 142

Herries, Cochrane, and Company, London, 139*n*.8

Hervey, ?Frederick Augustus, Bishop of Derry, *later* 4th E. of Bristol, 309

Hervey, James, devotional writer, 52

High Church, Glasgow, 79

High Street, Lisburn, 204

Hill, Robert W., xxvi

Hilles, Frederick W., xxv

Hillsborough, Wills Hill, 1st E. of, *later* 1st M. of Downshire, 205

Hillsborough, 205

Hillsborough Arms, inn at Donaghadee, 198

Hoadly, Benjamin, dramatist, *The Suspicious Husband*, 115, 149

Hoggan, Capt. James, 208

Holland, 2, 18, 44–45

Holmains. *See* Carruthers, John

Holyroodhouse, Henry Bothwell, *titular* Lord, 122

Home, John, *Douglas*, 286

Home, Patrick, of Billy, 167, 222

Horace, 314; *Epistles*, 24, 41, 64, 104, 235, 250; *Odes*, 9, 23, 43, 51, 90, 157, 180, 182; *Satires*, 314

Hounslow, 286

House of Commons, 286*n*.8

House of Lords, 70, 88, 236*n*.9

Howard, Hon. Edward, *The British Princes*, 334*n*.1

Howell, Mr., farmer, 267–268

Hume, David, characterized, 82, 153, 262, 293, 332; finds no venom in JB's song on the Hamilton cause, 27; agrees to transact publication of JB's *Account of Corsica*, 28, 35, 46; quarrel with Rousseau, 34; appointed secretary to Conway, 34; admired by Dr. John Smith of Oxford, 150; visits JB, 256; *History of England*, 182; mentioned, 46, 165 *and n*.3

Hunt, William, town clerk of Stratford, 283

Hunter, Andrew, D.D., professor at Edinburgh University, 239

Hunter, James, bailie of Edinburgh, 123

Hunter, Robert, professor at Edinburgh University, 35*n*.1, 91, 144, 215

Hunter, Veronica (Murray), wife of Robert Hunter of Polmood, 122

Hyde, Donald F., 132*n*.2

Hyde, Mary (Crapo), 132*n*.2

Hyndford, Janet (Grant), Countess of, 114

Hyndford, John Carmichael, 3d E. of, 251

Hyndford, John Carmichael, 4th E. of, 114

Hyndford, family, 144

Ireland, 177, 179–180, 183, 192, 198–208, 237

Irvine, 194, 337

Irving, John, solicitor, 290

Isham, Lt.-Col. Ralph Heyward, xxii, xxiii, xxiv

Italy, 2, 13*n*.9

Jachone, Corsican mastiff, 142*n*.5

Jamaica, 292

James, footman to Mr. Dilly, 296

James, waiter at Ayr, 195

James IV, King of Scotland, 68*n*.9

James and ——, ship, 198

Jedd, Mrs., Edward Dilly's housekeeper, 296

Jeffries, Joseph, LL.D., 300

JOHNSON, SAMUEL, LL.D.

[Part I, *Miscellaneous;* Part II, *Relations with JB;* Part III, *Opinions and Observations;* Part IV, *Works.*]

I. *Miscellaneous.* SJ characterized, xii, 177, 263, 274, 314; meets Wilkes, 83*n*.7; tests Mrs. Macaulay's republican principles, 160*n*.9; admired by Dr. Smith of Oxford, 150; helps Robert Chambers write lectures, 146*n*.6; entertained by Sir Alexander Macdonald and his wife on tour of the Hebrides, 143*n*.7; invites Dr. Gibbons to tea, 238*n*.; meets Paoli, 314–316; mentioned, x, xxiii, 151, 181, 197, 252–253, 284

II. *Relations with JB.* Introductory account of his relationship with JB, xi–xii, 1; letters to JB, 14–15, 164, 287–288, 342; letters from JB, 16–17, 164–165; JB's first meeting with, 1, 159*n*.5; disapproves of JB's enthusiasm for the Corsicans, xv, 164, 314, of JB's proposed *Account of Corsica*, 15; JB wishes him to read *Corsica*, 104; praises *Corsica*, but refuses to review it, 166, 287–288; JB visits or entertains, 2, 146–150, 152–154, 155–156, 163, 165–166, 175–177, 311–316, 317–334, 343; JB finds him away at Oxford, 145,

FINE SCHE

Books:

(Reserve,

and 10¢ for ev
that the Librar,

id Fines:

the

per day

A MAP OF ENGLAND

locating many of the places mentioned in the text